UTILITARIANS AND THEIR CRITICS IN AMERICA, 1789–1914

Edited by
James E. Crimmins
Huron University College
and
Mark G. Spencer
Brock University

History of American Thought

Printed in England by Antony Rowe Ltd, Chippenham

UTILITARIANS AND THEIR CRITICS IN AMERICA, 1789–1914

Volume I

With an Introduction by
James E. Crimmins

thoemmes

This edition published by Thoemmes Continuum, 2005

Thoemmes Continuum
11 Great George Street
Bristol BS1 5RR, England

http://www.thoemmes.com

Utilitarians and their Critics in America, 1789–1914
4 Volumes : ISBN 1 84371 110 9

Introduction © James E. Crimmins, 2005
Editorial selection © James E. Crimmins and Mark G. Spencer, 2005

British Library Cataloguing-in-Publication Data
A CIP record of this title is available from the British Library

Publisher's Note

The Publisher has gone to great lengths to ensure the quality of this reprint but points out that some imperfections in the original book may be apparent.

This book is printed on acid-free paper, sewn, and cased in a durable buckram.

ACKNOWLEDGEMENTS

Rudi Thoemmes came up with the original idea for this collection and, without being facetious, we would have to say it was a pretty good one. Of course, the work must stand for itself, but we believe it has opened up several intriguing lines of research. The input of Dr. Mark Bailey, when the idea was in its formative phase, gave it considerable impetus. We received help from many other quarters to bring the project to fruition. Our thanks are due to Toby Schwartz for her energetic research, and to Maryanne Harkins, Cam Bishop, Daniela Grech and Nadine Sant for other incidental assistance in preparing the texts for publication. In locating and delivering texts we greatly appreciate the assistance of the Department of Interlibrary Loans at the James A. Gibson Library, Brock University, and David Murphy and the staff of the Department of Interlibrary Loans at the D.B. Weldon Library, The University of Western Ontario. For financial support of various kinds we are indebted to Huron University College, St. Michael's College at the University of Toronto, the Institute for Ulster Scots Studies, and the Social Sciences and Humanities Research Council of Canada. Warm thanks are due, too, to Philip de Bary, our editor at Thoemmes Continuum, whose enthusiasm for this collection, and later patience when it threatened to go off the rails, was just what was needed. As ever, the work required to bring large-scale projects such as this to a satisfactory conclusion could never proceed smoothly, were it not for the encouragement and support of two very special people in our lives – Johanne and Kelly.

James E. Crimmins
Huron University College

Mark G. Spencer
Brock University

2005

CONTENTS

Volume I

Preface   xv

Note on Texts   xvii

Introduction by James E. Crimmins   xix

1. [Anon.], Review: *An Introduction to the Principles of Morals and Legislation. Printed in the Year 1780, and now first published. By Jeremy Bentham, of Lincoln's Inn, Esq.*, in *The American Monthly Review; or, Literary Journal*, vol. II (1795), pp. 339–48

2. Thomas Ewell, 'Essay on the Laws of Pleasure and Pain', in *Philosophical Essays on Morals, Literature, and Politics, By David Hume, Esq. To Which is Added the Answer to his Objections to Christianity, By the Ingenious Divine Dr. Campbell. Also, An Account of Mr. Hume's Life, an original Essay, and a few Notes* (Georgetown, D.C. and Philadelphia 1817); vol. I, pp. 525–33

3. Selections from *The Yankee* and *The Yankee and Boston Literary Gazette*, 1828–1829
   (1) 'Utility', vol. I, no. 6 (6 February 1828), pp. 46–7; vol. I, no. 7 (13 February 1828), p. 51; vol. I, no. 22 (28 May, 1828), pp. 169–71
   (2) 'Newspapers. Utility', vol. I, no. 26 (25 June 1828), p. 207
   (3) 'Jeremy Bentham', vol. I, no. 11 (12 March 1828), pp. 81–3; vol. I, no. 12 (19 March 1828), pp. 92–3
   (4) G.R.A.[?], 'Political Economy', vol. I, no. 23 (4 June 1828), p. 179
   (5) 'Bentham's Evidence', vol. I, no. 33 (13 August 1828), p. 259
   (6) R.[?], 'Metaphysics', vol. I, no. 36 (3 September 1828), pp. 281–2
   (7) 'Westminster Review', vol. I, no. 39 (24 September 1828), pp. 305–7
   (8) 'Bentham's Reminiscences', vol. II, no. 7 (12 February 1829), pp. 53–4

(9) 'Moore's New Poem', vol. II, no. 8 (19 February 1829), p. 63
(10) 'Penitentiary System. NO. I', vol. II, no. 15 (9 April 1829), pp. 113–14; 'Penitentiary System. NO. II', vol. II, no. 17 (23 April 1829), pp. 129–30; 'Penitentiary System. NO. III', vol. II, no. 20 (14 May 1829), pp. 154–5; 'Penitentiary System. NO. IV', vol. II, no. 24 (11 June 1829), pp. 187–8; 'Penitentiary System. NO. V', vol. II, no. 25 (18 June 1829), pp. 194–6; 'Penitentiary System. NO. VI', vol. II, no. 26 (25 June 1829), p. 202
(11) 'Jeremy Bentham. Extract from a letter from Mr. Lawrence, our charge at St. James's, dated Paris, March 10, 1829', vol. II, no. 24 (11 June 1829), p. 186
(12) 'Bentham's Principles of the Civil Code', vol. II, no. 25 (18 June 1829), pp. 196–7
(13) 'Jeremy Bentham', vol. II, New Series no. 1, no. 79 (July 1829), pp. 1–9

4. Thomas Cooper, Review: *Rationale of Judicial Evidence specially applied to English Practice. From the Manuscripts of Jeremy Bentham, Esq. Bencher of Lincoln's-Inn. London. 1828*, in *Southern Review*, vol. V, no. X (May 1830), pp. 381–426

5. [Hugh Swinton Legaré], 'Jeremy Bentham and the Utilitarians', *Southern Review*, vol. VII, no. XIV (August 1831), pp. 261–96, in *Writings of Hugh Swinton Legaré*, 2 vols. (Charleston, S.C. 1846), II. 449–81

6. [Caleb S. Henry], Review: *Morals and Legislation. By Jeremy Bentham. Translated into French by M. Dumont, with notes; and from the French* (2d. ed. corrected and enlarged) *with Notes, and a Biographical Notice of Jeremy Bentham and of M. Dumont, by John Neal. Boston, Wells & Lilly. 1836. Bentham's Deontology. Westminster Review. No. XLI. Art. I. The Principles of Moral and Political Philosophy. By Willam Paley, D.D.'*, in *New York Review*, vol. I (March 1837), pp. 58–75

7. [Anon.], Review: *Theory of Legislation, by Jeremy Bentham, translated from the French of Etienne Dumont. By Richard Hildreth, author of Banks, Banking and Paper Currencies, etc., etc. ol. I. Principles of Legislation – Principles of the Civil Code. Vol. II. Principles of the Penal Code. Boston: 1840. Weeks, Jordan, & Co.*, in *New York Review*, vol. VII (July 1840), pp. 263–7

8. [John L. O'Sullivan?], 'Jeremy Bentham', *The United States Magazine and Democratic Review*, vol. VIII, no. XXXIII (September 1840), pp. 251–71

9. [W. Phillips?], Review: *Theory of Legislation; by* Jeremy Bentham. *Translated from the French of* Etienne Dumont, by R. Hildreth, Author of "Banks, Banking, and Paper Currencies," Despotism in America," "Archy Moore," &c. Boston: Weeks, Jordan, & Co. 1840, in *The North American Review*, vol. LI, no. 109 (October 1840), pp. 384–96

10. [John L. O'Sullivan?], 'Edward Livingston and his Code', *The United States Magazine and Democratic Review*, New Series, vol. I, no. 1 (July 1841), pp. 3–20

11. [John L. O'Sullivan?], 'Early Life of Jeremy Bentham', *The United States Magazine and Democratic Review*, vol. X, issue 48 (June 1842), pp. 545–60

12. [G.H. Smith], Review: *The Works of Jeremy Bentham*. Published under the superintendence of his Executor, John Bowring, M.P. Edinburgh: W. Tait, in *National Quarterly Review*, vol. III, no. V (June 1861), pp. 51–70

Volume II

13. Richard Hildreth, *Theory of Morals: An Inquiry Concerning the Law of Moral Distinctions and the Variations and Contradictions of Ethical Codes* (Boston 1844)

14. [John L. O'Sullivan?], Review: *Theory of Morals: An inquiry concerning the law of moral distinctions and the variations and the contradictions of ethical codes*. By Richard Hildreth. Boston: Charles C. Little & James Brown. 1844, in *The United States Magazine and Democratic Review*, vol. XV, issue 73 (July 1844), pp. 103–4

15. [J. Walker], Review: *Theory of Morals: An Inquiry concerning the Law of Moral Distinctions, and the Variations and Contradictions of Ethical Codes*. By Richard Hildreth. Boston: Little & Brown.

1844, in *Christian Examiner and Religious Miscellany*, vol. XXXVIII (1845), pp. 125–6

Volume III

16. [Orestes A. Brownson], Review: *Theory of Morals: An Inquiry concerning the Law of Moral Distinctions, and the Variations and Contradictions of Ethical Codes*. By Richard Hildreth. Boston: Little & Brown. 1844, in *Brownson's Quarterly Review*, vol. I (1844), pp. 328–49

17. [Andrew P. Peabody], Review: *Theory of Morals: an Inquiry Concerning the Law of Moral Distinctions and the Variations and Contradictions of Ethical Codes*. By Richard Hildreth. Boston: Charles C. Little and James Brown. 1844, in *North American Review*, vol. LX, no. CXXVII (April 1845), pp. 393–403

18. Richard Hildreth, *Letter. A Joint Letter to Orestes A. Brownson and the Editor of the North American Review: In which the Editor of the North American Review is proved to be no Christian, and little better than an Atheist*. By Richard Hildreth, Author of 'Theory of Morals' (Boston 1844?)

19. [Orestes A. Brownson], Review: *A Joint Letter to O. A. Brownson and the Editor of the North American Review*. By R. Hildreth, Author of "Theory of Morals", in *Brownson's Quarterly Review*, vol. II (1844?), pp. 341–52

20. [Anon.], Review: *Principles of Political Economy, with some of their Applications to Social Philosophy*. By John Stuart Mill. Boston: Little & Brown. 2 vols., in *Graham's American Monthly Magazine*, vol. XXXIII (1848), p. 367

21. [Anon.], Review: *Principles Of Political Economy, with some of their applications to Social Philosophy*. By John Stuart Mill. In two volumes. Charles C. Little & James Brown, Boston, in *The United States Magazine and Democratic Review*, vol. XXIV, issue 127 (January 1849), p. 94

22. [Anon.], 'Law Reform in England. With Notices of Bentham, Romilly, Macintosh, Dumont, Mill, Brougham, Buxton and Bowring', *The United States Magazine and Democratic Review*, vol. XXVIII, issue 151 (January 1851), pp. 33–49

23. [Anon.], 'The Beautiful Streamlet and the Utilitarian', *The International Magazine of Literature, Art, and Science*, vol. III, issue 3 (June 1851), pp. 307–308

24. H.L. Baugher, 'Faith and Utilitarianism', *Evangelical Quarterly Review*, vol. VI (October 1854), pp. 209–25

25. John C. Hurd, Extract: *Topics of Jurisprudence connected with Conditions of Freedom and Bondage* (New York 1856), pp. 1–52

26. [Anon.], Review: Political Science. *Considerations on Representative Government* – Mr. John Stuart Mill, in *New Englander and Yale Review*, vol. XXI, issue 80 (July 1862), pp. 639–41

27. [Anon.], Review: *Principles of Political Economy, with some of their Applications to Social Philosophy*. By John Stuart Mill. New York: D. Appleton & Co. 1863. 2 vols., in *The North American Review*, vol. XCVIII, issue 202 (January 1864), pp. 270–3

28. [Anon.] Review: 1. *The Province of Jurisprudence determined, being the First Part of a Series of Lectures on Jurisprudence, or, the Philosophy of Positive Law*, By the late John Ausin, Esq., of the Inner Temple, Barrister at Law. Second Edition. London: John Murray. 1861. 2. *Lectures on Jurisprudence, being the Sequel to "The Province of Jurisprudence determined." To which are added Notes and Fragments now first published from the Original Manuscripts.* By the late John Austin, &c., &c. London: John Murray. 1861. 2 vols., in *North American Review*, vol. C (January 1865), pp. 246–53

29. John Neal, 'Jeremy Bentham', *The Atlantic Monthly*, vol. XVI, issue 97 (November 1865), pp. 575–84

30. [Anon.], Review: 'John Stuart Mill's Dissertations and Discussions', in *New Englander and Yale Review*, vol.XXV, issue 94 (January 1866), pp. 166–8

31. John Bascom, 'Utilitarianism', *Bibliotheca Sacra*, vol. XXIII (July 1866), pp. 435–52

32. [Anon.], Review: *Dissertations and Discussions; Political, Philosophical, and Historical*. By John Stuart Mill. Vol. IV. Boston: William V. Spencer. 1867, in *The North American Review*, vol. CVI, issue 218 (January 1868), pp. 300–3

33. Oliver Wendell Holmes, 'Codes, and the Arrangement of the Law', *American Law Review*, vol. V, no. 1 (1871), pp. 1–13

34. Oliver Wendell Holmes, '*The Law Magazine and Review*. No.3, April 1, 1872', *American Law Review*, vol. V (1871), pp. 723–5

35. Oliver Wendell Holmes, 'The Arrangement of the Law. Privity', *American Law Review*, vol. VII (1872), pp. 46–66

36. Borden P. Browne, 'Moral Intuition vs. Utilitarianism', *New Englander and Yale Review*, vol. XXXII, issue 123 (April 1873), pp. 217–42

37. [Anon.], Review: 'Sidgwick's *Methods of Ethics*', in *New Englander and Yale Review*, vol. XXXIV, issue 131 (April 1875), pp. 379–80

38. [Anon.], Review: *The Methods of Ethics*. By Henry Sidgwick, M.A., Lecturer and late Fellow of Trinity College, Cambridge. London. Macmillan & Co. 1874, in *The North American Review*, vol. CXXII, issue 251 (April 1876), pp. 446–52

Volume IV

39. [M.D. Conway], 'John Stuart Mill', *Harper's New Monthly Magazine*, vol. XLVII, issue 280 (September 1873), pp. 528–34

40. [Anon.], Review: *Autobiography*. By John Stuart Mill. New York: Henry Holt and Company. 1873, in *The North American Review*, vol. CXVIII, issue 242 (January 1874), pp. 185–8

41. [Anon.], Review: 'John Stuart Mill's Autobiography', in *New Englander and Yale Review*, vol. XXXIII, issue 126 (January 1874), pp. 193–5

42. [Anon.], Review: '*Autobiography* of John Stuart Mill', in *New Englander and Yale Review*, vol. XXXIII, issue 129 (October 1874), pp. 605–22

43. C.B. Crane, 'John Stuart Mill and Christianity', *The Baptist Quarterly*, vol. VIII (1874), pp. 348–62

44. [Anon.], Review: 'John Stuart Mill's *Three Essays on Religion*', in *New Englander and Yale Review*, vol. XXXIV, issue 130 (January 1875), pp. 181–3

45. [James E. Cabot], Review: *Three Essays on Religion*. By John Stuart Mill. New York: Henry Holt & Co. 1874, in *The North American Review*, no. 120 (1875), pp. 461–9

46. Noah Porter, 'John Stuart Mill as a Religious Philosopher', *Dickinson's Theological Quarterly* (October 1875), pp. 492–507

47. Lyell Adams, 'John Stuart Mill', *New Englander and Yale Review*, vol. XXXVI, issue 138 (January 1877), pp. 92–114

48. Daniel S. Gregory, 'John Stuart Mill and the Destruction of Theism', *The Princeton Review*, n.s. II (1878), pp. 409–48

49. Irving Berdine Richman, 'Law and Political Fact in the United States', *Atlantic Monthly*, vol. LXIV (August 1889), pp. 205–19

50. John A. Jameson, 'National Sovereignty', *Political Science Quarterly*, vol. V, no. 2 (June 1890), pp. 193–213

51. Janet Ross, 'John Austin', *The Atlantic Monthly*, vol. LXIX, issue 416 (June 1892), pp. 763–9

52. Woodrow Wilson, 'The Study of Politics' and 'Political Sovereignty', in *An Old Master and Other Political Essays* (New York 1893), Chs. II–III, pp. 29–57, 59–96

53. John Dewey, 'Austin's Theory of Sovereignty', *Political Science Quarterly*, vol. IX, no. 1 (March 1894), pp. 31–52

54. Winthrop More Daniels, 'A Letter To John Stuart Mill', *The Atlantic Monthly*, vol. LXXXVI, issue 517 (November 1900), pp. 664–71

55. Irving B. Richman, 'From John Austin to John C. Hurd', *Harvard Law Review*, vol. XIV (January 1901), pp. 353–71

56. [Anon.], 'Jeremy Bentham, the First Law Reformer', *American Law Review*, vol. XLV (May–June, 1911), pp. 388–400

PREFACE

In these four volumes the editors have put together a representative sample of writings by utilitarians and their critics that may serve as a starting point for further research. Many more items might have found a place in this collection, but considerations of space have required a more selective approach. Should the reader wish to investigate further, there are several paths of enquiry he or she might pursue. There are a good number of reviews of Paley's theological writings, in which comments on his 'religious utilitarianism' are very often to be found. Bentham's *Defense of Usury; Shewing the Impolicy of the Present Legal Restraints on the Terms of Pecuniary Bargains* (1787), first published in the U.S. in Philadelphia in 1796, seems to have stirred up considerable debate, as is evident by the writings of Thomas Cooper, Francis Walker Gilmer, John Whipple, and John Russell Hurd, among others. Utilitarian themes can be found in other places which, while not at the core of the debates over utilitarianism itself, possess a certain interest of their own, such as the rear-guard action to defend the 'utility' of the classics in university education, closely scrutinized in Jacob Bigelow's *Remarks on Classical and Utilitarian Studies, Read before the Academy of Arts and Sciences, Dec. 20, 1866* (1867), and in the various reviews of that address. James McCosh published *An Examination of Mr. J.S. Mill's Philosophy, Being a Defence of Fundamental Truth* (1866) in the year he became the eleventh president of Harvard University, but this study is over 400 pages long and is part of a series of philosophical writings and debates with Mill that date back to his earlier life in Scotland, during McCosh's tenure as chair of Logic and Metaphysics at Queen's College, Belfast. The writings of Oliver Wendell Holmes bear compelling testimony to the influence of Bentham and Austin on American jurisprudence in the nineteenth century. We have included several of Holmes' essays, but many more could have found a place in these volumes. In the many volumes of the celebrated jurist's writings on law can be found an abundance of material containing developments from, and critical comments on, the writings of the utilitarians. Writings published in the U.S. by British writers, such as Sir James Mackintosh's essay on international law published in the *Journal of Jurisprudence* volume I (1821), have been omitted. Also, omitted are many of the journal articles in which utilitarian ideas were discussed in an incidental fashion. The interested reader will find much to consider related to the reception of utilitarian ideas in America in journals such as *The Beacon* and *The Diamond* (both edited by Gilbert Vale), *Journal of Law*, *South Literary Journal*, *United States Magazine and Democratic Review*, *United States Law Intelligencer and Review*, *Western Law Journal*, *North American Review*, *American Quarterly Review*, and *The Yankee and Boston Literary Gazette*. Other publications in which occasional reviews and articles of interest can be found include *The Boston Morning Post*, *New Hampshire Patriot*, *New Hampshire Sentinel*, *New York Evening Post*, *New York Tribune*, *New England Magazine*, and *New York Albion*, among others.

A useful insight into the many debates concerning utilitarianism in these publications can be found in Peter J. King, *Utilitarian Jurisprudence in America: The Influence of Bentham and Austin on American Legal Thought in the Nineteenth Century* (New York and London 1986). King's book is by far the best introduction into the dissemination of utilitarian ideas in nineteenth century America, and it was particularly helpful in the writing of the introduction to this collection.

The dates marking the period covered by the items in these four volumes – the long nineteenth century – are a trifle arbitrary: 1789 was the year of publication of Bentham's path-breaking *An Introduction to the Principles of Morals and Legislation*, while the final essays were published at the turn of the century prior to the First World War. These years bracket, approximately, the period in which utilitarian theory became one of the prominent strands of moral philosophy and political economy in Britain and assumed a leading role in jurisprudence. One of the questions that stands behind the selection of the writings in these volumes, therefore, is what impact did utilitarians and utilitarian ideas have on the other side of the Atlantic during the same period?

NOTE ON TEXTS

Wherever possible facsimiles of original texts have been used, and their sources indicated both in the list of Contents and in the title pages which precede each item. The antiquarian spelling of words has been retained in reset texts, but the typeface has been modernised in each instance, obvious typographical errors have been silently corrected, and numerals have replaced other symbols in endnotes. Every effort has been made to identify the authors of the writings contained in these volumes, but in the instance of many of the reviews and journal articles this was not possible. The ubiquitous author 'Anon.' has been made responsible for these particular orphans.

INTRODUCTION

Utilitarian ideas in nineteenth-century America have been given short shrift in recent historical and philosophical scholarship. It is generally thought, Austin's theory of sovereignty aside, that utilitarian moral and legal theory is all but absent from the American political and philosophical tradition. In Bruce Kuklick's otherwise splendid book, *A History of Philosophy in America, 1720–2000*, a major survey of American philosophy, there is not a single mention of utilitarian theory and, with the exception of a few brief mentions of J.S. Mill, none of the leading utilitarians figure in this history.[1] Even Richard Hildreth, once known as 'the American utilitarian', who made a concerted effort to introduce utilitarian ideas into mainstream American thought, no longer warrants an entry in the most recent edition of the *American National Biography*.[2] In Elizabeth Flower and Murray G. Murphey's monumental study, *A History of Philosophy in America*, Paley, Bentham, Austin, and Sidgwick are mentioned only in passing.[3] Mill's debate with William Hamilton and its impact on American psychology is given rather more attention, as is the influence of Mill's empiricism on the Americans Chauncey Wright, William James, Clarence Irving Lewis, and John Dewey. But, Hildreth, America's leading utilitarian philosopher, is not mentioned at all.[4] Indeed, we might be justifiably concerned that Hildreth has very nearly disappeared from the American philosophical radar.

The reasons commonly offered to explain the failure of utilitarians to have an impact in the United States include the '*odium theologicum*' that wafted around Bentham and his school, the crudeness of their moral principles, and the 'immoveable obstacle' posed by the 'deep-seated Lockean tradition' of natural law and natural rights.[5] As a summary of the sources of the opposition to utilitarian ideas there is a good deal of substance to this analysis. However, it is simply not the case that utilitarian ideas did not penetrate the American mind. How influential were utilitarian ideas in American political thought? As the contents of these volumes amply demonstrate, the writings of Bentham, Austin, Sidgwick and Mill were frequently read and commented upon in the fields of moral and legal philosophy, political economy, penal reform, and law codification, and utilitarian theory garnered a good number of disciples among the American intelligentsia – utilitarian fellow-travellers, who either counted themselves as utilitarians or were at least supportive of the utility principle as the foundation of law. For example, John Neal (1793–1876) styled himself as Bentham's utilitarian spokesman in America and edited *The Yankee*, a journal devoted to the spread of utilitarian ideas which frequently featured excerpts from Bentham's writings, published with the banner heading 'the greatest happiness of the greatest number'.[6] Thomas Cooper (1759–1839), the English-born Unitarian friend of Joseph Priestley with whom he emigrated to the United States in 1794, was a lawyer and Jeffersonian reformer, a materialist and atheist who taught chemistry at the University of South Carolina, and liberally laced his theological and political writings with anticlericalism. Cooper employed utilitarian principles in his writings on political economy and legal philosophy. Edward Livingston (1764–1836) was the famous author of several codes of law for the state of Louisiana, and freely professed that his work was shaped by Bentham's utilitarian principles and ideas on codification. Richard Hildreth (1807–65) translated the first two volumes of Etienne Dumont's famous redaction of Bentham's utilitarian legal philosophy, *Traités de législation civile et pénale* (1802),[7] and wrote one of the few explicitly utilitarian moral treatises in the United States [II. 13]. John L. O'Sullivan (1813–95), the editor of the *United States Magazine and Democratic Review* and famous for coining the phrase 'manifest destiny', advocated utilitarian principles in legal reform, especially as they relate to capital punishment. Writers later in the century influenced by Austin's jurisprudence, in particular his analysis of political sovereignty, include John C. Hurd, Oliver Wendell Holmes, Woodrow Wilson, and Irving Berdine Richman.

There are occasions in the writings contained in these volumes when it is relatively clear that these and other Americans borrowed directly from utilitarian writers in Britain, while at other times, despite similarities of thought and expression, the connections are not readily transparent. At the same time, there are also instances in which utilitarian ideas were explicitly rejected.[8] Clearly, there is an interesting story to tell here, in terms of (1) the place of utilitarian ideas and principles in American philosophy, (2) the absorption of utilitarian perspectives into the broader intellectual culture of nineteenth-century America, and (3) the relative neglect by modern scholars of this area of the history of ideas. Collecting together in one place examples of the relevant published work is an essential starting point for a serious investigation of these issues.

1. Jeremy Bentham

Peter King's *Utilitarian Jurisprudence in America* is one of the few studies in the past twenty years to venture in a substantial way into this area of the history of ideas, though its focus is confined to the influence of Bentham and Austin.[9] King acknowledged that Bentham developed an extensive network of links with American politicians during the last twenty years of his life, to many of whom he wrote offering his services as a disinterested codifier of the law,[10] but argued that these connections failed to produce any tangible results either in reforming or codifying law. Nevertheless, it is equally clear that Bentham's name, and the basic elements of the philosophy associated with that name, were widely known. And, even if his ideas were not sufficiently appreciated at first to have a genuine practical impact on the existing law of the American states, the two foremost utilitarians in this early period, John Neal and Richard Hildreth, were far from preaching utilitarian ideas in a vacuum. Indeed, King's own concern with 'the broader sweep of Bentham's ideas in America' directs our attention to the activities of a wide range of scholars, legislators, political commentators, law reformers, and moralists. In general, he located three principal areas in which the utilitarian influence was felt in American political and legal thought. First, the critique of the American inheritance of English common law, its chaos and uncertainty, made Bentham's critique of this branch of law particularly relevant. Second, the issue of sovereignty, highlighted in the context of the Civil War and its aftermath, leant urgency to the consideration of Austin's ideas on this pressing subject. Third, the economic and social changes taking place in America, spawned by the rapid expansion of industry and commerce, produced a new middle class amenable to Bentham's *laissez-faire* political economy and the utilitarian ideas that lay behind it.[11] Against this background, King need not have been quite so hesitant about Bentham's impact on American social and political thought, and might have been encouraged to say considerably more about the influence of utilitarian ideas in moral philosophy, in particular.

The first known American journal review of Bentham's *Introduction to the Principles of Morals and Legislation* (1789), the foundational text of his legal philosophy, appeared in 1795 in the *American Monthly Review*, an important but short-lived miscellany, published in Philadelphia by the law reporter Samuel Harrison Smith (1772–1845). In this review Bentham is praised as a thinker with 'no ordinary share of understanding, penetration, and discernment', and described as an ambitious systemizer of the law who had made considerable progress toward that end [I. 1: 1].[12] The reviewer summarized Bentham's 'principle of *Utility*' and other related concepts and reproduced key passages of Bentham's text, demonstrating his familiarity with Bentham's plan to execute a comprehensive utilitarian code of law, to which the *Introduction* was intended to be an 'introduction' only to the penal part of that code. However, the reviewer offered no commentary on the substance of the parts quoted from Bentham's text, and the article ended with a note promising a later continuance of the article – which never came. Interest in Bentham's moral and legal philosophy, with the notable exception of Hoffman's lectures at the University of Maryland, was thin from that point until Neal founded *The Yankee* in 1828, specifically to promote utilitarian ideas.

David Hoffman (1784–1854) was the first professor of law at the University of Maryland, where he taught from 1822 to 1832, and the first legal scholar in America to introduce Bentham's ideas into the academic study of the law (several years before this occurred in Britain).[13] In his law lectures – originally published as *A Course of Legal Study* (1817), and later expanded to a two-volume edition in 1836 – Hoffman recommended that students study closely the first seven chapters of Bentham's *Introduction to the Principles of Morals and Legislation*, and chapters 12–17 of Dumont's redaction of Bentham's writings on rewards and punishments, *Théorie des peines et des récompenses* (1811).[14] Of the latter Hoffman wrote: 'It is a matter of no less surprise than regret that a work of such extraordinary merit ... should so long have continued unknown, not only to the students, but to the learned of our country.' Nor did he think this was putting it too strongly, for 'nowhere among ancient or modern productions, is the philosophy of criminal legislation so ably and happily illustrated', and in doing so Bentham had 'left his predecessors at an immeasureable distance.'[15] When Hoffman revised his text for the second edition he reconsidered elements of his initial appraisal, and now pointed out that what faults were to be found in Bentham's theory could be traced to his 'veins of eccentricity; his censorial passions ... his want of minute and accurate knowledge.'[16] But this did not prevent him from teaching that Bentham's central claims – that happiness was the only proper end of legislation, and that the sanctions of the law should be based on a clear understanding of the pleasures and pains which constituted human motivation – were correct. The comprehensive codification of the law recommended by Bentham, was also endorsed by Hoffman. Nor did the retention of natural law as rules of conduct for the production of happiness significantly alter the utilitarian thrust of his teaching.[17] To what extent Hoffman's teaching of Bentham's philosophy influenced his students is difficult to say without reviewing the records of the students who attended his lectures and determining whether that influence is detectable in their later careers. John Neal is one of the few we know to have been influenced in this way, but in general terms the question presents an intriguing avenue for further investigation.[18]

We know rather more about the interest created by Bentham's political economy in the United States, at least in so far as it addressed the issue of money lending regulations. Many of Bentham's American correspondents commented on the difficulty of obtaining his published work on that side of the Atlantic, and Bentham did his best to make up the deficiency by personally distributing his writings through his various American contacts. However, prior to the efforts of Neal and Hildreth the only one of his writings to achieve a general currency in the United States was the *Defence of Usury* (1787).[19] The arguments of this short text are entirely consistent with the commitment to *laissez*-faire economic principles Bentham inherited from Adam Smith and which he enunciated in several other economic tracts.[20] However, in this instance Bentham used these principles as the basis for a sharp invective on Smith's defence of the laws stipulating interest rates for lenders in *The Wealth of Nations* (1776). In 1820 Francis Walker Gilmer (1790–1826), a prominent Virginian lawyer and scholar, published anonymously 'A Vindication of the Laws Limiting the Rate of Interest on Loans, from the Objections of Jeremy Bentham and the Edinburgh Reviewers', in which he defended Smith's justification for legal restrictions on rates of interest.[21] A few years later Thomas Cooper took Bentham's side in his popular *Lectures on the Elements of Political Economy* (1826).[22] In 1836 John Whipple (1784–1866), a Rhode Island lawyer, took the opposite view, and published his position as part of the debate over a bill to repeal the usury law then before the New York legislature.[23] He received a vigorous reply from John Russell Hurd, the father of the Austinian legal philosopher John Codman Hurd, in which the elder Hurd relied on the evidence of past experience to demonstrate the benefits of a free market in interest rates.[24]

Bentham was sufficiently apprized of Cooper's utilitarian credentials to ask John Quincy Adams, with whom he had become acquainted in London in 1817, to forward copies of several of his writings on codification, education, and political reform.[25] In his *Lectures* Cooper rejected both natural rights and natural law in favour of utilitarian principles as the correct foundation for policy and law. He announced that the only 'legitimate aim of all politics is the greatest good for the greatest number', which is 'the true origin of moral obligation, whether applied to national aggregates of individuals, or to any individual of the number.' There could be no 'stronger or higher obligation ... than to pursue and practice systematically those rules of conduct which can most effectually and permanently secure our own happiness'.[26] In stridently Benthamic vein Cooper declared that 'rights are the creatures of society, founded on their real or supposed utility, and requiring the force of society to protect them'. In developing this line of argument he demonstrated that he had thoroughly imbibed Bentham's positivist perspective:

> The very terms – right, duty, obligation, law – are relative, ——— A right is ——— that which is commanded, ordered, directed. To be effectual, it must be the command of a competent authority, – of a superior who has the means of enforcing it. A right abstracted from the power necessary to protect it is a non-entity. A right founded entirely on the power of ordering, commanding, directing, wants the great principle of voluntary acquiescence founded on a conviction of its utility. All laws, therefore, are the directions and regulations of a body of men, combined for mutual convenience into a society or community, prescribing what is for the common good, and enforcing obedience by their combined power.[27]

In 1830 Cooper penned a lengthy review of Bentham's *Rationale of Judicial Evidence* (1825) in *The Southern Review*, a journal published in Charleston, South Carolina, by Stephen Elliott (1771–1830), a member of the American Philosophical Society and president of the Literary and Philosophical Society of South Carolina. In an otherwise friendly review, Cooper registered a frequently voiced complaint that Bentham's style often posed an obstacle to the dissemination of his ideas: 'We could have wished that the present editor [J.S. Mill] had translated the work out of the obscure, involuted Bentham dialect in which it is written. A book more disgustedly affected and so nearly unintelligible it is not possible to imagine, with the exception of some of Mr. Bentham's former works, which equally exhibit specimens of what may, by courtesy to Mr. Bentham, be called English, but on no other score.' [I. 4: 1] Nevertheless, Cooper declared that Bentham's analysis had left him 'with a perfect conviction that the English system of common law is not the "perfection of reason" but needs the most radical, thorough going reform' [I. 4: 1], and to the extent that the

English common law had been adopted in America it was equally deficient and subject to reform [I. 4: 2]. He recommended that a commission be appointed to codify the various branches of American law on Benthamite principles and that it be reconvened every ten years to review the effectiveness of the several codes [I. 4: 42]. In the same year Cooper published a *Treatise on the Law of Libel* (1830), in which he explicitly followed Bentham's anti-clerical critique of oaths laid down in the pamphlet *Swear Not at All* (1817): 'The supposed utility of the Christian religion, as furnishing a sanction for oaths has been greatly overrated', he wrote. '[A]ll oaths of every description in or out of courts of justice, are morally and religiously indefensible.'[28] Finally, in his 1832 'Introductory Lecture to a Course of Law' Cooper voiced the utilitarian conviction that 'The polar star of morals and law is the greatest happiness of the greatest number.'[29] However, that he could also use this formula to justify slavery leaves a question mark against the consistency of his utilitarian thinking.[30] On the other hand, this could be cited as evidence of the pliability of utilitarian theory in different hands.

Bentham's influence on Edward Livingston has often occasioned comment.[31] Livingston openly avowed himself a supporter of Bentham, with whom he became a correspondent, and in the introduction to his Louisiana penal code declared his support for utility as the only principle of law. However, caution is warranted when considering the invocation by public figures, in speeches or print, of the names of reputed authorities, such as Bentham had undoubtedly become by the 1820s. All too often this is merely a way of bolstering their own stature by association, or an attempt to win an audience over to their position by claiming an allegiance to the respected authority, whereas they may not necessarily be pursuing the kinds of policies or reforms that their icons recommended.[32] Indeed, scholars have too often mistaken rhetoric for genuine conviction in these matters. With this in mind, we should look beyond Livingston's professions of discipleship to his legal writings to determine whether there was in fact an affinity between his own opinions on law and Bentham's.

Livingston had for long applied his considerable energies to codifying the law of Louisiana, which was a mix of Spanish and French law. The majority of the population was French, but the laws were written in Spanish, and legal proceedings could be conducted in any of three languages. Recognising the pressing need for reform, Livingston advocated a completely new code of law against those who favoured adopting the common law found elsewhere in the union.[33] Livingston's initial effort produced a code governing court procedure – the first code of law in America – and was adopted by the state legislature in 1805. Later he explained that it was a simple, straightforward set of guidelines of which Bentham would approve.[34] When Louisiana turned its attentions to civil law, the state legislature appointed a law commission to undertake the task of codification, and Livingston played only a minor role as a sort of advisor. The resultant code, based on the French and Roman model, was adopted in 1808, but it retained elements of the common law and owed little to Bentham's ideas.[35] Many years later, in 1825, Livingston was able to introduce certain amendments to the civil code that moved it further away from its dependence on Spanish cases and statutes. However, when he was appointed to codify Louisiana's penal law he did so with the explicit guidance of Bentham's ideas before him, and announced that the principle of utility was the sole object of the code.

The first, indirect communications between Livingston and Bentham occurred in 1820. In a letter to José Joaquín de Mora Bentham reported that he had received from Richard Rush (1780–1859), the son of Benjamin Rush, 'communication of a letter to him from Livingston of New Orleans, stating a determination there to make a Penal Code, and requesting information from England.'[36] Rush, who had been U.S. Attorney-General and formerly Minister in London, visited Bentham in late November to discuss the letter from Livingston.[37] Subsequently, Bentham wrote to Rush expressing his disappointment with Livingston's views on prisons:

> Mr L. has it in contemplation to introduce solitary imprisonment. For short-lived instrument of compulsion, yes: for every thing else, bad and enormously bad, in every respect: unseen misery is waste: misery up to madness, without any assignable good effect to the offender himself, that I can think of: unseen by others, unconceivable by others, therefor (sic) without effect on them; and if carried into effect to any extent, the expence enormous.
>
> A copy of my Panopticon work is at his service, if you think there is any chance of its being looked at.[38]

Rush responded, thanking Bentham for procuring the several parliamentary papers he had asked for on Livingston's behalf, and requesting a copy of *Panopticon; Or the Inspection-House* (1791) for Livingston.[39] Two years later Livingston made a report to the Louisiana General Assembly (Senate and House of Representatives) on his 'Plan of a

Penal Code' in which he acknowledged receiving the parliamentary papers sent to Rush, praised Bentham – 'whose writings have thrown so much light on the subject of criminal legislation' – and noted that he had adopted Bentham's suggestion to abandon 'solitary confinement' as the principal form of imprisonment.[40] There are many similarities to Bentham's ideas on penal law and legal procedures discernible in the report, including remarks on codification, jury trials, the deterrence value of different types of punishment, legal procedure and evidence, prison discipline, and the death penalty. In 1824 Livingston produced a second report updating and making amendments to the report of 1822, and in the process gave a lengthy quotation from Bentham's *Theory of Rewards and Punishments* in which Bentham's principal argument against the death penalty – its irremissibility and the fact of frequent miscarriages of justice – is made part of Livingston's case for abolition. The quotation is described as from 'a man to whom the science of legislation owes the great attention that is now paid to its true principles, and to whom statues would be raised if the benefactors of mankind were as much honoured as the oppressors of nations'.[41] A few more years then passed before Livingston was again held up to Bentham as a reformer who might benefit from the philosopher's assistance.

William Plumer Jnr. (1789–1854), a New Hampshire legislator and son of the former Governor, wrote to Bentham on 15 September 1826 to report the progress being made in the United States in law reform and legal theory, commenting: 'In many of these inquiries, your labours have been noticed, your principles, to a certain extent, adopted; and a disposition manifested to do that justice to your extraordinary merits, to the benevolence of your designes (sic), and the sagacity of your views, which, first or last, must universally prevail.' To this he added, 'I am glad to learn that you are not unacquainted with the labours of Mr Livingston of New Orleans in the field of legislation. He is a man of real talents, of great industry and perseverance, and of high standing and influence in his country. He has often spoken of you to me in terms of the highest veneration and respect, and informed me, more than once, that his attempts at Codification grew out of what he learnt of your views in the works published by Dumont.'[42]

Livingston wrote to Bentham for the first time on 10 August 1829, sending him parts of his proposed Code of Criminal Law for Louisiana, and informing him that it remained incomplete until such time as he could study Bentham's *Rationale of Judicial Evidence*, a copy of which he had only recently been able to procure. Livingston also confirmed that it was his reading of the *Traités de législation* which 'fortified me in a design to prosecute the subject' of penal reform. Sending a copy of his code for Bentham's consideration, he wrote: 'In laying before you this work, I offer you little that you have not a legitimate title to; for, hereafter no one can, in Criminal Jurisprudence, propose any favourable change that you have not recommended, or make any wise improvement, that your superior sagacity has not suggested.'[43] Early the following year Bentham informed Livingston that Dr Southwood Smith, the utilitarian social reformer, had been commissioned to write an article advertising Livingston's *Code of Criminal Law* in the British journal *The Jurist*.[44] Livingston replied, thanking Bentham for the several books he had sent, and commenting on the news from Bentham that his previous letter (probably that of 10 August 1829) had been printed, fearing that 'it should have imperfectly expressed how much my work is indebted to yours for those parts of my attempts to reform the laws of my State'. In the same letter he wrote 'the perusal of your works first gave method to my ideas, and taught me to consider legislation as a science governed by certain principles applicable to all its different branches.'[45]

In sum, the evidence suggests there is good reason to describe Livingston as a disciple of Bentham's. The final word on the matter is from a review of Livingston's *A System of Penal Law for the State of Louisiana* (1833) – probably by John O'Sullivan – who argued that the Louisiana reformer 'reduced to practice what Bentham had only suggested; who, taking up the subject of law-reform where the master had left it, pursued important parts of it to a complete consummation; and who, not satisfied with the speculations of the closet, succeeded in inducing the legislative power of a magnificent state to request him to make law of that which had been before only theory.' [I. 10: 4]

From 1837 to 1846 John O'Sullivan edited *The United States Magazine and Democratic Review*, the leading voice of law reform at that time. O'Sullivan was also a critic of death penalty legislation, and in 1841 published a report to the New York legislature on the subject, in the hope that it would lead to the total abolition of capital punishment in the next legislative session.[46] In this lengthy report he quoted from a wide range of sources, including like-minded reformers on both sides of the Atlantic, including Pastoret, Montesquieu, Basil Montagu, Gilbert Wakefield, Robert Rantoul, Livingston, and Bentham. The latter O'Sullivan twice quoted from the *Theory of Rewards and Punishments*, in the first instance in support of the argument that the death penalty was not an effective deterrent to murder, and secondly to underscore the fatal weakness of its irremissibility (the same passage quoted by Livingston).[47] Prior to this O'Sullivan had already given sufficient indication of his utilitarian credentials in one of the few journal reviews of Hildreth's translation of the *Traités de législation* [I. 8; see also I. 7 and 9]. The review provides a relatively acute and succinct account of the moral and legal theory contained in Hildreth's edition. O'Sullivan described Bentham as 'the father of law reform, the founder of legislative science, the powerful advocate of political emancipation, and a distinguished friend of the moral advancement of the human race.' [I. 8: 252] Hildreth is praised for his efforts in making Bentham's ideas 'more widely known to the American public ... at a time when the subject of law reform is beginning to be agitated in the legislatures of several of the States, and when the young men of the nation, as we fondly believe, are attaching themselves to sentiments of democratic freedom and progress. ... The legislator who should go forth armed with the weapons of this magazine of thought would prove an invincible champion in the cause of justice and truth.' [I. 8: 256]

O'Sullivan was not without criticisms of the moral theory contained in *The Theory of Legislation*, but unlike the *North American Review* [I. 9] he avoided the charge of atheism and ignored the subject of religion altogether. The principal issues which concerned O'Sullivan were first, whether pleasure and pain are the sole governing motives of men, and second, whether the tendency of an act to produce the greatest amount of happiness is the only reason why it is binding upon the consciences of men [I. 8: 259]. The reservations, however, pale alongside the great service Bentham is said to have conducted for legislative science and political reform. The systematic manner in which he set about his analysis of existing law, the stress on the practical business of the law, his arguments for codification, his influence upon law reformers like Samuel Romilly, are all commended in the strongest language [I. 8: 264–9]. Moreover, the reviewer credited Bentham with making plain 'the true functions of government'. Unaware, it seems, of the existence of Bentham's writings advocating democratic institutions, nevertheless O'Sullivan praised the political tendencies of *The Theory of Legislation*: 'He has stated with more clearness than any preceding writer the real objects of the civil law, and the best methods of attaining them. If he has not carried his ideas to the extent to which American statesmen are disposed to push their theories of government, he has made a near approximation to it. Indeed, the most radical of American statesmen can find much instruction in what he has uttered on this head.' [I. 8: 269]

xxx *Introduction*

Reflecting further on the principles of civil law stated in *The Theory of Legislation*, O'Sullivan summarised Bentham's recommendations to the legislator in these terms:

> the single aim of the legislator should be to promote the greatest possible happiness of the community. But happiness is increased as our sufferings are lighter and fewer, and our enjoyments greater and more numerous. As the care of his enjoyments ought, however, to be left entirely to the individual, it becomes the principal duty of government to guard against pains. If it protects the rights of personal security, if it defends property, if it watches over honor, if it succors the needy, it accomplishes its main purposes. Government approaches perfection in proportion as the sacrifice of liberty on the part of the subject is diminished, and his acquisition of rights is increased two hundred guineas for his trouble. [I. 8: 269]

It is in this way, O'Sullivan believed, that Bentham contributed most to our understanding of the correct functioning of the law in relation to the individual, his liberty, property, and security.[48]

John Neal's familiarity with the *Traités de législation*, evident in his translation of the fourteen chapters of the introductory 'Principes de législation' as *The Principles of Legislation* (1830), provided the basis for his dissemination of Bentham's ideas in the pages of *The Yankee* (later *The Yankee and Boston Literary Gazette*) in 1828–9 [I. 3 (1–13)].[49] When Hoffman asked for a volunteer from among his students to undertake a translation of Dumont's French text, Neal volunteered but could not find a publisher [I. 5: 267–8]. While visiting Bentham in London in 1825 he was persuaded to begin the work of translation by John Bowring, Bentham's close friend and later editor, who promised him two hundred guineas.[50] Bowring did not pay any part of the agreed fee, and Neal stopped short of completing the work of translation. When *The Principles of Legislation* appeared, Neal informed Bentham that four hundred copies of the five hundred printed were sold.[51] However, reviews of the work were few and generally critical.

Hugh Swinton Legaré (1797–1843), former U.S. Attorney General and diplomat, panned Neal's translation in the *Southern Review*: 'We do not know whether the publication of this book is to be considered any proof of the growing popularity of Bentham and Utilitarianism in the United States. But sure we are ... that it will do nothing to increase that popularity.' [I. 5: 449] Legaré preferred Paley's religious version of utilitarian theory enunciated in *Principles of Moral and Political Philosophy* (1785), but concluded: 'enough of utilitarianism – a philosophy, the very reverse of that so justly, as well as beautifully, described in Milton's Comus:

"How charming is divine philosophy –
Not harsh and crabbed as dull fools suppose ..."' [I. 5: 481]

Caleb Henry (1804–84), a congregational minister, theologian, and professor of philosophy, who helped found the *New York Review*, was also highly critical of Neal's translation, not because of the style in which he rendered it but on account of its unpalatable philosophy. Clearly angered by Bentham's atheism [I.6: 63], Henry was yet more antagonistic to the 'selfish' principle, which he viewed as underpinning the theory in both Paley's religious and Bentham's secular versions. The utilitarian theory, he argued, confounded virtue with prudence and, worse still, confounded it with vice, in the process obliterating 'all intelligible distinction between right and wrong' [I. 6: 66] According to Henry this consequence followed directly from the principle: 'Once admit the principle that man acts and ought to act only from a regard to his own happiness, be it in this or in a future world, and it must be followed out till there remains no place for moral distinctions. Duty sinks till it becomes synonimous (sic) with prudence, virtue with skill, vice with error, remorse with regret, and indignation with pity.' [I. 6: 67] Henry's critical analysis turned to a plea to the American people not to become corrupted by this doctrine, not to put their own interest above knowledge and virtue. In a prescient pronouncement he exclaimed: 'A nation ignorant as well as depraved – imbecile in mind as well as corrupt at heart, may be governed, and in some sense saved. But a nation composed of strong and unprincipled minds, endowed with a thousand-fold energy, but restrained by nothing but self-interest – ready whenever passion indicates its expediency for wrong or outrage – such a nation contains within its bosom elements of woe and discord which must soon explode; and with a shock too that will convulse the world.' [I. 6: 71] Nor did Henry think the insidious tendency of the 'selfish' principle could be obviated or qualified by the principle of the greatest happiness, the standard by which the morality of our actions and conduct is to be judged. The problem is that the tendencies of actions to serve the end of public utility are rarely obvious, and disputes are frequent even between well-meaning individuals in elected legislatures as to what is the best way to achieve this objective. In the absence of any other guide to action, how much more difficult must it be for a private individual to correctly ascertain the bearing of his conduct on the public good? [I. 6: 73][52]

How Neal responded to these reviews is not known, but he was unlikely to be moved by such attacks. Neal, who was a guest at Bentham's home in London for eighteen months in 1825–6, was an enthusiastic supporter of Bentham, describing him in the pages of *The Yankee* as 'the High Priest of legislation' [I. 3 (3): 5].[53] He made clear his own commitment to the utilitarian cause in the following terms:

> we acknowledge no rights that can interfere with the *greatest happiness* of the *greatest number* – none whatever, not even that "of life, liberty, and the pursuit of happiness" (to borrow the awkward and either very unmeaning or very untrue phraseology of most of our constitutions). If it be better for the greatest happiness of the greatest number that a man should die – whoever he may be, and whatever he may be, *cut him off without mercy*. And so with his liberty, and so with his property. But have a care – be *certain* that it *will* promote the greatest happiness of the greatest number, before you do so; ay, before you cut off the greatest criminal that walks the earth; before you spoil the highway robber of his liberty, or deprive him of *his* property.' [I. 3(1): 1–2]

Oblivious to the seeming contradiction in what he says here (the pursuit of happiness is at the core of the utilitarian doctrine), Neal believed his grasp of the requirements of utilitarian theory was clear and comprehensive. All the dimensions of an action and its consequences need to be assessed before a correct view can be reached about its morality, particularly when the actions are those of the legislator: 'To see the point perfectly [the imposition of punishment], it must be observed, that the bad consequences of actions are twofold, *particular* and *general*. The particular bad consequence of an action, is the mischief which that single action directly and immediately occasions. The general bad consequence is, the violation of some necessary or useful *general* rule.' The general rule that would be violated in this instance is 'that no man be put to death for his crimes but by public authority.' [I. 3 (1): 4]

Having declared himself to be Bentham's spokesman in America, Neal, who was also fascinated by Bentham as a person, took it upon himself to explain the man behind the utilitarian system of morals and law [I. 3 (3), (8), (11), (13), and III. 29], and to defend him against those who dismissed the philosopher as an absurdity [I. 3 (2), (3)].[54] In this context he reprinted an 'Ode to the Sublime Porte' by the Irish poet Thomas Moore (1779–1852),[55] which satirized Bentham, the Mills, father and son, and other Benthamites. Neal introduced the poem as 'no more than a happy specimen of the whole concentrated bitterness of Moore's nature.' [I. 3 (9)][56] He even sought to familiarize his readers with Bentham's likeness, and reproduced at the front of one of these articles an outline portrait of the philosopher writing at his desk [I. 3 (13)].[57] He lamented the fact that Bentham and his writings had been misunderstood and frequently misrepresented, and that so few of his works had appeared in English while many more were 'to be found in every public library of Europe ... and upon the table of every statesman, jurist, or philosopher of the continent ...' [I. 3 (13): 2]. Neal generously praised Dumont for introducing Bentham's ideas to a European audience in a style designed to appeal to a broader readership [I. 3 (13): 3]. One of Neal's most helpful contributions was a six-article treatment of Bentham's panopticon scheme [I. 3(10)], which he hoped to impress upon prison reformers among his countrymen as a major improvement on existing penitentiaries. 'If Bentham's plan had been adopted forty years ago,' he announced, referring to its initial date of publication, 'there would have been a saving of millions for us – a profit of millions upon the labor of convicts, the safety of the public, and the diminution of crime.' [I. 3 (10): 2]

Ironically, much of the criticism of Bentham in the American journals drew sustenance from Neal's biographical sketch prefixed to his translation of Dumont, which provided ready ammunition for those bent on character assassination. The statement that there could be no doubt Bentham was an atheist proved especially harmful. Those inclined towards utilitarianism but offended by its atheistic character in the hands of Bentham, found Paley more to their liking, but even Paley was criticized for undermining the divine law by his conviction that expediency determined what was right. Bentham's critique of the theological sanction and belief that the utility principle did not require the support of religion made him appear so much more dangerous to many.[58] However, as time went by in the 1840s the treatment of the utilitarian philosopher in the journals softened, and it came to be appreciated that his analysis of law need not require acceptance of his ethical theory lock, stock and barrel.[59] Moreover, Bentham's writings were becoming more well known and read first hand, rather than his ideas being gleaned only from the summary (and often distorted) accounts in the reviews.[60] The emerging interest in law reform in

America in the 1840s further stimulated a closer look at Bentham's recommendations.

Richard Hildreth's most significant contributions to utilitarian theory in America were his 1840 translation of the main parts of the *Traités de législation*, published in two volumes as *The Theory of Legislation* (1840), and his own *Theory of Morals* (1844), one of the few recognisably utilitarian texts on ethics published in the United States in the nineteenth century [II. 13]. It was in Dumont's French that Bentham's utilitarian moral and legal philosophy received its widest distribution in nineteenth-century Europe, and this impetus was continued with Hildreth's English translation.[61] Hildreth's declared mission was to promote Bentham's utilitarian ideas in the United States, where his writings had been little read up to this point. In particular, he believed that the contemporary widespread interest in legal reform in the United States would benefit enormously from an English translation of the ideas expounded in the *Traités de législation*, the most extensive statement of Bentham's philosophy circulating in America up to this point.[62]

Several reviews of Hildreth's translation appeared in the American journals of the day [I. 7–9]. In a brief notice in the *New York Review* an anonymous writer hailed it 'with a pleasure unqualified by any fear of consequences.' Anticipating the opposition to the utilitarian philosophy expressed in the book, the reviewer asserted 'we Americans can have nothing to dread from a voice like the present, that summons them in the name of reason to the bar of utility.' At the same time, however, he argued that the benefits of the utilitarian philosophy should be confined to the law; on moral reasoning he declared himself 'at open war with Bentham and the Benthamese philosophy' [I. 7: 264]. Duty could not be reduced to expediency in the manner Bentham proposed, and his whole approach to moral questions is mistakenly based upon a 'one-sided philosophy of man's nature' [I. 7: 265]. Hildreth was commended for his wisdom in distancing himself from the application of the principle of utility to moral questions, and applauded for recommending it as 'the only safe rule in legislation' [I. 7: 266].

We have already mentioned O'Sullivan's sympathetic review of Hildreth's translation [I. 8]. A more critical anti-Benthamic opinion was expressed by W. Phillips in the *North American Review*.[63] Phillips noted that while the *Traités de législation* enjoyed an 'immense circulation' in Europe, 'The force of his [Bentham's] ethical writings is almost spent; the principle of utility as the sole foundation and criterion of morals is about passing into the limbo of vanities.' [I. 9: 385]

However, in agreement with O'Sullivan and the anonymous reviewer in the *New York Review*, Phillips believed that the real value of Bentham's theory lay in its application to the science of legislation, 'a science which has come to be much more studied, and better understood, on the continent of Europe, than in either England or this country.' [I. 9: 395] But, according to Phillips, even this was purchased by the reader at too heavy a price, and it is only Dumont's editorial surgery that made Bentham readable at all [I. 9: 388]. Similar sentiments had been expressed before about Bentham's unreadable style and about Dumont's efforts in rendering the philosopher's ideas more readable and more palatable. But even among those well-disposed to Bentham's science of legislation, and this includes Neal and Hildreth, reservations were nearly always present in comments by Americans on his utilitarian moral theory.

2. Richard Hildreth

Richard Hildreth is best known today as the author of several anti-slavery tracts and the crowning work of his later life, a six-volume *History of the United States*, which went through several editions, and received some attention in American historiography.[64] His anti-slavery writings include the popular *The Slave: Or Memoirs of Archy Moore*, reputedly the first anti-slavery novel in the United States.[65] Though educated as a lawyer, early in his life Hildreth planned a career as a writer on philosophical subjects. The *Theory of Morals* was the first significant product of this commitment. It contains the most substantial statement of utilitarian principles by any American moralist in this period. In 'The Advertisement' at the front of the book Hildreth explained it was intended to be the first of a six-volume series, collectively titled 'Rudiments of the Science of Man', and amounting to a complete and systematic philosophy of the science of man and society. Only, the *Theory of Morals* and *Theory of Politics* (1854) were completed and published; left incomplete were the *Theory of Wealth*, *Theory of Taste*, *Theory of Knowledge*, and *Theory of Education*.[66] Notable for its absence from the proposed series was a 'theory of legislation', but it is likely Hildreth believed Bentham had said all that was required on this subject in the *Traités de législation*. He was particularly impressed with that part of Bentham's science of legislation that dealt with civil law. When Hildreth discussed rights and duties, for example, he stated no more than Bentham, and cited *The Theory of Legislation* specifically when he explained that property rights are 'nothing but a *Basis of expectation*', one of Bentham's keenest insights into the basic principles of civil law. What the legislator must take care to do is to prevent the pain of disappointing legitimate expectations, especially when they are related to property [II. 13: 159].[67] Nevertheless, Hildreth eschewed the name 'utilitarian' when it came to moral theory, and at times deliberately distanced his own theory from Bentham's.[68] The crucial difference between the two men turned on Hildreth's interpretation of Bentham – together with the Stoics, Epicurean, semi-Stoics, semi-Epicureans and Mystics – as a partisan of the 'Selfish Theory of Morals', who believed that 'the only conceivable motive to act which a man can have is the promotion of his own happiness', and that the happiness of others 'never can be the primary motive to the performance of any action.' [II. 13: 30; see also 29–30n] Hildreth argued that the facts of human experience tell a different story [II. 13: 33]. He realized that Bentham did not always promote the selfish theory of action, and when it came to 'practical morals' he made 'general utility' the test of right and wrong [II. 13: 3n]. However, Hildreth did not believe Bentham was entirely consistent when he sought to tether personal utility to general utility.

On the other side of the balance sheet similarities are not hard to find between the theories of the two philosophers. Whatever defects might appear in Bentham's theory, Hildreth allowed that 'no man has contributed more than Bentham to advance the science of morals, of which ... the science of Utility is a most important branch.' He declared that Bentham's *Introduction to the Principles of Morals and Legislation* 'contains a complete and beautiful development of that science', and referred the reader to his own translation of Dumont 'for a more easy and agreeable explanation of the doctrines of Bentham' [II. 13: 30n]. Like Bentham, Hildreth left no doubt that a properly constructed ethical theory must be secular in character, and his writings exhibited a high degree of scepticism about religion. He spent a great deal of time on religion in the *Theory of Morals*, offering a naturalistic account of the genesis of gods and a conjectural chronology of the development of monotheism, modern religions, and the belief in futurity [II. 13: 23–6, 139–40; see also Ch. IX]. Moral theories founded on such tenets he criticized as 'mystical theories', and repeatedly illustrated their inconsistencies and paradoxes.

Hildreth's theory might have been called a 'theory of benevolence', since it was the 'laws' of the operation of benevolence that his theory of morals was designed to explain. He defined right action as that which gives pleasure to others: 'those actions which we call morally good are *such as tend to promote the pleasure, either immediate or prospective, of some sensitive being other than the actor;* while those actions which we call morally bad are *such as tend to produce pain, immediate or prospective, to some sensitive being other than the actor.*' [II. 13: 9] In stating his theory this way – deliberately excluding the pleasure of the agent from the calculation of the morality of an action – Hildreth knew he was taking a significant step away from the standard Benthamic position, trusting that this would make his theory impervious to the usual objection that utilitarianism was a crass theory premised on the self-centred motivation of the individual. Where his theory retained the utilitarian dimension is in its focus on consequences and the calculation of utility in terms of pleasure and pain. Like Bentham, too, Hildreth held that actions 'are the only original subject-matter of moral judgment' [II. 13: 9], though he qualified this by drawing a distinction between 'virtue' and actions which produce happiness: 'In speaking of actions we use the words *right* and *wrong* principally with an eye to the external event and with little or no reference to the motive of the actor. We use the words *virtuous* and *vicious* principally with reference to the motive of the actor, and with little or no regard to the external event.' [II.13: 10] This distinction between the meanings of 'right' and 'virtue' in relation to actions and motives, respectively, underscores a further difference from Bentham's theory. Bentham, who spent a good deal of text delineating types of motives in *An Introduction to the Principles of Morals and Legislation*, refused to employ positive or negative epithets to describe the individual's motivation in engaging in particular actions. Simply put, there are no such things as 'good' or 'bad' motives; the only elements that count in determining the virtue (i.e. the utility) of an action are the consequences that result. All motives, including the most extensive benevolence, are rooted in self-interest in one form or another; in these terms, the notion of a *dis*interested motive is implausible. We commonly speak of actions as proceeding from good or bad motives, but in Bentham's account the expression is inaccurate. Even 'ill-will' is still a kind of pleasure, or pleasure in prospect, that constitutes a person's motive.

Another variation from Bentham, though it is not one that constitutes more than a refinement of the analysis of the 'springs of action', is Hildreth's argument that 'all human actions originate in pains.' [II. 13: 33] In stating this, Hildreth claimed to be following Hobbes and Locke,[69] but he may also have encountered this understanding of the primacy of pain in an essay by the American moralist, Thomas Ewell (1785–1826). Ewell was a well-known writer and physician, whose medical writings were especially popular in the early nineteenth-century, and who produced an edition of David Hume's *Philosophical Essays on Morals, Literature, and Politics* in 1817. Ewell's 'Essay on the Laws of Pleasure and Pain' was first published in this edition of Hume's writings, but has been overlooked entirely by modern scholars [I. 2]. Hildreth's *Theory of Morals* contains an impressive echo of Ewell's discussion of the relationship between pleasures and pains. If we view pain as the motivation for action, then pleasures are 'motives of action only secondary; that is, when the contemplation of them produces in us that particular sort of pains, called *desires*' [II. 13: 34]. In this account, happiness 'consists merely in the avoidance of, or escape from present pains ...; and it may be safely alleged that no action, from the most trivial up to the most important is ever performed, of which some present pain, either a simple pain, or a pain of desire, is not the immediate motive.' [II. 13: 35] Moreover, motives are frequently a mix of pains and pleasures. Hildreth acknowledged Bentham's contribution to our understanding of 'simple pains and simple pleasures', but pointed out that many pains and pleasures are in fact 'complex' [II. 13: 39n]. This means that the relationship between pleasure and pain, on the one hand, and action, on the other, is by no means as straightforward as Bentham assumed. Hildreth explained: 'Any pleasure coexisting with any pain, whether a simple pain or a pain of desire, tends, in proportion to the keenness of the pleasure, to diminish the force of that pain as a motive of action'. Furthermore, it is possible that pains of different sorts may exist together, impelling to action 'sometimes in the same, and sometimes in contrary directions; for the same action that may tend to relieve one pain may tend to aggravate or to produce another.' There is also the consideration that the pains experienced by an agent may be separated in prospect, thus the agent's 'contemplation of a future pain, as probable or certain, produces a present pain which may be called a pain of Anticipation.' [II. 13: 39] The same analysis applies to pleasures, such as when the agent's 'contemplation of a future pleasure as probable or as within our power produces a present pleasure, which may be called a pleasure of Anticipation.' Commonly called 'hopes', such pleasures 'are never quite unmixed, being uniformly attended in a greater or less degree by pains of desire, pains of doubt, and pains of fear.' [II. 13: 40] The complexity of the pains motivating action, and the modification of their force by pleasures experienced at the same time, makes the determination of which action to undertake 'an exceedingly complicated and nice calculation.' [II. 13: 42] But this is where the 'science of Utility' comes in, the purpose of which is to determine 'whether acts are, in fact, beneficial or not.' This objective science is intended to leave the subjective judgment of individuals out of the decision as to the rightness or wrongness of an action [II. 13: 131].

At bottom the difference between the theories of Bentham and Hildreth turned around the latter's distinction between 'virtue' and 'utility' [II. 13: 10]. Whereas Bentham equated virtue with utility, in Hildreth's account the concept of virtue is not a simple supposition, but in its most general sense is constituted of 'all that part of human nature which cooperates in impelling and enabling men to perform actions beneficial to others; first, the pains and pleasures of benevolence; secondly, certain impulses of the pains and pleasures of self-comparison; thirdly, those pains and pleasures of anticipation included under the heads of the fear of punishment and the hope of rewards; and fourthly, all those temperaments indicated by the epithets Wisdom, Courage, Fortitude, Constancy, Hopefulness, Activity and Ability.' [II. 13: 100–1] However, Hildreth recognized that this is not what is commonly meant by the term 'virtue' in ordinary language; rather a more limited meaning is intended to refer to those impulses *'whereby men are induced to confer benefits upon others, without the expectation of any reward beyond that which arises from the consciousness of having conferred them.'* [II. 13: 101]

Hildreth took both Helvétius and Bentham to task for confounding the meaning of the concept. When Helvétius and Bentham include the pleasure and pains of benevolence under the term 'self-interest', or in other words '*Interest well understood*', according to Hildreth they employed ambiguous language. When they say that self-interest, including the sentiment of benevolence, is the only source of human action, technically they are correct, but 'it is to use a form of expression almost certain to deceive both those who hear it and those who use it.' [II. 13: 45]. More importantly, in a practical view, without the pains and pleasures of benevolence 'the "greatest happiness of the greatest number" would be an unmeaning jingle, incapable of exercising the slightest influence over conduct.' [II. 13: 45n] Helvétius and Bentham frequently reason 'as if benevolence were a chimera and as if human conduct were wholly uninfluenced by it', but this is 'a course of procedure quite inconsistent even with their own systems, according to which benevolence does in fact play a considerable, though subordinate part.' [II. 13: 45n] In the same critical vein, later in the book Hildreth claimed that Helvétius and Bentham 'made an ingenious but desperate attempt to amalgamate together the doctrines of pure selfishness and entire self-sacrifice', but this only resulted in 'the paradox, that pure selfishness may require of us the entire sacrifice of ourselves for the benefit of others.' [II. 13: 103, 104]

Having distinguished virtue from utility, what then is the relationship between the two? Hildreth resolved the issue into two separate questions: 'First. Does the increase of virtue in a community tend to increase the happiness of that community. Second. Are individuals happy in proportion as they are virtuous?' [II. 13: 255] In answering the first question Hildreth returned to his theory of benevolence to remind us that 'just in proportion as virtue exercises an influence over the conduct of man, just in that same proportion does the happiness of others become an object to be aimed at; and just in that proportion will men be likely to contribute to the happiness of each other.' [II. 13: 256] In answering the second question he dismissed the claim, commonly made by moralists and legislators, that the increase of virtue in an individual tends directly to increase his own happiness [II. 13: 257]. The claim that personal happiness is the necessary concomitant of virtue and that misery inevitably follows vice, Hildreth denounced as 'notions better fitted for the sycophant and the parasite, than for the philosopher or the moralist.' [II. 13: 261] Nevertheless, at times Hildreth did associate virtue with personal happiness, for example when he prescribed that 'it ought to be the aim of the enlightened moralist not so much to produce individual instances of extraordinary virtue, individual instances of self-sacrifice for the benefit of mankind, as to raise the general standards of morals, and thereby to produce a general increase of virtue, and at the same time of happiness; and that too without any sacrifice of individuals, and those the most meritorious.' [II. 13: 262] Hildreth's reasoning is that in acting benevolently and serving the general happiness, each individual will indirectly serve his own interest by creating a social climate in which virtue is fostered, benevolence is increased, and everyone's happiness is enhanced as a result. How is the general standard of morals to be raised? Hildreth suggested two primary methods of encouraging the sentiment of benevolence: (1) education and the formation of good habits at a young age, which are then reinforced in later life at the hands of tutors and moralists; and (2) a general improvement in living conditions, since it is evident that in more advanced civilizations there is greater scope for benevolence, while in more rudimentary societies people are forced to focus on their own basic needs [II. 13: 268–71]. Hildreth's thinking is novel on this point: 'The progress of civilization doubtless tends to relieve the whole community from certain pains, especially those terrible pains of famine, to which savage communities are particularly exposed and to create a large class of persons, who, as they enjoy a superior degree of knowledge and wealth, and which are the means of many pleasures, become capable in consequence, of a superior degree of happiness, and of a superior degree of virtue.' [II. 13: 270] Hildreth believed that the growth in the middle class throughout Europe was primarily responsible for the rise in the standard of morals during the most recent centuries. However, he thought that the uneven distribution in property and wealth left many exposed to 'new pains of inferiority' and 'new pains of desire' and might 'prove hardly less fatal to happiness and to virtue, than the worst evils of the savage state.' [II. 13: 270-1] It was this dilemma that Hildreth proposed to address in the *Theory of Wealth* and *Theory of Politics* [II. 13: 272] – only the latter of which was completed and published.[70]

For the most part the *Theory of Politics* proceeds in a pedantic, descriptive manner detailing the origins, development, and forms of government, from ancient and feudal to modern times, all abundantly illustrated with examples from historical record. In the course of this descriptive analysis Hildreth explained the elements of 'power' – the core concept of politics – in the several political arrangements discussed, but predictably demonstrated the advantages of democracy over all other forms of government.[71] However, his analysis of democracy was not uncritical; he noted several defects in American democracy. First, following Bentham, Hildreth argued that the common law basis of American jurisprudence inherited from England is 'hostile to the spirit of democracy'. The common law, correctly viewed, is nothing but 'a contrivance for setting aside the laws, and defeating the intentions of the legislative body, whenever those laws and those intentions fail to meet the approbation of the judges'. Secondly, the 'mystical ideas' of religion are a 'disturbing force' with 'no inconsiderable degree of influence in all social manners.' The consequence is 'intolerant bigotry and bitter opposition to all freedom of inquiry'.[72] Third, the existence of slavery stands 'in direct contradiction to the fundamental principles of democracy'.[73] Finally, it must be recognized that the United States is 'a country very recently settled, where the accumulation of wealth is but just beginning'; in these early stages of development in many parts of the country 'the dispersion and poverty of people form serious, and as yet insurmountable, obstacles in the way of social improvements, especially the cultivation of the sciences and the elegant arts'.[74] It is only in the last twenty or so pages of the book (274 pages long), and especially the concluding chapter headed 'Hopes and Hints as to the

Future', that Hildreth addressed the question raised at the end of the *Theory of Morals* – what are the means to social improvement (and thereby the means, in addition to education, of promoting the sentiment of benevolence and enhancing social happiness)? The answer he gave is that it lies in the continuing democratization of political life and in the advance of social equality through a steady improvement in the rewards of labor. Hildreth argued, again following Bentham's civil law prescriptions, against a legislated redistribution of property and wealth – an approach bound to cause insuperable conflicts between classes – and counseled that all political and socio-economic advances must be achieved through peaceful reforms over the course of time. With political and social advances will come, he believed, the general rise in those moral standards prescribed at the end of the *Theory of Morals*.

Several reviews of Hildreth's book appeared in the journals of the day [II. 14–15; III. 16–17], drawing the author into a bitter dispute with two of his opponents [III. 18–19]. Not surprisingly O'Sullivan's *United States Magazine and Democratic Review* published a sympathetic notice of the *Theory of Morals* [II. 14], but other responses were highly critical. Hildreth's main opponent was Orestes A. Brownson (1803–76), a well-known critic of utilitarianism. In *Brownson's Quarterly Review* he denounced Hildreth's atheism, and argued that there can be no moral theory or morality without a belief in God. In the process Brownson also fired off a few critical remarks on Bentham and utilitarian theory in general. 'Hildreth', he concluded, 'has studied Benthamism until his own head is more confused, if possible, than ever was Bentham's own head.' [III. 16: 2] Andrew Preston Peabody (1811–93), a unitarian minister who had been a classmate of Hildreth's at Harvard, and was now the editor of the *North American Review*, also entered the lists against the *Theory of Morals*. Despite its being 'grave, decent, dignified, in its tone and manner', Peabody claimed 'its reasoning is all vitiated by the assumption of false premises, and its sober, didactic style is made the vehicle for conveying the most licentious sentiments in morals and theology.' [III. 17: 393] Peabody was particularly exercised about the first chapter of the second part of *The Theory of Morals*, devoted to rights of personal security: 'we are met by propositions abhorrent from every sentiment of humanity, and in accordance with the morality of the least enlightened nations and ages.' [III. 17: 397] Hildreth's defence of suicide when employed to avoid disgrace, of duels when resorted to in defence of honour, of private revenge and infanticide in extreme situations, Peabody found acutely distasteful. He praised the chapter on the rights of property and Hildreth's attacks on slavery, but denounced the anti-christian character of its final chapter [see II. 13: 397]. Peabody was also critical of the chapter on promises, contracts, and truth in general, in which Hildreth voiced the unpalatable argument that deception and falsehood are permitted when it is likely that more beneficial results will follow than by an adherence to the truth [see II. 13: 167, 169–70]. Finally, he declared Hildreth's remarks on the marriage contract and the obligation of chastity to be 'most offensively loose and licentious.' [III. 17: 398] In sum, the whole book is nothing but 'an undisguised profession of bald, blank atheism', in which the author does not 'omit a single convenient opportunity of casting ridicule on religious ideas'. [III. 17: 399]

Incensed by these attacks, Hildreth issued *A Joint Letter to Orestes A. Brownson and the Editor of the North American Review: In which the Editor of the North American Review is proved to be no Christian, and little better than an Atheist* (1844). He denounced the slurs on his character by Brownson and Peabody, and referred to the conduct of the latter as that of a 'skulk, a coward, a sycophant, a hypocrite, and a liar.' [III. 18: 30][75] Brownson, never one to miss an opportunity to continue a debate, published a reply in which he criticized Hildreth for ignoring the *a priori* existence of a moral law and 'a moral law-giver', defiantly reiterated his condemnation of Hildreth's atheism, and condemned the *Theory of Morals* as blasphemous. According to Brownson, Hildreth's book was 'as absurd as Bentham, as skeptical as Hume, and as atheistic as D'Holbach' [III. 19: 333, 328].[76]

3. Paley, Religion and J.S. Mill

The charge of atheism dogged the acceptance of utilitarian theory almost from its first appearance in the United States. However, it is one of the notable ironies of the British political tradition that utilitarian principles were first expounded and nurtured in association with Christian principles, beginning with the Anglican divines John Gay (1699–1745) and John Brown (1715–66), and continuing in the eighteenth century in the writings of Edmund Law (1703–87), Abraham Tucker (1705–74), and Paley, among others.[77] In the first few decades of the nineteenth century it was Paley's religious version of the utilitarian doctrine that dominated discussions of the theory. Only when Neal and Hildreth took upon themselves the task of popularising Bentham was Paley gradually unseated from the utilitarian pedestal in America. Paley was a powerful influence on the teaching of moral philosophy and theology in the universities of nineteenth-century

Britain. In America his theology received explicit attention in several journals of the day and, more significantly, ten editions of the *Principles of Moral and Political Philosophy* were published in the United States prior to 1821.

Though the influence of Paley's writings in America is well known, not everyone was convinced by his appeal to expediency to indicate the substance of God's benevolent will.[78] Scandalized by Bentham's secular version of utilitarianism, in the words of a modern scholar, 'they were seduced by Paley, the vicar who sugar coated the pernicious doctrine of expediency with theology, into acquainting their charges with utilitarianism.'[79] Nevertheless, by preaching the utilitarian message in a more palatable form Paley was able to assume the place of leadership in expounding utilitarian ideas in America, at least until the 1830s, after which Bentham increasingly assumed prominence.[80] One early reviewer of Paley's *Evidences of Christianity* (1794) described the *Principles* as 'an excellent treatise' in which the author excelled 'in clearness of conception, propriety of language, and pertinency of illustration.'[81] A good illustration of Paley's influence can be found in Nathaniel Chipman's *Principles of Government* (1833). Though an adherent of natural law, Chipman drew upon utility as a secondary and supplementary line of defense in asserting natural rights. The right of property, for example, originated in natural principles, but received its formal sanction from the principle of utility – 'the general interest which is the greatest end of all the laws of nature.'[82] This form of argument was derived from Paley, who stressed happiness as a test of morality not in its own right but rather as an index to the natural law. Other utilitarian elements in Chipman's theory included the claim that no obligation could exist without a regard for utility, which was the end and purpose of the law. Also, he argued that since men were primarily self-interested, benevolence was required to achieve the general end of happiness. He granted benevolence the status of a natural law, but stated that the only certain test that a rule requiring obedience was a genuine law of nature was the rule of utility.[83]

Even though it came dressed in Christian theology, not many other American commentators accepted unequivocally the moral theory contained in Paley's *Principles*. An anonymous reviewer in *The Christian Examiner*, one of the foremost religious journals of the day, praised Paley's writings for their 'practical bearing' and Paley for 'his felicity in selecting illustrations of his arguments, his sound judgement, and the candour, benevolence, and devotion, which he everywhere exhibits'.[84] These qualities are best exhibited in Paley's *Natural Theology* and *Evidences of Christianity*. By comparison, the reviewer was far less impressed by the *Principles*, which, he opined, 'we should not be sorry to see banished from the collegiate course of study.'[85] The gist of his complaint follows: 'we cannot but feel that a treatise which rests moral obligation on utility, a treatise in which this unsound principle is frequently brought forward, and in which some questionable positions of an important practical tendency are maintained, ought not to be presented to young persons, with the authority which it must have when stamped with the apparent approbation of their instructors.' If Paley's text must be used, then 'it should be with notes in which the unsafe foundation of his system is exposed, and the errors into which he has fallen are carefully corrected.'[86] Another commentator, this time in a review of several works by Henry Brougham, in which Brougham provided elaborations and supplementary material on Paley's theology, commented on the 'extraordinary influence and popularity' of Paley's writings. His philosophy, says the reviewer, is marked by 'unrivalled clearness of statement', 'terseness of language', 'abundance of forcible but homely illustration', 'close and orderly array of argument', and by 'brief, but nervous touches of eloquence with which the whole composition is seasoned.'[87] However, the reviewer's tone changed dramatically when he turned to the *Principles*; he condemned the 'exceptional' character of its moral philosophy as 'unsound in doctrine and pernicious in its results'. The root cause of Paley's errors lay in his starting point, in the definition of virtue: 'Virtue consists in doing good to mankind, in obedience to the will of God, and for the sake of everlasting happiness.' It is the narrowness and irreligious aspects of this definition that the reviewer found anathema: 'It is enough to say, that benevolence is not the whole duty of man, that right is of inherent and necessary obligation, anterior to all command, and that a selfish regard to our future welfare, far from constituting the only proper motive, vitiates the whole act, and is destructive of the very essence of virtue.'[88]

If Paley's 'religious' version of utilitarian moral philosophy could not win over the American critics, how much less likely to succeed were the openly anti-religious Bentham and Hildreth. More problematic still was the response to the views on religion of J.S. Mill, Bentham's self-described 'spiritual godson' whose writings, more than any other utilitarian, were read and critically received in America, including *Principles of Political Economy* [III. 20–1, and 27], *Considerations on Representative Government* [III. 26], *Dissertations and Discussions* [III. 30, and 32], and his famous *Autobiography* [III. 40–2, 47]. The influence of Mill's empiricism on pragmatism in the United States is well-enough testified by William James' *Pragmatism* (1907), dedicated to Mill 'from whom I first learned the pragmatic openness of mind and whom my fancy likes to picture as our leader were he alive today'.[89] When first published, Mill's work did not always register with the American public, but the proliferation of editions of writings often elicited a belated appreciation. Such was the case, for example, with *Principles of Political Economy* (1848). When a new edition was published in New York in 1863, a short but well-informed review appeared in the *North American Review*, in which the reviewer noted that the first edition of this work had made little impression in America. The reason for this, the explained, 'can be attributed only to the circumstances that many of the questions discussed in it have not hitherto been regarded as of immediate interest to ourselves.' [III. 27: 271] For example, customs like 'primogeniture' and 'entails' are of little interest in America, and Mill's discussion of colonies and the governance of dependencies could have little impact in a country that had dispensed with the practice of colonization. Nor could Mill's discussion of the Malthusian doctrine of population or Ricardo on rent have much meaning in a country with a seemingly inexhaustible supply of land for settling. But times had changed since Mill first published the *Principles*, and there are subjects examined in its pages that are of vital interest to America. Of these, the reviewer lists the following: the best method of managing an 'inconvertible' paper currency; the expediency of income tax; whether extraordinary expenditures are best defrayed by an increase in direct tax or an increase in the national debt; the influence on commerce of a sudden increase in bank-notes; the effect of an increase in paper currency on foreign exchange and international trade; the circumstances determining the demand and supply of loans and alterations in the rate of interest; the benefits and inconveniences of establishing a national bank responsible for issuing all banknotes; the effect of great extensions and contractions of credit; and the influence of speculators on value and prices – 'upon all these Mr. Mill has made suggestions of the highest value, and destined erelong to make their way into the public mind of this country, as they have already done into that of England.' [III. 27: 272] Above all, Mill's chapter on peasant proprietorship would be invaluable in a society in which slavery had been abolished and which must decide how an expanded free labour force will function. Americans could also benefit from Mill's discussion of several other pressing issues, including the debates over free trade, the rights of women, and the representation of minorities [III. 27: 272–3]. The same journal also featured a generally positive review of Mill's *Dissertations and Discussions*, published in

Boston in 1867 [III. 32], which began by commenting on Mill's reputation in America: 'The time has gone by when it would be thought necessary to introduce Mr. Mill to the readers of America or any other civilised country. Mr. Mill's reputation rests upon a foundation too strong to be shaken, upon an eminence too conspicuous to need pointing out.' [III. 32: 300] However, when the reviews turned to Mill's opinions on religion an entirely different tone exuded from the journals.

Most critics, especially in reviews of Mill's *Autobiography* (1873), were appalled by the lack of exposure to religion in Mill's early education, which they held accounted for the narrowness of his utilitarian perspective, and on this basis sought to prove the deficiencies of his philosophy. Even in reviews of his publications in which he spent little time on religious matters, such as *Considerations on Representative Government* (1862), a reviewer could find room to disapprove of Mill's 'air of condescending recognition toward ... "Christian Ideas",' and 'regret that a book so able as this should be deformed by such opinions as these, so needlessly introduced and so offensive to multitudes of readers.' [III. 26: 2] The attack on Mill was part and parcel of the general dismay in America at the anti-religious thrust of utilitarian philosophy.

Henry L. Baugher (ca. 1805–68), a theologian and professor of Greek, criticized the materialist focus of utilitarianism in an 1854 article on 'Faith and Utilitarianism' in the *Evangelical Review*: 'Nowhere but in the school of the atheist and the unbeliever are we taught that the end of this life is wealth, or fame, or knowledge, or happiness. If it be, then have all men failed most sadly.' [III. 24: 216–17]. According to Baugher, the 'evils of utilitarianism' can only be corrected by faith [III. 24: 223] John Bascom (1827–1911), the president of Wisconsin University and lecturer in the well-known Concord School summer series in philosophy, launched his attack on the theory in the *Bibliotheca Sacra*, the mouthpiece of the Andover Theological Seminary. In this 1866 article Bascom compared the utilitarian and intuitionist theories: the first 'refers knowledge to perception and reflection', the second 'to perception, intuition, and reflection'. The first school of thought, associated with Locke, Hartley, the Mills, Bain, and Spencer, 'is more immediately connected with the scientific and positive tendency of human thought'; the second school, associated with Kant, Coleridge, Reid, Hamilton, and Hickock,[90] 'has been developed largely in the interest of religion, of our higher nature, and stands associated with a devout spirit, putting itself in communion with

God, and resting on a providence more immediate and personal than that of law.' [III. 31: 435] Mill was singled out for special attention as the principal representative of utilitarian school, and Bascom included many lengthy quotations from Mill's *Utilitarianism* (1861) [III. 31: 436–41], including what he had to say about the distinction between higher and lower pleasures – a distinction Bascom held to be unintelligible and too subjective to be practical. Not surprisingly, he argued against Mill that the primary determinant of what is right is the 'moral sense':

> The mind is left by utilitarianism to judge between pleasures independently of morality – to measure them in quantity before it can secure a moral verdict for either. The theory of an intuitive right affirms that the sense of obligation arises because of a primitive perception, and accounts therein for the firmness and decision with which the balance is brought down. Utilitarianism, affirming that this sense attends on all pleasures, cannot call it in to determine in favor of any one pleasure, till this has been shown, on independent grounds, to be greater than any and every competing good. [III. 31: 447]

It is right which judges of utility, Bascom concluded, not the other way round, and the source of what is right is located in the will of God [III. 31: 451–2]

Moncure Daniel Conway (1832–1907), who later published books on Paine and Carlyle among other subjects, was one of the very few to see in Mill's writing 'his essential religiousness', explaining that it 'did not express itself in conventional ways, nor his devotion ascend to popular symbols.' [IV. 39: 11] Another sympathetic reviewer, James Elliot Cabot (1821–1903), the editor of Emerson's writings,[91] argued that Mill's 'Religion of Humanity is capable of fulfilling every important function of religion, and would fulfil them better than any form of supernaturalism.' [IV. 45: 463] However, the general reaction in America to Mill's posthumously published *Three Essays on Religion* (1874) was highly critical. One reviewer described the essay 'Nature', the first of the three essays, as 'singularly paradoxical and offensive to the common judgement of men in respect to the so-called Law of Nature as the foundation and standard of rectitude.' [IV. 44: 181] The essay 'Theism' faired no better; Mill's remarks on Christ and Christianity were denounced as 'eminently pathetic ... and inconsistent' [IV. 44: 182]. The reviewer concluded: 'Those who are believers will find abundant confirmation of the excellence and reasonableness of their faith, in the weakness and occasional fatuity of this rejector of God and of Christ.' [IV. 44: 183] C.B. Crane was equally forthright in summoning the defenders of Christianity to reply to Mill: 'He is too great, too confident, too plausible, too fascinating to remain unchallenged.' [IV. 43: 349] It is the arrogance of Mill's analysis of Christianity that cried out for a response. On the one side stands Mill, 'proud, self-righteous, self-sufficient', and on the other side is Christianity, 'teaching humility, penitence, faith in God.' Which of these, Crane demanded, 'is the more admirable, the spirit of the man, or the spirit of the religion?' [IV. 43: 352] In a similar vein the theologian and president of Yale College, Noah Porter (1781–1866), declared 'Nature' to be 'one of the feeblest of Mr. Mill's productions, for the ambitiousness of its pretensions, the narrowness of its definitions, the defectiveness of its logic, and the repulsiveness of its conclusions.' [IV. 46: 493] The argument of 'The Utility of Religion', the second of the three essays, that the Religion of Humanity is superior to supernatural religion, and that the more cultivated man becomes the less he will need the belief in immortality, was similarly dismissed as 'lame and impotent' [IV. 46: 493]. While the third essay, 'Theism', is generally the better of the three essays, Porter argued that it was fatally weakened by Mill's incapacity to appreciate and adequately represent the views of those who believe in the existence of God:

> That the belief in an intelligent originator is the necessary assumption to the belief in an orderly universe, and therefore the condition of all special induction, is a proposition which Mr. Mill would seem to be incapable of understanding, so far as to conceive how any sane man should hold it. That a man, with these limitations, should fail to find what he calls an argument decisively proving that God exists, is to us altogether intelligible. [IV. 46: 504]

The theologian and educator Daniel S. Gregory (1832–1915) subjected 'Theism' to an even more searching analysis in *The Princeton Review*, describing Mill's argument against the existence of 'a First Cause' as a 'marvellous combination of intricate sophistry and utter confusion of thought, with an extraordinary show of candour and fairness, and a tone of supreme confidence such as is ordinarily begotten only by a certain and infallible grasp of truth.' [IV. 48: 411]

4. Henry Sidgwick, intuitionism and utilitarianism
The issue of religion was dealt with far more judiciously by Henry Sidgwick, often described as the most philosophically sophisticated of

1   *Introduction*

the classical utilitarians. Sidgwick shared with other nineteenth century utilitarians the urge to provide a comprehensive and practical ethical theory. However, he was never a utilitarian in an unqualified sense of the term, and on the question of religion he tended to side with Paley and Austin, rather than with Bentham, Hildreth, and Mill. Sidgwick believed that only some form of theological postulate about the moral harmony of the universe could plausibly resolve the potential conflict between the moral point of view and the personal point of view – usually described in terms of the dualism of practical reason.[92] The utilitarian perspective he thought was the correct point of view for those in political power and administrative positions in the state – their enlarged responsibilities required this, since they are most likely to be able to put such a view into practice – but this is simply not expected of private individuals.[93] This is suggestive of the elitism that is detected elsewhere in Sidgwick's thinking, but is also related to his reluctance to discuss openly his doubts about religion. He demonstrated his intellectual honesty when he resigned his Fellowship at Cambridge because he could not bring himself to subscribe to the Thirty-nine Articles.[94] Generally, however, he kept his deeper religious doubts private, as Bart Shultz has explained, 'out of the conviction that public morality, at that time and place, still very much required the religious buttress. Hence, for utilitarian reasons, he did not want to do anything to further the decline of popular religious belief'. On the other hand, Shultz pointed out that Sidgwick's elitism is further evidenced by his membership in the Cambridge Apostles, a discussion society 'out to undermine, typically in a behind-the-scenes way the hold of orthodox Anglican religion on such social institutions as Oxbridge.' Based on this, Shultz concluded that for Sidgwick 'what was appropriate for the educated elite was one thing, what was appropriate for the general public was something else'.[95]

Sidgwick's ethical theory, adumbrated in *The Methods of Ethics* (1874) and other works, is an amalgam of intutionist and utilitarian principles. The criterion for utilitarianism is the general happiness; the criterion for intuitionism is the conformity to duty, as defined by fundamental and self-evident principles. By comparison, egoism, included by Sidgwick as one of the 'methods' of ethics, offers an account of motives in terms of the happiness of the individual alone. One recent commentator regards this as the source of the incoherence in Sidgwick's moral theory.[96] While the cognition of utilitarianism and intuitionism may recommend action contrary to the good or happiness of the individual, egoism can only recommend what the individual would himself desire to do and there is no potential conflict for the moralist to navigate or adjudicate. In the context of egoism the 'ought' has a decidedly different status as an imperative to action, and it is therefore problematic whether egoism counts as a 'method' of ethics at all.[97]

The Methods of Ethics received a good deal of attention in American journals, praised by one reviewer as 'one of the most important contributions to scientific ethics which has been made in the present century by any English writer.' [III. 37: 379] Sidgwick's project to develop a synthesis of utilitarianism and intuitionism was also undertaken by others in the United States, notably by Borden Parker Browne (1847–1910), professor of philosophy at Boston University [III. 36]. In the *New Englander and Yale Review*, in the year before the publication of *The Methods of Ethics*, Browne compared the schools of moral intuitionism and utilitarianism and argued that 'though each party has held the other in detestation, still neither, when pressed by argument, has been able to avoid assuming the positions of the other.' [III. 36: 217] To demonstrate this claim Browne quoted from the theories of William Whewell, Paley, and Mill [III. 36: 217–18]. His own position is that only God's law can be a sure guide in morals: 'implicit faith in our Heavenly Father's commands is the only becoming attitude for us to assume.' However, Browne revealed his utilitarian tendencies when he followed this by saying 'nothing is obligatory which is not helpful; and nothing is wrong which is not hurtful.' [III. 36: 223] Would Paley or Bentham have said anything different? On the other hand, Browne argued that in yielding to the utilitarian that consequences matter in the assessment of the morality of actions 'we by no means agree with him in denying moral intuition ...' Furthermore, 'We look upon our moral instincts as a part of the primary furniture of the soul, and, like all the intuitions, as authoritative in their sphere. The attempt of the utilitarians to reduce them to some operation of the intellect, or some affection of our sensitive nature, we look upon as a complete failure.' [III. 36: 226] In the course of this discussion Browne quoted Paley on the measurement of pleasures [III. 36: 230], and complained of Bentham's narrow view of happiness [III. 36: 231]. He preferred the theory of Mill, who included in his account of agency 'the spiritual bearing of actions.' [III. 36: 231] But, according to Browne, Mill, like other utilitarians, was confused in his understanding of motives. Are men motivated by their own happiness or the happiness of others? Why are some forms of happiness to be preferred over others? Motives, says Browne, 'are of different rank, else there is no good or evil.' But how is the utilitarian to determine 'their relative authority?' [III. 36: 232] Browne was not persuaded by Mill's account of experience as the basis upon which to distinguish between higher and lower pleasures. Rather, he sided with the moral intuitionists, holding (not without paradox) that 'as two motives appear in the mind, we intuitively know which is higher', while the utilitarian 'can only test them by their subjective consequences.' The truth is that our 'moral estimate of motives always precedes approval or condemnation.' On this view, we do not act rightly because we are happy, but are happy because we act rightly. Browne concluded that 'the utilitarian makes far too much of happiness as the cause of action. Happiness is rather the end of action than its cause. The bulk of human action is instinctive, and though it would cease if it were found to be resultless, yet the primary cause is the promptings of the instinct.' [III. 36: 234] Browne explained his own position in these terms: 'We believe, then, with the intuitionist in the absolute authority of conscience. We believe with the utilitarian that the end of all action should be to secure our own or others' good, but what particular good we shall seek, or how we shall seek it, cannot be determined without reference to our moral affections as well as to our sensitive nature.' [III. 36: 236] Both intuitionism and utilitarianism, then, are necessary to a complete science of morals: 'When the intuitionist attempts to construct an *á priori* code, he falls into the most ludicrous extravagances; when the utilitarian denies that we have the power of moral insight, he reduces morality to the lowest selfishness, and does violence to universal experience.' Perhaps erring more than he intended on the side of the intuitionists, Browne summed up his synthesis of the two theories as follows: 'The end of all action is not to do right, but to do good, either to ourselves or others; but what kind of good we shall do will depend more upon our moral affections than upon our sensitive nature.' [III. 36: 242]

5. Austin's jurisprudence and the theory of sovereignty
It is arguable that Austin's writings had a greater impact on American legal thought than Bentham's, from whom Austin derived the essential foundations of his jurisprudence.[98] Austin was the first to hold the chair in that field at the newly established University College London, where he gave the lectures that formed the basis for *The Province of Jurisprudence Determined*. He insisted on a clear division between the study of laws and theories of morality and, at a time when the academic divisions between the various disciplines were beginning to take hold, this was generally welcomed as an advance on Bentham. In addition,

Austin's ethical doctrine was far more acceptable to American tastes than Bentham's had been, both on account of his less critical position on natural law and his sympathetic theological views. Moreover, in the context of the troubles that afflicted the union in the mid-century, Austin offered some welcome analyses of the location and operations of sovereignty.[99] By the 1890s Austin's concept of sovereignty was firmly entrenched in American political science – law was to be understood as the command of the sovereign, and the sovereign was the determinate law-making authority. King points out as a measure of Austin's influence on this topic that even those most closely associated with the 'popular sovereignty' school, like Philemon Bliss and John Jameson, resorted to Austin's concept in order to establish their own positions on sovereignty and the function of law.[100]

It may seem chronologically eccentric to discuss the influence of Austin last – his great work *The Province of Jurisprudence Determined* was first published in 1832, the year of Bentham's death – but his influence was only really visible in the United States in the last third of the nineteenth century. The first review of Austin appeared in the *North American Review* in 1865. Reflecting on the little that he had published and bemoaning the incomplete form of the *Lectures on Jurisprudence* (published posthumously in 1861), the reviewer was yet convinced that 'Austin is conspicuous among the most distinguished jurists of the present century. ... Incomplete ... as his works are, we gain from them the highest opinion of Mr. Austin's juridical talents.' [III. 28: 246] Had he finished his planned study of the philosophy of positive law 'he might have produced a work which would have marked an era in modern legal history, and given a strong impulse to scientific legal study in England and America.' [III. 28: 247] In summarizing the principal elements of Austin's jurisprudence and delineating the sorts of law according to Austin's division (the law of God – further divided into revealed and unrevealed law – positive law, positive morality, and metaphorical laws), the reviewer underscored the point that Austin 'is a disciple of the school of Bentham' who employed the theory of utility as the index to all laws, including 'unrevealed divine commands.' [III. 28: 251] It remained unsaid that Bentham had little time for this mode of reasoning about God's supposed benevolence. The study of Austin's *Lectures* was recommended to students of the law by this reviewer in the strongest terms: while they 'cannot be supposed to recommend themselves very strongly to the general reader ... they should be read repeatedly by every student of law.' Austin demonstrated great skill in unraveling even the most baffling topics, such as in his remarks on 'vested and contingent rights', which

liv *Introduction*

'offer the only satisfactory clew we have ever met to that labyrinthine subject,' and posited ideas on legal subjects 'particularly important to the American people, and which might tend somewhat to replace our present vague and rusty ideas connected with law and morality by precise and definite conceptions.' [III. 28: 253]

Austin's influence is evident in the legal writings of Oliver Wendell Holmes (1841–1935), the foremost American jurist of the period and a scholar well-read in the whole tradition of British legal thought. Holmes was one of the first to subject Austin's jurisprudence to serious critical analysis, and frequently recommended his writings to students of the law.[101] While he voiced doubts about Austin's theory of sovereignty, he accepted without reservation his concept of rights and critique of natural law. Invariably, he found greater lessons in Austin's writings than in Bentham's, though he declared on one occasion that Bentham's *Fragment on Government* and Austin's *Lectures* together are 'worth the whole *Corpus*' of Roman law.[102] In the 1871 essay on 'Codes, and the Arrangement of the Law' [III. 33] Holmes tackled Livingston, and by extension Bentham, on the desirability of constructing codes of law. He was not opposed to codes in general, but was sceptical about some of the claims made for their benefits. Holmes took the side of the common law in this debate, finding significant drawbacks to fixed codified rules: 'New cases will arise which will elude the most carefully constructed formula. The common law, proceeding ... by a series of successive approximations – by a continual reconciliation of cases – is prepared for this, and simply modifies the form of its rule.' Though this could not be said of Bentham's approach to codes of law, Holmes charged that it was one of the failings of codifiers that they tended to make their codes short, an error that 'probably springs from the thoroughly exploded notion that it is to make every man his own lawyer ...', a goal famously proclaimed by Bentham. But a code will not get rid of lawyers, and they should be drafted with a view to encompassing 'the whole body of the law in an authentic form.' [III. 33: p. 2] The main advantage of a code, Holmes claimed, is that 'the whole work being under the control of one head, it will make a philosophically arranged *corpus juris* possible. If such a code were achieved, its component treatises would not have to be loaded with matter belonging elsewhere, as is necessarily the case with text-books written to sell.' Another advantage is that not only would it be useful to 'train the mind of the student to a sound legal habit of thought, but would remove obstacles from his path which he now only overcomes after years of experience and reflection.' [III. 33: 3] Explicitly following Bentham and Austin, Holmes asserted that the method of arrangement of a code should be based on duties and not on rights: 'Duties precede rights logically and chronologically. Even those laws which in form create a right directly, in fact either tacitly impose a duty on the rest of the world, as, in the case of patents, to abstain from selling the patented article, or confer an immunity from a duty previously or generally imposed, like taxation.' [III. 33: 3; see also III. 35: 46] However, seemingly at odds with Bentham, Holmes also asserted that law is not a science 'but is essentially empirical', and therefore 'although the general arrangement [of law] should be philosophical, even at the expense of disturbing prejudices, compromises with practical convenience are highly proper.' [III. 33: 4]

Holmes then proceeded to examine Austin's theory of a law as 'a command (of a definite political superior, enforced by a sanction), which obliges (intelligent human beings) to acts or forbearances of a class.' His terse comment on this definition is that while it may be 'accurate enough' for lawyers 'it seems to be of practical rather than philosophical value.' In practice, who has sovereign power, and whether such a power exists at all, are questions of fact and degree [III. 33: 4]. For example, the decisions of judges often form precedents which thereafter function as rules, though they are not the commands of a sovereign. Furthermore, international law established rules of conduct with sanctions to enforce them (i.e. the threat of war), even though there exists no sovereign body [III. 33: 5]. Holmes reiterated his misgivings about Austin's definition of law in his discussion of Frederick Pollock's views on Austin in a subsequent number of the *American Law Review*,[103] including the opinion that Austin's definition was not satisfactory 'from a philosophical point of view', and argued that custom and judicial precedent have a greater force than Austin allowed [III. 34: 723, 724].

Not surprisingly, Austin's theory of sovereignty received careful attention in a political society marked by conflicting positions on this most important of political issues. John C. Hurd (1816–92) presented an Austininian analysis of law and sovereignty in the first of two chapters published as *Topics of Jurisprudence connected with Conditions of Freedom and Bondage* (1856).[104] This often-cited book had a major impact on the slavery debate and on the debate over sovereignty. Hurd took as his starting point Austin's theory of positive law, and his view of jurisprudence as the science of positive law, 'that is, the science of what the rule given or allowed by the state *is*.' Like Austin, Hurd stressed the need for a clear distinction between law and ethics; the latter is the science of 'what *ought to be*', and laws exist and are enforced by the state without regard for what ought to be law, or any other rules of conduct not enforced by the state [II. 25: 14–15]. Hurd found Austin's analysis of sovereignty particularly helpful in explaining the American constitution and as a framework for assessing the secession claims of the southern states.

Irving Berdine Richman (1861–1938), a disciple of Hurd, followed him in delineating the command theory of law in an essay in the *Atlantic Monthly* in 1889 [IV. 49; see also IV. 55]. Richman's essay set forth a discussion of sovereignty and law in American constitutional theory and practice. In Part II of the essay he quoted extensively from Hobbes, Bentham, and Austin to illustrate the command theory of law, or law as the expressed wish of the sovereign. He applauded Bentham's reliance on 'fact' not fiction, and Austin as the chief expositor of the idea of 'positive' law. In Part III Richman argued that the rhetoric of divided sovereignty and popular sovereignty found in the U.S. constitution did not square with the facts of American political life, which he thought better represented in the theory of the English jurists. A concise summary of the positions of both Austin and Hurd then followed, which he contrasted with traditional American political thought and its failure to appreciate that law was a mode of conduct set by a superior political authority and not by the people. Richman offered numerous examples as proof of the illusory character of American political thinking on this subject, citing vague notions of equality, the divisibility of sovereignty, the sovereignty of the people, and the sovereignty of the states. By contrast, 'the ideas of Austin and of the whole English school of jurists are that law exists in strict subordination to political fact, – the fact of supreme despotic power lodged in a determinate, come-at-able aggregate of natural persons; that political fact or sovereignty precedes law, creates law and sustains law.' [IV. 49: 216]

A few years later Woodrow Wilson (1856–1924) published his influential *An Old Master and Other Political Essays*, in which he made explicit use of Austin's *Province of Jurisprudence Determined* to reject the theory of popular sovereignty advocated by John Jameson and others [IV. 50]. Like Richman, he sought to adapt Austin's view of sovereignty to more clearly base it upon the observed facts of political life, something theorists of popular sovereignty had singularly failed to do. Sovereignty could never lie with the people as a whole and it could never be unlimited in practice [IV. 52: 80]. The authority of the government ultimately depended on force, the instrument through which the will of the sovereign was enacted, but Wilson, like Bentham and Austin, understood that it was the habit of obedience that made the sovereign's power effective. These two elements of sovereignty should be kept clearly distinct; power is located in the specific institutions of government, while the control of the community lies with the voters. The crucial vehicle of sovereignty is the legislature, the executive is the agent of the legislator, and the courts interpret the commands of the sovereign. The community's limits on sovereignty were a significant element in Wilson's analysis, but this should not be confused with sovereignty itself. Sovereignty, he explained, is 'to sit at the helm and steer, marking out such free courses for the staunch craft as wind and weather will permit. This is the only sort of sovereignty that can be exercised in human affairs. But the pilot is sovereign, not the weather.' [IV. 52: 96]

John Dewey (1859–1952) was among those not persuaded by the arguments of Hurd, Richman, and Wilson. Indeed, despite his apparent familiarity with the writings of the utilitarians, Dewey was not readily persuaded about very much contained in or spawned by utilitarian thought. King, who argued that Bentham had laid 'the foundations for the rise of pragmatism, America's major contribution to the development of modern philosophy',[105] also thought that he had 'paved the way for two important positions in Dewey's instrumental logic': (1) the classification of acts into 'genera' and 'species' for legal purposes; and (2) the division between the 'real entities' of sense perception and 'fictitious entities', such as power, right, and duty, which have no real presence though they may be reducible to real entities. The latter division foreshadowed Dewey's distinction between existential and symbolic levels of reference.[106] In other respects, however, Dewey was far less impressed by the propositions of utilitarian moral and legal thought. In an essay in March 1894 he rejected Austin's theory of sovereignty on the grounds that it was unverifiable as a matter of fact and useless as theory. Austin confused the nature of sovereignty with the organs of its exercise, the institutions of government. He had declined to associate sovereignty with public opinion because it was not determinate (in Austin's account this was an essential quality of sovereignty), but Dewey questioned whether Austin could be precise in locating the determinate character of sovereignty when applying his theory. The problem for Dewey was made manifest in representative democracy, where the majority of decision-makers could only be known *post facto*, once the vote had been taken. Moreover, Austin's analysis could not resolve the dilemma of what becomes of those who vote with the minority – they could not be said to have issued the command. Austin would have to maintain that their participation alone was sufficient for them to be counted as sharers of sovereignty, but this effectively divorced sovereignty from command, according to Dewey. Even so, Dewey accepted Austin's emphasis on determinateness as a valuable element of the nature of sovereignty, since this indicated both the idea of definite institutions and the determinateness of the specific persons responsible for making decisions and issuing commands – without these elements sovereignty would not be a coherent concept [IV. 53: 51–2].

Conclusion

Perhaps enough has been said in these introductory pages to convey to the reader the central claim of the editors: that utilitarian ideas were far more significant in American moral, legal, and political thought than is usually acknowledged. Nor should we be misled by the amount of critical writing in America on utilitarians and their philosophy. The strength of opposition engendered by ideas is frequently an impressive indicator of the vibrancy and impact of those ideas – they are viewed as something worth combating. Critics of utilitarianism in the United States were many and formidable. They challenged utilitarian moral theory because it was a secular and godless doctrine, because it gave priority to the expedient in place of rights, and because it was premised on a narrow and contested view of human nature. However, many of the same critics readily acknowledged the value of utilitarian principles in legal philosophy and government, and it is probably in this domain that we should recognise that utilitarian ideas had their most significant influence in the American political tradition. Undoubtedly, an investigation of this aspect of American thought in the twentieth century would take us still further in illustrating the continuities that link the present with the past in this strand of the history of ideas.

* I would like to express my appreciation to my fellow editor, Mark Spencer, for his suggestions for improvements to this introduction, and to the Georgia Political Science Association for welcoming the presentation of a paper on the subject at its annual meetings in Savannah, November 2004.

James E. Crimmins, 2005

NOTES

1 Bruce Kuklick, *A History of Philosophy in America, 1720–2000* (Oxford 2001).

2 *American National Biography* (New York 1999), formerly *Dictionary of American Biography*; Hildreth featured in earlier editions of the latter (New York 1931), vol. V. 19–20.

3 Elizabeth Flower and Murray G. Murphey, *A History of Philosophy in America*, 2 vols. (New York 1977).

4 Oddly, Flower and Murphey insert an endnote (ibid., I. 361n) in which they express the view that, contrary to conventional wisdom, utilitarian political theory was 'shared by many Americans beyond William Beach Lawrence and Fanny Wright, the two avowed Utilitarians', but then omit all discussion of these utilitarians as well as Hildreth.

5 Paul A. Palmer, 'Benthamism in England and America', *The American Political Science Review*, vol. 35, no.5 (Oct. 1941), pp. 859, 868.

6 This emblematic phrase, together with Bentham's name, was also used as a motto by the Paineite free-thinker Gilbert Vale (1788–1866) on the title-page of each issue of the *Diamond* (1840–2), a journal he edited, devoted to legal and political reform.

7 *Traités de législation civile et pénale. ... Par M. Jérémie Bentham, ... Publiés en François par Ét. Dumont, ... d'aprés les Manscrits confiés par l'Auteur*, 3 vols. (1802; 2nd edn. Paris 1820); *Theory of Legislation; by Jeremy Bentham. Translated from the French of Etienne Dumont, by R. Hildreth*, 2 vols. (Boston 1840).

8 On occasion, the rejection was based on a caricature; for an example of this see III. 23.

9 Peter J. King, *Utilitarian Jurisprudence in America: The Influence of Bentham and Austin on American Legal Thought in the Nineteenth Century* (New York and London 1986).

10 Among Bentham's American correspondents were Aaron Burr (1756–1836), John Quincy Adams (1767–1848), James Madison (1751–1836), Abraham Gallatin (1761–1849), Simon Snyder (1759–1819), De Witt Clinton (1769–1828), Henry Francis (n.d.), Francis Walker Gilmer (1790–1826), George Hay (1765–1830), William Plumer (1759–1850), his son William Plumer Jnr. (1789–1854), Richard Rush (1780–1859), John Adams Smith (1788–1854), Charles Jared Ingersoll (1782–1862), and Frances Wright (1795–1852).

11 King, *Utilitarian Jurisprudence in America*, pp. ii–iii.

12 References to writings in this collection appear in square brackets in the text, indicating the volume no., item no., and, where appropriate, the relevant page number; hence [I. 1: 1] indicates vol. I, item 1, page 1.

13 King, *Utilitarian Jurisprudence in America*, p. 139. Austin was appointed to the Chair of Jurisprudence at the newly established University College London shortly after its founding, and began lecturing there in 1828; this was the earliest date Bentham's legal philosophy was introduced into the law curriculum in Britain.

14 *Théorie des peines et des récompenses. Par M. Jérémie Bentham ..., rédigée en Français d'aprés les manuscits. Par Et. Dumont*, 2 vols. (Londres 1811).

15 David Hoffman, *A Course of Legal Study; Respectfully Addressed to the Students of Law in the United States* (Baltimore 1817), pp. 4–6.

16 David Hoffman, *A Course of Legal Study, Addressed to Students and the Profession Generally*, 2 vols. (Baltimore 1836), I. 364.

lx *Introduction*

17 King claims (with what evidence is not apparent) that Hoffman's understanding of moral obligation was initially derived from Paley, and was reinforced by his reading of Bentham; *Utilitarian Jurisprudence in America*, p. 168.

18 Neal was first introduced to Bentham's legal philosophy by Hoffman at the University of Maryland. Hildreth may have had his first encounter with Bentham reading Hoffman's *A Course of Legal Study* at Harvard; Donald E. Emerson, *Richard Hildreth* (Baltimore 1946), p. 91.

19 See William Plumer Jnr. to Bentham (2 October 1818), in *The Correspondence of Jeremy Bentham (Collected Works of Jeremy Bentham)*, vols. 8–10, ed.. S.R. Conway (Oxford 1988–9), IX. 276–7. Henceforth items in the *Collected Works of Jeremy Bentham* are indicated by (CW).

20 See *Jeremy Bentham's Economic Writings*, 3 vols., ed. Werner Stark (London 1952–4).

21 Reprinted in Francis Gilmer Walker, *Sketches, Essays, and Translations* (Baltimore 1828). The law on usury had been a pressing matter in Virginia a few years before; see George Hay, *Speech, Delivered in the Legislature of Virginia, in the session of 1816–17, in support of a bill to repeal all laws concerning usury* (Richmond 1817).

22 Thomas Cooper, 'Of Interest of Money; Usury; Bottomry and Respondentia', in *Lectures on the Elements of Political Economy* (Columbia, SC 1826).

23 John Whipple, *Free Trade in Money, or Note-Saving, The Great Cause of Fraud, Poverty and Ruin: Stringent Usury Laws, The Best Defence of the People Against "Hard Times." An Answer to Jeremy Bentham* (Boston 1855); parts published in *New York Daily Express*, December 1836.

24 [John Russell Hurd], *A Familiar View, of the Operation and Tendency, Of Usury Laws; ... Being a reply in part, to the essay of a "Rhode Islander," published in the New-York Daily Express, of Dec. 1936* (New York 1837).

25 Bentham to John Quincy Adams (7 June 1817), *Correspondence* (CW), IX. 14–15.

26 Thomas Cooper, *Lectures on the Elements of Political Economy* (1826; 2nd edn. 1830, reprt. New York 1971), p. 22.

27 Ibid., p. 63.

28 Thomas Cooper, *Treatise on the Law of Libel* (New York 1830), p. 127.

29 Quoted by Dumas Malone, *Public Life of Thomas Cooper* (New Haven 1926), p. 370.

30 Thomas Cooper, 'Slavery', *Southern Literary Journal*, I (November 1835), p. 189.

31 See, for example, C.W. Everett, *Anti-Senatica: An Attack on the United States Senate, sent by Jeremy Bentham to Andrew Jackson*, in *Smith College Studies in History*, vol. 11, no. 4. (1926), introduction; Mitchell Franklin, 'Concerning the Historic Importance of Edward Livingston', *Tulane Law Review*, vol. 11 (1937), pp. 163–212; Palmer, 'Benthamism in England and America', p. 862; and King, *Utilitarian Jurisprudence in America*, pp. 226–7, 270–80.

32 In the context of constitutional reform in Greece, see Fred Rosen's detailed exposition of the disjunction between Bentham's position and that taken by his supposed disciples in *Bentham, Byron and Greece: Constitutionalism, Nationalism, and Early Political Thought* (Oxford 1992).

33 King, *Utilitarian Jurisprudence in America*, p. 226.

Introduction lxi

34 Livingston to Bentham (1 July 1830), *The Works of Jeremy Bentham, Published under the Superintendence of his Executor, John Bowring*, 11 vols. (Edinburgh 1838–43), XI. 52. Henceforth Bowring.
35 King, *Utilitarian Jurisprudence in America*, p. 275.
36 Bentham to José Joaquín de Mora (23–4 November 1820), *Correspondence (CW)*, X. 177. Bentham's secretary John Colls recorded in his journal that Bentham received the letter from Livingston to Rush (dated 1 August 1820) on 23 November; Bentham Papers at University College London, UC CVI. 256; *Correspondence (CW)*, X. 182n.
37 Bentham to Adam Weidman and de Mora (1 December 1820), ibid., p. 218.
38 Bentham to Rush (11 December 1820), ibid., p. 240.
39 Rush to Bentham (14 December 1820), *Correspondence (CW)*, X. 240.
40 *Report made by Edward Livingston to the Honourable the Senate and House of Representatives of the State of Louisiana in General Assembly convened* (1822), in *The Complete Works of Edward Livingston on Criminal Jurisprudence*, 2 vols. (New York 1873), I. 8. In the parts of the report devoted to 'the establishment and government of public prisons' (pp. 72–4), Livingston indicated the requirements of an effective penitentiary, including the education of young offenders and the substitution of 'amendatory to vindictive punishments' (p. 73).
41 *Introductory Report to the Code of Crimes and Punishments* (1824), in *The Complete Works of Edward Livingston on Criminal Jurisprudence*, I. 209n. An extract from this report and the report in note 40 are reprinted in James E. Crimmins (ed.), *The Death Penalty: Debates in Britain and the US, 1725–1868*, 7 vols., (Bristol and Tokyo 2004), III. No.21, pp. 7–76, 185–224. The quotation appears to be an English translation from *Théorie des peines et des recompense* (see above note 14); the *Théorie* was first published in English as *Rationale of Reward* (London 1825) and *Rationale of Punishment* (London 1830), both translated by Richard Smith.
42 Bowring, X. 556, 556–7. The reference is to Dumont's *Traités de législation*; see above note 7.
43 Livingston to Bentham (10 August 1829), Bowring, XI. 23.
44 Bentham to Livingston (23 February 1830), ibid., p. 35; Southwood Smith had arranged for a copy of Livingston's Code to be published in London.
45 Livingston to Bentham (1 July 1830), ibid., p. 51. Bentham alluded to the similarities between his ideas and Livingston's in a letter to President Jackson, accompanying a copy of his *Papers Relative to Codification and Public Instruction* (1817); ibid., p. 40.
46 John L. O'Sullivan, *Report in Favour of the Abolition of the Punishment of Death by Law* (2nd edn., New York, 1841), in Crimmins (ed.), *The Death Penalty*, VII. No.39, pp. 1–168.
47 Ibid., pp. 56–7, 122–3.
48 O'Sullivan followed this review with an account of the early life of Bentham [I. 11], and also reviewed Hildreth's *Theory of Morals* [II. 14], both in the same journal.
49 Much of what Neal had to say on the subject of utility [I. 3 (1)] was later reprinted as 'Chapter on Utility' in *Principles of Legislation: From the Ms. of Jeremy Bentham; ... By M. Dumont, ... Translated from the Second Corrected and Enlarged Edition [Paris 1802]; with Notes and a Biographical Notice of Jeremy Bentham and of M. Dumont. By John Neal.* (Boston 1830), pp. 119–47. In *The Yankee* Neal also published extensive

lxii   Introduction

extracts from his translations of Dumont's *Traités*: 'Dumont's Bentham [with notes by Neal]', *The Yankee*, vol. II, no. 3 (15 January 1829), pp. 20–1, vol. II, no. 9 (26 February 1829), pp. 68–9, vol. II, no. 12 (19 March 1829), pp. 93–4; vol. II, no. 16 (16 April 1829), pp. 122–4, vol. II, no. 19 (7 May 1829), pp. 145–6.

50   John Neal, *Wandering Recollections of a Somewhat Busy Life* (Boston 1869), p. 286.

51   John Neal to Bentham (11 March 1830), cited by Palmer, 'Benthamism in England and America', p. 863.

52   The harshest criticism of Neal's efforts came from the *Boston Morning Post* (16 May 1840): 'Bentham's views, we believe, are not appreciated in this country owing to two causes – the fact that they were originally published in the French language, and the more unfortunate fact, that that versatile and unbearably egotistical genius, John Neal, undertook from the very best of motives, to introduce them to the American public.'

53   In Neal's 'Biographical Notice of Jeremy Bentham' in *Principles of Legislation* the eulogium was elevated to 'the great-high priest of legislation' (p. 14).

54   In I. 3 (3) Neal responded to the *North-American Review*, vol. XXVI (1828), pp. 188–9, which repeated the account of Bentham's eccentricities from William Parry's notoriously unreliable *The Last Days of Lord Byron* (London 1825), pp. 155–9. The author of this article reported that Bentham was suffering from 'a partial aberration of intellect', and that his ideas were consequently unworthy of detailed consideration; see J.R. Dinwiddy, 'Early-Nineteenth-Century Reactions to Benthamism', *Transactions of the Royal Historical Society*, 5th series, vol. 34 (1984), pp. 47–69, in Parekh (ed.), *Jeremy Bentham: Critical Assessments*, I. 257.

55   From Moore's *Odes on Cash, Corn, Catholics, and other Matters* (London 1828).

56   Moore, it seems, had been severely reviewed by Albany Fonblanque in the Benthamite *Westminster Review*.

57   Neal says it was 'engraved from the copy of a very faithful and spirited sketch of him, by Robert M. Sully, a young Virginian of great promise, to whom Bentham sat in the year '27', and noted the likeness to Franklin [I. 3 (13): 9]. The engraver was George Washington Appleton (1805–31) from Portland Maine, who also painted a portrait of Neal in 1829; *The Old Radical: Representations of Jeremy Bentham* (London 1998), p. 42.

58   King, *Utilitarian Jurisprudence in America*, pp. 239–40.

59   Ibid., pp. 248–51.

60   See, for example, III. 22, which bears ample testimony to the growing awareness of Bentham's contributions to legal philosophy and law reform, and the influence he had upon other notable reformers, such as Romilly, Macintosh, James Mill, Brougham, and Buxton.

61   A second corrected edition appeared in 1864, and many more reprints 1871–1931. Most recently Hildreth's text has been reprinted by Thoemmes Continuum (Bristol 2004), with a new introduction by James E. Crimmins; for the background to Hildreth's translation see the introduction to this edition.

62   It should be noted that Bowring's edition of Bentham's *Works* (1838–43) was not reviewed in the United States until 1861 [I. 12].

63   Possibly Wendel Phillips (1811–84), the anti-slavery agitator and advocate of women's rights, or William Wirt Phillips (1796–1865), Presbyterian clergyman, trustee of both Princeton and the University of the city of New York, later a director and trustee of the theological seminary in Princeton, and president of its board of directors 1861–5.

64 Richard Hildreth, *The History of the United States of America from the Discovery of the Continent to the Organization of Government under the Federal Constitution, 1497–1789*, 3 vols. (New York 1849), and *The History ... from the Adoption of the Federal Constitution to the end of the Sixteenth Congress, 1788–1821*, 3 vols. (New York 1851-2). On Hildreth as historian see Alfred H. Kelly, 'Richard Hildreth', in William T. Hutchinson (ed.), *The Marcus W. Jernegan Essays in American Historiography* (1937; reprt. New York 1958), pp. 25–42.

65 Richard Hildreth, *The Slave: Or, Memoirs of Archy Moore* (New York 1836), *Despotism in America; or, An Inquiry into the Nature and Results of the Slaveholding System in the United States.By the author of "Archy Moore"* (Boston 1840), and *The White Slave; A True Picture of Slave Life in America* (Boston 1852). The claim that *The Slave* was America's first anti-slavery novel is made by Emerson, *Richard Hildreth*, p. 73.

66 For the extant mss. of the *Theory of Wealth* and *Theory of Taste* see Martha M. Pingel, *An American Utilitarian: Richard Hildreth as a Philosopher, with selections from his published and unpublished works* (New York 1948), pp. 44–74, 75–120.

67 See also Richard Hildreth, *Theory of Politics: An Inquiry into the Foundations of Governments, and the Causes and Progress of Political Revolutions* (New York 1854), pp. 55–6, where he extends the implications to include a property in power or political office.

68 Hildreth's utilitarianism and its differences from Bentham are discussed in David Baumgardt, 'The Forgotten Moralist: Richard Hildreth's Theory of Morals', *Ethics*, vol. 57, no.3 (April 1947), pp. 191–8, in part a reply to the version of Bentham's influence in Arthur M. Schlesinger Jnr., 'The Problem of Richard Hildreth', *New England Quarterly* (June 1940), pp. 237–9; see also Pingel, *An American Utilitarian*, pp. 11–23.

69 The idea may also be traced to an older progeny in the Latin prefix *com*, meaning 'with', combined with *passio*, meaning 'suffering'.

70 See note 67 above.

71 See esp. Hildreth, *Theory of Politics*, pp. 255–9, 262–3.

72 Ibid., p. 264.

73 Ibid., p. 265.

74 Ibid., pp. 265, 266.

75 On this exchange see Emerson, *Richard Hildreth*, pp. 105–11.

76 Later, Brownson found Austinian ideas helpful in his analysis of the U.S. constitution; see 'The Federal Constitution' and 'Are the United States a Nation?', *Brownson's Quarterly Review*, national series I (January 1864), pp. 12–44, and (October 1864), pp. 385–420. King doubts whether Brownson had read Austin, but is certain that he read the work of one of Austin's most prominent disciples, John C. Hurd, and made no secret of his borrowings from this source [see III. 25]; King, *Utilitarian Jurisprudence in America*, p. 421.

77 See James E. Crimmins (ed.), *Utilitarians and Religion* (Bristol 1998), Part I.

78 On Paley's influence in America see Wilson Smith, *Professors and Public Ethics: Studies Of Northern Moral Philosophers before the Civil War* (Ithaca 1956), esp. Ch. II.

79 Wendell Glick, 'Bishop (sic) Paley in America', *New England Quarterly*, vol. XXVII (1954), p. 352, quoted King, *Utilitarian Jurisprudence in America*, p. 145.

lxiv Introduction

80 King, *Utilitarian Jurisprudence in America*, p. 145.
81 [Anon.], Review of Paley's *A View of the Evidences of Christianity*, *The American Monthly Review; or, Literary Journal*, vol. III (1796), p. 216.
82 Nathaniel Chipman, *Principles of Government* (Berlington, Vermont 1833), p. 71.
83 King, *Utilitarian Jurisprudence in America*, p. 143.
84 [Anon.], 'Natural Theology: or Evidences of the Existence and Arttributes iof the Deity, collected from the Appearance of Nature. By William Paley, …', *The Christian Examiner*, vol. VI, no. XXXIII, New Series III (July 1829), p. 389.
85 Ibid., p. 392.
86 Ibid., p. 393.
87 Review of Henry Brougham: '1. A Discourse of Natural Theology, showing the Nature of the Evidence and the Advantages of the Study (London 1835); 2. Paley's Natural Theology, with Illustrative Notes [by Brougham and Sir Charles Bell] (London 1836); 3. Dissertations on Subjects of Science connected with Natural Theology; being the concluding Volumes of the New Edition of Paley's Works', *The North American Review*, vol. LIV (Jan. 1842), p. 105.
88 Ibid., p. 107.
89 William James, *Pragmatism: A New Name for Some Old Ways of Thinking* (London 1907).
90 Laurens Perseus Hickok (1798–1888), professor of theology at Western Reserve and Auburn Seminaries, later president of Union College, and author of *Rational Psychology; Or the Subjective Idea and Objective Laws of all Intelligence* (Auburn 1848), among other publications.
91 *Emerson's Complete Works*, 11 vols. ed. James Elliot Cabot (London 1883–6).
92 Bart Shultz, 'The Methods of J.B. Schneewind', *Utilitas*, vol. 16, no. 2 (July 2004), p. 150.
93 Ibid., p. 156.
94 Ibid., p. 157.
95 Ibid., p. 158.
96 John Deigh, 'Sidgwick's Conception of Ethics', *Utilitas*, vol. 16, no. 2 (July 2004), pp. 168–83.
97 Ibid., pp. 173–4.
98 King makes the point in *Utilitarian Jurisprudence in America*, p. 337.
99 Ibid., p. 338.
100 Ibid., pp. 482–3. P. Bliss, *Of Sovereignty* (Boston 1885); and John A. Jameson, 'National Sovereignty', *Political Science Quarterly*, vol. V, no. 2 (June 1890), pp. 193–213 [III. 50].
101 See, for example, Holmes's review of James Bryce, *The Academical Study of the Civil Law* (London 1871), *American Law Review*, vol. V (1871), pp. 715–16.
102 Oliver Wendell Holmes, 'Summary of Events [*American Civil Law Journal*]', *American Law Review*, vol. VII (1873), pp. 578–9.
103 For Pollock's position see *The Law Magazine and Review*, New series, no. 3 (1 April 1872).

104 The second chapter examined 'private' international law; John C. Hurd, *Topics of Jurisprudence connected with Conditions of Freedom and Bondage* (New York 1856), pp. 53–113. In the Advertisement Hurd mapped out a twenty-five chapter work, later published as *A View of the Laws of Freedom and Bondage in the United States*, 2 vols. (Boston and New York 1858–62). Hurd was the son of John Russell Hurd; see above p. xxiii.

105 The evidence for this, according to King, lies in the 'entirely pragmatic' attitude demonstrated by Hildreth and Livingston, for which they were indebted to Bentham's empiricism; *Utilitarian Jurisprudence in America*, p. 141.

106 Ibid.

1

[Anon.]

Review

An Introduction to the Principles of Morals and Legislation.
Printed in the Year 1780, and now first published.
By Jeremy Bentham, of Lincoln's Inn, Esq.

in

The American Monthly Review; or, Literary Journal
vol. II (1795), pp. 339–48

[Anon.]

Review

An Introduction to the Principles of Morals and Legislation.
By Jeremy Bentham

The American Monthly Review; or, Literary Journal,
vol. II (1795), pp. 339–48.

WHOEVER has perused this author's former writings must have perceived that he possesses no ordinary share of understanding, penetration, and discernment; and whoever reads the present work will find abundance of additional matter to confirm him more thoroughly in the same sentiment. Like many other men, however, of great and comprehensive minds, he here seems to have engaged in a pursuit too extensive, perhaps, for the powers of any individual of the human race to execute with precision and propriety.

The present work was originally much more limited in its design than is indicated by the title-page now affixed to it; being intended only for an introduction to a plan of a penal code *in terminis*, which was designed to follow it in the same volume; but the author, by his own observations and those of his friends, having detected some flaws in his performance, found himself, by his endeavours to ascertain the source of his errors, so involved in the metaphysical maze, that by degrees he grew disgusted with his book; and laying aside the idea of completing it, he turned his thoughts to those considerations which had led him to engage in it. Here 'every opening which promised to afford the light he stood in need of was still pursued; and as occasion arose, the several departments connected with that in which he had at first engaged, were successively explored; insomuch that, in one branch or other of the pursuit, his researches have nearly embraced the whole field of legislation.'

In attempting to ascertain, in the course of his inquiries, wherein consisted the iden[ti]ty and completeness of a law? – what is the distinction and where is the separation between a *penal* and a *civil* law? and what is the distinction and where is the separation between the *penal* and *other branches* of the law? – the author found that, to give a proper solution of these questions, it was necessary to have before him a complete system of legislation, to survey carefully all its parts, and to comprehend their several relations and dependencies with respect to each other: but, as the existence of such a fabric is as yet no where to be found, what follows? – 'that he who for the purpose just mentioned, or for any other, wants an example of a complete body of law to refer to, must begin with making one.' Still farther: 'There is,' says Mr Bentham, 'or rather their ought to be, a *logic* of the *will*, as well as of the *understanding*: the operations of the former faculty, are neither less susceptible, nor less worthy, than those of the latter, of being delineated by rules. Of these two branches of that recondite art, Aristotle saw only the latter; succeeding logicians, treading in the steps of their great founder, have concurred in seeing with no other eyes. Yet so far as a difference can be assigned between branches so intimately connected, whatever difference there is, in point of importance, is in favour of the logic of the will. Since it is only by their capacity of directing the operations of this faculty, that the operations of the understanding are of any consequence.

'Of this logic of the will, the Science of *law*, considered in respect of its *form*, is the most considerable branch, – the most important application. It is, to the art of legislation, what the science of anatomy is to the art of medicine: with this difference, that the subject of it is what the artist has to work *with*, instead of being what he has to operate *upon*. Nor is the body politic less in danger from a want of acquaintance with the one science, than the body natural from ignorance in the other. One example amongst a thousand that might be adduced in proof of this assertion, may be seen in the note which terminates this volume.

'Such then were the difficulties: such the preliminaries: – an unexampled work to atchieve, and then a new science to create: a new branch to add to one of the most abstruse of sciences.

'Yet more: A body of proposed law, how complete soever, would be completely useless and uninstructive, unless explained and justified, and that in every tittle, by a continued accompaniment, a perpetual commentary of *reasons*: which reasons that the comparative value of such as point in the same directions may be estimated, and the conjunct force of such as point in the same direction may be felt, must be marshalled, and put under subordination to such extensive and leading ones as are termed *principles*. There must be therefore, not one system only, but two parallel and connected systems, running together, the one of legislative provisions, the other of political reasons, each affording to the other correction and support.

'Are enterprizes like these atchievable? He knows not. This only he knows, that they have been undertaken, proceeded in, and that some progress has been made in all of them.'

Some idea of the progress which Mr. Bentham has made in his extensive undertaking may be formed, and the nature of his arrangements may be collected, from the titles of the works, 'by the publication of which his present designs would be completed. They are exhibited in the order which seemed to him best fitted for apprehension, and in which they would stand disposed, were the whole assemblage ready to come out at once: but the order, in which they will eventually appear, may probably enough be influenced in some degree by collateral and temporary considerations.' They are divided into ten parts, treating of *the principles of legislation*; 1st, in matters of *civil*, more distinctly termed, *private distributive*, or for shortness *distributive, law*: – 2dly, in matters of *penal law*: – 3dly, in matters of *procedure*: uniting in one view the *criminal* and *civil* branches, between which no line can be drawn but a very indistinct one, and that continually liable to variation: – 4thly, in matters of *reward*: – 5thly, in matters of *public distributive*, more concisely as well as familiarly termed *constitutional, law*: – 6thly, in matters of *political tactics*; or the art of maintaining *order* in the proceedings of political assemblies, so as to direct them to the end of their institution, viz. by a system of rules which are to the constitutional branch, in some respects, what the law of procedure is to the civil and the penal: – 7thly, in matters between nation and nation, or to use a new though not inexpressive appellation, in matters of *international* law; – 8thly, in matters of finance: – 9thly, matters of *political œconomy*: – and lastly, a plan of a body of law, complete in all its branches, considered in respect of its *form*; in other words, in respect of its method and terminology; including a view of the origination and connection of the ideas expressed by the short list of terms, the exposition of which contains all that can be said with propriety to belong to the head of *universal jurisprudence*; such as *obligation, right, power, possession, title, exemption, immunity, franchise, privilege, nullity, validity*, and the like.

Here, we believe, most of our readers will be of opinion that there is work enough, cut out for the powers and abilities of any one man to execute: but the author goes on to inform us that the use of the principles laid down under the above several heads is only to prepare the way for the body of law itself exhibited *in terminis*; and which, to be complete with reference to any political state, must consequently be calculated for the meridian, and adapted to the circumstances, of some one such state in particular.

Such is the immense extent of Mr. Bentham's views; such the magnitude of the object of which he is in pursuit! an object which he himself begins at last to *suspect* to be too large for his grasp; as he tells us that, *if he had* an unlimited power of drawing on time, and every other condition necessary, it would be his wish to postpone the publication of each part to the completion of the whole; especially as the exact truth of the ten parts, which are intended to furnish reasons for the corresponding provisions in the body of law itself, cannot be precisely ascertained till the provisions, to which they are destined to apply, are themselves ascertained, and that *in terminis*. – The infirmity of human nature, however, as he observes, rendering all plans precarious in the execution, in proportion as they are extensive in the design; and as he has already advanced considerably farther in his theory than in his corresponding practical applications; he deems it more than probable that the order of publication will not be that which, were it equally practicable, would appear most eligible; though the unavoidable result of this irregularity will be a multitude of imperfections, which, if the execution of the body of law *in terminis* had kept pace with the developement of the principles, so that each part had been adjusted and corrected by the other, might have been avoided.

The foundation, on which Mr. Bentham builds his whole system of morals and legislation, is the principle of *Utility*, which he thus unfolds and explains in the present work – a work now made to serve, by the help of some alterations and additions, as an introduction to his enlarged plan; though it was originally drawn up for the purpose of introducing only a confined part of it:

'I. Nature has placed mankind under the governance of two sovereign masters, *pain* and *pleasure*. It is for them alone to point out what we ought to do, as well as to determine what we shall do. On the one hand the standard of right and wrong, on the other the chain of causes and effects, are fastened to their throne. They govern us in all we do, in all we say, in all we think: every effort we can make to throw off our subjection, will serve but to demonstrate and confirm it. In words a man may pretend to abjure their empire: but in reality he will remain subject to it all the while. The *principle of utility* recognizes this subjection, and assumes it for the foundation of that system, the object of which is to rear the fabric of felicity by the hands of reason and of law. Systems which attempt to question it, deal in sounds instead of sense, in caprice instead of reason, in darkness instead of light.

'But enough of metaphor and declamation; it is not by such means that moral science is to be improved.

'II. The principle of utility is the foundation of the present work: it will be proper therefore at the outset to give an explicit and discriminate account of what is meant by it. By the principle[1] of utility is meant that principle which approves or disapproves of every action whatsoever, according to the tendency which it appears to have to augment or diminish the happiness of the party whose interest is in question: or, what is the same thing in other words, to promote or to oppose that happiness. I say of every action whatsoever; and therefore not only of every action of a private individual, but of every measure of government.

'III. By utility is meant that property in any object, whereby it tends to produce benefit, advantage, pleasure, good, or happiness (all this in the present case comes to the same thing) or (what comes again to the same thing) to prevent the happening of mischief, pain, evil, or unhappiness to the party whose interest is considered: if that party be the community in general, then the happiness of the community: if a particular individual, then the happiness of that individual.

'IV. The interest of the community is one of the most general expressions that can occur in the phraseology of morals: no wonder that the meaning of it is often lost. When it has a meaning, it is this. The community is a fictitious *body*, composed of the individual persons who are considered as constituting as it were its *members*. The interest of the community then is, what? the sum of the interests of the several members who compose it.

'V. It is in vain to talk of the interest of the community, without understanding what is the interest of the individual.[2] A thing is said to promote the interest, or to be *for* the interest, of an individual, when it tends to add to the sum total of his pleasures: or, what comes to the same thing, to diminish the sum total of his pains.

'VI. An action then may be said to be conformable to the principle of utility, or for shortness sake, to utility, (meaning with respect to the community at large) when the tendency it has to augment the happiness of the community is greater than any it has to diminish it.

'VII. A measure of government (which is but a particular kind of action, performed by a particular person or persons) may be said to be conformable to or dictated by the principle of utility, when in like manner the tendency which it has to augment the happiness of the community is greater than any which it has to diminish it.

'VIII. When an action, or in particular a measure of government, is supposed by a man to be conformable to the principle of utility, it may be convenient, for the purposes of discourse, to imagine a kind of law or dictate called a law or dictate of utility: and to speak of the action in question, as being conformable to such law or dictates.

'IX. A man may be said to be a partizan of the principal of utility, when the approbation or disapprobation he annexes to any action, or to any measure, is determined by and proportioned to the tendency which he conceives it to have to augment or to diminish the happiness of the community: or in other words to its conformity or unconformity to the laws or dictates of utility.

'X. Of an action that is conformable to the principle of utility, one may always say either that it is one that ought to be done, or at least that it is one that ought not to be done. One may say also, that it is right it should be done; at least that it is not wrong it should be done; that is a right action; at least that it is not a wrong action. When thus interpreted, the words ought, and right and wrong and others of that stamp, have a meaning: when otherwise they have none.

'XI. Has the rectitude of this principle been ever formally contested? It should seem that it had, by those who have not known what they have been meaning. Is it susceptible of any direct proof? it should seem not: for that which is used to prove every thing else, cannot itself be proved: a chain of proofs must have their commencement somewhere. To give such proof is as impossible as it is needless.'

'XII. Not that there is or ever has been that human creature breathing, however stupid or perverse, who has not on many, perhaps on most occasions of his life, referred to it. By the natural constitution of the human frame, on most occasions of their lives men in general embrace this principle, without thinking of it: if not for the ordering of their own actions, yet for the trying of their own actions, as well as of those of other men. There have been, at the same time, not many, perhaps, even of the most intelligent, who have been disposed to embrace it purely and without reserve. There are even few who have not taken some occasion or other to quarrel with it, either on account of their not understanding always how to apply it, or on account of some prejudice or other which they were afraid to examine into, or could not bear to part with. For such is the stuff that man is made of:

in principle and in practice, in a right track and in a wrong one, the rarest of all human qualities is consistency.

'XIII. When a man attempts to combat the principle of utility, it is with reasons drawn, without his being aware of it, from that very principle itself.[3] His arguments, if they prove any thing, prove, not that the principle is *wrong*, but that, according to the applications he supposes to be made of it, is it. *misapplied* [sic] Is it possible for a man to move the earth? Yes; but he must find out another earth to stand upon.

'XIV. To disprove the propriety of it by arguments is impossible; but from the causes that have been mentioned, or from some confused or partial view of it, a man may happen to be disposed not to relish it. Where this is the case, if he thinks the settling of his opinions on such a subject worth the trouble, let him take the following steps; and at length perhaps, he may come to reconcile himself to it.

'1. Let him settle with himself, whether he would wish to discard this principle altogether; if to let him consider what it is that all his reasonings (in matters of politics especially) can amount to?

'2. If he would, let him settle with himself, whether he would judge and without any principle, or whether there is any other he would judge and act by?

'3. If there be, let him examine and satisfy himself whether the principle he thinks he has found is really any separate intelligible principle; or whether it be not a mere principle in words, a kind of phrase, which at bottom expresses neither more nor less than the mere averment of his own unfounded sentiments; that is, what in another person he might be apt to call caprice?

'4. If he is inclined to think that his own approbation or disapprobation, annexed to the idea of an act, without any regard to its consequences, is a sufficient foundation for him to judge and act upon, let him ask himself whether his sentiment is to be a standard of right and wrong, with respect to every other man, or whether every man's sentiment has the same privilege of being a standard to itself?

'5. In the first case, let him ask himself whether his principle is not despotical, and hostile to all the rest of the human race?

'6. In the second case, whether it is not anarchical, and whether at this rate there are not as many different standards of right and wrong as there are men? and whether even to the same man, the same thing, which is right to-day, may not (without the least change in its nature) be wrong to-morrow? and whether the same thing is not right and wrong in the same place at the same time? and in either case, whether all argument is not at an end? and whether, when two men have said,

"I like this," and "I don't like it," they can (upon such a principle) have any thing more to say?

'7. If he should have said to himself, No: for that the sentiment which he proposes as a standard must be grounded on reflection, let him say on what particulars the reflection is to turn? if on particulars having relation to the utility of the act, then let him say whether this is not deferring his own principle, and borrowing assistance from that very one in opposition to which he sets it up: or if not on those particulars, on what other particulars?

'8. If he should be for compounding the matter, and adopting his own principle in part, and the principle of utility in part, let him say how far he will adopt it?

'9. When he has settled with himself where he will stop, then let him ask himself how he justifies to himself the adopting it so far? and why he will not adopt it any farther?

'10. Admitting any other principle than the principle of utility to be a right principle, a principle that it is right for a man to pursue; admitting (what is not true) that the word *right* can have a meaning without reference to utility, let him say whether there is any such thing as a *motive* that a man can have to pursue the dictates of it: if there is, let him say what that motive is, and how it is to be distinguished from those which enforce the dictates of utility: if not, then lastly let him say what it is this other principle can be good for?'

[*To be continued.*]

NOTES

1 '[Principle] The word principle is derived from the Latin word principium; which seems to be compounded of the two words *primus*, first, or chief, and *cipium*, a termination which seems to be derived from *capio* to take, as in *mancipium*, *municipium*: to which are analogous *aucepts, forceps,* and others. It is a term of very vague and very extensive signification; it is applied to any thing which is conceived to serve as a foundation of beginning to any series of operation: in some cases, of physical operations; but of mental operations in the present case.'

'The principle here in question may be taken for an act of the mind; a sentiment; a sentiment of approbation; a sentiment which, when applied to an action, approves of its utility, as that quality of it by which the measure of approbation or disapprobation bestowed upon it ought to be governed.'

2 '[Interest, &c.] Interest is one of those words, which not having any superior *genus*, cannot in the ordinary way be defined.'

3 '"The principle of utility," (I have heard it said) "is a dangerous principle: it is dangerous on certain occasions to consult it." This is as much as to say, what? that it is not consonant to utility, to consult utility: in short, that it is *not* consulting it, to consult it.'

2

Thomas Ewell

'Essay on the Laws of Pleasure and Pain'
in

Philosophical Essays on Morals, Literature, and Politics, By David Hume, Esq. To Which is Added the Answer to his Objections to Christianity, By the Ingenious Divine Dr. Campbell. Also, An Account of Mr. Hume's Life, an original Essay, and a few Notes (Georgetown, D.C. and Philadelphia 1817); vol. I, pp. 525–33

ESSAY

ON THE LAWS OF PLEASURE AND PAIN.

THE philosophers and common people agree, that nature, in all her works, observes a remarkable uniformity; operating by established rules in every thing visible. No where the man of sense will say, is chance permitted to wheel her blind events at random: 'Tis all system—all order—all regulated events.

No one can fail having these general reflections, on viewing the innumerable bodies and operations around us. We behold regularity, from the arrangement of the stars, to the direction of water courses: From the deposit of the strata of the earth, to the formation of plants. Above all, uniformity is most striking in animals: They breathe, they eat, they sleep, by rules inconsiderably varied. Nevertheless, there is not a man who does not at all times believe, that irregularities occur; and most, in the most important objects of creation. "Happiness, our being's end and aim," is sought after with as much solicitude and hope of success, as pain is avoided with unceasing industry. The excitement of pleasure and the encountering of pain, present themselves to every observing mind, as the most important feature in animal existence. How then men can imagine, that in the most important points, there are irregularities; no laws to govern; no fixed rules for pleasure and pain; is as remarkable as it is universal: It becomes the more extraordinary, as every man will declare, that, in defiance of every effort, he has had to encounter pains at one time; and, at another, has partaken of unexpected pleasure: He will declare, that with whatever care he may have laid up in store for future enjoyment, that he has been disappointed; his joys expiring even with a succession of the most probable sources.

In order to understand this subject, and to settle the fact of the universal belief in the inequalities of pleasure and pain, I would refer to the excitements in our bosom on surveying the supposed good or bad fortune of others. If we believed, that the persons, with whose glories or disasters we sympathized, were under the operation of feelings common to all mankind; we should not—would not be so highly excited: we would never weep over the sorrows of the dead, or rejoice at the successes of the oppressed.

The maiming and execution of the martyrs to a peaceful religion: Men represented to have done no harm; who strove to teach others the way to happiness on earth, and to the Heaven of the other world: To find these men, without giving a provoking word, conducted to prison; denied all the comforts of the body: then to have their limbs dismembered, their flesh torn with heated instruments; and their mangled bodies, with sufficient life for sensation, tied to stakes and slowly burnt 'till death! have produced almost the universal excitement of the deepest concern and sorrow. Next, accounts of little babes: Some cruelly burnt to death: Others with their bodies ulcerated; and shewing, by their incessant cries, the agony they endure: Others lost and left to savages; in vain saying, to appease the relentless destroyer, as wont to tell the parent, "I will be good:" Others clinging to the breast of the frozen mother, in vain sucking for sustenance, 'till the pains of hunger and cold gradually produce the fatal exhaustion! These I urge, with the innumerable, various accounts of particular distress, which so deeply affect mankind, unquestionably prove that the impression exists that there is unequal suffering.

With equal certainty, the belief prevails that some persons have an unusual proportion of happiness. Some are represented as enjoying a perfect round of pleasure: One joy to another rapidly succeeding. They have princely estates, and uncontrouled power, securing the love and respect of all who approach: Every sense is gratified in rapid succession: With a healthy and prosperous family, and the most entertaining society at agreeable intervals: In short many are represented as too happy to have an encrease of pleasures on earth.

In most of the novels acceptable to the public taste, the characters are represented in the extremes of felicity or misery. Moreover, every man in the community will tell of some case of perfect wretchedness: In like manner all speak of characters deemed in enviable enjoyment. With these facts before us, I do not comprehend how any one can deny the truth of the statement, that men believe in the inequalities of the distribution of pleasure and pain.

Philosophers and common men probably never committed a greater error, than in entertaining this belief. It is interwoven in every man's mind; yet, most obviously, it is an error. After glancing at the operations of God, can a rational mind come to the conclusion—that the chief desires of our life, to receive pleasure and avoid pain, are left to caprice—to varying rule: That the creator of all, would give to one of the same kind a greater pleasure or greater misery than another. The father who gives to one of his children, that which a just equality requires should be distributed among the whole, is universally condemned. The partial views of narrow sighted man, prompt him even to complain of the distribution of the heavenly father, when conspicuous griefs assail his mind. Why are these afflictions! is uttered in dissatisfied spirit, by almost every being encountering torments.

I have discovered the great law upon this subject, which dispels the darkness that has so long over-shadowed it; which is in unison with all the operations of God, that proclaim him a being of intelligence, of benevolence, and of impartiality.

For the ready comprehension of the law, regulating the pleasures and pains of the mind, I will refer to the laws of the actions of our body. The great Dr. Brown has incontrovertibly established, that the life, the actions of our body, called excitement, are produced by stimulants acting upon the excitability of the system : That, for animal life to be in perfect state, excitement and excitability should be equal: That, when excitement is too high, the excitability is exhausted ; and that the healthy state can only be produced by the abatement of the excitement, so that the excitability shall return to its proper standard. In like manner, when excitement is too low, the excitability is accumulated, and requires exhaustion for the restoration of health. The power of exhausting excitement and excitability in excesses, is in the constitution ; often to be aided by art: never failing, however, to be done perfectly when health is restored. The doctrine is illustrated, by supposing a scale of an hundred degrees of excitement, and another of excitability; perfect health in the middle: Thus,

Excitement, 1, 10, 20, 30, 40, 50, 60, 70, 80, 90, 100.
Excitability, 100, 90, 80, 70, 60, 50, 40, 30, 20, 10, 1.

Healthy action being, when excitement and excitability are all fifty, when there is a variation in one the other is affected according to the degrees in the scale. The one, as before remarked, is never higher or lower without returning to the middle; when health is restored.

This rule, as law of the body, I extend somewhat to the mind, in its pleasurable and painful excitements.

Every mind has a capacity for pleasurable feeling; and the feeling, when indulged, exhausts this capacity or excitability, in proportion to the degree of indulgence. The restoration of this excitability is a retrograde motion; which is called pain. To make the idea more clear and familiar, I shall define pain the counter-action of pleasure.

Accordingly, when our intellect has the excitement of pleasure, to any fixed degree, we have afterwards a counteraction of pain corresponding precisely. When we have indulged in the excesses of joy, we have to pass through the excesses of pain, 'till the mind is restored to its natural equilibrium. This is in conformity to a remark of the oldest philosophers, that those readily excited to greatest happiness are liable to greatest depressions or sufferings. Every one remarks that the cold insensible man of phlegm, is never troubled with the pains of those devoted to mirth.

This simple theory, is nothing but an induction from facts. I had scarcely arrived to manhood, before I was impressed with its truth. In every situation where pleasure was enjoyed, in defiance of every effort, pains equal in degree, sooner or later, would ensue. I could only preserve my mind from suffering, by preserving it from the operation of pleasure: When preserved from pleasure, no occurrences could excite one painful feeling.

I had no sooner established, in my own case, the truth of this law of pleasure and pain; than it presented itself, as the only means of explaining the innumerable variety and sources of misery in others: It unfolded the whole secret of suffering; establishing the uniformity of the ways of providence: It ascribed to system and order, what had been marked by confusion and folly.

At one time a man shall have great pleasure from events, which another time he will view with indifference: At another time with great pain. In some cases, the most trivial causes excite an agony of feeling: In others, sources, we would believe, of infernal pains are received with calm indifference. The martyr has gone coolly to the flames, and viewed, unmoved, the bursting of his limbs 'till death released him: Men have been flogged with hundreds of stripes; as king for a few more, to relieve some pleasurable excitement: Others have had pleasure, from feeling the scales of their sores, from picking the vermin from their bodies: Most monstrous of all, from destroying the lives of brother man! To conclude, what is it that has not produced pleasure? And what is it, to which pain has not been ascribed. The answer, on an extended survey of mankind, is that there is nothing.

The explanation of this phenomena is easy. When pleasure has existed, the mind having its excitability to be restored, any cause that it may seize hold of is considered as the source of the pain; so that if some event did not occur as the supposed cause, the uneasiness would be felt at apprehensions of the stars, the colour of the clouds, or any thing as irrelevant. On the other hand, when the counter-action to pain has taken place; when the mind has no farther retrogade operation to encounter for its preceding pleasures—let what will ensue—no pain can be produced. Such the powers of the constitution—such the eternal operation of the law—that mutilation, mangling, consignment to the flames, are encountered with insensibility; sometimes with an intermixture of pleasure and pain, in obvious—marked—proportion.

The ascertainment of truth, the main object of all for honest inquiry, is not the only gain by the discovery of this great law of feeling: It leads to important practical benefits. We learn from it, that, by refraining from immoderate mirth, we guard against immoderate pains. By preserving the equilibrium of the mind, that is keeping it, fixed in its great operations in pursuit of knowledge, never allowing it to be ruffled with the trifling excitements of pleasure, we perfectly insure our total exemption from every pang. It teaches us, that, having indulged in pleasure, pain will inevitably ensue; and, therefore, that when under its operation, we should endure whatever may happen with perfect resignation.

Our Saviour was never seen to smile. Many philosophers and saints have spent years without one pleasurable laugh. Such gravity comports with the dignity of intellectual beings, while it insures an insensibility to supposed sufferings: Our commiseration may cease for all beings in torture: The law of nature cannot be violated; "The Lord tempers the shorn lamb to the winds," not the winds to the shorn lamb.

The greatest benefit to be derived from the discovery of the laws of feeling, is in our conduct to criminals or offenders against the public. In early ages it was customary to deliver offenders to the party injured, that they might be punished. The severity with which they were treated caused the discontinuance of this practice. To hang and mutilate the bodies of men, is now consigned to the public officers of justice. The object of such inflictions, is stated not to take revenge, but to operate in deterring others from the commission of similar offences. Governments the most enlightened now prefer attempting the improvement of the criminals, by keeping them at hard labour in the public work-houses, called Penitentiaries. But this mode is as improper as the preceding; for as certainly as that crimes are most frequently committed, where public exhibitions of punishment are most common, so certainly do those returning from the penitentiary return to their vicious habits. As a punishment to the criminal it is unavailing: Habit reconciles him to his circumstances: He becomes attached to the very thing designed for his affliction.

The punishment of a man, whatever may have been his crime, is unnecessary: Nothing can prevent his having pains in proportion to his pleasures; no art can give him sensibility, to suffer more than the share of misery corresponding to preceding enjoyment. Cease then with tortures, infuriated man! The greatest pain is in your angry mind! "Viper you bite against a file."

The natural—the humane—the christian course is, when an injury is done, let the offender make reparation to the injured party. There should be but one motive in the proceedings against him; and that should be utility to the injured.

Suppose a brother—a husband—to have been murdered: A poor woman to have had imposed upon her forged bills, or any property to have been stolen; the criminal should be made to work for the good of the injured party; he should become their property, in the public penitentiary, according to rules to be settled in the laws. Instead of a penitentiary, it should be called *a house of reparation.*

The influence of such a system would eventuate in the improvement of all mankind. The prospect of having to labour for the family of the murdered man, would arrest the murderer! the thief would find that he could gain more by working for himself, than by working in reparation for the one defrauded? Thus interest would clearly lead to the abandonment of vice; and, in the restoration of the golden age of universal virtue, would proclaim anew the majesty of man.

3

Selections from
The Yankee
and
The Yankee and Boston Literary Gazette,
1828–1829

(1) 'Utility', vol. I, no. 6 (6 February 1828), pp. 46–7; vol. I, no. 7 (13 February 1828), p. 51; vol. I, no. 22 (28 May, 1828), pp. 169–71

(2) 'Newspapers. Utility', vol. I, no. 26 (25 June 1828), p. 207

(3) 'Jeremy Bentham', vol. I, no. 11 (12 March 1828), pp. 81–3; vol. I, no. 12 (19 March 1828), pp. 92–3

(4) G.R.A.[?], 'Political Economy', vol. I, no. 23 (4 June 1828), p. 179

(5) 'Bentham's Evidence', vol. I, no. 33 (13 August 1828), p. 259

(6) R.[?], 'Metaphysics', vol. I, no. 36 (3 September 1828), pp. 281–2

(7) 'Westminster Review', vol. I, no. 39 (24 September 1828), pp. 305–7

(8) 'Bentham's Reminiscences', vol. II, no. 7 (12 February 1829), pp. 53–4

(9) 'Moore's New Poem', vol. II, no. 8 (19 February 1829), p. 63

(10) 'Penitentiary System. NO. I', vol. II, no. 15 (9 April 1829), pp. 113–14; 'Penitentiary System. NO. II', vol. II, no. 17 (23 April 1829), pp. 129–30; 'Penitentiary System. NO. III', vol. II, no. 20 (14 May 1829), pp. 154–5; 'Penitentiary System. NO. IV', vol. II, no. 24 (11 June 1829), pp. 187–8; 'Penitentiary System. NO. V', vol. II, no. 25 (18 June 1829), pp. 194–6; 'Penitentiary System. NO. VI', vol. II, no. 26 (25 June 1829), p. 202

(11) 'Jeremy Bentham. Extract from a letter from Mr. Lawrence, our charge at St. James's, dated Paris, March 10, 1829', vol. II, no. 24 (11 June 1829), p. 186

(12) 'Bentham's Principles of the Civil Code', vol. II, no. 25 (18 June 1829), pp. 196–7

(13) 'Jeremy Bentham', vol. II, New Series no. 1, no. 79 (July 1829), pp. 1–9

John Neal

(1)

'Utility'

The Yankee, vol. I, no. 6 (6 February 1828), pp. 46–7.

We have long intended to give our readers some idea of what we mean by UTILITY. One way of doing so would be to refer them to the preceding numbers of the Yankee; and another way would be to refer them to the future. But the best way of all is – to give them a fair and straight forward history of the truth. Jeremy Bentham is the head of a party who have adopted the name of *Utilitarians*. We are of that faith – although not of the *party*; for some of their doctrines we do not subscribe to, and a few of the practices, and teachings, particularly of certain of the more youthful among them, are absolutely hateful in our eyes, and worthy of punishment by law. But, nevertheless – we are a *Utilitarian*, to the full extent of what we understand by the word *Utility*, or by the motto affixed to our paper – "*The greatest happiness of the greatest number.*" To that law we suffer no exception – we recognize no duties, no rights in opposition to it. We preach Bentham heartily and without qualification so far. We do not stop half way, with the late president Adams, who in speaking of the institutions of Lycurgus, the Spartan lawgiver, says, "But as a system of Legislation which *should never have any other end than the greatest happiness of the greatest number* – SAVING TO ALL THEIR RIGHTS, it was not only the least respectable, but the most detestable of all Greece." We do not say, "The greatest happiness of the greatest number – *saving to all their rights* – no! – for we acknowledge no rights that can interfere with the *greatest* happiness of the *greatest number* – none whatever, not even that "of life, liberty, and the pursuit of happiness" (to borrow the awkward and either very unmeaning or very untrue phraseology of most of our constitutions). If it be better for the greatest happiness of the greatest number that a man should die – whoever he may be, and whatever he may be, *cut him off without mercy*. And so with his liberty, and so with his property. But have a care – be *certain* that it *will* promote the greatest happiness of the greatest number, before you do so; ay, before you cut off the greatest criminal that walks the earth; before you spoil the highway robber of his liberty, or deprive him of *his* property.

Here is a rule of conduct which never can deceive us – though, to be sure, it may give to a bad man, here and there, an outward justification for misbehaviour; just as every other great truth may. And so far it may be called, what the chief adversary of Bentham called it, nearly fifty years ago, a *dangerous doctrine*. But fire arms are dangerous – and that very law which requires of man to do as he would be done by, is dangerous in precisely the same way. If we are weak, or blind, or perverse, we may judge wrong; if we are wicked or too ingenious for truth, we may pretend to judge, as we do not.

However – this magnificent rule of conduct, which we regard as the greatest discovery in morals that ever was made, did not originate with Bentham. Ages ago, people talked about the *fitness of things*, and Helvetius, that extraordinary Frenchman, had got his foot upon the shadow of the pyramid, and was preparing to measure its altitude for the benefit of all who were at sea, in the vast ocean of morality, when Mr. Archdeacon Paley appeared, and brought forth a new instrument, under the name of UTILITY, and gave us what we required – a name for that, which will hereafter be a guide for the nations – a pillar of light, for the journeying ages that are to follow in the footsteps of this.

And after Paley, came Bentham – who looking abroad with the eye of one that is able to read the universe of thought like a map, and fixing upon two or three first principles, in morals and Legislation, as clear and as satisfactory, as the law of gravitation in physics, laid the foundation of a new science, which, for the want of a better, we may call by the name of UTILITY.

He has written much upon the subject – enough, we should say, if he had written it in English; but he has not – and he is pretty generally misunderstood, even by the very few that have the courage to look into a part of his fifty or sixty volumes of one kind of stuff and another.

Now – as we know the man well, and his works well; and as we know that there are treasures of wisdom and beauty in them, we shall try to give our countrymen, gradually, and step by step, some idea of both. His character we shall give at length hereafter, when we have come to that part of our labors on ENGLAND. The character of his works in general, we mean also to give, in a chapter exclusively devoted to the purpose. At present therefore, we shall confine ourselves to this one subject – UTILITY. And here we begin with an extract from Paley,[1] to show what he understood by the word; after which (though not in this paper) we shall show how strangely both have been misunderstood and misrepresented by the whippersnappers of the age, who have pretended to give the world an account of them.

'Utility'
The Yankee, vol. 1, no. 7 (13 February 1828), p. 51.

We referred in our last to the notions of PALEY on the subject of UTILITY; and we now give the whole chapter. By and by we shall have occasion to refer to it.

So then actions are to be estimated by their tendency.[2] Whatever is expedient, is right. It is the utility of any moral rule alone, which constitutes the obligation of it.

But to all this there seems a plain objection, *viz.* that many actions are useful, which no man in his senses will allow to be right. There are occasions in which the hand of the assassin would be very useful. The present possessor of some great estate employs his influence and fortune, to annoy, corrupt, or oppress, all about him. His estate would devolve by his death, to a successor of an opposite character. It is useful, therefore, to despatch such a one as soon as possible out of the way; as the neighborhood will exchange thereby a pernicious tyrant for a wise and generous benefactor. It might be useful to rob a miser, and give the money to the poor; as the money, no doubt would produce more happiness, by being laid out in food and clothing for half a dozen distressed families, than by continuing locked up in a miser's chest. It may be useful to get possession of a place, a piece of preferment, or a seat in Parliament, by bribery or false swearing; as by means of them we may serve the public more effectually than in our private station. What then shall we say? Must we admit these actions to be right, which would be to justify assassination, plunder, and perjury; or must we give up our principle, that the criterion of right is utility?

It is not necessary to do either.

The true answer is this; that these actions, after all, are not useful, and for that reason, and that alone, are not right.

To see the point perfectly, it must be observed, that the bad consequences of actions are twofold, *particular* and *general*.

The particular bad consequence of an action, is the mischief which that single action directly and immediately occasions.

The general bad consequence is, the violation of some necessary or useful *general* rule.

Thus, the particular bad consequence of the assassination above described, is the fright and pain which the deceased underwent; the loss he suffered of life, which is as valuable to a bad man, as to a good one, or more so; the prejudice and affliction of which his death was the occasion, to his family, friends, and dependants.

The general bad consequence is the violation of this necessary general rule, that no man be put to death for his crimes but by public authority.

Although, therefore, such an action have no particular bad consequences, or greater particular good consequences, yet it is not useful, by reason of the general consequence, which is of more importance, and which is evil. And the same of the other two instances, and of a million more which might be mentioned.

But as this solution supposes, that the moral government of the world must proceed by general rules, it remains that we should show the necessity of this.

'Utility'
The Yankee, vol. 1, no. 22 (28 May 1828), pp. 169–71.

The most extraordinary notions are abroad respecting UTILITY, and the followers of Utility – the UTILITARIANS; the former is seldom alluded to without a sneer, and the latter never. The very name is enough. To call a man a Utilitarian – what is it but to call him by a very odd name? And what are odd names good for but to be laughed at? Ask the newspaper-people.

The Greeks had their notions of utility, and so had the Romans; but they were the vague, shadowy, imperfect type of the substantial doctrine which has lately begun to be thought of, studied and understood, by certain of the ablest men of Europe. Among the moderns, Helvetius and Paley, the latter of whom borrowed his whole groundwork from the former, though the superstructure is entirely his own, are entitled to the chief praise for having stripped the doctrine of all mystery and qualification, and made it what it deserves to be considered – *a perfect rule of conduct* – a rule even more perfect than that, which appears at first view to be incapable of improvement – i.e. – the rule which bids you do unto others as you would that others should do unto you: for that, in some cases would not be a sure guide for the understanding. As for example – a judge is about to give sentence of death, or an executioner is about to do execution. What if the culprit were to turn upon either and say – Art thou of a truth a christian? If so – do as thou would'st be done by – Let me go free. How could the judge escape – what plea could he offer? It might be said, to be sure, that the criminal after setting aside the law, for his own gratification, should not be allowed to set it up again, for a defence against the consequences of his act. But how would that excuse the judge? for he, whether the criminal pleaded or not, would be bound *ex officio*, to take notice of the law; and therefore to do as *he* would be done by. It might be said too – for it has been said – that the judge who proceeds to give sentence of death on a fellow creature, notwithstanding the law, *Thou shalt do as thou wouldest be done by*, does so, not in violation but in confirmation of that law, inasmuch as if *he* had done what the culprit has done – he would be willing to receive sentence of death. But this is a wretched fallacy, a mere subterfuge; and the law itself, so far, is imperfect.

Now – suppose that instead of being told to do as we would be done by in all cases; we were told to do that, which would produce the greatest happiness to the greatest number. Here then would be a *law* about which there could be no dispute. It would apply in all cases – in every age. Now this in fact is the law of utility – the great pervading and abiding principle of that new sect, not in religion, but in morals, who are known abroad, and are beginning to be known here, as *Utilitarians*.

If the readers of the Yankee will refer to page 46, no. vi. and to page, 51, no. vii. they will see what the notions of the Editor are, and what Archdeacon Paley's notions were on the subject of utility; after which, if he will return to this paper and bear with me patiently for a good half hour, I will try to give him a sort of general view of the doctrine, with a sketch of its history, and a few samples of the kind of error that prevails generally on the subject, – I might almost say universally among those who pretend to write about it. He will be surprised undoubtedly, to find such men as the late president Adams erring egregiously in the very outset of a paragraph, meant to be a serious and formal annunciation of his faith; and he will perhaps be more astonished when he comes to see the celebrated Mr. Colton, the author of *Lacon*, that severe thinker, and otherwise extraordinary man, absolutely blundering about the same subject, with a pertinacity and a composure only to be equalled by some parts of "De Lolme on the constitution of England," or by that man, the author of a reply to Beccaria, who by way of showing, to the utter confusion of all those who alluded to perpetual motion, even as a figure of speech, that the very *idea* was impossible, profoundly observed, that as all materials were perishable, there could be no such thing as perpetual motion. Just so with a multitude more – they have erred as strangely in what they have said of this new doctrine and of its followers; and for my own part, I can allege that I have seldom or never seen either alluded to in a book, or heard either alluded to in conversation, without perceiving that the writer or the speaker was meddling with that, of whose elementary principles he was inexcusably ignorant.

Now let us lay down the rule without fear or favor; and try it with a becoming courage – carry us where it may.

Do anything, says the advocate of utility, if by doing it you produce more good than evil. – Murder, lie and steal. Stop at no crime. Butcher your parents or your children. Make war upon your country – do what you please – make war upon heaven if you will. But before you move one step in the work – before you breathe your purpose aloud – be *sure* that you are going to produce more good than evil. If you are not certain – stop – if you are not *certain* that the act must produce more good than mischief, whatever happen – though the sky should fall – do not lift a finger. But are you never to do some evil, that good *may* come of it? – Yes, if that be your motive; and if it be such evil as you, yourself, would not be ashamed to avow. Suppose a madman were pursuing a little child. Suppose the child were to pass you, and escape into a hiding place, without being seen by the pursuer; and suppose he were to ask you if the child had gone that way – and you were to say he had not – you would be telling a falsehood, not with a *certainty* of saving the child's life, but with a prospect of doing so. Would you be justified? – that would depend upon your own views of utility? If your untruth, on account of your character, the station you occupied, or the incapacity of those who were about you, were likely to introduce a habit of untruth in trivial cases, it might be questionable whether you had done most evil or good? But suppose you *knew* that by telling the untruth you would save a fellow creature's life – and suppose the pursuer, instead of being a madman, were a man capable of committing murder, and suppose you knew therefore, that by telling the untruth, you would not only save the life of the child, but the life of the murderer – and perhaps his soul – what then? Would you be justifiable? You might be – or you might not. If you were the high priest of a nation that could not perceive the why and the wherefore of such distinctions – if they were likely to stop at no untruth for any purpose, or even to disregard truth in their daily intercourse with each other, in consequence of your example, it *might* be better for both to perish, the child and the murderer, than for you to be guilty of untruth.

It comes to this, then, you will say – Every man is to judge for himself. Certainly. But is not that a dangerous doctrine? – Assuredly it is, and so is every other doctrine of power – if it be willfully perverted. He who would steal or lie, under pretence of consulting the great principle of utility, is the very man who would steal or lie, under pretence of doing as he would be done by. If he would excuse himself by saying that he did the mischief under an idea that more good than evil would come of it – he must either speak the truth, or not speak the truth. If he does not speak the truth, he would not scruple to say, if he were pressed, that by taking another's property, he *had done as he would be done by*. And if he did speak the truth, he is only to be pitied like every other conscientious man who errs, not for lack of honesty, but for lack either of judgment or education. The result is, that you are to teach people to see the truth, to look ahead, to judge fairly. In other words, you are to educate them.

Now, without stopping to inquire into the doctrine of utility, as it appeared by glimpses in the writings or teachings of the ancients, let us go straightway to such of the moderns as have contributed to give it a shape.

Of the *greatest-happiness-principle*, we have a pretty decided view in the works of two or three lawyers, and political writers about the time and immediately after the time of –

HOBBES –

Who in his LEVIATHAN, declares that the *safety of the people* should be the supreme law; that public good in every case whatever, should prevail over private.[3] Hobbes was followed by Mandeville, Swift and Chesterfield, in England; and by Helvetius and Rochefoucauld and Rousseau in France.[4]

SWIFT – ROUSSEAU

"Swift in his detached thoughts observes, that there are some whose self-love inclines them to please others, and some whose self love inclines them to please themselves; the first he designates as the virtuous; and the second as the vicious. Rousseau saw the difficulty of the egotistical creed and to avoid it, divides self-love into two orders, a higher and a lower, a sensual and a spiritual; and labors to convince us that his higher order of self-interest is compatible with virtue, the lower not."

Here we have the beautiful doctrine trying to work itself up to the light. Nothing however was made of it, till Paley undertook the matter in a serious way; nor did Paley carry it far enough – if was left for Mr. Bentham to give it power and plausibility, and to apply it as a perfect law to all the business of life.

OLIVER GOLDSMITH.

But leaving these, let us go to another class of writers. Oliver Goldsmith had his notions too of this new rule; and as they happen to be like those of many a sensible head, they are worth refering to here.

In part of the Vicar of Wakefield – I forget where now, for I have not read the book for many years, though I have the most exalted opinion of it as a story, the kind-hearted author goes into a heavy argument to show that evil may not be done for the sake of good to follow. And the very marrow of what he says amounts to this – that between the evil done by you and the good that follows, even if it should follow, there must be an interval: that you may be cut off, and called up to your final account, during that interval: and that therefore you must suffer for the evil you did, without having advantage from the good you hoped. Now all this, though very like the reasoning of Oliver Goldsmith in general, I take to be such reasoning as would not satisfy anybody now – save perhaps here and there a novel-reader. Why did he not perceive that if a man be judged at all, hereafter, he must be judged by his *motives*, and by them alone; or more carefully speaking, by the *purposes of his heart*? And if so, what would he have to fear, who should be able to say to the judge of the quick and the dead – Lo! I appeal to thee – *our Father!* – Thou knowest that I meant good and not evil, when I did this thing.

BENTHAM.

To Jeremy Bentham we are indebted for the establishment of the sect of Utilitarians, and for setting forth the whole ground-work of their sublime and simple faith so clearly and so energetically, that people are converted every day by merely reading over the chapter headed Utility – a chapter I mean to republish before long. It is already translated, but I have no room for it now, and shall content myself for the present with repeating and exposing a few of the many cruel and absurd slanders that have been heaped upon him and his doctrines within a few years. One of the first to assail him was a Blackwood writer; and he did so, not because he knew anything about, or cared anything about, the doctrine of Utility, but because Jeremy Bentham was the head of the Radicals; because he had been attacked by the Quarterly Review, the chief Tory Journal; and because he had been well treated by the Edinburgh Review, the chief Whig Journal. For many years they lost no opportunity of sneering at the sage – "the white headed sage." Nor was anything ever said in his favor by Blackwood, till I introduced the following paragraph, into a paper I furnished him. This was before I had ever seen Bentham, and a long while after I had given up all idea of it; for I had learnt something of his habits, and much as I wanted to meet him, and though I would have crossed the Atlantic to meet him, after reading his great work on Morals and Legislation, I would not have gone a step out of my way to *request* an introduction.

Speaking of the revised codes and of the several constitutions of America, I said, "Setting aside John Locke's constitution for Carolina, and Jeremy Bentham's conundrums in legislation, to speak reverently of what we cannot speak irreverently of – *a truly great and incomprehensible man*, whose thoughts are problems, and whose words (when they are English) miracles," &c. &c.

I give this merely to show what my notions of the Philosopher were before I was acquainted with him. I had read but few of his works then, though I had read all that I knew of, and they gave me the idea of an extraordinary man. But I saw the newspapers and journals in travail with absurd stories about him and his writings; a few unconnected, incomprehensible *parts* I had met with – and these I called his *conundrums in legislation*. But after I had an opportunity of knowing and studying the man, I thought very differently of these same conundrums. Not that I agreed with him in everything. No indeed – for many a tough battle have we had concerning several of his favorite opinions; but I saw so much to agree with, that I became a disciple and follower of the faith he taught; and this without even wishing to be so – nay before I was master of the whole of it; for after he had put me in the path, having his clear and beautiful maxim of utility for a guide, I anticipated him at every step of the demonstration.

But the poison that Blackwood poured into the waters of literature, had circulated with them through every channel of public opinion. And Jeremy Bentham at last came to be regarded as a sort of moral and political Swedenbourg.

After Blackwood, came Hazlitt, who pretended to give a full length portrait of Mr. Bentham. This passed for something, very true – nevertheless it hardly contains a word of truth. He mentions the ring sent by Alexander, but he makes a sad story of it. He describes Bentham's eyes at one time as "lack-lustre," and before he gets through the page as glittering with vivacity. I have not Mr. H. to refer to, or I would quote the passage. He then affects to enter into a sober investigation of the mind of Jeremy Bentham – Good God! – William Hazlitt trying to sound the depths of Jeremy Bentham's mind – as well might he hope to sound the Pacific with a chain of flowers, or with the trinkets at the end of a watch ribbon. – But so it was, he talked of Godwin, and he talked of Paley, and he at last concluded to conclude, that Bentham was "no great things after all" – a mere getter-up of other men's cast-off ideas. But, if Mr. Hazlitt's love of truth was what I have acknowledged it to be, and what Hunt says it is, how could he say such things of Bentham, if they were not true? Simply because he did not *know them to be untrue*. He had never interchanged a word with Mr. Bentham, I believe – at any rate, he was not at all acquainted with him – he had a book to make – Mr. Bentham was a good subject for a chapter – and he had lived in one of Mr. Bentham's houses (the rent of which he never paid,) overlooking a large garden, in which the dear old man used to trot for exercise, with his white hair blowing about his face, like the hair of a child. – So much for William Hazlitt's portraiture of Bentham. He has made two, I am told, though I never saw but one.

After this followed captain Parry, already exposed in the Yankee, friend Griscomb of New-York, and about forty more; but as they have meddled, some with one and some with another part of his works or theories, I shall pass them by. Friend Griscomb, however, had better read Mr. Bentham's *Panopticon*, before he proses again about the Bridewell of Edinborough, which he supposes to have been built according to Mr. B's panopticon-plan.

But there is one writer whom I cannot overlook so readily, so shrewd, so keen, so otherwise to be depended on are his remarks. I allude to the author of Babylon the Great. "I know not" says he, "why I should conceal the parties for whom THE CHRONICLE, at least at one time labored – they were Richard Carlisle, and a *soi-disant* philosopher somewhere westward of Temple bar; the one of whom labored (perhaps he did it through terror of starvation which was at least some extenuation of his labor) to set men altogether free from the restraints of religion, and the other labored (and if he did it without any necessity of pecuniary reward, that was no extenuation of his labor – (indeed!) *to introduce among the most heartless of his fellow subjects, notions which would have gone far to subvert not only the moral principles, but the rational feelings of a large proportion of the poorer classes.*" A grave charge that, my masters, a very grave charge; but luckily for Mr. B. without one word of truth in it. Mr. Bentham preached *utility*; and certain of his followers did, I acknowledge, attempt to do what they narrowly escaped the exposure they merited and the punishment they would have received at law *for* doing. But *he* had no hand in it – he saw with shame and sorrow the precipitate and foolish misconduct of those, who while they pretended to do good, were in reality sowing the whole neighborhood with mischief.

KANT.

Now apply what has been said to a familiar case. The great German Philosopher, Kant, would not allow a man to tell a falsehood even to save a friend from death, by the hand of a ruffian or a maniac. He would not allow you "to do evil that good might come, or that good and evil were only good and evil with reference to their consequences." And here laying aside the authority of Dr. Johnson, it would not be difficult for one who professed to be governed by the principle of Utility, to decide against the great German, without wavering or misgiving. Where would be the mischief to the moral sense of the community, were it published to the world that Kant or another had told an untruth to stop a ruffian or a maniac on his way to butchery? Would others feel themselves privileged on his authority, to utter untruth, not for the *advantage*, but for the *injury* of a fellow creature? In the case supposed, a great immediate evil is prevented – the consequent mischief is, if any, but small and remote. If otherwise, or even if it appear so one would be justified in coming to a different conclusion.

JACOBI.

But another German metaphysician denies the existence of any fixed or definite rule, by which the interpreter of God in the heart of man is bound – the moral sense – for both he and Kant, like the *Friends*, allow an innate moral sense – something not the growth of education, nor subject either to be stifled or produced by circumstances. Jacobi would leave the conscience at full liberty to decide in every case – that being what he considers the voice of God in the heart. Now, so far, without stopping to show whether what is called conscience is or is not the growth of education – for the conscience of a Jew and a Christian, of a Hindoo and a Turk, are always according to the faith in which they were brought up, the Utilitarian would agree with Jacobi. Let your conscience, or in other words, your judgment judge in every case. Being satisfied that you are going to produce more good than evil, by a given step – take it – by a given act, do it. If you mistake, the fault is not yours – you are safe, so long as you are honest. But says Mad. de Stael, speaking of this very philosopher and of this very subject – He is so well guided by his own feelings, that he may not have sufficiently reflected on the consequences of such a rule of morality to the mass of mankind. For what could we say to those, who are going aside from the path of duty, and who should pretend that they were but yielding to the impulses of the conscience? Undoubtedly it would be seen that they were hypocrites in what they said; but they have been helped to an argument, which may seem to justify whatever they do; and it is a good deal for men to have a few phrases ready to urge in favor of their deeds. They make use of them at first only to deceive others; but they finish by deceiving themselves." This is very well said, but what does it amount to? – Only to this, that by urging utility as the standard of morals, you urge that which is capable of abuse – that which a hypocrite may avail himself of, that which may help a wicked man to a plausible word or two. But after all, what do we care for plausible words in the mouth of a hypocrite or knave? He may urge the finest and boldest of arguments – he may reason like a god – but there stands the fact, there goes the judgment of his fellow – he cannot alter the one, nor stop the other. Few believe a bad man to be sincere; and they who do, are rather inclined to pity than to copy him.

Few are they that ever believe *anybody* to be sincere who, having done what they consider a bad action, declares that he did it with a good motive – with a view to some high purpose. If you are doubtful of the truth of what I say, call to mind a case, if you can, where on being satisfied a neighbor that had perpetrated any unworthy act, you have acquitted him immediately on the strength of his tried virtue. How little danger therefore in the pretences of a bad man? Take a very decided case. Not many years ago, Purinton murdered his whole family – but one of a large household survived to narrate the awful circumstances. Till that event, Purinton bore the best of characters. He was of an amiable temper, and brimful of religious hope. He had been a good father and a good husband. Yet when he hewed his whole family to pieces with an axe – they who had known him for years, were doubtful of his sincerity – he was dead, he had offered up his own life to *prove* his sincerity – he had died with his beloved children – and yet how few were they that believed him to have put them to death from the best and holiest of motives? And of those few that did believe, what in truth there can be no doubt of – namely – that he strove to obey, not to disobey what he mistook for the promptings of divinity, did any one ever believe that Purinton was right? – No – they looked upon him as a poor bewildered wretch, who had offered himself up in sacrifice to the unknown god, under a fearful mistake – a sort of hallucination like that described in one of Brown's novels, where a father destroys his wife, and I believe a family in the same way, under an idea that he has been commanded to do so, even as Jacob was, to offer up Isaac to the God of the Hebrews. Of what are we to be afraid then – of the hypocrite – of the man that lives and flourishes after the violation of that law, which others are swayed by – when we are not to be convinced by one that lays himself down in his grave, red with the blood of his little ones, to show that he has faithfully applied the great maxim of utility? I say no – and I say therefore, that Mad. de Stael has gone wide of the mark in the little she has urged against Jacobi.

LACON.

But, leaving Mad. de Stael, a writer who could not reason, let us go to another – one who was always reasoning or pretending to reason, even while he uttered a joke.[5] I allude to the reverend Mr. Colton – the author of Lacon. Of his merit as an author I shall have occasion to say a few words hereafter – at present I will concede to him the high place that appears to be generally awarded to the sententious and watchful, and vigorous, and keen. They who are able to say much in few words are very apt to pass for more than they are worth – and he may be like others; but I shall not stop now to examine the foundation of his work; it is enough that in his two volumes of maxims, he has thought proper on three several occasions, to allude to the doctrines of utility with a sneer, and that in two out of the three, he has actually entered into a serious argument to prove that to be absurd – that of which he knew just nothing at all.

In maxim cccxxviii – after saying a good deal (for him) about Socrates, and selfishness, and the present state of society, he says, with what in him was almost a spirit of prophecy, he being ignorant at the time, as I shall show hereafter, that the very thing which he foretold and foresaw, was actually in existence while he was writing the prediction, – "*But I foresee the period,*" "*when some new and parent idea in morals, the matrix of a better order of things shall reconcile us more completely to God, to nature and to ourselves.*" Now this, the Utilitarian believes to be the very definition of the great principle of *utility*, and if the Rev. Mr. Colton had been well acquainted with what he afterwards attempted to ridicule, he would never have written that passage, or having written it, he would have referred to it as either a description, or a prophecy, relating to the *greatest-happiness-principle*, or in other words, which I have adopted for the motto of this paper – *The greatest happiness of the greatest number.*

But this odd prediction appeared in the first volume of the reverend author's maxims. After a while another volume appeared, and he, wishing to have the credit of a discovery which he had not made, or wishing to fulfil his own prophecy, undertook to provide the very law he had spoken of, the new and parent idea in morals – the "matrix" of truth. But how did he do it? Here are his words –

"There are two principles, however, of established acceptance in morals; first, that self-interest is the main spring of all our actions, and secondly, that utility is the test of their value. Now there are some cases where these maxims are not tenable, because they are not true; for some of the noblest energies of gratitude, of affection, of courage, and of benevolence, are not resolvable into the first. If it be said indeed, that these estimable qualities may, after all, be traced to self-interest, because all the duties that flow from them are a source of the highest gratification to those that perform them, this I presume savours rather too much of an identical proposition, and is only a round-about mode of informing us that virtuous men will act virtuously. Take care of *number one,* says the worldling, and the Christian says so too; for he has taken the best care of number one, who takes care that number one shall go to heaven; that blessed place is full of those same selfish beings who, by having constantly done good to others, have as constantly gratified themselves. I humbly conceive, therefore, that it is much nearer the truth, to say that all men have an interest in being good, than that all men are good from interest. As to the standard of utility, this is a mode of examining human actions, that looks too much to the event, for there are occasions where a man may effect the greatest general good, by the smallest individual sacrifice; and there are others where he may make the greatest individual sacrifice, and yet produce but little general good. If indeed the moral philosopher is determined to do all his work with the smallest possible quantity of tools, and would wish to cope with the natural philosopher, who has explained such wonders, from the two simple causes of impulse and of gravity, in this case he must look out for maxims as universal as those occasions to which he would apply them. Perhaps he might begin by affirming with me that – *men are the same*, and this will naturally lead him to another conclusion, that if men are the same, they can have but one common principle of action, *The attainment of apparent good*; those two simple truisms contain the whole of my philosophy, and as they have not been worn out in the performance of one undertaking, I trust they will not fail me in the execution of another."

Let us now look a little into our author's reasoning. If you take the whole passage together, it would appear to be a decided attack upon the strong holds of the Utilitarian faith. But if you examine it piecemeal, and receive what he offers for a substitute as well as for a discovery, you find the Rev. Mr. Colton himself, to be a Utilitarian though probably without either knowing it or suspecting it. And so with a multitude more.

In the first place, the Utilitarian says that *selfishness* – or in the language of Bentham, who being aware of the mischief done every day, and at every breath by the word selfishness, thought proper to call a proper selfishness, that which looks to the future – *a self-regarding interest* – is the main-spring of all our actions.

Now this the reverend Mr. Colton flatly denies. He says "there are some cases where this maxim is "*not tenable, because not true*;" for that "some of the noblest energies of gratitude, of affection, of courage, and of benevolence, are not resolvable into it." Having said this, which for a common author, who disdains to reason, would be enough to say, he proceeds to the proof. And here we have it – "If it be said indeed that these amiable qualities may after all be traced to self-interest, because *all the duties that flow from them are a source of the highest gratification to those that perform them*, this I presume, savors too much of an identical proposition, and is only a roundabout mode of informing us that virtuous men act virtuously. Take care of *number one* says the worldling, and the christian says so too; for he has taken the best care of number one, who takes care that number one shall go to heaven; *that blessed place, is full of those same selfish beings, who by having constantly done good to others, have as constantly gratified themselves.*" Now laughable as it may appear, these very passages contain the whole pith and marrow of the Utilitarian's faith. They are just exactly what he teaches and what he believes. He believes that heaven is full of these selfish beings; and that *they* only are happy, *they* only wise, who are selfish on earth in the same way. But is there no distinction to be supposed between the selfishness that sacrifices the future to the present, and that which sacrifices the present to the future? None to be made between that which leads one wretched creature to destroy another for the gratification of a brief and base appetite, whether of the soul or the body; and that which leads another to offer himself up, in sacrifice for the good of others, of a wife or a child, of his country or of the world? Both are influenced by the vary same motive – both seek their own happiness – both *enjoy* the reward they look for, though that of one may be the anticipation of what others will say of him hereafter. Are we to have it called a dispute about words then, if we desire to have all selfishness denominated – not *selfishness*, for that word has been so long applied in an ill sense, that it cannot now be used in a good one – but a *self-regarding interest*? Are we to be told that we do not know what we teach, if we say that every man is to be judged by the manner in which his self-regarding interest may show itself? or that when it is long-sighted and provident, regarding the greatest happiness of the greatest number, it is *virtue*; when short-sighted, and regardless of the greatest happiness of the greatest number – either vice or weakness? But the Rev. Mr. Colton would have you believe that we assert an identical proposition – that when we say the virtuous man acts in a certain way, or the wise man in a certain way; we do but assert that the virtuous man acts virtuously, and the wise man wisely. – If so, then every syllogism is an identical proposition; every protracted argument another. But the Rev. Mr. Colton does not appear to understand rightly what is meant by an identical proposition – suppose we help him to one out of the passage quoted. "I humbly conceive," says he, "that it is much nearer the truth to say that *all men have an interest in being* good, than that *all men are good from interest!*"

Now *I* humbly conceive that to say that *all men have an interest in being good*; and that *all men are good from interest*, is to say the very same thing in different words. And to say the very same thing in different words, I take to be an identical proposition, whatever may be the play of syllables. Young logicians, who are just beginning to learn the names of their tools, are always meeting with adversaries who *beg the question*, who *argue in a circle*, or who delight in *identical propositions.* To such, the best tri-angled syllogism that ever was framed, would appear a circle.

But as the Rev. Mr. C. has a high character in the commonwealth of literature, and as they who read such authors, are very apt to take what they say for granted, let us try the truth of the charge here made against the teachers of Utility. Let us see if they have been so absurd as to assert an identical proposition; or so childish as to say that virtuous men act virtuously. What is their doctrine? – they teach that all men are governed by the fear of evil, or the hope of good; that the weak and ignorant however, being prone to judge precipitately, are led into many mistakes in their estimate of both – and particularly with regard to the present and future value of both; that as they become wiser and better, they learn to be more and more long-sighted in their calculations, to deal with more liberality, to make better bargains; in a word to believe that their own happiness is best promoted by promoting *the greatest happiness of the greatest number.* This is the substance of what they say; and this the Reverend Mr. C. would have it, is an identical proposition.

To show by a familiar example what is understood by a Utilitarian, who speaks of that self-regarding interest alluded to above, let us imagine two men seated at the same table with a favorite bird between them. Let us further suppose that each has fixed upon the same part, for his own share. Now, if these two men are short-sighted *"worldlings,"* rude, coarse, uneducated men, there would most likely be a struggle between them for the knife. Each would be anxious to carve, *that he might help himself first, and secure the part he liked.* But, on the contrary, if these two men were a little better educated, a little longer-sighted, the strife would be, not who should get the knife, but who should get rid of it – for *each would expect the favorite piece to be offered him by the carver.* – You see plainly now, that he who has got forward but a step or two in the mystery of Utilitarianism, has already arrived at his object – *the very same object* he had in view before, with less trouble, and with less heart-burning. But to carry this a step further – if he be long-sighted enough to look to to-morrow, instead of to-day, when the favorite part is offered him, he will either propose to divide it, or he will waive his share entirely. The better educated he is, and the further he advances in the new faith, the more easy it will be for him *to gratify himself without interfering with the happiness of others*; nay, by promoting the happiness of others.

All our chief pleasures are social – very few are solitary. We cannot bear to live alone – we neither eat nor drink alone – we are unwilling even to pray alone, or to sleep alone – so much and so delightfully are we dependent upon each other for happiness. After all therefore, a self-regarding interest is but another name for a social-regarding interest, *concentrated* and made more effectual for the good of the human race.

But Mr. Colton proceeds to judge and rejudge the other maxim, that "*Utility* is the test of value." And here too, just as he did with selfishness, he begins with denying what he ends with admitting. Let the reader refer to that part of the passage quoted, beginning with "As to the standard of utility," and then proceed to the paragraph, where the author, pretending to a discovery of the very *matrix* he had alluded to years before – a sort of philosopher's stone, or elixir of life, in morality – says first, that *men are the same* – being just what the Utilitarians say; and secondly, that "if men are the same, they can have but one common principle of action, *the attainment of apparent good*" – which is also just what the Utilitarians say; it is but another name for their *self-regarding interest* – it is in fact the very language of Bentham. Who would believe it! – who would believe that in the same breath, a logician like the reverend Mr. C. would gainsay and admit, deny and acknowledge the very same thing? But so it is, and so it ever will be where men are weak enough, or presumptuous enough to talk about what they are ignorant of.

HUME.

But Mr. Hume, on the other hand, says Lacon, "seems inclined to make utility the test of virtue; and this doctrine he has urged so speciously as to draw after him '*a third part of the Host of Heaven.*' Paley has been in some degree seduced, but Paley's authority is on the decline."

Do not regard what Mr. C. says of Paley – he had never read him. It is quite impossible that a man should be so silly as to say what Mr. C. says in the following passages marked in italics, if he had read Paley, or indeed anybody else on the subject of Utility. Let the reader judge for himself by referring to the chapter from Paley, quoted in Yankee No. 7, p. 51.

But continues Mr. C. "If one were disposed to banter such a doctrine, by pursuing up its conclusions to the absurdities to which they would lead us, one would say that *if a building were on fire, a philosopher ought to be saved in preference to a fool, and a steam-engine, or a loom, in preference to either; no parent ought to have any affection or tenderness for a child that was dying of a disorder pro-*

nounced to be incurable; and no child ought to take any trouble for a parent that was in a state of dotage. If we met with a beggar with one leg, we ought to give him nothing, but reserve a double alms for a beggar who had two, as being the most useful animal."

Now all this is a sheer nonsense. And so utterly untrue that no Utilitarian that ever breathed, ever held such a doctrine. Hereafter I shall give a short chapter on the subject, from the untranslated works of Bentham. Like that chapter in Paley, it is worth a score of idle essays on Utility, after the reader has been prepared for it.

However, the Rev. Mr. C. is not alone. The most laughable ideas have got abroad concerning the object, and views, the doctrines and the faith of the sect – as if there were any mystery in the matter. Read the Westminster Review, and there you have a sample of the work which is not only mediated, but achieved by a few of the Utilitarians of England – see if that encourages immorality. See if it is in battle-array against all the beauties and graces, all the affections and sympathies of the human heart. You will say no – and yet, the Westminster review goes much further than the great body of those who have adopted the creed of the Utilitarian. They say – give us poetry, music, all the fine arts, all the higher and nobler feelings, – the poetry of the stage, of trick, and art, and of oratory – and of youth – for all have their use. But do not prefer them to what is more useful, *truth, wisdom, courage, probity – the greatest happiness of the greatest number.*

But as if people are determined not to know any better, the last Edinburgh Review, by way of criticising a volume of poetry, has attacked the *Utilitarians*, pretty much as it did the phrenologists not long ago, talking itself out of breath about a subject of which it was so ridiculously ignorant, that they who knew anything of it, could not read a page of Mr. Jeffrey's essay without laughing. And the clever editor of the ALBION, at New-York (certainly one of the two or three best papers of the time) has thought proper to say what follows of the said attack, – while enumerating the articles in the last Edinburgh.

"*Cunningham's Songs*, which follows, is chiefly to be noticed for its very able *defence of poetry against the levelling and barbarous charges of the utilitarians*. This is a class, we are sorry to say, fast rising into notice in England; they profess to deal only with the useful, *discarding all the more polished graces of the intellect as so much worthless lumber*; and cling to the driest and the tritest matters of fact, *from what they term their ardent love of truth. They are, in fact, the Puritans of literature*, and richly merit the reprehension they here meet with from the Reviewer."

In reply to all which, I have but two or three words to say. The writer in the Edinburgh Review is dreadfully mistaken – the editor of the Albion yet more so. Let those who doubt, read over the YANKEE – *that paper is edited by a thorough-bred and thorough-going Utilitarian.*

NOTES

1 Paley next week.
2 Actions in the abstract are right or wrong, according to their tendency: the agent is virtuous or vicious, according to his design. Thus, if the question be, Whether relieving common beggars be right or wrong? we inquire into the tendency of such a conduct to the public advantage or inconvenience. If the question be, Whether a man, remarkable for this sort of bounty, is to be esteemed virtuous for that reason? we inquire into his design, whether his liberality sprang from charity or from ostentation? It is evident that our concern is with actions in the abstract.
3 Blackstone says the same thing, but he does not mean what he says, where he speaks of pursuing criminals into their castles or houses, or rather – he means what he says not for a general law, but for a law in that particular case.
4 In his *"Maxims"* and *"Falsity of human virtue."*
5 Some authors, in a vain attempt to be cutting and dry, give us only that which is cut and dried. *Lacon*, xxxiv.

John Neal

(2)

'Newspapers. Utility'

The Yankee, vol. I, no. 26 (25 June 1828), p. 207

Not long ago that inconceivable chatter-box who manages the PHILANTHROPIST, and who in the hope of being cuffed into notoriety, is eternally popping his head out and snapping at the Yankee as he sees it sweeping by, on its upward career, took into his head to prattle a paragraph or so about UTILITY – the sum and substance of which was to declare that all *governments had been instituted with reference to Utility, – in other words to the greatest happiness of the greatest number*. This was so pitiable, that though I cut out the passage intending to rap my gentleman over the knuckles for venturing so far out of his depth, yet when I came to make up the paper which appeared last week on the subject of *Utility*,[1] I had not the heart to do it – I threw the extract into the fire.

Emboldened by impunity, the courageous block-head has come out again, and after extracting a passage from the paper alluded to above about Utility, he adds what, most undoubtedly, he believes to be a refutation of what I say: and as *this* is a fair specimen of the style and reasoning of these whipper-snappers, who occupy the public prints, to the exclusion of men, I shall give the passage as it appears in the Philanthropist.

After quoting the following from the Yankee.

"'Among the moderns, Helvetius and Paley, the latter of whom borrowed his whole ground-work from the former, though the superstructure is entirely his own, are entitled to the chief praise for having stripped the doctrine of all mystery and qualification, and made it what it deserves to be considered – a *perfect rule of conduct* – a rule even more perfect than that, which appears at first view to be incapable of improvement – i.e. – the rule which bids you do unto others as you would that others should do unto you; for that, in some cases, would not be a sure guide for the understanding. As for example – a judge is about to give sentence of death, or an executioner is about to do execution. What if the culprit were to turn upon either and say – Art thou of a truth a christian; If so – do as thou would'st be done by – Let me go free. How could the judge escape – what plea could he offer? It might be said, to be sure, that the criminal after setting aside the law, for his own gratification, should not be allowed to set it up again, for a defence, against the consequences of his act. But how would that excuse the judge? for he, whether the criminal pleaded or not, would be bound *ex officio*, to take notice of the law; and therefore to do as *he* would be done by. It might be said too – for it has been said – that the judge who proceeds to give sentence of death on a fellow creature, notwithstanding the law *Thou shalt do as thou wouldest be done by*, does so, not in violation but in confirmation of that law, inasmuch as if *he* had done what the culprit has done – he would be willing to receive sentence of death. But this is a wretched fallacy, a mere subterfuge; and the law itself, so far is imperfect."'

After quoting the above, the PHILANTHROPIST proceeds to reply; and this, dear reader, is the refutation of what I say.

"An improvement upon the *Golden Rule*, with a vengeance! Mr. Neal, we believe, is a lawyer; but if this be a fair specimen of the gentleman's ratiocination, we hope that his clients will not work him *to the death*. It is the prettiest cob-house ever put together by childish ingenuity, or a crazed imagination; and our only surprise is, that the wing of a lazy fly, or the weight of a falling mote, did not tumble it into ruins before its completion. Let us look at this most profound speculation. Should you like to be hung? says the murderer to the judge. No, indeed! very naturally replies the latter. Then, gravely rejoins the convicted scoundrel, you disobey that inestimable rule which says, "Do unto others as you would have others do unto you!" There, exclaims our Portland Utilitarian, after listening to the conversation, does not that last reply irrefragably prove that "the law itself, so far, is imperfect?" Not so fast, my philosopher! *It proves no such thing. On the contrary, it establishes the perfection of the law.* Suppose that the victim to the cut-throat's knife had made a similar appeal to his destroyer – would not the reply have been the same? And if the criminal had acted in accordance with the golden rule, where would have been the necessity for the judge or jury?"

There – there – is not that reasoning "with a vengeance?" Observe what I said. – The rule, excellent as it is, is not perfect; since if it were, it would apply to *all cases, and to every case*; and therefore, a judge who pretended to be a christian, and to do as he would be done by, ought to let the criminal go free; for it *he* were the criminal, and the criminal the judge, *he* would wish to go free. I then say that if this be true – and who will deny the *fact*? – the rule is so far imperfect. And how does our logician of the Philanthropist get over the difficulty? How? – Simply by denying it, point blank – and *then, admitting it.* He says first. "Not so fast my philosopher! *It proves no such thing. On the contrary, it establishes the perfection of the law.*" But how? – Behold the "ratiocination" of this clear-headed writer. – "Suppose that the victim to the cut-throat's knife had made a similar appeal to his destroyer – *would not the reply have been the same!*" Ergo – the moon is made of green cheese. But, we have more to look at. – "And if the criminal," says the Philanthropist, by way of clenching to the Q. E. D. of his demonstration, "had acted in accordance with the golden rule, where would have been the necessity of the judge or jury?" – "*Ergo* the YANKEE is adrift and the Philanthropist ashore. Let us vary the proof.

Major – Is not the dome of St. Paul's higher than a two-year-old boy? Admitted.
Minor – Very well – can you deny that two and two make four? No.
Conclusion. Then sir – does not that make one hundred and twenty miles to Boston?

There, that I take to be a pretty fair illustration of the reasoning of the Philanthropist.

Now what the blockhead was trying to say, though he failed to say it, is exactly what I said in the paragraph he finds fault with. After admitting that a criminal might so address the judge, his argument goes to show that the judge in the case supposed need not *do as he would be done by* – observe that – *because* – because the criminal had not done as *he* would be done by. What a rule for a wise and good man to follow! – a rule that A. may depart from, if B. does; and what a pity that the PHILANTHROPIST would not confine itself to the path it has been praised in this very paper for pursuing so zealously? – Hereafter it may be able to reason; but just now, it would be better for it to spend its time in flying kites, or in trundling hoops.

"Little boats should keep near shore,
"But greater boats may venture more." *Byron.*

Since the above was written – a PHILANTHROPIST has come to hand, charged to the muzzle with matter, about "Mr. Neal," the greater part of which is rather complimentary. To that I have nothing to say; but for the following paragraph, extracted, it would appear from the PROVIDENCE INVESTIGATOR, I have a word or two in store. The first is that I have never read a page of anything that Godwin ever produced, except his Caleb Williams, his St Leon, and a review of his reply to Malthus. The second is that my *infidelity*, whatever else it may be, is not very *subtle*, and whatever else it may be, is not borrowed from anybody, and is moreover that for which *I* hope to be accountable to the only proper judge of infidelity – JEHOVAH. Have you anything more to say?

SUBTLE INFIDELITY.

"Mr. Neal, of the Portland Yankee, is endeavouring to resuscitate the *Utility* Scheme of the French Philosophists, by which Godwin so modestly proved that our Saviour's *golden rule* was "not modelled with philosophical accuracy." Mr. Neal is rather too late in the day. He might as easily restore the "etherial whirlpools" of Des Cartes, or the "substantial forms" of the Peripatetics. And then, the awkward work he makes of it? David, in the hands of Sternold and Hopkins, never fared worse than does Godwin, in the hands of his excentric expositor. Heaven save the cause of *Truth* from *such* a defender. *Error* is welcome to him. Mr. Neal *once undertook to write against* Lotteries. No doubt he has repented of it; since his marvellous discoveries in moral philosophy have been made."

NOTE

1 This was written two or three weeks ago.

John Neal

(3)

'Jeremy Bentham'

The Yankee, vol. I, no. 11 (12 March 1828), pp. 81–3;
vol. I, no. 12 (19 March 1828), pp. 92–3.

In the NORTH-AMERICAN REVIEW, for Jan. 1828, among several papers of which we mean to speak, by and by, just as they deserve, is one of a character so worthy of immediate and exemplary reproof, that we cannot suffer the author to escape.

We should have taken him in hand before, had we seen the article; but strange as it may appear to the writers of the North-American Review, it is nevertheless the simple truth, and as a truth, more mortifying perhaps than anything else could be, that we never knew a word of it, until a week or two ago; nor should we have known it then, had not a fellow-laborer informed us that Jeremy Bentham – one of the greatest and best men that ever breathed, a man whose whole life and whose large fortune has been employed for more than fifty years in the promotion of the welfare of the whole human family – a man to whom the kings and princes of our earth have literally sent ambassadors, and whose works are to be had in almost every language of Europe – had been vehemently assailed in the North-American Review. Nor did we believe it when we heard the story: we *could* not believe that the editor of so respectable a journal would suffer anybody to attack such a man, with the forty-times-refuted follies and levities of Blackwood or the John Bull newspaper; or that any decent writer in our country would be found so destitute of a regard for truth, or so presumptuous, if he did not know the truth, as to assail one of the greatest benefactors of the human race, with downright ribaldry too, in the pages of the chief journal of North-America. Yet, although we put no faith in what we heard – believing it to be some other work, we went again to the table of contents for the North-American Review, and ran our eye over it again. – It was not there – no sign nor shadow of a sign was to be met with where it should be looked for. We then tossed over the pages, and stopped to read whatever we met with, which appeared to bear upon a subject having any sort of relation to the chief among lawgivers; but all to no purpose. Nor should we have discovered the thing at all, had we not taken up the whole review at last for the purpose of reading it through, and saying to the public what our notions of it were. Then it was, and not till then that we saw the following passage – it occupies a part of a paper on *De Stael's*[1] *letters on England*. Thus much to show, that if the review has been suffered to escape hitherto, it has not been so much our fault (for knowing Mr. Bentham as we do, on *us* would devolve the duty of seeing that he is not treated with outrage or indignity by our countrymen) as the good luck of the writer.

We now give the passage alluded to, in the very words of the North-American; after which, what we have to say will be added, not in the usual form of notes, for we regard this offence as one of too high an import for such a thing, but in the shape of serious and deliberately-written paragraphs.

"Baren de Stael enters into a somewhat detailed examination of the sentiments of the two parties denominated Whigs an Radicals on the question of *parliamentary reform*. We have not room to follow him in this, and the subject, though always important in theory, has for some years past been but little agitated in England, and has lost a great part of its immediate interest. The well known Jeremy Bentham is referred to by our author as his principal authority in regard to the Radical opinion. We believe that this philosopher is in fact acknowledged as the leader of the sect, and as entitled to the honor, whatever it may be, of having supplied them with something like a theory. As respects the character and pretensions of this person, we have thought, that with a good deal of natural talent and acquired information, he has the misfortune to labor under a partial aberration of intellect, which has grown upon him as he advanced in life. His first publications, though not of much importance, were judicious and well written. He afterwards engaged in inquiries of greater extent and interest, but as he went on prosecuting them, his understanding seems to have become confused, perhaps from too intense and exclusive application to study. He found himself incapable of bringing out his own ideas in an intelligible form, and committed his manuscripts to a clear-headed Genevan, named Dumont, who arranged and published them in French, and to whom we probably owe most of what there is valuable about them.

"It seems at least but natural and fair to draw this conclusion, since the numerous works which Bentham has since published are entirely of a different stamp as respects both tone and substance. They are written in a strange and incomprehensible jargon. The matter of his latter writings is also nearly or quite as extravagant as the manner: and his conduct is of a piece with both. Our readers doubtless recollect the pleasant account given by Captain Parry, in his work on the life of Lord Byron, of a visit which he made to Bentham at his residence in London, and of the would-be Solon's race through Fleet Street and Cornhill, which he ended, if we remember rightly, at Moorfields, from an instinctive consciousness, perhaps, that he should be more at home there than anywhere else. This little circumstance, like straws that show which way the wind blows, decided our opinion on the condition of his understanding, and explained at once how a person, who in the maturity and vigor of life was avowedly incapable of expressing his own thoughts in his native language, should feel himself called upon in his old age to reform the legislation of the whole civilized world from China to Peru, and should actually enter into correspondence with most of the sovereigns and other rulers of the day upon the subject. With these impressions respecting his character, we should of course deem it unnecessary to examine in detail his political system, had we even the necessary space at our disposal.

"We may remark, however, that it exhibits in many parts evident symptoms of a complete incoherence of ideas in the author. Thus our legislator thinks it necessary that in a perfectly free government, where all the magistrates are elective, measures should be taken for enabling each citizen to conceal his opinion on the public affairs, lest forsooth he should be called to account by – we are not informed whom. For the better effecting of this object, our modern Numa enters into a large dissertation upon the proper shape and constitution of a balloting box, and directs that the citizen, when he comes to the polls, shall be required to take an oath that he will regard every attempt to discover for which candidate he means to vote, as an act of oppression, and will not feel himself bound to give a true answer. How poor to this the wisdom of the Lockes, Montesquieus, and the Madisons, whom Bentham thinks it his vocation to supersede. Baron de Stael pronounces these regulations to be *de grades pauvretés,* or *much ado about nothing.* We should rather class them with what the Spaniards call *disparates* or *sheer nonsense* – the natural fruit of an unsound intellect.

What do we mean by the freedom of speech and the press, if the citizen's lips are to be hermetically sealed, and his way of thinking an impenetrable mystery? Is it not the precise object of a free government, to give him the opportunity, as Tacitus has it, of thinking what he pleases, and saying what he thinks, – *sentire quæ velis, et quæ sentias dicere?* What would be the surprise of our people, who have now for two years past been publicly discussing from one end of the Union to the other, the question for whom they shall vote as President two years hence, if they were told that it was essential to liberty that every man's opinion should be kept a profound secret! It is evident that Bentham's notions are not merely trifling and unstatesmanlike, but actually incoherent, and in gross violation of the laws of plain common sense."

Having now suffered the writer in the North-American Review to speak for himself, we shall add what we have to say, in as few words as possible, consistent with our respect for justice and our great love for Jeremy Bentham, whose true character, and the true character of whose labours we intend to give our countrymen a fair and full idea of, at some future period, if we are not prevented by death, or by something as fatal to the purposes of men.

And 1st. We pray the reader observe to the manner in which this great and good man is alluded to – a man who, whatever else he may be, is now fourscore and upwards, and who, whatever else he may have done, has brought forth, according to this writer's own acknowledgment, publications that were both *"well written* and judicious." "The well known Jeremy Bentham" – "this *philosopher"* – "has supplied them (the Radicals,) with something like a theory" – "As respects the character and pretensions of *this person"* – "the *would-be Solon"* – "our *modern Numa"* – "our legislator." And this language is held in the North-American review toward a man upwards of eighty years of age, whose character and worth, and writings are what we are now to describe.

II. "As respects the character and pretensions of this person *we have thought,* that with a good deal of natural talent and acquired information, he has the misfortune to labor under *a partial aberration of intellect* which has grown upon him as he advanced in life." Now we have an idea that if this writer had ever read a fiftieth part of the works which are alluded to here in the lump, he would have been rather more careful about his phraseology, and rather more select in his authorities. All – we do not choose to qualify the remark – *all* that he appears to know of Bentham he has picked up, as we have said before, from the most unprincipled and least clever of the Blackwood-gang and the John-Bull-newspaper. And why do we say this? Because he repeats just what they say – people who have no means of knowing the truth; for Mr. Bentham has lived the life of a hermit for nearly half a century, seeing hardly five strangers a year, refusing himself to the most celebrated of his countrymen, and actually suffering one of Alexander's counsellors of state, who had came to London from Paris, chiefly if not entirely to see the High Priest of legislation, to go away without an interview. The Blackwood writers know nothing at all of him; and they who do know him, the writers of the Westminster Review, being his disciples and followers, do not speak of him – aware that if they do, no attention would be paid to what they say. Some at least of their number we know to be actuated by this consideration; but others are too discreet for the truth. – Like Mr. Mill, the author of British India, who is indebted to Bentham for the very groundwork, and for the best part of the materials of his own reputation – having borrowed largely from him in almost every chapter, and the whole of Warren Hasting's trial, without acknowledgment; – they are far too polite and selfish to do justice to a benefactor, when it can only be done by betraying themselves. And others, like master John Mill, the son, the cleverest lad of the day[2] so far as the head is concerned, for he was never suspected of a heart, have no time to look after the reputation or welfare of a man who has literally been feeding them for years – feeding not only their minds with the very wisdom and strength for which they are celebrated, where they are celebrated at all, but their very bodies with food. To say no more now of Mr. John Bowring, who has met with a terrible overthrow since we spoke of him last, and of whom therefore we shall say nothing just now, there are some fifty of the most promising men of England, who are under the heaviest obligations to Bentham (which we are not – for we have been rather losers than gainers by our knowledge of him, except so far as intellectual matters are concerned; and there, we have no words to express our obligations to him) and of this whole fifty there is not one to put a stop to the stupid lies that are permitted to circulate year after year about him through all the two-penny pamphlets of England.

But let us state a few facts. Jeremy Bentham, as we have said before, is now upwards of eight. While he was yet in his boyhood, he distinguished himself by a masterly attack on Blackstone's Commentaries.[3] It appeared in one volume, and was so remarkable for beauty of style and strength of argument, as to be ascribed to the first writers of the age – and among others to Lord Mansfield; who used to speak of it in the highest terms. After this (we do not stop to preserve the chronological order of his works, nor to mention a fiftieth part of them) – After this, he took up the doctrine of usury, at that time regarded rather as a theological, than as a political question, and in an essay which never has been refuted and never will be, though it is very brief, and a perfect model for clearness and simplicity of style, demonstrated the absurdity of regulating the interest of money by law. From that day to this, all that has ever been said; by certain of the ablest writers and statesmen of Europe, may be referred immediately and directly to this very essay by Bentham. About the same period (we speak from memory, meaning to be more particular hereafter) he came forth as the advocate of *free trade*, laying down a large part of the very theories which have since made Mill, the father, so celebrated, and urging the French who had made him a citizen of the Republic, to "*Emancipate their colonies.*" This was one of the most eloquent pamphlets of the age. The celebrated letters, on the subject of *prisons and prison discipline*; succeeded – letters to which the whole world have been directly or indirectly indebted for the improvements that have been made and yet are making in the structure of prisons and treatment of prisoners; and all this without any acknowledgment in favor of the author. – Our *Prison Discipline Society* at Boston, among the rest: – If they would look into Bentham, they would find most of their discoveries and suggestions, and hopes and views originated with him; that he was ahead of them half a century ago in the best part of their plan; and that if they would, they might have their mistakes rectified, and their deficiencies supplied, by a paragraph or two borrowed whole, here and there, out of his Panopticon. This work received so much attention, that a bill was brought into parliament, and the appropriation was actually made under the administration of Mr. Pitt, for carrying the project into full operation. But, owning to a personal grudge on the part of the reigning monarch against Bentham for a review of one of his majesty's papers, he, George the third, would not sign the order for the money, and the affair dropped through. And just so was it in France – there an appropriation was made; but the breaking out of the revolutionary war put a stop to the erection of the buildings. And so in Spain – while that country was under the sway of the Cortes, large appropriations were made for the same purpose; but change followed change, and the money, if it was ever collected, which is doubtful, was directed into other channels more immediately affecting the safety of the state.

These works were followed by others – a great body in fact which we have no time to give the titles of; but among them was one which we regard, and which Dr. Parr – and scores and scores of such men have regarded, as the greatest work that has appeared since the days of Bacon. We allude here to Bentham's *Theory of morals and legislation.* We acknowledge that the wording is rather obscure; that it requires a painful degree of attention to master it; that as a work it might be greatly improved; and that so far as the English and our people are concerned, it has been from that day to this, very shamefully neglected; but nevertheless we repeat what we have said before. It is the *Novum Organum* of morals and legislation. It contains the seeds and elements of all truth in these two great sciences – the greatest the human mind was ever yet employed upon. Before Bentham wrote, all was chaos in the whole history of legislation. But now it is beginning to wear the shape of science; and to him are we entirely indebted for this. What we say now, we shall prove hereafter.

To this succeeded a number of works – perhaps twenty volumes of one sort and another in England; and half as many more in French – a part of them being written in French by the author himself, perhaps for the oddest of all reasons in the view of an ordinary writer. He could not find words in English, wherewith to express himself clearly and unequivocally; and as he knew that from the imperfection of language it never could be otherwise while he lived, and while the very elements of the new science, the very tools thereof, had no name, he concluded to write – as he would talk – in a foreign language – and leave it for others to make what they could of it hereafter. He was overburthened with vast ideas; but they were not to be communicated in the every-day language of ordinary men. He had no time to contrive a new language; and therefore he had recourse to one which, though he was well acquainted with it, he was not so severe a critic in, as to be troubled with metaphysical misgivings in every paragraph he formed, as he was with English. This very reason we give out of his own mouth.

After some years, a clever Frenchman, who had been for a while an associate of Mirabeau, and who (as we have been told by Mr. Gallatin, the townsman of both) used to write the very speeches that Mirabeau delivered, came to England, where he got acquainted with Mr. Bentham. These manuscripts, partly in French, and partly in English, were thrown into his hands; and out of them he has extracted about ten large volumes of *readable* matter, which but for him would never have been popular. This much we admit, with pleasure; though we say – and he says the same, and so does everybody that knows anything of the two – one a sever thinker, the other a mere rhetorician, a beautiful writer – we say that instead of improving Bentham, he has only *preserved* a portion of his greatness, and that he has added nothing to him – absolutely nothing.

Most of these ten volumes have gone through three editions in France, each of three thousand copies, and have been multiplied and distributed in most of the languages, and through all the states of Europe.

As Mr. Bentham grew older, he grew more and more dissatisfied with the *inaccuracy* of language, with the want of exactness in it; and he therefore began to prepare a new system of logic for himself – a few chapters of which have lately been booked into a readable shape by his nephew, Mr. George Bentham, one of the most promising men of the age, both for acuteness and for strength. From this he went on, growing less and less elegant, and to the careless reader, – the novel-reader, or the newspaper reader, less and less perspicuous every year; for he went on abridging volumes into chapters, and chapters into tabular views, till it was impossible for anybody to understand him, who had not gone step by step through his preliminary demonstrations; till at last he has come to a style, which cannot be defended – such as that of the article he wrote for the Westminster Review, and which if we could have had our way, and we told him so, should never have gone forth to the world in that work. And yet, though we say this of that particular paper, we owe it to him and to the public to add, that as he has grown older he has grown wiser; that the style we speak of grows out of his exceeding honesty, – for he does not allow himself to separate his assertions from their qualifications – so that his periods are encumbered on every subject of interest: that in ordinary matters where a newspaper style would do, no man alive writes a more off-hand, free or natural style than Jeremy Bentham; and that – after all – the very difficulties we complain of, are attributable more to the *subject* handled by him, than to the style in which they are handled; more to the nature of the science treated of, than to anything else; and that for people who are not acquainted with his early works, to complain of his late works for not being clear, is about as absurd as it would be for a man who had never studied his multiplication table, to find fault with Newton's Principia for not being as intelligible – straight-forward and agreeable as a newspaper-essay upon the private character of a political adversary.

III. But continues the writer in the N. A. R. "His first publications *though not of much importance* were judicious and well written." *Though not of much importance!* Really now we should like to know the author of this remark. It would be pleasant to understand out of his own mouth what his ideas are of the things that *are* of much *importance* in this world. If laying the foundations of an immutable science; if going forth to the four quarters of the earth as a benefactor and a legislator, thinking nothing too small for notice which concerned the happiness of the great human family, nothing too weighty nor too large to be grappled with, if it affected their welfare, either now or hereafter, – if these things be not of much importance, then peradventure it may turn out that the tie of a cravat, or the title of a book, or the writing a paper for the North-American Review, or the correcting of other men's proofs, may be so. But the truth is – to put the writer we are dealing with into a dilemma from which he cannot escape – the truth is, either that he never saw the early works, nor a fiftieth part of the early works of Jeremy Bentham, which he has the impudence to allude to here; or – that he is guilty of a base and wilful untruth. And we are inclined to believe that the former is the case; for if he *had* ever seen the early writings of Bentham, he would not have been such a fool as to say what he has said. It is charity therefore to say of him, that he ought to be pardoned, for he knew no better.

IV. "He afterwards engaged in enquiries of greater extent and interest, but as he went on prosecuting them, his understanding *seems.*" – Seems to whom? to this reviewer, who is utterly ignorant of what Bentham's works are. – "Seems to have become confused, perhaps *from too intense and exclusive application to study.*" Perhaps –! Now the truth is that Mr. Bentham never studies at all; he seldom or never reads a book, and as for study, he has not studied anything, but his own mind, and what he had stored up in his youth, for full fifty years; though even at this age, he sits all day long at his table with his pen in his hand, laboring upon the parts of a well adapted and a vast, though to the mere multitude, a disjointed, unintelligible, system.

V. "*He found himself incapable of bringing out his own ideas in an intelligible form*, and committed his manuscripts to a *clear-headed* Genevan, named Dumont, who arranged and published them in French, and to whom we probably owe *most* (observe the word) *most* of what there is valuable about them." – Very admirably managed. – If this Genevan was so *clear-headed*, how came he to be humbugged with the manuscript of a man who was *incapable of bringing out his own ideas in an intelligible form*? and how came such ideas to be intelligible even to the clear-headed Genevan, if the author himself was incapable of bringing them out in an intelligible form? But what says the *clear-headed* Genevan himself? We shall give what *he* says hereafter in detail; but the substance of it is, that instead of our being indebted to him for the *most* of what there is valuable in Bentham's works, we are indebted to him for nothing – absolutely nothing, but the *arrangement*. And this we happen to know is true. M. Dumont, as we have said before, though a beautiful writer, is a very insecure and vague writer; and all that we have to thank him for is, for having made Bentham more palatable and more popular. – But how has he done it? Now by judiciously abridging, we confess; and now by omitting passages and parts which they, who know the strength and acuteness of Bentham, would no more part with or give up, than they would part with or give up the brains of the man. In a word – we are largely indebted to Dumont, though not for improving Bentham; but for making him popular with those who would never have read nor understood him in his original gothic simplicity, severity and strength; – to say all in a single word – for having *Frenchified* him.

But if this be true, and if Mr. Dumont himself has publickly and repeatedly acknowledged it to be true, how durst the writer in the North American Review, say that we probably owe "*most* of what there is valuable about them," to M. Dumont? The answer is clear – the writer cannot escape – he has either not read the works of Bentham by Dumont (for they all contain this and other acknowledgments to the same effect) or he is unprincipled enough to say that which is utterly untrue of those works. To unpardonable ignorance, and therefore to unpardonable presumption; or to downright knavery we are obliged to refer such criticism.

IV. "It seems at least but natural and fair to draw this conclusion, since *the numerous works which Bentham has since published, are entirely of a different stamp, as respects both tone and substance. They are written in a strange and incomprehensible jargon.*" – Really the impudence and ignorance of a writer, capable of saying this – even if it were said in a barber's shop or a newspaper, would merit instantaneous reproof; but said as it is in the first Journal of North America, and therefore of both Americas, – what, if we show it to be utterly and ridiculously untrue, what would be too severe to say in reply, either to the writer of such an article, or to the publisher of such an article? Nothing. The paper would be a disgrace to the whole country – every honest, every honorable man would say that, and therefore we hasten to the proof.

The "*Plea for the Constitution*" was written in 1803; the "*Introduction to the Rationale of Evidence,*" about 1812; "*Scotch Reform*" in 1806; "*Elements of the Art of Preaching*" 1810; "*Swear not at all*" in 1813; "*Springs of Action*" 1815; "*Defence of Economy,*" vs. Edward Burke and George Rose, 1810; "*Chrestomathia*" (perhaps the profoundest work of the age – including a critical examination of Lord Bacon's table by D'Alembert) in 1816–17. "*Church of Englandism*," and the "*Catechism*" after this – a work on "*Evidence*," in five large volumes, just out; and a multitude more.

(Remainder in our next.)

Jeremy Bentham.
(Continued from page 83).

Such are a part of the writings of Jeremy Bentham, since Dumont published the selections alluded to above; most of them are distinguished for strength and simplicity, though not so much for *style* as were his early works; yet either of them would be enough to show that Jeremy Bentham, and not M. Dumont, is the author of every profound and every extraordinary thought in the whole of the ten volumes, edited by Mr. Dumont; and not only that, but of the very form and felicity of expression, where either is remarkable for strength or directness, for grasp or comprehensiveness.

We might enumerate more – they crowd upon our memory now from all quarters; but we shall content ourselves with referring to the "*Book of Fallacies*," reviewed in the Edinburgh Review, by the Rev. Sidney Smith; and to the review of "*Humphries*", by Bentham, which appeared in the Westminster Review, – and which, though it contains most of Bentham's peculiarities, and more of that which comes nearest to *incomprehensible jargon*, than anything else to be found in any of his works, we ourselves would appeal to, if there were nothing else, to show the amplitude, the elevation, or the depth of the writer's mind. Allow what you please for the gossip, and the trifling, and the hard words, and the affected phraseology (as it would appear to a reader of novels and story-books, or North American Reviews) there would still be enough left to show that the writer was a great man. We may add that when such men as Sir Samuel Romilly; Mill, the author of British India; Austin, the professor of Jurisprudence for the New London University; Colson, the editor of the Globe and Traveller; Parkes, the editor of the Journal of Jurisprudence;[4] Bingham, a lawyer and reporter of high character;[5] Mill, the son, and a multitude more, of the first men of their age and country, are his avowed disciples – to say nothing of Sir Francis Burdett, and Mr. Secretary Peel, who are charged with being so, and who most undoubtedly were to a considerable extent; nor of

Aaron Burr, nor of Mr. President Adams, Mr. Rush, and others of our country, who with fair opportunities of judging of him, have the highest opinion of his integrity and benevolence of heart, vigor and acuteness of mind, – when such men are his avowed followers, we may be pretty sure, in the absence of all other proof, that he neither talks nor writes "*incomprehensible jargon.*"

But why make the charge? Simply because, though the writer may not read Bentham – and we refer what he says rather to ignorance than to malice, for we love charity, – he does read the Edinburgh Review, Blackwood, and perhaps the John-Bull-newspaper; and having seen 'our philosopher' joked at there; as all our writers are prone to imitation – praising what they praise over sea, laughing at what they laugh at, and sneering at what they sneer at, without caring to know why, he has undertaken to serve up Jeremy Bentham for the amusement of our public – *hashing* over what had been hashed over forty times before. But he will be taught better before we have done with him; for we intend to give two or three of his authorities for the foolish and impudent things he has been allowed to say in the North American Review, – and then teach him the value of those authorities.

VII. "The *matter* of his later wirings is also nearly or quite as extravagant as the *manner, and his conduct is of a piece with both*. Our readers doubtless recollect the pleasant account given by Captain Parry, in his work on the life of Lord Byron, of a visit which he made to Bentham at his residence in London, and of the would-be Solon's race through Fleet-street and Cornhill, which he ended, if we remember rightly, at Moorfields, from an instinctive consciousness, perhaps that he should be more at home there than any where else" – (A bad joke spoilt for want of understanding the topography of London) "*This little circumstance,* like straws that show which way the wind blows, *decided our opinion* on the condition of his understanding, and *explained at once* how a person, who in the maturity and vigor of life, was *avowedly* incapable of expressing his own thoughts in his native language, should feel himself called upon in his old age to reform the legislation of the whole civilized world, from China to Peru, and should actually enter *into correspondence*[6] with most of the sovereigns and other rulers of the day upon the subject. With these impressions respecting *his character* we should of course deem it unnecessary to examine in detail his *political system* (!) had we even the necessary space at our disposal."

Now, it would appear from this passage, that the writer having taken up a notion that Jeremy Bentham was mad, from the story of captain

Parry – being in fact, as he acknowledges himself, "*decided*" in that belief, by the circumstance alluded to – the "*straw*," he did not deem it necessary to examine the Political System of Bentham. And yet – he has the audacity to attack not only the system, but the man himself, with language, that stripped of a little of its seriousness, would be downright ribaldry. But, as in all cases of this kind, the faith of the believer, and the good sense of the believer is to be judged of, by the nature of the testimony that has *decided* him; let us inquire a little into the character of captain Parry, and the testimony of captain Parry above alluded to. In the first place, it may be proper to observe, (and we dare say the reviewer will jump when he hears it) that *this* captain Parry is not *the* captain Parry whose polar expedition has made such a noise in the world. He is not only another and a different, but a totally opposite character; and as Mr. Bentham has already suffered by the same mistake, we consider it worth our while to say who and what this captain Parry is. He is a worthless fellow, with a good share of downright cunning, mixed up with a great deal of sheer buffoonery, who got introduced to Bentham, which is a very difficult thing;[7] under pretence of being about to devote himself to the Greeks. Mr. Bentham, whose high and holy sympathy with every people on earth, is only to be equalled by his great wisdom and child-like simplicity – took every thing for granted, till he found his visiter going too far in his direct and beastly adulation. He took the alarm then – grew reserved, and they parted with no very favorable opinion of each other, certainly with no very favorable opinion of captain Parry, on the mind of Jeremy Bentham. One of the last things, the captain said, was, that in three weeks after he met Byron, he would have him under his thumb. – Yet he kept his word. For he flattered Byron into the most ridiculous confidence in him; a confidence which in the result grew pitiable. And this he did by the very grossness of his adulation. Had it been more admirably managed, or more delicately expressed, his lordship would have seen through it, and taken fire; but as it was, it appeared to be the spontaneous and abrupt outpourings of a rude nature – a something which could not be affected, and which no human being that knew Byron would ever have the audacity to affect; and therefore Byron trusted him, and petted him, and played with him, for his own amusement & for that of his friends, as he would with a great slobbering bear; never dreaming the while that so very a beast could have any design whatever in his head. But while he romped with the bear – the bear grew up, and at length overmastered him.

But to go back. The story that was afterwards published, under the name of Parry, describing his interview with 'our philosopher,' though a very laughable story, and though exceedingly well got up, was not strictly true in any one particular. Being rather curious to know the history of the whole affair, we asked Mr. Bentham and his two secretaries about it – and were quite astonished to find how little truth had been made use of by the narrator. In fact, so little was known of the habits of Bentham by his very next neighbours, by lady C—— herself, who occupies one of his next houses, that almost any thing might be said of him with impunity. It was much more difficult to see him, than it ever was to see the reigning monarch of the three united kingdoms – and of all the persons now living, there are perhaps not one thousand that ever saw his face. When Parry go alongside of Byron, he might tell what he pleased therefore of the head of the radicals. Few are they that care whether a good story be true or not; and Byron was not of those few. He was an aristocrat in heart and blood and pulse – he avowed it – and used to show his little hands, and write poetry about them, to prove his unadulterated lineage, and swim with white kid gloves on, that the proof might not be spoiled by the too familiar touch of plebeian waters.[8] Being an aristocrat, he loved nothing so much as to hear the radicals abused. Bentham being the radical chief – and Parry being what he was, a flatterer and a knave, he made up the story upon which, after it was prepared for the press by a London hack-writer, the grave judgment of a North American reviewer, upon the works of the most extraordinary man of the age, has been made up forever; and that in a parenthesis.

What a capital N.A. Reviewer might have been made of the boy, who, when he saw Sir Isaac Newton blowing soap bubbles in his old age, was "*decided* by that *little circumstance*, in his opinion of the understanding" of the said Sir Isaac Newton. Sir Isaac himself – to render the parallel complete, was avowedly incapable sometimes (and so was Lord Bacon) of expressing his thoughts in his native language; and this little "*straw*," the blowing of soap bubbles, would be enough to explain the why and the wherefore to a shrewd thinker.

VIII. "We may remark, however, that it exhibits (i.e. the Political System of Bentham!) in many parts evident symptoms of a complete incoherence of ideas in the author. Thus *our legislator* thinks it necessary that in a perfectly free government, where all the magistrates are elective, measures should be taken for enabling each citizen to conceal his opinion on the public affairs, lest forsooth he should be called to account by – we are not informed whom. For the better effecting of this object, our modern Numa enters into a large dissertation upon the proper shape and constitution of a balloting box (?)

and directs that the citizen, when he comes to the polls, shall be required to take an oath that he will regard every attempt to discover for which candidate he means to vote, as an act of oppression, and will not feel himself bound to give a true answer. How poor to this the wisdom of the *Lockes,* the *Montesquieus,* and the *Madisons,* whom Bentham thinks it his vocation to supersede."

Now – joking apart, all this happens to be not only very silly, but very old. The N. A. Reviewer borrows it from De Stael; De Stael from the Rev. Sidney Smith, in the Edinburgh Review; and the Edinburgh Review from the sheer pleasantry of one of Mr. Bentham's hearty admirers. It is very true that Mr. Bentham has invented or tried to invent a ballot-box; which would not betray the hand that put in the vote; a very difficult thing to do, if we look at the general shape of these boxes, and consider how utterly worthless the institution itself would be, if it could be *guessed* by a bystander from the position of the arm or the direction of the hand, of the person voting, into which of the *two apartments* of the box (for there must be two,) he has deposited his vote. Mr. Bentham, at the age of fourscore, had thought enough and read enough to know, that in proportion to the fastness and beauty and perfection of machinery, should be the care of the projector to have it in complete order, to start with. A little dust, or the lack of a little oil, might hinder the movement of the most perfect orrery ever constructed on earth. Therefore it was that Mr. Bentham, though a great man, was not too great to wipe away the dust from the very life-spring, or to let fall a drop of oil into the secret chamber of power, before he set his machine at work before the universe.

But – apart from the unworthy littleness of detail, which "our philosopher" is charged with; is there not a something yet more fatal to his high character, in what is said of the "complete incoherence of ideas," by the N. A. R? Let us see. Mr. Bentham requires not only that every voter should be allowed *by law* to vote as he likes, in a free government – but that he should be allowed so to vote, by prejudice, and power, and wealth, and secret influence. We all know that most men are afraid to express their opinions openly, when they are likely to lose by it; that on all occasions of little moment, they prefer taking no side at all, or taking the profitable side, to going against their interest. Nothing can be more true than this. – All such people would be secured for the right side, by a ballot box. But influence of every sort is beginning to be felt in our country. It is the *few* and not the many that elect our magistrates: –

few are they that prepare the names; a multitude are they that give their votes in favour of the names, after they are prepared. At present the privilege of voting is not cared for in this country – men regard it rather as a tax than as a prerogative; and unless they are dragged to the polls or excited by strong party or personal feeling, they do not go, without considering it, and speaking of it as a hardship. The time will come however, when a vote will be worth weighing, when every rich man will have his voters, and every proud man his followers – who, if they are not protected by these precautionary measures, will at least have a *check*, if nothing more, upon the free expression of their choice. Ought we to mock the legislator who, perceiving this, provides for it perhaps a whole century before it may be indispensable in every free country of our earth? It is not open, declared power – it is not bare-faced authority we are to be endangered by – it is a secret *untouchable* power. To keep free, we must have a *secret* power of defence.

But, "How poor," says the N. A. Reviewer, "to this, the wisdom of the Lockes, the Montesquieus, and the Madisons!" Very true – we should reply; if John Locke's constitution for Carolina be referred to; or the everlasting brilliancy and skittishness of Montesquieu in his Esprit des Loix; – for, with the exception of the supposed discovery of three elements of government, and of the necessity of keeping them always apart, about which he says a multitude of showy things, no one of which is true, and every one of which is contradicted, not only by the combined and mixed powers of our Federal and State governments, but by those of the British monarchy, and of almost every other he refers to, what is there of real worth in all that the president Montesquieu has said? Of Mr. Madison, we do not think so lightly – he was a disciple of Montesquieu, and he committed his part well, and worked out a system with admirable effect, from the vague and shadowy half-understood principles of his teacher.

IX. "What would be the surprise of our people," continues the North American reviewer, "who have now for two years past (?) been publickly discussing, from one end of the union to the other, the question for whom they shall vote as president two years hence, if they were told that it was essential to liberty *that every man's opinion should be kept a profound secret!*"

Now – we ask of you, readers of the North American Review, if that paragraph would not be a disgrace to a country newspaper, edited by a country lawyer, trying to blackball himself into the place of a political adversary? What incompatibility pray is there between the two ideas? May not a people be canvassing for two years about which of the two, A or B shall be president; and yet, when they have decided in favor of either, by possibility desire to give a vote without having it known to their *employers*, or *creditors* of a different political faith, for whom they voted? May not men give their vote, pray, and yet be rather unwilling – if it could be avoided, to have the vote known? Is not such a thing possible? And if possible, is it not worth guarding against? How many people are prevented every day of their lives from speaking the plain truth, because they have no ballot-box to fly to? How many more, who if there were a lion's mouth, in which to deposit their inward belief – how many that would speak a language that nobody dares to breathe now?

But concludes the Reviewer – "It is evident that Bentham's notions are *not merely trifling and unstatesman-like, but actually incoherent, and in gross violation of the laws of plain common sense.*"

We leave the reader to judge between the two. We have not undertaken to show all the goodness or the greatness of Jeremy Bentham, for that would require a book; but we have merely tried to give the public an idea of the truth – to show these unhappy scribblers of our country who dare to sit in judgment over such men as Jeremy Bentham, that where they least know it, they are prattling blasphemy.

X. But we must conclude. Hereafter we shall give the authorities referred to above; with a remark or two upon each. Just now, all that we can say more, is – that although we neither know nor suspect who the author of this review of De Stael is, we are heartily ashamed of him, and more ashamed of the North American Review, for giving it a place. But although we neither know nor suspect the author, this much we do know: Having given them, whoever he is, a paper which was too long, and which therefore they made two papers of; and they being afraid to lose any part of the precious gossip, cut a few pages out, and called them "*Art. VII. Speeches in Congress, as published in the newspapers!* 1826, 1827," and the remainder, they let go as "*Art. VIII. Lettres sur L'Angterre, &c.*" A most admirable trick wasn't it? The North American Review, employed in reviewing newspapers by the lump, without quoting a single passage from any! But how happened this? – we'll tell you. The paper about De Stael – as we have said before, was too long. Some part was to be dropped. But the author was ticklish, or it may be interested in the N. A. Review, and the proprietor was either very timid, or very blind. So the former was obliging enough to allow a part of it to be taken out, and christened with a title which had nothing on earth to do with it; and put back and dove-tailed into another part of the Review; and the latter was fool enough to preserve a part, which to be sure did well enough, or at least as well as the talk about Cobbett or Bentham, or newspapers, in the original Review of De Stael, but was entirely absurd as a review of the DEBATES IN CONGRESS.

But how do we know this? – How do we know they are both written by the same author chopped over and re-christened? Simply by the circumstantial evidence to be found in the two papers – and from nothing else. 1. In both papers, Bentham is alluded to (p. 163, p. 168.) 2, in both papers, a plan is proposed, which the author, after shewing how well he knows its value – proposes to give away. One is about speeches in Congress p. 163; the other about newspapers, p. 182. 3. In both, we have pretty much the same style, upon precisely the same subject. 4. The *Seventh* article, if it had been published under the head of the *Eighth* would have had, at least, a show of relationship with it; while now, it is what, if we had seen it quoted by a foe of the N. A. R. we should have called a capital hoax. 5. In both papers we met with the *very same quotation*. "Speeches in congress have increased, are increasing, and ought to be diminished," p. 159 – "The influence of the crown had increased, was increasing, and ought to be diminished." p. 190. And 6 – The seventh article is as much too short, as the eighth is too long – the first containing les than *six pages!* the latter no less than *thirty three pages!*

Now really, if the North American Review hopes to humbug us into a respectful idea of the fruitfulness or variety of its literary contributors, it must take another course. A book, by dividing it into chapters, each having a head of its own for a title, one may get through with; but a Quarterly Review – written altogether by one man, upon one subject, and so divided and so entitled, we have an idea would not be exactly the thing. We have done – for the present.

NOTES

[1] In the North-American Review, which is eternally going out of the way to let off its borrowed gibberish, or to blunder about the alphabet of some language its readers are not acquainted with; now printing a received and familiar English word in *italics* (like *fanfaronade*) as if it were a foreigner, and now foreign phrases which mean nothing at all; or nothing but *touch* or *taste*, in a way to startle the pure English reader – in this work *De Stael*, or *DeStäl*, (for it may be written either way) is always written *De Stäel*, which to a German scholar, and such orthography is meant as a show of German scholarship, is about as bad as their old way of writing the name of *Goethe*. – In the N.A.R. and in the Quarterly Review of England it used to written Goëthe! Now the *diaeresis* in German is a mere corruption of the vowel e, which used

to be written *over* certain of the other vowels, the *a*, the *i*, and the *u*. In German therefore, De Stäl with as an *e* on the top of the *a*, or with two little commas or dots, means the same as De Stael. But to write the word in the way the N. A. Review does, not only *with* the vowel, but with the *substitute* for the vowel; and what is more, with the substitute placed over the *e* instead of the *a*, is just as great a blunder in orthography as it would be to write de Sta-æ-l, or Go-œ-the.

2 At the age of eighteen, he wrote some of the best articles in the Westminster Review; he has neither wit, nor imagination, beauty of style nor eloquence of feeling; but he writes like a sensible man, and reasons like a very superior man. At the age of six or seven, he was yet more extraordinary than he is now. We have heard of his having discussed the character of Marlborough at the cafe with a descendant of the Duke, before a large company.

3 Called a "Fragment on Government, or a Comment on the Commentaries."

4 We are not certain of the *title* of this work; nor do we know certainly that Mr. Parkes is *editor*; but he is a large contributor and most favourably disposed toward our country.

5 Mr. Bingham is the editor of the late Parliamentary Register and Review – we forget the title.

6 Mr. B. *did* enter into correspondence with the powers of Europe and America; and was treated with, by most of them through their ambassadors, and highest functionaries. Pay was offered him – but he refused it; honors and presents, but he rejected them, for he could not afford to be *suspected*, at any price, that an emperor could pay. But more of this hereafter.

7 Mr. Bowring the poet and philanthropist was two or three years, if we may believe what he himself says, at trying to get a peep at the Philosopher of Q. S. P. He saw him at last by accident. It was just so with ourself. After reading the *Theory of Punishments and Rewards*, which we undertook to translate years and years before we ever thought of seeing Europe – and before we know it was the work of a Frenchmen, or an Englishmen, or whether the author was dead or alive, we would have crossed the atlantic to see him. Yet we have been above a year in his immediate neighbourhood before we met him, or had any hope of meeting him. And we see by a letter now before us, that Mr. Wheaton, or minister in Denmark, has just been presented to him, by Mr. Lawrence, our *charge d'affaires* – who himself was not introduced till after a negotiation of more than six months.

8 Since this was written, we have met with Leigh Hunt's lively and free sketch of Byron; he goes yet further in what he says of Byron's worship of his own little hand – of his foppery. "He often appeared holding a handkerchief, upon which his jewelled fingers lay imbedded as in a picture."

G.R.A.

(4)

'Political Economy'

The Yankee, vol. I, no. 23 (4 June 1828), p. 179

"Try all things, and hold fast that which is good."

"This science, we imagine, has not yet arrived at maturity; but still retains a prejudice for the good old way of its father, who was a sensible man enough, and broad awake to what was going on in the world sixty years ago. In plain English, Adam Smith was a man of talent and research; but he wrote before our revolution, before the French Economists had carried their views into practical operation; before Cartwright, Franklin, Paine, Jefferson, Bentham, Hamilton, and others had endeavored to explore the sources of public justice, and establish a standard of right by which every part of their country's constitution should be tried.

Practice is a good judge, and experiment a credible witness. Almost any one can now perceive the utility of the steam-engine, and the advantages of applying it to navigation, the idea of which a few years ago, was thought chimerical; and it is said that an idle boy, who loved play better than his work, cheated himself out of employment, by a very simple contrivance for opening and shutting the valve; and perhaps it was a nincompoop that first enquired why the pot-lid rose and fell so regularly. Much in the same way every machine and every science slowly approximates to perfection, casting off incumbrances and receiving new impulses, now from an accident and now from a profound investigation. Political, even more than houshold economy, depends upon a long series of observations and experiments. The immediate effects of any simple plan of operations are obvious; but where the plan is complicated, and requires years fully to develope itself, the prophetic eye of genius cannot clearly discern the consequences, through the intervening cloud of circumstances, unless the scattered rays of historic light are concentrated and properly directed.

It is much easier to make theories and suppositions, or even to book them, than it is to arrange facts, and deduce from them a general rule. Hence we frequently find in our text books, a long talk about the origin of rent, or something equally unimportant, where all the economy seems of a negative kind – a waste of labor and stationary. We hear too a continual gabbling about our free institutions, equal laws, &c.; but to what standard work can we direct a foreigner wishing for something more than bare assertion, with regard to their utility? To the Federalist, says one. But the Federalist was written in the spirit of prophecy, and the enquirer would wish to know how our constitution operates when reduced to practice. It seems to me that we might and ought to have something like a continuation of the Federalist, a national work, showing how and why we have been more successful than the Romans under Brutus, the English under Cromwell, and the French under Bonaparte; what laws have been particularly useful, and what have endangered the safety of our republic. We have the old, but we want a new testament. We have scattered about Congressional debates, debates in conventions for forming and for accepting constitutions – here a defence of the guess-work of the English constitution, there a comment upon a legal decision. We want them melted together, and moulded into some useful shape.

Our lawyers know more of political economy than any other class of men; but their business leads them to inquire what law is, not what it ought to be; they have the materials, but it is out of their line to make a book of the kind wanted, so that one of our best universities has to put up with a womanish compilation from old authors, for a text book. This compilation however is interesting and useful; the author first shows that this science is a subject of every-day conversation, and then discusses the enquiries that would naturally arise in the mind of an English beginner: she has discovered no new substance, but formed a compound agreeable to delicate stomachs.

The importance of this branch of learning, as well as the entertaining manner in which its maxims may be illustrated may perhaps indicate that it will ere long be extensively cultivated. It takes notice of every thing that has ever called for legislation in any part of the world. It consults the pin maker and the shipwright, the savage and the philosopher, the poet and the miser, the ruler and the ruled. It certainly is of importance, that the principles by which one can ascertain what is good or bad in each law, be thoroughly investigated and firmly established, that some of those not connected with government, who best know what national customs and the safety of the people require, should examine the institutions of their respective countries, discover their defects, and propose alterations. When called upon to make laws, as all men of common sense and common honesty are liable to be in this country, we do not wish to be ignorant of their effects, till they have ruined thousands; but we wish before they are promulgated to try them by some standard; to find out in some expeditious manner what have been the effects of similar laws under similar circumstances; in short to understand political economy. It may not be important that our representatives comprehend fully the theory of rent, or know whether a physician is a productive or an unproductive laborer; but it is of importance, that he should know whether an abundance of paper money is a blessing or a curse; whether a great amount of silver and gold is beneficial; or whether the restrictive system taxes one part of the nation, for the benefit of another.

As to the interesting manner in which its principles may be explained, those who have read Adam Smith, Franklin's essay upon luxury, Conversations on Political Economy, &c. will need no illustration. The object of the science is to observe the causes which have accelerated nations in their progress towards wealth and refinement; to reduce history to a system, and arrange facts as they confirm or refute some political theory. It embraces a great variety of men and things. The admirer of chivalry can learn the influence of the Feudal system upon society; the manufacturer finds his conduct discussed, and the man of letters indignantly seizes his pen to overthrow a science which ranks him among unproductive laborers.

Thus the number of those who turn their attention to this subject has increased, is increasing, and ought not to be diminished.

G. R. A.

John Neal

(5)

'Bentham's Evidence'

The Yankee, vol. I, no. 33 (13 August 1828), p. 259.

This extraordinary man has lately published a work on evidence, which will probably overthrow the whole system of what we regard as the most rational part of our law. A correspondent, who has furnished me with a copy, writes thus.

"I expect you will have received Evidence before you get this. You will be delighted with the 4th volume, it is the one of all others to make extracts from. Luckily the work required no editor to recommend it, or it would have miscarried wofully;[1] what has been done, is slovenly, with the exception of one excellent note. There is one note, however, which shews that the editor cannot have read the text, or that if he did, he has not understood it: he combats what he supposes to be an opinion of the author's, although in the text of the preceding page it is given as an hypothesis, and with the author's dissent to its truth. The work has been much read here, even among our lawyers, and has added considerably to that splendid reputation which Bentham enjoys, more especially among enlightened men. The editor of his works, which have appeared in French, M. Dumont, has been staying in London for about two months, and has been as usual most favorably *accueilli*, in our first circles. He has lately published in Paris, "*Organization Judiciare*, &c. *par* Bentham," – an enlargement of the English "Judicial Establishment," which I believe Bentham drew up for the French National Assembly."

NOTE

1 The editor is John Mill, jun. son of the author of "British India." The son has no superior of his age, for reasoning power. He is hardly twenty-one yet.

R.

(6)

'Metaphysics'

The Yankee and Boston Literary Gazette,
vol. I, no. 36 (3 September 1828), pp. 281–2.

The author of the following paper has dealt intrepidly with his subject, and is heartily welcome to our columns. N.

"MR. NEAL – in giving your readers Bentham's opinions on the great subjects of morals and legislation, in simple, intelligible English, you are doing us a service of no small value. Valuable indeed, they are to every body, but peculiarly valuable to us, since it is a curious fact, but no less true than curious, that at this very moment, when the study of metaphysics has become almost obsolete in England, and a great portion of the continent, it is pursued in America, and especially in New-England, with a higher sense of its importance and interest than ever. Brown's Philosophy of the Mind passed through three or four editions in this country before the first was exhausted in Britain; and with the Waverly Novels, and Lord Byron's poetry, was for a season, one of the most fashionable topics of drawing-room literature. In young ladies' boarding-schools, a book about metaphysics is one of the indispensables; and the female who would establish beyond doubt a character for high cultivation, must talk of the purity and elegance of Stewart, and be all enthusiasm in her admiration of Brown. In our colleges even, where our youth are supposed to be fitted for the business of life by the acquisition of practical knowledge, and good habits of thinking, it forms a most prominent item in their course of studies. At the richest and most venerable literary institution in our land, the old scholastic question, "do spirits occupy space?" is, year after year, given out for the serious contemplation and discussion of young men, whose minds are just expanding into maturity and vigor, ready to grapple with those all-important subjects that involve the highest interest of their fellow-men, and consume the noblest talents that earth can produce.[1]

That an intellectual taste of this kind should prevail thus extensively among a people, so new in their existence as a nation, so matter-of-fact in their habits, and moreover, so fond of the superficial and trashy in literature and science, seems at first thought utterly unaccountable. It is readily explained, however, when we look back for a moment, and examine the peculiar character, condition, and religious sentiments of our puritan ancestors. With them, speculative opinions in religious matters, many of which were of a metaphysical nature, were all in all. For the free and unmolested enjoyment of these, they determined to quit their very homes forever, and set up their Ebenezer in a distant and dreary land; – for these, this little band dared to persecute one another, before the fires of persecution from which they had escaped, were scarcely gone out. These points were strenuously insisted on by the clergy, and early inculcated upon the rising generation as necessary to their eternal safety. No sermon was preached in which they were not dwelt upon with a peculiar sense of their importance; and seldom did the "seventeenthly and lastly" conclude the pious man's reflections, without an additional "improvement" to encourage an unwavering hold upon them, as the very pillars of the faith. Dissentions would necessarily break out; and in the paper warfare that was incessantly going on, the people manifested a deep concern, not more from a belief of the intrinsic importance of the subjects, than from a taste they had insensibly acquired for such discussions. The progress of the combatants was watched with an intenser interest than the strife of knights in times of chivalry; a fondness for these disputes increased upon the people, and the uncouth and unintelligible jargon in which they were conveyed, became real music to their ears. Thus it was that polemical theology, the most subtle and incomprehensible of all metaphysics, was the popular literature of the times among all our ancestors. Connected as it is with our eternal welfare, and cultivated still with unabated spirit and fervour, is it strange that a taste for metaphysical studies should continue among us, even after it had ceased to exist every where else?

In a country like ours, where the most favorable conditions exist for the highest developement of the mental powers, and at a time, too, when *Utility* is becoming the grand test of all knowledge, it is a question worthy of the serious consideration of those who have an influence over the intellectual tastes of the people, whether the study of metaphysics does not receive a degree of attention of which it is wholly undeserving. For our own part, we have no hesitation in saying, that so far, metaphysics present us no great, nor useful results, and therefore that the study is altogether vain and unprofitable. Such a flagrant heresy, as this will appear to most people who see it, we cannot defend with reasonings and argument, for we have neither room nor inclination. A few facts and a few remarks, rather calculated to make men *think* upon the subject themselves, than to convince their understandings on the spot, are sufficient for our purpose.

Seriously, we put the question to the advocate of metaphysical studies, and let him reply deliberately and with an unprejudiced mind, as if he were accountable for his answer – What good thing has ever come out of the science? Are the laws of the mind better understood *now*, than they ever were? Do men reason more logically, or with increased facility? Are judgments formed with more dispatch and accuracy? Does the imagination soar higher? Has the memory greater power of retention? That we can see a little farther into the operations of the intellect now than formerly, may be very true; but it is solely because thy are displayed upon a wider and more varied field, not from any light received from metaphysics. But have we any more control over these operations? Have we received from metaphysics one jot more of intellectual power?

Without insisting any farther on the inutility of metaphysics, let us see what has been the certainty of its results. After all its host of professors and defenders, from Plato to Brown downwards, (lights indeed in the dark pathway of time,) after all its eternal reasonings about truth, its discussions, its dogmatism, its doubts, what has it proved? Nothing – but the ignorance of metaphysicians and the utter uncertainty of their science. They have not even *proved* the existence of the mind itself. There are more materialists at this moment, we do not hesitate to say it, than in all previous time together. The whole history of metaphysics is but one dull tale of hypotheses built up, merely to be pulled down.

This could not have been otherwise; for, till lately, they had all gone the wrong way to work, and though each saw the error of his predecessors, yet he could not detect its source. The first source of error, was their entire ignorance of anatomy and physiology. This objection strikes at the root of the science, for the very starting-point of the knowledge of the mind, is the knowledge of the body. So intimately connected are the body and the mind that we can hardly conceive of their separate existence, and yet for a series of ages, they have been studied as if they had no necessary relation together.

Secondly, mind was the grand object of their investigations, – *mind*, wherever it existed. But instead of looking at its manifestations in the brute creation, where they are few, simple, and unaffected by cultivation, they confined their researches exclusively to the mind of man. This partial method of studying their subject, must necessarily have given rise to erroneous and limited notions. As well might the anatomist say, I will confine my researches to the human structure, and thus become acquainted with the whole science of organization; or the botanist declare that he would examine only the bright and gaudy flowers and neglect the unattractive weed.

Another source of error – a necessary consequence, in fact, of the last – was, that they speculated upon man as a being, insulated from the rest of creation, whose passions, instincts and faculties were regulated by laws altogether peculiar, in whose whole moral nature nothing was found analogous among the crowds of other beings that share with him the beneficence of a common Maker. Hence all their wild reasonings about good and evil, and their foolish presumption in defending the government of the Deity, from the cavillings of others more foolish than themselves. With some, man was a monster of evil from birth. Every passion, every desire, every faculty was depraved, and tended to iniquity continually. With another set, he was a cipher from birth – his mind was a *tabula rasa*, a blank tablet, ready to receive any impression that was made upon it by things around it. For the mind, said they, came from God, and God is the source of no evil. As if the tempest, the lightning, the pestilence were not from God. In short, man with them was any thing but what he actually is, an animal – morally, as well as zoologically, an animal. They forgot that *like* other animals he is endowed with passions and instincts, as much a part of his constitution and just as necessary to his well-being as his bones and muscles and nerves; – as capable, too, of being abused and converted into fruitful sources of evil, as the organs of the body are, in consequence of intemperance, of becoming the seats of pain and disease. They forgot that *unlike* other animals he has a mind that is susceptible of almost indefinite improvement, and that man will be in a state of nature only when all his faculties have received all the developement of which they are capable. They saw moral evil in the world; and compromised the power and goodness of the Deity in every step of their explanations. They did not see, however, that moral evil was necessary to our very conceptions of an infinitely perfect being. Moral evil exists, because the universe is imperfect, – for how can the created be perfect like the Creator? Can Deity make Deity? These things, thus strangely overlooked, are the ground-work of all good philosophy of the mind; and the superstructure that is raised on any other basis must fall, for it is built on the sand.

The metaphysical books most read in this country, are the productions of the Scotch school, which, whatever may be thought of them here, are in little repute any where else but in the country of their authors. The cause of their popularity in America is very manifest. Possessing real merits as literary compositions, people were induced to read them, who otherwise would as soon have thought of becoming acquainted with Thomas Aquinas, or the early Fathers. Pleased with their fine writing, they concluded very rationally that their metaphysics must be good of course, just as people every day admire a portrait, because the chairs, or table, or trinkets, are so like chairs, and tables, and trinkets, that it is hardly possible to take them for any thing else. It would be difficult to tell on what the Scotch school rests its claim to originality, much less to eminence; for as to any light they have thrown on the science, we think it would be just as clear at the present moment, as if they had never existed. Instead of taking deep and extensive views of the intellectual phenomena, their works are filled with discussions about things that are either beyond our comprehension, or of no manner of importance if they could be comprehended. Instead of taking up facts and reasoning about them, they begin in hypothesis, and end where they begin.

Reid, the founder of the school, is an excellent writer, and his works are more capable, we think, of affording pleasure and profit to his readers, than those of his successors. And yet, what think ye, is considered his chief claim to distinction as a metaphysical writer? Why, for declaring that Hume's doctrine of man's being a mere bundle of impressions, and not composed of real body and soul, passions and instincts, head, trunk and limbs, is false *because* nobody in his sober senses believes it. O! the wisdom of metaphysics! A strong recommendation to Reid's works is their liberality of feeling, and a freedom from little prejudices and narrow views, as far as was possible, considering the circumstances under which he wrote. Beattie – what shall we say of him? Nothing; his vapid milk-and-water essay on Truth is almost obsolete: Let it be. Stewart's writings have had a more extensive circulation than any other metaphysical books that have ever been put forth, and are more generally read in this country, than those of his brethren of the same school. His highly cultivated taste, his classical allusions, the rich but chaste dress in which he has clothed his thoughts are the causes which make him a favorite with general readers. It would seem as if these qualities had no such harm to his own eyes, since he finds fault with Condillac, because "he never elevates the imagination, or touches the heart;" – (Hist. Phil. Part II.

p. 192) an objection most certainly to a dramatist, or novel-writer, but a merit we should think in a metaphysician. As a reasoner, Stewart's chief fault is that he every where labors indefatigably about trifles, but seldom has courage to work up a great and original idea. His merits are beginning to be better understood however, – his late volume has been reprinted here, but has been little read.

Brown is the star-ascendant now, in the metaphysical firmament. He is a fine writer too, as well as Stewart, but very much like those who enrich magazines and reviews with their precious effusions. Hence his works are exceedingly admired by sophomores, boarding-school misses, and such like, to whom the best recommendation of a scientific book, is the frequent prospect of rivulets of poetry flowing gracefully through meadows of prose. He pretends to something new, and as some of our readers may not have a very distinct idea of what metaphysical discoveries are, we shall quote a specimen or two from this writer.

Memory, consciousness, abstraction, conception, imagination, &c., instead of being each a distinct faculty of the mind, as has been generally believed among metaphysicians, are all merely modifications of one and the same faculty. Thus saith Dr. Brown, and so said the phrenologists long before, and proved in a much better way; and so would everybody of common-sense say, whose minds were not mistyfied by metaphysics.

Again, as in vision, our notions of the distance of objects are acquired by experience, so, says, Dr. Brown, our notions of the distance and direction of sounds are obtained in the same way. That he must have learnt this extraordinary fact while a student in medicine, we can easily conceive, if the medical lecturers in Edinburgh are acquainted with the standard works on physiology, that have been published within the present century; but he must have been laboring under a strange hallucination, when he thought of promulgating it as his own discovery.

Lastly, people are accustomed occasionally to *classify* objects, but the precise operations of the mind in this business, has always been a bone of contention to the metaphysicians; and from Aristotle down to Dugald Stewart, they have all marshalled themselves in the ranks of one or the other of the two adverse factions, the realists and the nominalists. The former believe that the ideas attached to genera and species have a real existence, as much as the individuals themselves. Thus, when we use the term house, we do not refer particularly to a two-story or a three-story house, a wooden, or a stone one, but we mean the essence of a house which has a real existence, and is seen by the intellect, just as a particular house is beheld by the senses. The nominalists, on the contrary, contended that in such cases, the mind contemplated no such existence, but merely a name – a word; that when we speak of *house*, we have reference to some particular thing designated by that word. Dr. Brown, however, denies them all, and avers that the principle which conducts us in our classifications of objects, is that of *resemblance* between those objects; and this, say his followers, settles the question which has been agitated for ages! We have not room to mention any more of this man's discoveries and improvements, to which his friends lay claim for him in abundance; we have selected these, because they have been insisted upon very strongly, as the most important and original. [N. A. Review, No. 44.]

Such are the metaphysical works that are read, quoted, and studied by every body; but which ere long, we trust, will be gathered to their fathers of the dark ages. A new spirit of philosophizing on the mind has arisen, and its success, thus far, will be as durable as it is now brilliant. The Phrenologists have begun upon a foundation as firm as nature, and which will continue, whatever may be the result of their doctrine of the brain. Bentham and his followers are in the right path, and though truth is aways in the minority at first, yet she is great and will finally prevail.

R.

NOTE

[1] Well do I remember having once to discuss the question whether a possible angel or a really-existent fly was highest in dignity? I took both sides, and proved both sides – to my own satisfaction, at least. N.

John Neal

(7)

'Westminster Review'

The Yankee and Boston Literary Gazette,
vol. I, no. 39 (24 September 1828), pp. 305–7.

People have an idea that reviewing at a guinea a page must be a very profitable kind of work over sea; but if they knew what was meant by reviewing there, and what was expected of a reviewer, they would think otherwise; and with any spirit, would rather go out a-washing, wheel dirt, or dig clams at the halves, than toil for a British reviewer. Talk of day-labor – day-labor is downright pastime to the toil of a reviewer, who gets his bread by Macadamizing authors, and paving the high-ways of literature with their bones and skulls.

That our natives may know something of the truth on this head, I shall now give them a review, and the whole history of a review, written above two years ago by particular request, paid for (in part) and printed, though never published, in the celebrated W. R.

In the month of Oct. 1826, Jeremy Bentham, the founder and proprietor of the Westminster Review, applied to me to write a review of a work, then just published in London – a presentation copy of which had been sent by Lord St. Helens, to Gen. Sir Samuel Bentham for the purpose. I did not much like the job; for I had written for the W. R.; and had enough to do with Mr. John Bowring, the senior editor, and Mr. Henry Southern, the junior editor, to know that neither was a man to be trusted. Still, however, as I could not well refuse to do any thing for Mr. Bentham – one of the best and greatest men that God ever put the breath of life into, I promised to read the book, and see Bowring, and explain my views to him; after which, if we agreed in our notions, I would review the work for him. I did so. Mr. Bowring called on me, and we talked the matter all over. He assented to every thing, promised every thing, and I went cheerfully to work – laying out materials enough, and taking pains enough to prepare a volume. Still, when it was completed, that there might be no after-claps in the affair, instead of sending it to him in the usual way, I sent it with a note, saying that unless it could be published *without material alterations and omissions*, I chose to have it returned to me. Being written with care, and with a most impartial spirit, I knew that in a half a day at furthest, I could prepare it either for the Edinburgh, or the Quarterly Review, to say nothing of a multitude of magazines for which I scribbled at the time. Instead of replying to my note, *by* a note. Mr. Bowring called on me in person, and expressed great satisfaction with the paper, saying that I had erred however in translating *lanternes*, and that he could not agree with me in my views of Mr. Bentham. "Very well" said I, after a hurried recapitulation of the arguments I had used, no one of which he understood, or was capable of understanding – "leave that whole passage out." – Here we were interrupted by the voice of Mr. Bentham at the door – "All that I ask of you, is not to make me say as you did, not long ago, what is entirely contrary to my opinion, and what I may have to contradict in some other Journal." I alluded here to the impertinent alterations and interpolations of Mr. John Bowring and Mr. Henry Southern, in a paper which I had published in the W. R. on the subject of this country; some of the errors of which I afterwards corrected in the Old Monthly.[1] The most offensive passages in it, and the silliest, were two by Mr. John Bowring, and Mr. Henry Southern; they were offensive to all parties; they were either untrue in point of fact, or inconsequential as a matter of reasoning, or excessively impertinent, unapt and foolish. "*Contrasted with the abominable systems of costly misrule which prevail in Europe, the comparison is no doubt highly advantageous to the United States. They get an infinitely greater sum of security at a low price than is obtained at a high price in our hemisphere.*" W. R. p. 179, 1826 – a remark, which though true enough, was altogether out of place.

The other passage, and there were but two, is longer, and occupies about a page and a half in the same paper. It commences with – "*It is now totally unnecessary to answer such idle talk as this,*" and it concludes with – "*Violent exaggeration is the character of American literature at the present day, and compared with the character and more natural style of our best writers, the style of North-American authors is usually the rant and unmeaning vehemence of a strolling Thespian, when placed beside the calm, appropriate and expressive delivery of an accomplished actor. We will proceed to give some specimens of the North-American style of fine writing from the books placed at the head of our paper.* (Pr. Message 1825; Webster, Everett,

Sprague and others) *We have distinguished a few of the remarkable passages by italics. Sometimes the reader will find these remarkable parts the worst,[2] sometimes the best of the paragraph, and – and what? – and often composed in a spirit worthy of a less viliated expression.*"

These two passages are the joint production of the two editors of the W. Review – all the rest of the article, was by the senior editor of the Yankee and B. L. Gazette; and I mention this here, partly to show what I meant by saying above, that they were not to be trusted; partly to show what I alluded to when I desired him, as I did in the presence of Mr. Bentham, to leave out the whole passage, but not to make me say the contrary of what I did say; and partly to show what my bitterest enemies have never yet been able to show, though defied over and over again to the proof – the true cause of that belief which *did* prevail, though it does not now prevail in this country, on the subject of what I have published abroad. The very things which have, in all human probability, produced the impression here that I was employed to attack our country, and the writers of our country, were written not by me, but by others – and by others too with whom I quarreled in consequence thereof. But why have I not said this before? Simply because knowing the strength of my case, I preferred waiting till some of them who had threatened to republish the slanders attributed to me, had redeemed the pledge – and then – *then* – I should have come out with a triumphant vindication of my whole career.

But enough – Mr. Bowring's reply to what I said was – "Oh no – certainly not." And here we parted – the condition being that he should leave out my whole review of Mr. Bentham's opinion about a double legislative body, and all that related thereto. I should remark here, however, before I go to the other part of the story, that in the course of conversation he offered to pay for the paper, and that I took about fifty dollars in advance, out of the one hundred and fifty which I was to have.

Dinner over, and Mr. Bowring gone, Mr. Bentham, with whom we both dined, not having understood the subject of our conversation, desired to know what it was about. I told him, and after hearing all I had to say against the favorite theory alluded to above, he replied, that he would tell Bowring to put it in – and to put it in too, in my own language, and just as I said it. All he wanted was fair play; and what he wanted for himself, he was willing to give another. If I was right, he would be glad to find himself in error; if otherwise, to publish what I said, might lead to a change of opinion with me. After this, I had another conversation with Mr. Bowring, who agreed to preserve the passage, with some such introduction observation as this – "We have heard the subject stated so and so." Here the matter ended, and I heard nothing more of the review till I got the proof, *unaccompanied* by the copy. Judge of my astonishment when I discovered that Mr. John Bowring had not only omitted whole passages that he had appeared to be much pleased with in conversation, together with all that related to the examination of Mr. Bentham's opinion about a legislative-body; but that he had actually taken advantage of a remark by the author, to introduce an opinion directly in the teeth of my whole argument, and wholly at war with fact and history – an opinion that nothing but his extraordinary ignorance of the subject he had presumed to meddle with could excuse for a moment.

I could not bear this, and I told Mr. Bowring so, in a brief and peremptory note, requiring him to publish the article as he had *promised*, or to return it to me forthwith. His reply was so altogether in character, that I would be doing both him and myself injustice not to publish it entire.

"Dear Sir – I have not seen the proof of your article – so you must not *understand* that it has passed through my *hand* in the way it will have to *stand*. I meant to do this after you had sent it, and I had received your observations upon it. You do not *say* how I have made you *say* the contrary of what you did *say*. The W. R. must speak the opinions of the W Reviewer, and not the opinions of any individuals when those persons differ from those of the W. R.

"I shall be very happy to hear any observation of yours in writing – but should your opinions differ from mine, and you be unable to convince me that mine is wrong – it must be my opinion (which in all doubted cases I wish to fortify by the best warrant) that must stand – at least in the W. R.

Yours ever,
J. BOWRING."

To this, I replied at length; for it was really high time to teach these quarterly reviewers that I for one, was not disposed to be trifled with. To show something of the temper in which it was written, I give the following extract.

"I do not wish the Westminster Review, nor the editor of the Westminster Review to be answerable for my opinions. Nor will I be answerable for the opinions of the Westminster Review, or its editor, when they disagree with mine – especially after having stipulated with due care that if the article I wrote for the W. R. could not be published without material alterations or omissions, it was to be returned to me; and yet more especially, after being assured that if a few paragraphs, about which we could not agree, were not published in the shape I gave them, they should be omitted altogether, and not published in a contrary shape.

"You cannot be surprised I think at what I have said to you[3] on receiving the proof (without the copy) of an article prepared under such circumstances, when I find that after all my care in stipulating before hand, many material alterations and omissions *have* occurred – some that are unintelligible to me, and some that would be unintelligible to anybody who knows much about America, or who had ever read the book under review; and not only this, but that an opinion *directly the reverse of mine* upon the subject, and the *only* subject upon which you appeared to disagree with me has been substituted for my opinion.

"You say to be sure that you had not read the proof; and that I must not understand that it has passed through your hands in the way it will have to stand – you meant to do this after I had read it, and after you had received my *observations* – *in writing* upon it. By which it would appear, that after I have written a paper for the W. R. which has been accepted on *my conditions*; and after the editor and I have agreed together concerning it, I am to write another paper of *observations* upon it, if I receive such a proof that I am hardly able to recognize a part of my own writing, on account of the changes that are made, not in words or phraseology, but in serious, thoughtful opinions. Thank God, I have something else to do."

The rest of the letter was occupied with a recapitulation of the sacrifices I had made for the Westminster Review, and of the treatment I had received, in common to be sure, with several more, from its presumptuous editor.

The result was, that, as I would not consent to the alterations and omissions and impudent changes of the editor, the article did not appear. I got possession of it however, and kept it till a few weeks before my departure to the continent, when it occurred to me that I would send it, *just as it was*, to the Edinborough Quarterly. I knew of course that if I had leisure I could make it more suitable for Mr. Jeffrey; but I was hurried to death by my business; and tired to death of reviewers and editors. They were almost without exception, a set of blockheads or knaves – or both. Mr. Jeffrey *kept* the paper, as he had some others which had been sent him by a friend of mine without either publishing it or paying for it. In the mean time the North-American Review arrived with an article on this very book, which though little to the purpose, gave to a part of what I said (especially of Roger Williams and Lord Baltimore) the appearance of having been prepared by the same writer. I was vexed by the delay, and wrote to Mr Jeffrey to return my paper; and I was the more in earnest, being about to leave the country, and having a right to expect from one to two hundred dollars for it. But I received no answer. I wrote again – Still no answer. At last, being ready to go, and having lost all patience with Mr. Editor Jeffrey, I sent him the following very respectful note – remembering as I did so, that he had once treated Mr. Mill, the author of British India, in the same way; *keeping* a paper that Mr. Mill had sent him, and neither paying him for it nor publishing it.

Q.S.P. 14th April, 1827.

"Sir – You are reputedly the editor of the Edinborough Review. If so, I look upon you as answerable to me for the parcel I sent you some months ago. I have paid postage enough about this matter and others (in which I had no interest) and as I have now given up the idea of going to Scotland, where I should have taken the trouble to say to you what I am now obliged to write, I must beg, not as a matter of favor, but of common decency and common honesty that you will return the article I sent you.

Whatever other people may do, I choose to hold an editor answerable as I do other men, for a breach either of courtesy or good faith.

"I shall soon be in America – I shall leave this country for the continent to-morrow; and in America, I shall expect to receive the article in question.

"Address to care of —, Baltimore.

Yours with respect, J. N.
F. JEFFREY, Esquire."

Two or three months after my arrival here, the review was returned to my address, and with it a reply to my note, which was forwarded to me.

"Edinburgh, 18th April, 1827.

"SIR – The printed paper, prepared for the Westminster Review, with the M.S. additions to which I understand your letter of the 14th refers, were this day dispatched for Liverpool, to be forwarded to your address at Baltimore academy.

"I must confess I see but slender grounds for the tone of impatience and resentment you assume in the letter. – That an article withdrawn from the journal should not be instantly inserted in another, really does not appear to me to be a very reasonable cause either of surprise or complaint. The truth is, that I thought favorable on the whole of the paper – and was inclined to admit it, though only with some retrenchments and variations, upon which my recent ill health and many avocations prevented me from consulting you. I am not aware that till the letter I am now answering, I have received any request of yours to have the paper returned – or indeed any inquiry with regard to it. How common decency, or common honesty are concerned in all this, I really am unable to comprehend.

"I understand as little what you refer to as to expense of postage. But as I never dispute on pecuniary matters, I beg leave to say that whatever you please to claim upon this head shall be instantly paid to any person you appoint."

I have the honor to be
   Sir, your very ob't. servant, &c.
      P. JEFFREY."

This letter was so gentlemanly and proper, that angry as I was, I could not forbear making an apology to him – for I had not heard of his illness, nor did I once imagine that my numerous letters, on account of myself and another, had miscarried; and this I did immediately, and without recollecting that the very practice which he had disclaimed with so much dignity and plausibility here, was a very common one with editors; nor that he himself had been guilty of precisely the same sort of trick, years before, with the author of British India.

So much for the history of the Review. And now for the Review itself, just as it was offered to the W. R. I might have altered it, and I certainly could improve it in many ways; but I have prefered publishing it exactly as it was written, so that others may judge of the value of the editorial emendations over sea. – The notes contain the alterations and amendments alluded to.

Aperçu de la Situation intérieure des Etats-Unis d'Amerique, et de leurs rapports politiques avec l'Europe. Par un Russe. London (J. Booth) 1826. 8 vo. p. 164.

This little work of only one hundred and sixty four pages octavo (as octavos are made now) contains more valuable information about the Anglo-American states[4] as a political body, than any other book of which, at this time, we have any knowledge. By this, we do not mean that the world are to be indebted to it, or to M. De Politica (the reputed author) for much that is new, or indeed for anything, apart from his own views of what he saw, which might not be gathered from books that have already appeared, if not here, at least in America, and which deserve to be, if they are not, accessible to every man of Europe, who deserves to be thought either a politician or a statesman, whether he be, or be not an hereditary legislator; but we mean that, as a whole, though it professes to be a mere outline, it gives a truer idea of the Anglo-American states, of their political and moral condition, their growth and resources, their future prospects, and their relationship to the rest of the world, than any other *book* that we know of – we might say *work*. – It is therefore well worth reading.

By the preface, it would appear that the author was in that country during the years 1810, 1811, and 1812, and again, after the great war in Europe during the years 1819, 1820, and 1821 – both memorable periods for America, and the former especially so; for, owing to the approach of war with this country, and to the exhausted condition of that, from a long series of what we are obliged to speak of as unworthy and hazardous experiments in political economy, the play of the State-machinery was impeded one day, and accelerated the next, for a considerable time, by circumstances more trying to it, perhaps, than had ever occurred before, from the day on which the Federal constitution was adopted – more trying, perhaps, than will ever again occur, till the confederacy be divided, or till some neighbor, with a differently constituted executive, has become powerful enough to withstand, or to drive back the tide of population, which is now settling toward Mexico; or powerful enough to block without being swept away, or swallowed up, the growth of the confederacy upon some other side, – as on that, where the British have still an empire of their own.

The author is a Russian too – a circumstance very favorable, we think, to impartiality, however it may lead him to over-appreciate common liberty; for he who has grown up in a jail may be delighted with the liberty of a lock-up-house, and the privilege of two rooms to himself; and, though the author (if M. de Politica, the Russian minister at Washington, at the very period we speak of, is the author) certainly did enjoy the favorable opinion of the Americans to a very high degree; and lived, as we happen to know, in habits of rather cordial and free intercourse, not only with the chief dignitaries, but with the people there, we are much gratified to see that he has been able to speak the truth of all parties; of the government, although he acknowledges himself to be a believer in monarchies – (a thing credible enough, to be sure, in the Russian Autocrat's representative) and of the people, though aware, we suppose, of their hatred for monarchy – a hatred so unappeasable, that, of their own accord, they would probably endow their chief magistrate with more privilege, if he stood before them as a president or governor, than they would refuse, with a knife at his throat, if he were to assume the title or the carriage of a king.

The work is divided and subdivided, with a superfluity of method, worthy of Montesquieu himself, into four parts; the *first*, containing a sort of GENERAL VIEW; the *second*, a chapter under each of the following heads – 1. *Extent of territory*; II. *Population*; III. *Confederacy*; IV. *Government*; V. *Army*; VI. *Navy*; VII. *Finances*; VIII. *Political relations with Europe*; the *third*, two chapters more, one about the *Administration of justice*; the other about *Penitentiaries*; and the *fourth*, a paper on the STATE OF SOCIETY. Our course will be to go along with our author, and supply, so far as our limits may allow, the deficiencies that appear – correcting on our way the few errors that we observe; some of which are of magnitude enough to require a detailed exposition, though most of them are trivial, and would not be worth correction, but for the *very* sensible, sober and impartial character of the work, which would be likely to ensure them a degree of perpetuity as well as favor, – especially in the present state of knowledge *here* concerning this part of America.

In the General View of which we spoke, he has touched upon the chief causes of the sudden growth and prosperity of the confederation, with remarkable rapidity and success. We shall render him without much regard for the *words* he may happen to use, if we are able to give their sense.

"Among the permanent causes, we are to place in the first rank," he says, "the geographical situation of the United-States, which enables them to participate in all the advantages appertaining to an insular position, with regard to security, from abroad, without excluding them from those which result from the possession of an immense territory, susceptible of almost every sort of culture."

"The great quantity of rich lands and the abundance of food were the more favorable to population, as the inhabitants were naturally active, laborious and enterprising. Therefore it was that population *doubled itself in the twenty years which followed the war of independence. This unexampled fact in the annals of statistics has not been repeated since.*"

In the paragraph just quoted, our author has been led into a mistake; from which follows another mistake of no small importance, we believe, though it may appear otherwise to him, and though it may be, as we are now ready to acknowledge it *is*, the mistake of almost every writer who has had occasion to speak of the growth of the United-States, and of the supposed ratio of increase, at different periods of their history; from the day of the emancipation, up to the year 1820, when the last enumeration was made. It would appear from what he says, that a material change has occurred in that ratio for the worse. Now the truth is that we have no census of the population at the period of the "war of independence;" neither at the breaking out, nor at the termination of that war; and if we are to understand him to mean what he says, that the population of the United States of America, doubled itself in the *twenty years that followed their war of independence*, there could be but one reply to be made. We should have to say that he had no authority for the remark, and that such a paragraph had no business in such a book.

But let us not be satisfied with general contradiction. The war to which he alludes, began in 1775, and ended in 1783. But no enumeration of the people of America was made between the years 1753,[5] and 1790. In 1790, the population was 3,929,326; in 1800, 5,309,558; in 1810, 7,239,903; in 1820, 9,638,166, without including the indians who are estimated, altogether, at 472,136, and who, while they rove about within the territory of the United-States, are independent of the federal sway. Now – suppose we take the period between 1790, and 1810; we shall have twenty years, and yet we see that instead of the population having been doubled in that time, which would make it for 1810, 7,858,652, it is only 7,239,903; or *six hundred and twenty eight thousand, seven hundred and forty nine* less than it should be to correspond with what we hear repeated almost every day. Let it not be said that such errors are trivial – they are not; errors of eight and a half per cent. in a population-table which is to be the ground work of rather grave political inferences are worth correcting, we should say.

Well, having shown that, in the *first* twenty years after the *first* enumeration, which followed the war, the population did not double – or, in other words, that the population did not increase quite so rapidly as our author says; we mean to show, that the ratio of increase now, is not only greater than he would appear to suppose, but very nearly if not altogether as great as it ever has been. Thus, if we take the population of two other periods, with an interval between them of twenty years – that of 1800, which was 5,309,558, and that of 1820, (the only two periods that our author *could* take, for the enumeration is made in America only once in ten years) which was 9,638,166, we shall find that the deficiency, after all, is but a little more than *ten per cent.* from the sum to which the population would have amounted to, if it had doubled every twenty years. And, now, having done thus, we would ask, if a writer should not be rather cautious in making calculations unfavorable to the future growth of a power, when it is found that the *variation* in the ratio of its increase from a given ratio, which is admitted to be without example, is only about *two per cent.* on the whole amount of population, for such twenty years?

Or if need be, we might show the *percentage* of growth for every ten years, from the period of the first enumeration; together with the ratio of increase for the coloured and the white people of the United States; and by the by, as we may have occasion for such a table before we get through, while occupied with what our author says of the black population, we may as well do it now.

From 1790 to 1800, the ratio of increase for the *whole population* of the United States of America for 10 years was – 35–1 per ct
   From 1800 to 1810 it was 36–3 ”
   From 1810 to 1820, it was 33–1 ”
        SLAVES for the same period.
   From 1790 to 1800. Ratio of increase for
     10 years was 28–7 ”
   From 1800 to 1810, it was 32–1 ”
   From 1810 to 1820, it was 29–1 ”
        FREE BLACKS.
   From 1790 to 1800 – ratio of increase for
     10 years, 76–2[6] ”
   From 1800 to 1810, it was 76–8 ”
   From 1810 to 1820, it was 19–8 ”

12 John Neal

From this table, which we take to be a very safe one, it would appear, that instead of *decreasing*, the ratio *increased*, after the first twenty years which followed the *war of independence* were over. So much for theory; so much for taking words instead of figures, for a ground of political prophecy.

NOTES

1 I find on referring to my letter-book, that I alluded to this in the note which accompanied the article, for I mention there that I had been obliged to unsay elsewhere what he had made me say in the W. R. – alluding to a paper afterwards written by me for the Old Monthly, about copy-rights in America.

2 A pretty way of distinguishing to be sure. But the truth is, that I had spoken much more highly of Mr. Sprague, than the Review does now, and as the editors could not alter my underscoring, they were driven to this whimsical expedient – obliged to *italicise* what they liked as well as that they disliked!

3 Alluding to the note abridged above – it ran thus: "Q.S.P. 24th Nov. 1826 Dear Sir – After all my guardedness in stipulating with you before-hand, you have not only left out the passage that I agreed to have "eliminated," but you have left out one or two more upon which my conclusions were founded – conclusions which would appear absurd, or not intelligible to those who know anything about the matter, if they were unaccompanied with the profess of proof; and you have not only done this, but you have actually made me say the very reveres of that I did say.

4 We do wish that people could agree upon a name for the old United-States of America. The *United-States* will not do; for United-States are to be found everywhere now; nor will the *Northern*-United-States – it would be equivocal, or might be so, now that another confederacy of the *north* has begun to wear a proud shape among the political powers of the earth.

5 In 1753, it was estimated, at 1,051,000. The grounds of the calculation were the militia-rolls, the bill of mortality, an the returns from the governors and other local authorities of the several colonies. *Marshall's life of Washington.*

6 This, it should be observed, is not the *natural*, increase, for it includes the manumitted blacks; nor do we know of anything to alter the view of the subject, which appears in the W. R. for Jan. 1826.

John Neal

(8)

'Bentham's Reminiscences'

The Yankee and Boston Literary Gazette,
vol. II, no. 7 (12 February 1829), pp. 53–4.

Above a year ago, Jeremy Bentham promised me some account of his editor and interpreter, *Dumont*. The following I have just received: it is not only from his own mouth, but undoubtedly in the very words he used in conversation. Hereafter, when I come to speak of his written language, I shall refer to parts of this, which are eminently characteristic of the man's natural style.   N.

Mr. Bentham, on his return from his travels in February 1788, found M. Dumont domiciliated in Lansdowne house. He had then been a year or two in England: he was a citizen of Geneva; his father and family had emigrated from thence to Petersburgh, where his father was court jeweller. Dumont, Stephen, with the addition of some others, was his christian name, had been bred to the church. At Petersburgh he became highly distinguished as a pulpit orator. About the year 1786, Col. Isaac Barrè, having become blind, had need of a companion to read to him; to occupy this situation, Dumont repaired from Petersburgh to London. Barrè was one of the two most confidential friends of Lord Lansdowne in the house of commons. Lord Lansdowne was the head of a party, and for somewhat less than a year, in the years 1782 and 1783, had been prime minister. How it happened, that from Col. Barrè's house Dumont passed into the Marquis of Lansdowne's family, is not remembered. Lord Lansdowne had two sons, one by his first wife, aged about 23, who succeeded him in the marquisate, but though married, died childless; the other, by his second wife, is the present Marquis, aged at that time nine years. The notion is, that Dumont was looked to, by him, as qualified to take a part in the education of the youngest, at least, of these sprigs of nobility, and that for this purpose Barrè, who owed every thing to his patron, was induced to give his consent to the transference.

Lord Lansdowne had been placed in the army, where he served with distinction, in the seven years' war, and formed his connexion with Col. Barrè. The literary, as well as every other part of his education, had either been neglected or misconducted. While yet a subaltern, it happened to him to be quartered in some obscure country town, where he found no society from which he could receive either improvement or amusement. Books, of some sort or other, there were in the town, and to these he was driven as the sole resource that he found open to him. To this incident he was indebted for that love of literature, and fondness of the society of literary men, by which he became so distinguished from his rivals.

In the year 1776, came out Mr. Bentham's first work, the "Fragment on Government." In the spring of 1781, the Earl of Shelburne called upon him to express his admiration of the work, and to solicit the acquaintance of the author. The acquaintance ripened into a close intimacy. In the year 1781 or 1782, the greatest part of Mr. Bentham's work, intituled, "Introduction to the Theory of Morals and Legislation," being in print, was put by him into Lord Shelburne's hands. The "Fragment" had been read by his lordship with a degree of enthusiasm, which he took every opportunity to communicate to such of his friends as afforded a promise of being susceptible of it. The work on Morals and Legislation, had been read by him with correspondent interest. At the time of Mr. Bentham's return to England, as above, he found Dumont, of course, not unacquainted with it. In the interval between the year 1781 and this year 1788, the matter of that work had received considerable additions in manuscript. Of their conversations on the subject, the result was, the papers being for a time communicated to Dumont and placed in his hands. The whole together, printed and manuscript, being in a state far short of completion, Mr. Bentham could not harbour any such thought as that of publishing it at that time, or at any other than a contingent, as well as indefinitely remote period. Dumont said, that with the help of a little labour, which would carry with it its own reward, he thought that if put into French, he could make such a work of it as need not be afraid of meeting the public eye. Mr. Bentham, considering that on this plan he should stand exempt from the responsibility attached to the publication of a work manifestly imperfect, embraced the proposal, not merely with acquiescence, but with alacrity.

This was in 1788: the next year opened the dawn of the French Revolution. Dumont repaired to Paris. Amongst other features by which the character of the Earl of Shelburne had become distinguished, was the intercourse he had formed and kept up with the most distinguished men of the most distinguished nations of the continent: Dumont failed not to reap the benefit of it. Amongst other persons, he became acquainted with the celebrate Comte de Mirabeau. Of all the active citizens of the time and place, Mirabeau was the most active: the most distinguished orator, and the most distinguished writer at the same time. But though on former occasions it was to his own pen that he was principally indebted for his reputation, on this occasion it was to others, that he was exclusively, or almost exclusively, indebted. Under his name, by the title of *"Lettres à ses Commettans,"* came out a periodical on the topics of the day: it was by Dumont that, at the outset, and for a considerable length of time, perhaps the whole of the time, – the pen was held. With him, but under him, was a man of considerable reputation, but whose name is not now remembered. Of these letters of Dumont, a great part of the matter, probably all that was new, was taken from Mr. Bentham's papers. During this interesting period, Dumont was sometimes at Paris, sometimes in London; at Paris he was, at the time the Elections for the second National Assembly were going on; that assembly, for which Joseph Priestly and Thomas Paine was returned: it is not remembered whether Thomas Paine sat. Brissot then, or soon afterwards, at the head of the party called the Girondists, had been in England not long before the year 1784: he had contracted an intimacy with Mr. Bentham. Dumont, on his arrival at Paris, had found him busy in canvassing for seats in the Assembly; among the names for which he had been most active, was that of Jeremy Bentham. Judging from the complexion of the times, Dumont thought it matter of obligation, laid on him by his duty to his friend, to do what he could to prevent his being stationed in a post of so much danger: without saying any thing to Mr. Bentham, he laboured and succeeded. This was, it is believed, somewhere about the year 1793, but the history of the times will show. After this, Dumont's stay at Paris, it may well be imagined, did not long continue. On his return, he resumed his situation in Lansdowne House, and retained it till about the year 18— , when he paid a visit to his own country, Geneva, where he took a prominent and efficient part in its political affairs. In 1802, came out the first of his translations of Mr. Bentham's works, that in 3 vols. 8vo. *"Traités de Legislation."* Out of this work, seems to have been formed the pretence for a pension of 500*l*. a year, which he enjoys at present. The history of this pension is curious enough, and not uncharacteristic of the matchless Constitution, the envy and admiration of surrounding nations. In the department of the Exchequer there existed, in those days, a sinecure called the Clerkship of the Pells: produce in fees, about 3,000*l*. a year. Soon after the accession of Lord Shelburne, this sinecure was found or made vacant, and Col. Barrè was invested with it. Under this clerk, were clerks in considerable numbers, by whom the business was carried on: of these under clerkships, the highest in pay and dignity (pay in fees about 400*l*. a year) was likewise soon after found or made vacant, and found or made a sinecure, and being so found or made, was given to M. Dumont: the said M. Dumont not being a native, this appointment was contrary to an express law, but there are times and seasons at which laws are silent, or tantamount to it. Since then, M. Dumont has figured in a double character and under two different names, – in England, in the Red Book, Stephen Dumont, Esq.; in Geneva, Citizen Etienne Dumont, with an intervening string of other christian names. In 18— , when Mr. Addington (now Viscount Sidmouth) became Premier, this Clerkship of the Pells was too precious a jewel to be left in non-ministerial hands. Col. Barrè was at this time blind – as such, an object of charity: the sinecure was taken from him, but 3,000*l*. a year, under the name of pension, was granted to him in *lieu of it*. A son of Mr. Addington's got the *clerkship*. In the year 1806, came a fresh ministerial change, to which the whigs were indebted for their short-lived reign – First Lord of the Treasury, Lord Grenville: Chancellor of the Exchequer, Lord Henry Petty, youngest of the quondam Earl of Shelburne's (now Marquis of Lansdowne's) two sons. On this occasion, the list of the clerks above mentioned came to be overhauled. For no inconsiderable length of time, Stephen Dumont, Esq. was in a state of trepidation: all this time the sinecure was tottering and threatening to slip from under him. He was not altogether destitute, having made some savings which he had invested in the French Funds, but these had undergone what was called consolidation; in plain English, two-thirds of the interest on the capital had been struck off. Of this little political earthquake, what was the result? The 400*l*. a year, instead of being struck off, was thrown up in the form of a pension, *and had a hundred a year added to it*.

Since then his time has been passed in vibrating between London, Paris and Geneva; of late years mostly in Geneva. When in England, a good part of it has been passed at Holland-house, Kensington: sometimes in Bowood, in Wiltshire, the seat of the Marquis of Lansdowne. At Geneva, some years were passed in the endeavour to obtain adoption for a Penal Code, which, as far as it went, was on the principles of Mr. Bentham, as explained in the first published work. During two years, prodigious, M. Dumont used to say, was the consumption of words that took place on the occasion, during that period. The persons with whom he had to do, were Aristocrats to the back-bone. Next to impregnable was the *vis inertiæ* which he had to contend against. In a more particular degree distasteful, was the Rationale, which constitutes so distinguishing an ingredient in those specimens of a Code which may be seen in that work. Without the reasons, it might have passed; but reason, and reasons made every thing dry into which they were introduced. At the end of a struggle of several years, M. Dumont has continued to introduce, in some indirect form, into that mixed Constitution in which Aristocracy has, in a high degree, the ascendant, some small additional spice of democracy, insomuch that with reference to the interest of this, his little State (the population of which, by the last changes, has been increased to 40,000 inhabitants) he has the satisfaction of felicitating himself on the not having lived in vain.

John Neal

(9)

'Moore's New Poem'

The Yankee and Boston Literary Gazette,
vol. II, no. 8 (19 February 1829), p. 63

ODES ON CASH, CORN, AND CATHOLICS. There is no reviewing a volume such as this. The flavour and spirit escape, while you are making up your mind how to describe them. As poetry, it is brimful of music – and if regarded as satire, a large portion of it is the very essence of biting truth. Lord Eldon, with all his doubts, and about half a score of the chief men of the day, are literally tickled to death.

The following Ode is no more than a happy specimen of the whole concentrated bitterness of Moore's nature. But a key is wanted. Jeremy Bentham is the proprietor of the Westminster Review: Mill the father, John Mill the son, Mr. Fonblanque (the sharp reviewer of Moore in that very work), are writers for the W.R., and the W.R. has been a very severe, and on some accounts a very unfair reviewer of Mr. Moore. Hence the ode below, and the bitter – bitter allusions that are found elsewhere in the utility, Bentham, and *breeding*.   N

ODE TO THE SUBLIME PORTE

Great Sultan, how wise are thy State compositions!
   And oh, above all, I admire that Decree,
In which thou command'st, that all *she* polititians
   Shall forthwith be strangled and cast in the sea.

'T is my fortune to know a lean Benthamite spinster –
   A maid, who her faith in old Jeremy puts;
Who talks, with a lisp, of "the last new West*minster*,"
   And hopes you're delighted with "Mill upon Gluts;"

Who tells you how clever one Mr. Fun-blank is,
   How charming his Articles 'gainst the Nobility; –
And assures you that even a gentleman's rank is,
   In Jeremy's school, of no sort of *utility*.

To see her, ye Gods, a new Number perusing –
   ART. 1 – "On the *Needle's* variations," by Pl—e;
ART. 2 – By her fav'rite Fun-blank – "so amusing!
   Dear man! he make poetry quite a *law* case.

ART. 3 – "Upon Fallacies," Jeremy's own; –
   (Chief Fallacy being, his hope to find readers); –
ART. 4 – "Upon Honesty," author unknown; –
   ART. 5 – (by the young Mr. M) – "Hints to Breeders."

Oh, Sultan, oh, Sultan, though oft for the bag
   And the bowstring, like thee, I am tempted to call –
Though drowing's too good for each blue-stocking hag,
   I would bag this *she* Benthamite first of them all!

And, lest she should ever again lift her head
   From the watery bottom, her clack to renew, –
As a clog, as a sinker, far better than lead,
   I would hang round her neck her own darling Review.

   N.B. – The "she-politician" alluded to here, is Mrs. *George Grote*, the banker's wife; she has made up an article or two for the W.R.; and her husband was the author of the Greek Papers.   N

John Neal

(10)

'Penitentiary System'

The Yankee and Boston Literary Gazette,
vol. II, no. 15 (9 April 1829), pp. 113–14;
no. 17 (23 April 1829), pp. 129–30; no. 20 (14 May 1829), pp. 154–5;
no. 24 (11 June 1829), pp. 187-8; no. 25 (18 June 1829), pp. 194-6;
no. 26 (25 June 1829), p. 202.

PENITENTIARY SYSTEM. NO. I.
Essays on Penitentiary Discipline. By Mathew Carey.[1]
Philadelphia. 1829.

This indefatigable man, who is never weary of well doing, is now engaged in the discussion of a subject perhaps of more importance than any other, to the prosperity of the whole human family. It is nothing less, indeed, than what may be regarded as the very foundation of law; the sanction, seal and authority of all human legislatures. Without punishment in some shape, the good are at the mercy of the vicious. With improper, inadequate, or disproportioned punishment, perhaps the evil to society is nearly as great as with no punishment at all. What then are we to do? After a thirty years' trial of the penitentiary system, are we to abandon it, because it may not have effected all that was expected or *hoped* for, by the ignorant, the weak, or the visionary? Our whole country – nay all the countries of earth are interested in the verdict. Some few years ago, when the measures were to be attended to hereafter, there seemed to be a settling down of the public mind in favour of *solitary confinement, without labour,* as the only proper and safe punishment for offenders. Great expenses followed – hundreds of thousands of dollars were lavished, with a view to render the mode of punishment effectual; and now the legislation of the country is at a dead stop with fear of its inefficiency. With a view to invite enquiry, and elicit truth, from every quarter on this momentous subject, it is intended to give a sort of historical sketch of the system, and to record such facts as are believed to be not generally known here. Prison statistics are plentiful now: they were not so, at the time of the last change of opinion throughout our country. Experiments have been tried now: they were but theories unsupported by proof, at the time referred to. But to do this effectually, it may be proper to go into a field yet unvisited by our writers. In the progress of the following discussion, therefore, I shall examine, either directly, or indirectly, the following publications.

I. BENTHAM'S PANOPTICON – London. 1791. To this work I shall refer, perhaps, at every step of the enquiry; for it is a positive fact that most, if not every one, of the evils now attempted to be provided for, by the whole body of writers upon the *penitentiary* system, and *Prison-discipline*, both here and in Europe, are provided for in the original draught of Mr. Bentham. And it is moreover a fact – a melancholy one to be sure – but nevertheless a fact, that all the discoveries and improvements, we are now making in the structure of prisons, in the treatment of prisoners, in their dress, diet and work, may be found, not merely suggested, but detailed with admirable propriety and clearness in this extraordinary work. And I do not scruple to say, in addition to all this, that if Mr. Bentham's plans had been adopted in this country forty years ago, there would have been a saving of millions for us – a profit of millions upon the labour of convicts, the safety of the public, and the diminution of crime; and that this declaration is actually proved by the *facts* that are now coming forth from every quarter – all of which are found to be satisfactory to our legislator and philanthropists, exactly in proportion as they approximate to the original plan of Mr. Bentham, in the structure of state-prisons, or penitentiaries, and in the treatment of prisoners.

II. PRISONS OF PHILADELPHIA – *By the Duke of Liancourt*. London. 1796. This work appeared originally in Philadelphia.

III. TRAVELS OF THE DUKE DE LA ROCHEFOUCAULT LIANCOURT – *Chapter on the Massachusetts convicts*. London. 1797.

IV. REPORT ON THE PENITENTIARY SYSTEM – New-York. 1822. This valuable work was prepared by certain of the ablest men of the State, and contains about 207 closely printed octavo pages.

V. ROBERTS VAUX – *on the discipline of the Philadelphia prison*. Philadelphia. 1826. This work immediately preceded the appropriation of something like half a million of dollars by the State of Pennsylvania, for building a penitentiary, where *solitary confinement without labour* should be the only punishment for any offence.

VI. MR. THOMPSON'S SPEECH in Congress, March 1: 1826. On the bill for establishing a penitentiary in the District of Columbia.

VII. FIRST ANNUAL REPORT *of the Prison Discipline Society* – June 2, 1826. Boston. 1827.

VIII. SECOND REPORT – *same.* June 1, 1827 – Boston. 1827.

IX. Sundry letters, reports and pamphlets, collected by the senior editor of the Yankee, while in England, in 1825–26.

X. ESSAYS ON THE PENITENTIARY SYSTEM – *by Hamilton.* Philadelphia. 1829.

HISTORICAL SKETCH. About ten years before Howard, the philanthropist, who went about doing good, where no other man had ever thought of going, in the last refuge and hiding-place of guilt – that is, in 1776, a society was formed in Philadelphia, for *assisting distressed prisoners*; and in 1787, at the very moment while Howard was traversing one hemisphere, like an angel of mercy, and risking his life wherever it might be risked with advantage to the miserable outcasts whom he had gone out to succour, another society was established in Philadelphia, for *alleviating the miseries of public prisons.* These were the first ever established for similar purposes.[2]

Here began the great enquiry, which is now waking up the best feelings and healthiest energies of our whole country. And in this very year, Jeremy Bentham, who was upon his travels in the north of Europe, having been led by the merest accident in the world to a consideration of the subject, wrote a series of letters, afterwards collected and published in London, and after that in Dublin, with a view to improving the structure and discipline of prisons. These letters were entitled the PANOPTICON or INSPECTION HOUSE, and were not only the originator, of a most extensive system of reform throughout Europe, as I shall have to show by and by, but they led afterwards to a series of works by the same author, – and of their value, but one opinion is now entertained by those who have studied them on the subject of criminal jurisprudence.

The following is an extract from the first of these letters dated

"*Crecheff in White Russia* – 1827.

"I observed, t'other day, in one of your English papers, an advertisement relative to a HOUSE OF CORRECTION therein spoken of, as intended for * * * * It occurred to me that the plan of a building lately contrived by my brother, for purposes in some respects similar, and which under the name of Inspection House, or the Elaboratory he is about erecting here, might afford some hints for the above establishment."

Here was the first idea of the Panopticon – of that very system of penitentiary-structure now prevailing in different parts of our country, where *discoveries* and *improvements* have been most plentiful. The brother alluded to here was General Sir Samuel Bentham, a philosopher, a soldier, and a man of extraordinary mechanical genius.

In this letter, Mr. Bentham proceeds to say – and however visionary the hope may have appeared at the time when he wrote, we are now justified in declaring that all he hoped for has been, or might, in all human probability be accomplished – if we may judge by recent facts, discoveries and experiments. To say all in one word, it will be found applicable, I think without exception, to all establishments whatsoever, in which *within a space not too large to be covered or commanded by buildings, a number of persons are meant to be kept under inspection.* No matter how different or even opposite the purpose, – whether it be that of punishing the incorrigible, guarding the insane, reforming the vicious, confining the suspected, employing the idle, maintaining the helpless, curing the sick, instructing the willing in any branch of industry, or training the rising race in any path of education: in a word, whether it be applied to the purposes of *perpetual prisons* in the room of death, or prisons for confinement before trial, or PENITENTIARY-HOUSES, or houses of correction, or work-houses, or manufactories, or mad-houses, or hospitals, or schools.

After this, he proceeds to develope the plan, carrying the same exact and philosophical views into the whole system of detail. The work is contained in two large duodecimo volumes, containing altogether 582 pages. In my next I shall give an abridgment or outline of the whole. Now, I have only to observe, that such was the settled and sure conviction of his mind, that immediately after having matured and published the plan, he made proposals to the British government which were acted upon, – to receive all the convicts for a certain period, at something less a-head than it cost to maintain them for a-year, or to transport them in the usual way; to keep them for the whole period of their sentence, *without any further charge to the government – to pay so much a-head for every death that occurred within that period, no matter how, among the convicts, and at his charge – and to pay so much a-head for every* RECONVICTION, *after their first term of service had expired.*

The plan was adopted, appropriations made by the British government, land purchased for the erection of a penitentiary, and a contract entered into with Mr. Bentham, who gave securities; and the order was actually made on the treasury for the appropriation. But the king refused his signature, in some stage of the proceeding, for the reasons that appear in the sketch of Sir Francis Burdett, which may be found in YANKEE, No. 10, Vol. 2, p. 74. Many years went by, before Mr. Bentham was indemnified for this breach of faith on the part of the British government; and then he was barely reimbursed for the money which he had spent – nothing was allowed for the loss of a fortune incalculably great, which he would have realized; nothing for the loss of time, nothing for the sacrifices of property; for he and his brother, a cool-headed, sagacious, practical man, and neither a theorist nor a visionary, had sold off their paternal inheritance at a considerable loss for ready money to begin the establishment with, and the same fatality has pursued the scheme from that hour to this. The French government appointed a committee of enquiry, and adopted the plan, and it was just about being carried into effect, when the Revolution broke out, and there was an end of the matter for half a century. And so in Spain – already were they preparing their panopticon asylums and penitentiaries there, in every circle of the empire under the constitutional government, when the restoration of Ferdinand put a stop to the whole. But here – in America – we have not even heard of the Panopticon, except as a joke – perhaps in the North American Review; and after fifty years of trial and conjecture, and thirty of actual and costly experiment, we are but just beginning to believe just what Jeremy Bentham published and *proved* at his own charge forty-two years ago.   N.

P.S. No. 2 will contain a sketch of the PANOPTICON PLAN as it is – not as it is represented to be by the *Prison discipline Society* of Boston, the managers of Edinburgh, or Mr. Sparhawk of New-Hampshire – the latter of whom alludes to it, as I would to the story of Aladdin or the wonderful lamp.   N.

PENITENTIARY SYSTEM. NO. II.

In the paper No. I. on this subject, there were two errors worth correcting. This passage in col. 1, page 113, "Some few years ago when the measures *were to be attended to hereafter,*" should be something like this, – When the measures were in contemplation which are to be alluded to hereafter. And, on the same page, col. 3, there is an extract from Mr. Bentham, which does not appear credited to him. It beings with, "To say all in one word," and finishes with the paragraph.

In this number, my object will be to give an outline of the Panopticon-scheme, as it was finally matured by the author. In 1790-91, the first twenty-one letters were published, containing the details of the original plan. They occupy a volume of 140 pages. But some time after this, much further consideration having been bestowed upon the subject, so many improvements and changes of one sort and another, not so much in the plan itself, as in the details, suggested themselves to Mr. Bentham, that he thought proper to publish another volume, called the PANOPTICON-POSTSCRIPT, and chiefly referring to penitentiaries. This volume is contained in 240 page, and accompanied with tables, calculations, and plates. And again, having thought still more of the subject, and being prepared to carry this magnificent system of reform into operation – to reach the law, and the source of law, all which he has effected since, by the unwearied, uninterrupted, undeviating pursuit of a single object, for nearly half a century, he published a third volume, under the title of the PANOPTICON-POSTCRIPT, No. II., occupying 232 pages, and devoted altogether to the details of the MANAGEMENT, under which, he particularly speaks of a provision for liberated prisoners, a sort of bettering-house, or half-way house to society, where they are allowed to labour, and receive pay for their labour, and establish a new character on their way back to the world. In this part of the plan we are deplorably deficient; our works of charity and reform, as well as of punishment and relief, are all unfinished. Our economy is that which would make us leave one plank up, on a bridge worth half a million, rather than exceed the sum we have appropriated, by so much as it would cost by a board or a nail. We seem to forget, that, if it would const 100,000 dollars to *complete* a thing, which when completed would be profitable – if we laid out 99,999 dollars, and stopped there, the whole might be a dead loss. And yet we are lavish enough in our expenditures after the fit of economy has gone off. Ours are what may be called the fever-and-argue of legislation: we are cold to-day and hot to-morrow. This year we refuse to appropriate five hundred dollars for an object already proved and acknowledged to be wise and profitable, and the next, away goes half a million upon a project or a theory.

The first idea of Mr. Bentham was to have the building circular; but, for reasons not necessary to be given here, he afterward thought proper to recommend a *polyognoal* shape – a double duodecagon, or polygon of twenty-four sides. This wall was to be full or cells, so contrived that when proper, for the encouragement of good behaviour, for economy in labour, and material, work tools, &c. or for the purposes of distinction, two might be thrown into one. The diameter of the building was to be 120 feet; it was to be furnished with cast-iron pillars, for economy of space and safely, with cast-iron galleries, doors and stair-cases – and he proposed flooring the cells with plaster; it was to be supplied with water (where practicable) by an annular cistern running round the top of the building, under the roof, immediately within the wall; the inspector's lodge was to be so contrived as to occupy the centre of the building, to be surrounded by a sort of annular well – or space – all the way up, and to be so divided that *one person could have a view of two stories of cells, and see what every prisoner was about, by merely turning his head, at any moment of the day;* to be altogether beyond the reach of attack, and to be commanded by the governor's lodge, so that *no prisoner nor inspector could ever be sure that he was not observed.* It was to be warmed by flues and pipes, leading fresh air through heated vessels. I need not stop here, to speak of the outward shape of the whole, the situation of the officers' houses, nor the structure of the chapel, which being in the place of one of the inspection lodges, would give all the prisoners the advantage of the services, *without bringing them together, or even permitting them to see each other.* It will be enough for the purpose I had in view, to give a sketch of the main features of the subject.

The annular wall, or space, surrounding the inspection tower, with "an uninterrupted sky-light, as broad and opening in as many places as possible," was adopted with a view to "airiness, lightsomeness, and increased security – above all things to *airiness*, the want of which, it might not by any other means have been very easy to remove." * * This vacuity does service in a thousand shapes: a *ditch in fortification; it is a chimney, and much more than a chimney in ventilation.* In this point of view, *the distance between the particular ceiling and the general sky-light* (observe this. – N) *is so much added to the height of ceiling in each cell,* so that instead of six cells, each eight feet high and no more, (the height proposed by Mr. B. N.) we have in fact six cells, one of sixty-six feet, another of fifty-seven, a third of forty-eight, a fourth of thirty-nine, a fifth of thirty, and the lowest not less than twenty-one, (that being the least distance from the bottom of the highest range of cells to the top of the sky-lights. N.)

Other advantages in the structure. "Communication impeded in as far as it is dangerous, is, instead of being retarded, accelerated where it is of use. To the inspector in his gallery, a single *pole* answers the purpose of many stair-cases. By this simple implement, without quitting his station," he opens and shuts the doors of the cells. "Machines, materials of work, and provisions, find a direct passage by help of a crane, without the tedious circuity of a stair-case: whence less width of stair-case may suffice. The ports, at which were iron gratings of no avail, it would be possible for a desperate prisoner to attack an inspector in his castle, are reduced to three narrow passages on each side; and these too crossed and guarded by doors of open work, exposing the enemy while they keep him at a distance."

With regard to the management, or facilities furnished thereto, by this mode of construction.

In the first place. "There is no cell of which *some* part is not *visible from every story in the Inspection Tower: and in the lowermost story, not only from the inspection gallery, but even from the included inspector's lodge.*"

II. "The part thus visible is considerable enough to receive *and expose perfectly to view, a greater number of prisoners than it can ever be proposed to lodge in the same cell.*"

III. "No prisoner can ever make any attempt upon the grating that forms the interior boundary of his cell, without being *visible to every one of the three stations in the inspection part.*"

IV. "During meal times, and at church times, by stationing the prisoners close to the grating, *two out of three inspectors may be spared.*"

V. "The cell-galleries are, *every one of them, commanded by every station in the inspection part.*"

VI. "An attempt can scarcely, if at all, be made on a window in the third story of cells, without being visible not only to its proper story (the second) of the inspection part, but likewise to the first; nor upon a window of the fourth story of cells, without being visible not only to its proper story (the second) of the inspection part, but likewise to the third. Those of the fourth story at least, as well as the two above it, are sufficiently guarded by their height; upon the supposition that the cells afford no ropes, nor materials of which ropes could be made in the *compass of a night, by persons exposed constantly to the eye of a patroling watchman.*"

VII. "To give an inspector at any time the same command over the cell of another inspector as over his own, there needs but an *order*, drawing a line of limitation in the cells, and *confining the inhabitants within that line.* So long as a prisoner (or inspector, N.) keeps within that line, he is visible; *and the instant he ceases to be so, his very invisibility is a mark to note him by.*"

Thus much to show the practical good sense of our philosopher. Here is a large building, crowded with convicts, set free at once from the greatest charge – that of watching and guarding it. Of the economy of the structure, and other circumstances and considerations, hereafter in No. III.   N.

PENITENTIARY SYSTEM. – NO. III.

Whatever may now be thought by the people of this county on the subject of penal jurisprudence, the time is rapidly approaching, when it will be regarded every where, as one of transcendant importance, not merely to the legislator and the philanthropist, but to the multitude.

At the time when the author of the Panopticon scheme was in travail with it, penitentiary prisons and jails were a most enormous tax to the nations of the earth. Nobody had ever dreamed of being able to do more than reduce the tax – nobody, certainly, of ever making them a source of revenue; a sorrowful source, to be sure, but still better in that shape, than in that of a drain. But the author alluded to, grappled with his subject in a new way; took the bull by the horns; and argued thus, *theoretically*. Theoretically, I say, for he knew little or nothing in 1787, while buried in the snows of White Russia, of what has occurred since 1820, in a few of the states of North America. The great penitentiary system of the British empire, was then about to go into operation. Act after act had been deliberated over, and passed, with a view to the complete reform of the criminal legislation of the day. Committee after committee had been making enquiries, by the month, on the subject of what had been hoped for and wished for, by the best practical men, as well as the greatest visionaries alive; but nothing, not even so much as a hint had they met with, in all their vast accumulation of matter, touching the possibility of a change like that alluded to here. The author is enquiring into the possibility and probability of lessening the charge upon governments, for the punishment of criminals, and the protection of society. He imagines a scale – he divides it into degrees – he would know whether the loss may be lessened, till it becomes a profit; and whether the profit may be augmented till it becomes a great and productive, though sorrowful source of revenue. I hope this will be read with attention; for I mean to refer to it hereafter, to show the wastefulness and prodigality of our most economical systems.

MANAGEMENT – A SOURCE OF REVENUE.

"Many distinct points for the eye to rest upon in such a scale, will readily occur. 1st. The produce might be barely sufficient to pay the expense of *feeding*. 2d. It might farther pay the expense of *clothing*. 3d. It might farther pay the expense of *guarding* and *instructing*, the salaries of visitors, governors, jailors, taskmasters, &c. 4th. It might pay the *wear* and *tear* of the working stock laid in. 5th. It might pay the interest of the capital employed in the purchase of such stock. 6th. The interest of the capital laid out in the *erecting* and *filling* up the establishment in all its parts, at the common rate of interest for money laid out in building. 7th. The *interest* of the money laid out in the *purchase* of the *ground*. Even at the first mentioned and lowest of these stages, I should be curious to compare the charge of such an institution with that of the least chargeable of those others that are as yet preferred to it. When it had arisen above the last, then, as you see, and not till then, it could be said to yield a *profit*, in the sense in which the same thing could be said of any *manufacturing establishment of a private nature*.

But long before that period, the objections of those whose sentiments are the least favourable to such an establishment, would, I take for granted have been perfectly removed. Yet what should make it stop any where short of the highest of those stages, or what should prevent it from rising, even considerably above the *highest of them*, is more, I protest, than I can perceive. On what points a manufacturer, setting up such an establishment, would be in a *worse* situation than an ordinary manufacturer, I really do not see; but I see many points on which he is in a *better*. His hands, indeed, are all raw, perhaps; at least with relation to the particular species of work which he employs them upon, if not with relation to every other. But so are all hands, every where, at the first setting up of every manufacture. Look round, and you will find instances enough of manufactures, where children, down to four years old, earn something; and where children a few years older, earn a subsistence, and that a comfortable one. I must leave you to mention names and places.[3] You, who have been so much of an English traveller, cannot but have met with instances in plenty, if you have happened to note them down. Many are the instances you must have found, in which the part taken by each workman is reduced to some one single operation of such perfect simplicity, that one might defy the awkwardest and most helpless idler that every existed, to avoid succeeding in it. Among the eighteen or twenty operations, into which the process of pin-making has been divided, I question whether there is any one that is not reduced to such a state. In this point, then, he is *at least upon as good a footing as other manufacturers*; but in all other points, he is upon a better. What hold can any other manufacturer have upon his workmen, equal to what my manufacturer would have upon his? What other master is there that can *reduce his workmen, if idle, to a situation next to starving, without suffering them to go elsewhere?* What other master is there, *whose men can never get drunk, unless he chooses they should do so?* And who, so far from being able to raise their wages by combination, *are obliged to take whatever pittance he thinks it most for his interest to allow?* In all *other* manufactories, those members of a family who can and will work, *must earn enough to maintain, not only themselves, but those who either cannot or will not work.* Each master of a family must earn enough to maintain, or at least, help to maintain a wife, and to maintain such as are yet helpless among his children. *My manufacturer's workmen, however crampt in other respects, have the good or ill fortune to be freed from this encumbrance*; a freedom, the advantage of which will be no secret to their master, who, seeing he is not to have the honour of their custom in the capacity of shop-keeper, *has taken care to get the measure of their earnings to a hair's breath.* What other manufacturers are there, who reap their profits at the risk of other people, and who have *the purse of the nation to assist them in the case of any blameless misfortune?* And, to crown the whole, by the great advantage which is the peculiar fruit of this new principle, what other master or manufacturer is there, who, to appearance, constantly, and in reality, as much as he thinks proper, *has every look and motion of each workman under his eye?* Without any of these advantages, we see manufacturers not only keeping their heads above water, but making their fortunes every day. A manufacturer in this situation, *may*, certainly, fail, because so may he in any other. But the probability is, he would *not* fail; because, even without these great advantages, much fewer fail than thrive, or the wealth of the country could not have gone on, increasing as it has done, from the reign of Brutus to the present."

Since that was written, how much has been done, how much more than must have been regarded as chimerical in 1787 – as the benevolent hope, the idle dream of a closet-philosopher. Already, some few of our penitentiaries nearly maintain themselves; and others quite, and here and there one, actually produces a revenue. But how far is the best from being what it might be? Take an example. One celebrated Auburn penitentiary or prison, with about five hundred convicts, found its receipts exceed its expenditures, in the year ending October 31, 1828 – by only $3336 97;[4] a very large sum, to be sure, considering what other *manufactories* of the same sort have hitherto done. But nothing, absolutely *nothing*, if we consider what might be done – here we have no allowance for the wear and tear of machinery – the interest or the waste of capital – and the convicts, one with another, are made to earn, in this country too, where labour is so high, *less than seven dollars a year, over and above their maintenance!* Simply stating the fact on paper, should be enough, of itself, to waken the four quarters of our whole country to a more serious investigation.

Having spread out the author's plan for the *structure*, and the groundwork of his plan for *converting a tax into a revenue*, I shall now give the outline of his *plan of government*, and a summary in his own language, of the several objects he had in view, for the general improvement of penitentiaries. Mr. Bentham, as every body is *beginning* to know, is a great lover of method. He lays down his principles, therefore, in the shape of rules – each having somewhat to do with every other; and all uniting to form the vast and beautiful whole, which we have now to do with.

"1. *Example*, or the preventing others by the terror of the example, from the commission of similar offences. This is the main end of all punishment, and consequently, of the particular mode here in question.

2. Good behaviour of the prisoners during their subjection to this punishment; in other words, *prevention of prison-offences* on the part of prisoners.

3. *Preservation of decency:* or prevention of such practices in particular, as would be offences against decency.

4. Prevention of undue hardships; whether the result of design or negligence.

5. *Preservation of health*, and the degree of *cleanliness* necessary to that end.

6. *Security against fire*.

7. *Safe custody*; or the prevention of escapes, which as far as they obtain, frustrate the attainment of all the preceding ends.

8. *Provision for future subsistence:* i.e. for the subsistence of the prisoners after the term of their punishment is expired.

9. *Provision for their future good behaviour:* or prevention of future offences, on the part of those for whose former offences this pun-

ishment is contrived. This is one of the objects that come under the head of *reformation*.

10. *Provision for religious instruction*. A second article belonging to the head of *reformation*.

11. *Provision for intellectual instruction and improvement* in general. A third article belonging to the head of *reformation*.

12. *Provision for comfort:* i.e. for the allowance of such present comforts as are not incompatible with the attainment of the above ends.

13. *Observance of economy*: a provision for reducing to its lowest terms, the expense hazarded for the attainment of the above ends.

14. *Maintenance of subordination:* i.e. on the part of the under officers and servants, as towards the manager in chief, a point on the accomplishment of which depends the attainment of the several preceding ends. No one of these objects but was kept in view throughout the contrivance of building; none of them that ought to be lost sight of in the contrivance of the plan of management. The management was indeed the end; the construction of the building, but one amongst a variety of means, though that the principal one.

1. *Rule of lenity*.

The ordinary condition of a convict doomed to forced labour for a length of time, ought not to be attended with a bodily sufferance, or prejudicial, or dangerous to health or life.[5]

2. *Rule of severity*.

Saving the regard due to life, health, and bodily ease, the ordinary condition of a convict doomed to a punishment which few or none but individuals of the poorest class are apt to incur, ought not to be made more eligible than that of the poorest class of subjects in a state of innocence and liberty.

3. *Rule of economy*.

Saving the regard due to life, health, bodily ease, proper instruction, and future provision, economy ought in every point of management to be the prevalent consideration. No public expense ought to be incurred, or profit, or saving rejected, for the sake either of punishment or of indulgence."

These being the general views of the author, let us now go into some detail with regard to *solitary confinement* – that last refuge for the benevolent of our country now. He argues thus:

"*For the purpose of example?* The effect in the way of example, the effect of the *spectacle*, receives little addition from the protracted duration of the term.

Are you afraid the situation should not be made uncomfortable enough to render it ineligible? *There are ways enough in the world for making men miserable, without this expensive one*; nor if their situation in such a place were made the best of, is there any great danger of their finding themselves too much at their ease.⁶ If you must torment them, do it in a way in which somebody may be a gainer by it. Sooner than rob them of *all society, I would pinch them at their meals.*

But solitude, when it ceases to be necessary becomes worse than useless. Mr. Howard has shown how. It is productive of gloomy despondency, or sullen insensibility.⁷ What better can be the result, when a vacant mind is left for months or years to prey upon itself?

This is not all. Making this lavish use of solitude is expending a useful instrument of discipline in waste. Not that of *punishments*, or even a proper variety of punishments, there can ever be a dearth. I mean of what is usually in view under that name – suffering employed in a quantity *predetermined, after an offence long past.* But of instruments of *compulsion*, such as will bear scrutiny, there is no such great abundance."

More detail in No. IV.   N.

PENITENTIARY SYSTEM. – NO. IV.

The faulty structure of all prisons, at the time this work appeared, was another subject of observation, by our author. It seems never to have entered the heads of the people of his country; and I might say almost the same of the people of ours, that a room may be *low* as well as *high*, if air enough is properly admitted. The following are his remarks on –

THE STRUCTURE OF THE CELLS.

"Of the waste of room observable in the common plans, a great part is to be placed to the account of *height*. Not more than eleven feet, but not less than nine, is the height prescribed by the penitentiary act.⁸ The Wymondham house takes the medium between these two extremes. Waste, it may well be called. I suspected as much at the time of writing the letters. I speak now with decision, and upon the clearest views. In respect to health, height of ceiling is no otherwise of use than as a sort of succedaneum to, or means of ventilation. In either view, it is beside the purpose: As a succedaneum, inadequate; as a means, unnecessary. If your air indeed is never to be changed, the more you have of it, the longer you may breathe it before you are poisoned. But so long as it is undergoing an incessant change, what signifies what height you have? Take a Panopitcon Penitentiary-house on one hand, and St. Paul's employed as a Penitentiary-cell, on the other. Let the Panopticon, aired as here proposed to be aired, and warmed as here proposed to be warmed, contain 400 or 500 prisoners. Let St. Paul's, hermetically closed, have but a single man in it. The Panopticon would continue a healthy building as long as it was a building; in St. Paul's, the man would die at the end of a known time, as sure as he was put there.[9]

In this one article, we may see almost a half added to the expense in waste. Ten foot from floor to ceiling, when less than seven foot would serve! When less than seven foot would serve, and does serve to admiration. I am almost ashamed of the eight foot I ask; it is for the mere look's sake that I ask it. The experiment has been tried, the result is known, though not so well known as it ought to be. Have the *hulks* ten foot of height? have they eight foot? have they seven? I look at Mr. Campbell's *hulks*, and to my utter astonishment I see that nobody dies there. In these receptacles of crowded wretchedness, deaths should naturally be more copious than elsewhere. Instead of that, they are beyond comparison less so. I speak from the Reports. I know not the exact proportion; my searches and computations are not yet complete; but as to so much I am certain. I speak of the ordinary rate. Now and then indeed, there comes a sad mortality. Why? Because where pestilence has been imported, hulks neither do, nor can, afford the means of stopping it. But, bating pestilences, men are immortal there. – Among 200-300 – quarter after quarter, I look for deaths, and I find none. Why? Because Mr. Campbell is intelligent and careful, Pandora's cordials unknown there, and high ceilings of no use."

Had Captain Cook ten foot, eight foot, seven foot between decks? Captain Cook, under whom, in a voyage that embraced all the climates of the globe, out of 80 men, not a single one died in a space of between four and five years;[10] out of 112 in the same time, but five, nor of those more than two in whom the seeds of death had not been some time before their embarkation.

No. V. will relate to the SYSTEM OF MANAGEMENT recommended by Mr. Bentham, forty years ago.　　　　N.

PENITENTIARY SYSTEM. – NO. V.

CONTRACT MANAGEMENT.

But the author of the Panopticon was not satisfied with the husbandry of prisons, or the *oversight* of prisoners at so much a year. He believed that more good might be done to the prisoners, more to the country, not only for much less cost, but really at a large and continually increasing profit to the state. But how? Not by allowing fixed salaries to every officer – not by leaving the management to persons who need not trouble themselves about the labour of prisoners. Let us now refer to the author, who was the *first* that ever alluded to such a thing as contract management, or indeed, to the possibility of any productive management.

"By whom then, says he, speaking of the management provided for in the celebrated penitentiary act of G. B. (and followed by every act of our country for years and years), ought a business like this to be carried on? By one who has an interest in the success of it, or by one who has none? By one who has a greater interest in it, or by one who has an interest not so great? By one who takes loss as well as profit, or by one who takes profit without loss? By one who has no profit but in proportion as he manages well, or by one who, let him manage ever so well or ever so ill, shall have the same emolument accured to him? These seem to be the proper questions for our guides. Where shall we find the answers? In the questions themselves and in the Act.

"To join interest with duty, and that by the strongest cement that can be found, is the object to which they point. To join interest with duty is the object avowed to be aimed at by the Act. The emolument of the Governor is to be proportioned in a certain way to the success of the management. Why? That it may be "his interest" to make a successful business of it – "*as well as his duty.*" How then is it made his interest? Is he to take loss as well as profit? No! profit only. Is he to have the whole profit? No; nor that neither; but a part only, and that as small a part as gentlemen shall please. Well – but he is to receive none however, if he makes none? Oh yes – as much profit, and that as secure a one as gentlemen may think fit to make it. He may have ever so large a share of any profit he makes, or ever so small a share; and whether he makes any or none, he may have a salary all the same. Let him get as much as he will, or get as little as he will, or lose as much as he will, or waste as much as he will, he is to have a *salary* for it, and in all these cases, *the same salary*, if they please. All this in the same section and the same sentence which lays down the junction of interest with duty as a fundamental principle."

After this, he proceeds to show in a manner peculiar to himself, how and why the management should be a thing of partnership.

"Economy has two grand enemies: *peculation* and *negligence*. Trust-management leaves the door open to both: Contract-management shuts it against both. Negligence it renders peculiarly improbable: peculation impossible.

"To peculate is to obtain, to the prejudice of the trust, a profit which it is not intended a man should have. But upon the contract plan, the intention, and the declared intention is, that the contractor shall have every profit that can be made.[11] Does the trust lose any thing by this concession? No – for it makes him pay for it beforehand. Does he pay nothing, or not enough? The fault lies, not in the contract plan in general, but in the terms of the particular contract that happens to be made: not in the principle, but in the application.

"As to negligence, to state the question is to decide it. Of whose affairs is a man least apt and least likely to be negligent? another's, or his own?

* * * * * *

"Turn to the *motives* which a man in this situation can find for paying attention to his duty. In the instance of the uninterested manager, what can they be? Love of power, love of novelty, love of reputation, public spirit, benevolence. But what is there of all this that may not just as well have fallen to the contractor's share? Does the accession of a new motive destroy all those that can act on the same side? Love of power may be a sleepy affection: regard to pecuniary interest is more or less awake in every man: public spirit is but too apt to cool: love of novelty is sure to cool: attention to pecuniary interest grows but the warmer with age.

"Among unfit things, there are degrees of unfitness. As trust-management is, in every form it can put on, ineligible in comparison of contract-management, so among different modifications of trust-management is board-management in comparison of management in single hands. When I speak of single-handed management as the better of the two, I mean in this sense only, that by proper securities, it may be made better than the other is capable of being made by any means. Pecuniary security against embezzlement: publicity in all its shapes, against peculation and negligence. In board-management, danger of dissension, want of unity of plan, slowness and unsteadiness in execution, are inbred diseases which do not admit of cure.

"The more confidence a man is *likely to meet with*, the less he is likely to *deserve*. Jealousy is the life and soul of government. Transparency of management is certainly an immense security; but even transparency is of no avail, without eyes to look at it. Other things equal, that sort of man whose conduct is most narrowly to be watched, is therefore the properest man to choose. The contractor is thus circumstanced in almost every line of management: he is so more particularly in the present. Every contractor is a child of Mammon: a contracting manager of the poor is a blood-sucker, a Vampire: a contracting jailor, a contracting manager of the imprisoned and friendless poor, against whom justice has shut the door of sympathy, must be the cruellest of Vampires. The unpaid as well as uninterested manager is of all sorts of managers the most opposite to him who is the object of this distinguished jealousy: He expects and receives confidence proportionable; though on several accounts not entitled, as we have seen, to so much, he enjoys more. A man who, in a station so uninviting, has the generosity to serve for nothing, while others who occupy the most flattering situations are so well paid for it, will assume to himself accordingly, and make in other respects his own terms: Unless the honour of serving the public *gratis* were generally put up to auction, a plan yet never proposed, this must always be the case. Standing upon the vantage ground of disinterestedness, he looks down accordingly upon the public, and holds with it this dialogue.

Gentleman Manager. *I am a gentleman: I do your business for nothing: you are obliged to me.*

Public. *So we are.*

Gentleman Manager. *Do you mind me? I am to get nothing by this: I despise money: I have a right to confidence.*

Public. *So you have.*

Gentleman Manager. *Very well, then, leave me to myself – never you mind me – I'll manage every thing as it should be – I don't want looking after – Don't you put yourselves to the trouble.*

Public. *No more we will.*

What is the fruit of all this good understanding? Frequently negligence; not unfrequently peculation. Peculation, where it happens, is not liked: but of what is lost by negligence, no account is taken. So good are the public, and in theory so fond of virtue, they had rather see five hundred pounds wasted at their expense, than five shillings gained.

Between the public and the candidate for a management-contract, there passes, or at least might be made to pass a very different conversation.

Public. *You are a Jew.*
Contractor. *I confess it.*
Public. *You require watching.*
Contractor. *Watch me.*
Public. *We must have all fair and above-board. You must do nothing that we don't see.*
Contractor. *You shall see everything. You shall have it in the newspapers.*
Public. *Contractors are thieves. Sir, you must be examined.*
Contractor. *Examine me as often as is agreeable to you, gentlemen: any of you, or all of you. I'll go before any court you please. Thieves stand upon the law, and refuse answering when it would show you what they are. I refuse nothing. I stand upon nothing, gentlemen, but my own honesty, and your favour. If you catch me doing the least thing whatever that should not be, let my Lord Judge say go, and out I go that instant."*

DETAILS OF GOVERNMENT – CLOTHING.

Here we have other notions of the author, which though promulgated more than forty years ago, our people are just beginning to *discover*.

"Two hints I will venture to offer to my contractor in this view.

For men, coat and shirt sleeves of unequal length – the left as usual: the right no longer than that of a woman's gown.

Economy is served by this contrivance in a small degree; safe custody in a greater. The difference of appearance in the skin of the two arms will be an essential mark. In point of duration, nothing can be more happily suited o the purpose: it is a permanent distinction, without being a perpetual stigma.

Exclusive of this pledge, I look upon escape out of a Panopticon, I have said so over and over, as an event morally impossible. But suppose it otherwise – how great the additional security which an expedient thus simple would afford!

A man escapes – minute personal description, *signalement*, as the French call it, is almost needless. One simple trait fixes him beyond possibility of mistake. His two arms wear a different appearance; one, like other men's; the other red and rough, like that of a female of the working class. No innocent man can be arrested by mistake. He bares his two arms: *Observe, they are alike. I am not the man; you see it is impossible.* The common expedient is one sleeve of a different colour. This costs something; it saves nothing; and when the coat is off, the security is gone.

Hardship, there can be none: the tenderer sex, even in its tenderest and most elevated classes, has both arms bare. Among the Romans, even the most luxurious and effeminate, not the fore-arm only, but the whole arm was bare, up to the very shoulder.

In both sexes on working days, shoes wooden; stockings, none; on Sundays, stockings and slippers.

Shoes wooden, for several reasons.

1. They are cheaper than leather.
2. Among the common people of England, they are known as a sort of emblem of servitude.
3. By the noise they make on the iron bars of which the floors of the cell galleries are composed, they give notice whenever a prisoner is on the march. Putting them off in order to prevent this, and escape observation, is an act which, if forbidden, will not be practised, when non-discovery will be so perfectly hopeless. Besides that, the bars would give pain to bare feet not accustomed to tread on them.
4. Were the prisoners to go barefoot, the bars which form the floor of the galleries must be so much the closer, consequently the more numerous and expensive.
5. In climbing with a view to escape, it would be impossible to make use of the feet either with the wooden shoes on, or with naked feet kept tender by the use of shoes. Common leather shoes, especially when stout and coarse, are of great assistance in climbing, and bare feet, hardened by treading on iron and on the bare ground, might find no great difficulty. Bare feet that were accustomed to shoes would serve as indifferently for running or for climbing; and a fugitive would hardly carry about with him so palpable a mark of his condition as a pair of wooden shoes.

Neither in this privation, fashion apart, is there any real hardship. Not to mention antiquity, or foreign nations, in Ireland shoes and stockings are rare among the common people in the country. In Scotland, these habiliments are not generally worn by servant-maids even in creditable families.

It is on account of fashion and the notions of decorum dependant upon fashion, and to avoid giving disgust to the chapel-visitors, that I propose stockings and slippers for Sundays. Slippers in preference to shoes, as helping to keep up the distinction, and being less expensive. Slippers, according to our customs, suit very well the conditions of those who it is not intended should ever be absent from home. But in the East, they are worn at all times in preference to shoes.

As to the rest, see the titles of *health and cleanliness*.

HEALTH AND CLEANLINESS.

Hints relative to this subject, are not noble in themselves; but they are ennobled by the end.

1. No blowing of noses, but with a handkerchief. (Very important *here*. – No.)
2. No spitting but in a handkerchief or spitting-box.
3. No tobacco in any shape.
4. Washing of hands and face at rising and going to bed; washing of hands before and immediately after each meal; washing of feet at going to bed.
7. Hair of the head to be shaved or cropt; if shaved, to be kept clean by washing; if cropt, by brushing.
8. Bathing to be regularly performed; in summer, once a week; in spring and autumn, once a fortnight; in winter, once a month.
9. Shirts clean twice a week.
10. Breeches washed once a week; coats and waistcoats once a month, in summer; once in six weeks in spring and autumn; and once in winter. Sheets, once a month; blankets, once in summer.
11. Clothes all white, and undyed. By this means, they can contract no impurity which does not show itself."

These last are the details which have subjected the author to so much ridicule. They are to be found in every thing he ever did – are they unworthy of him; or of any other philanthropist? Look them over, and see whether you can place your fingers upon *one* which ought not to be provided for in some way or other; and if so, by whom? Why should it be thought beneath a wise man to make others happier in trifles?   N.

PENITENTIARY SYSTEM. – NO. VI.

This paper will conclude the abridgment, or general view rather, of the Panopticon scheme.

DIET.

On the subject of diet for the prisoners, a matter of exceeding moment, as we shall have an opportunity of being satisfied by and by, Mr. Bentham says –

On the important head of diet, the principles already established leave little to add:

1. Quantity, unlimited; that is, as much as a man chooses to eat.
2. Price, the cheapest.

3. Savour, the least palatable of any in common use.
4. Mixture, none.
5. Change, none unless for cheapness.
6. Drink, water.
7. Liberty to any man to purchase more palatable diet, out of his share of earnings.[12]
8. Fermented liquors excepted, which, even small beer, ought never to be allowed on any terms.[13]

And going further into detail, he provides thus, for

THE DISTRIBUTION OF TIME.
Example for working days.

	Hours.
Meals, (two in a day,)	1 1-2
Sleep,	7 1-2
Airing and exercise in the wheel, for those employed in sedentary work within doors, at two different times, in the whole, at least	1
Sedentary work,	14
	24

Example for Sundays and Church Holidays.

	Hours.
Meals,	2
Sleep,	10
Morning service,	1
Evening service,	1
Schooling, including catechising and psalmody,	9

These preliminaries adjusted, the question of employment occurs; on which we have the following.

EMPLOYMENT.

1. Of what quality? To that question I must give three answers.

1. The most lucrative (saving the regard due to health) that can be found.

2. Not one only, but two at least, in alternation; and that in the course of the same day.

3. Among employments equally lucrative, sedentary are preferable to laborious.

1. What then are the most lucrative, will it be asked? Who can say? – least of any body the legislator. Sometimes of one sort, sometimes of

another. No one sort can possibly, unless by dint of secrecy or legal monopoly, stand in that predicament forever. But there are those which are essentially disqualified from ever standing in it. – They are those, as we shall see, which stand foremost on the list recommended by the Penitentiary Act.

2. Thus far, however, may be answered in the first instance: – No *one* sort at any time: two, at least, should succeed one another in the course of the same day. Why? Because no one sort will answer all the conditions requisite. Health must never be neglected: the great division is into *sedentary* and *laborious*. Consult health, a sedentary employment must be sweetened every now and then by air and exercise: a laborious employment, by relaxation. But exercise is not the less serviceable to health, for ministering to profit; nor does relaxation mean inaction. When inaction is necessary, sleep is the resource; a sedentary employment is itself relaxation, with regard to a laborious one. And though the body should even be in a state of perfect rest, that need not be the case with the mind. When a man has worked as long as, without danger to health, he can do at a sedentary employment, he may therefore add to his working time, by betaking himself to a laborious one; when a man has worked as long as, without pain and hardship, he can do, at a laborious employment, he may work longer by changing it for a sedentary one. No one employment can therefore be so profitable by itself, as it might be rendered by the addition of another. *Mixture of employment*, then, would be one great improvement in the economy of a prison.

* * * * * *

Could a man be made even to find amusement in his work, why should not he? and what should hinder him? Are not most female amusements works? Are not all manly exercises hard labour?

LABOUR WASTED.

According to Desaguliers, the force which a man can exert in towing, is upon an average equal to no more than 27lb.: that is, a force that would serve to raise a weight to that amount: for instance, so much water out of a well. But "drawing in a capstern" is towing. According to the same philosopher, 140lb. may be reckoned the average weight of a man: with this whole force a man acts, when walking in a wheel. The principle of the walking-wheel is therefore more than five times as advantageous as that of the capstern.

But Jeremy Bentham was not a man to stop here. He saw that a reformed criminal, if he were turned adrift upon society, helpless, friendless, and thoroughly stigmatised by the apprenticeship he had gone through, might be starved into a relapse; and therefore he made the following *provision for liberated prisoners*, and gave bonds for the faithful discharge of what he undertook, not on paper, but in fact, and as a governor.

PROVISION FOR LIBERATED PRISONERS.

How to make provisions for the prisoners at the expiration of their terms? How to ensure for the future, with least hardship on their part, with due regard to their respective characters and connexions, and at the least expense, their good behaviour and their subsistence? It is time to be short – here follows a slight sketch.

1. The prisoner not to be discharged, but upon one or other of three conditions:

1. Entering into the land-service.
2. Entering into the sea-service for life.
3. Finding some responsible house-holder who will be bound in the sum of (50*l*.) for his good behaviour by a recognizance renewable from year to year, with a stipulation of surrendering the body in case of non-renewal.

2. To furnish an inducement capable of engaging not only relations or other particular friends, but strangers, to take upon them such an obligation, authority given to the prisoner to enter into a contract for a term of any length, conferring on his bondsmen the powers following, viz:

1. Power of a father over his child, or of a master over his apprentice.
2. In case of escape, powers of recaption, the same as by 17 G. H. ch. 5. § 5, in case of vagrants; with penalties for harbouring or enticing, as by 5 Eliz. ch. 4. § 11, in case of persons bound for want of employment, to serve as servants in husbandry.
3. The contracting Governor of the Panopticon Penitentiary-house to be bound to keep the prisoner there, after the expiration of the term, though it should be for life, until discharged in one or other of the three ways just mentioned; and that upon terms at any rate not exceeding those on which he would be bound to receive a fresh prisoner; and so in case of a surrender by a bondsman.
4. The prisoner's parish to be bound in such case to give the crown an indemnification, not exceeding the utmost amount of the charge borne by reason of any pauper by that parish.
5. The bondsman to be bound for the *maintenance*, as well as the good behaviour of the liberated prisoner during the term of the engagement.

6. The Governor of the Penitentiary-house to be bound, on failure of the particular bondsman, to the extent of half the penalty specified in his recognizance in case of forfeiture.

7. The Governor bound also, on such failure, for the prisoner's maintenance; but without being obliged to grant him relief on any other terms than those of his returning to the Penitentiary-house, or engaging in his service for such time as shall have been agreed on.

8. Such bondsman's recognizance to be taken before Justices in quarter or petty sessions, with power to the Governor to oppose and cross-examine, as in the King's Bench in case of bail.

9. The recognizance to be registered with the Clerk of the Peace, and annually renewed; upon failure of renewal, the responsibility of the Governor to revive, and with it the power of recaption.

10. Power to the Governor and the Prisoner to enter into a contract of engagement for any number of years, and that before the expiration of the term, subject to attestation before a Justice, as in case of enlistment, and examination touching his consent, as in the Common Pleas in case of a *femo convert* joining in the disposal of an estate.

11. In case of a dispute between the Governor, or any other master-bondsman, and any such servant, Justices to have cognizance, as at present in case of servants in husbandry.

12. Any such contract so made with a prisoner, not to give him a fresh settlement.

13. Power to Government to remove to his parish any such *Remanent* remaining on the Penitentiary establishment after the expiration of his term.

14. Power to the parish to bind over to the Governor a Remanent removed or liable to removal; and that for a term not exceeding seven years in the first instance, nor one year ever after.

NOTES

[1] *Hamilton* is the signature.   N.

[2] *Roberts Vaux*.

[3] Yet labour is cheap in England – very cheap.   N.

[4] About 800 pounds sterling!   N.

[5] The qualification applied by the epithet *ordinary*, and the words *length of time*, seemed necessary to make room for an exception in favour of temporary punishment for prison-offences, at the expense of bodily ease.

[6] Query to this. We *have* made the best of their situation, and so have they sometimes; fed them better, and clothed them better at the public charge, than they were ever fed

or clothed before. Hence most of the augmentation of crime here. But the author is *plain* hereafter. His views are sound. N.

7 And the benevolent Howard is corroborated by the testimony of our wardens at the State's Prison of Maine. We have tried solitary confinement out and out. N.

8 Alluding here to the penitentiary act of England. N.

9 In the letter on hospitals, the reader may recollect what is said in commendation of an idea of Dr Marat's with respect to ventilation, and the from of construction proposed by him in consequence. What he says, is very just, as far as it goes; but the truth is, that so long as proper air-holes are made, and proper means employed for determining the air to pass through them, there is no form but may be made as ventilative, and by that means as healthy as his. At that time I had never experienced the heart-felt satisfaction I have since enjoyed, of visiting a London hospital. I had not seen either St. Thomas's or Guy's. I had no idea of the simple, yet multiplied contrivances, for insuring an unremitted, yet imperceptible change of air, nor the exquisite purity and salubrity that is the result of them. If I had, I should little have thought of sending Englishmen to France, or any other country, for Hospital practice, or theories of ventilation.

10 Four years two months and twenty-two days. See Cook's Second Voyage. Introduction.

11 This is to be understood only in as far as profit and loss is the avowed object. As to sacrificing to schemes of profit some other of the ends in view, such as good morals, proper severity, or proper indulgence, it forms a separate consideration, and will be spoken of in its time.

12 Rule of economy. Few cases I believe there are, if any, in which it wil not be found advantageous, even in point of economy, to allow a man, in the way of reward, a proportion of his earnings. But reward must assume the shape of a present gratification, and that too, of the sensual class, or, in the eyes of perhaps the major part of such a company, it can scarcely be expected to have any value; and if it takes a sensual shape, it cannot take a more unexceptionable one.

13 The mischief done to health by the use or abuse of fermented liquors, is beyond comparison greater than that effected by all other causes put together. The use, is in fact, none at all, where habit is out of the question. It would be next to impossible to tolerate a moderate enjoyment without admitting excess. The same beverage that produces no sensible effect on one man, will overcome another. Even small beer ought not to be excluded from the general proscription; for there can be no commonly practicable test for distinguishing small from strong; and I have known constitutions to which even ordinary small beer has afforded the means of intoxication.

Jeremy Bentham

(11)

'Extract from a letter from Mr. Lawrence, our charge at St. James's, dated Paris, March 10, 1829'

The Yankee and Boston Literary Gazette, vol. II, no. 24 (11 June 1829), p. 186.

"The thirst for knowledge, which now prevails among the young men in France, is no where more fully manifested than by the crowds that frequent the public lectures at the Lorbourne. To see two or three thousand persons rush to hear a metaphysical disquisition of Causin, almost reminds one of the age of the revival of learning. When the Professors who had been suspended by the late Ministry, resumed last spring their Courses, much of the interest might well have been ascribed to political feeling, but there has now been sufficient time for this enthusiasm to abate.

"Mr. Bentham's name I hear frequently introduced in the public lectures, and always in terms of the highest respect. A new edition of his works, in seven volumes, translated by Dumont, is advertised in the Constitutionnel of this morning. I have long been desirous of writing to the Philosopher in Queen-Square-Place, to express those sentiments of gratitude and reverential respect, which I shall never cease to entertain. I have only been deterred from not having found the proper topics, on which I thought I could venture to address him. He must, I can well conceive, be highly gratified with the attempt now making, with every prospect of success, to remove one foul stain on the British constitution. With the mere admission of Catholics to office, the people of Ireland will not, I feel confident, be long satisfied. Though prudently nothing is now said on the subject; this point gained, Catholics and Dissenters will unite to put themselves on a real equality with their fellow-subjects, which can only be done by adopting, as to religion, the system of France, or the still more rational one of the U.S."

Extract from the first No. of the "*Utilitaire,*" published at Geneva – p. 29.

See what an immense advantage a writer is sure to obtain, by his neutrality between contending parties! Bentham penetrates every where; his works are read by every body; they are found in all libraries, in those of the *Anti*-liberals, as well as those of the Liberals. And yet, he tramples under foot those errors which are most in vogue, those prejudices which are most universal; he spares none of the favourite notions of the day, none of those principles styled sacred, in short, none of the *inviolabilities* of Politics or Legislation. Armed with the sword of analysis, he undermines the foundations of absolutism, with much greater freedom than was ever done by the philosophers of the last century, or by the leaders of the revolution, which terminated it. Why then are they the objects of the unceasing invectives of a whole generation? Why does it repulse them with horror as dangerous sophists? It is because they formed themselves into a party which had its particular interests, and was almost as much opposed to men as to measures. Bentham, on the contrary, derives his strength from the evidence of the very abuses which he attacks. From the height where he has fixed himself, he looks down upon all our social relations, without being the slave of any one of them. Without interest, as without passions, he knows neither friends nor foes: nobody can feel humiliated by yielding to him, or consider it a triumph to have convicted him of error. Nevertheless what an attraction, what a charm has he contrived to throw over the exposition of his theories! With what force does he take possession of the mind, without flattering any weakness, or truckling to any prejudice![1] If his works have not been attended with that *éclat*, that notoriety, which every now and then accompanies the results of great labours, their success is not the less real, and no one can without manifest injustice, refuse to allow him a share in the improvements which have been made in the science of legislation for the last twenty years. Of what importance is a vain and transitory glory to a man of genius, who has dared to conceive a plan for the general reform of our social order? He aims not at the surprising effects of a mine, which after being excavated in darkness and mystery, overthrows, by a sudden explosion, the earth which covered it; but rather, at the slow and progressive action of that nourishment, which, spread openly over uncultivated or sterile lands, mixes with the natural elements, encourages the development of the seed, accelerates the march of vegetation, and at last renders that soil which was formerly obstinate and ungrateful, fruitful in all kinds of culture.

Perhaps it is to be regretted that the ideas of Bentham have hitherto only been contained in complete works, by which means they present a whole so extended, that the mind can scarcely grasp it; such a great number of reforms to effect, that doubts arise as to the possibility of their realization; in short, so vast a field to travel over, that the imagination is frightened, and dares not commence the task. The only thing, perhaps, which is required for the complete triumph of his principles, is their appearance in the form of a periodical publication, undoubtedly the most favourable as regards the action of thinking, because the truths thus proclaimed, pursue you without intermission, reach you in all social positions, in all the phases of your humour, and uniting themselves with the events of the day, share that attention which they would otherwise absorb entirely.

Hitherto we have merely spoken of rules, which are in great measure negative. We have seen what it would be proper to avoid, in order to exercise by means of the press, a direct action on masses of men. Remains, to speak of positive rules, to point out the path which should be followed, the subjects which ought to be treated of, the particular end, which should always be kept in view. On these matters I have but a few words to say.

Social philosophy, like any other science, ought to follow a logical march, and proceed from beginnings to their consequences; from known things to unknown things. All the relations between man and man, may form part of the subject matter of its researches, and, as elements and powers of physical nature fall within the province of chemistry, so does religion, education, social organization, and every thing which exercises a good or evil influence on the condition of man, in society, belong to that science which we have named social philosophy. Its most immediate end, is THE GREATEST HAPPINESS OF THE GREATEST NUMBER – the universal application of the principle of utility; and I should say that the tendency of this journal was *Benthamic*, were it not for the inconvenience of making a party name for an enterprise eminently free from all party spirit, eminently neutral and independent.

After this, my friend says, jumbling a variety of things together – "I am almost overwhelmed with all sorts of things – politics, law, and music. Having just heard that Sparks was going to leave, I manage to scrawl two or three lines to you. I thought you might like to see the accompanying extract from Lawrence's (the American) letter, and the do. from the *Utilitaire*, which I have hastily translated. We do not know who or what the editor is. The Catholic question will undoubtedly be carried: at the last two divisions in H. C. the night before last, the majority for ministers was 180.   Yours, ever.

20th March, 1829.

NOTE

[1] Can it be necessary to call to mind that this eulogium of Bentham regards more particularly his eloquent interpreter? Their names ought never to be separated, any more than those of Kepler and Newton.

John Neal

(12)

'Bentham's Principles of the Civil Code'

The Yankee and Boston Literary Gazette,
vol. II, no. 25 (18 June 1829), pp. 196–7.

Dumont's Introduction. (*Translated by J. N.*)

Of all the branches of legislation, civil law is that which has the least attraction for those who do not study jurisprudence for a livelihood. I may go further; it produces a kind of affright. Curiosity has been a long while occupied with political economy, with penal laws, and with the principles of government. Celebrated works have given credit to these studies, and under pain of acknowledging a humiliating inferiority, we are obliged to know them, and even to sit in judgment on them.

But the (law of) civil rights has never passed beyond the obscure boundaries of the bar. The commentators sleep side by side with the controversial writers, in the dust of libraries. The public are ignorant even of the name of the sects which divide them, and regard with silent respect, these numerous folios, those enormous compilations ornamented with such pompous titles, as *Bodies of Right*, and *Universal Jurisprudence*.

The general repugnance toward that study, is owing to the manner in which it has been treated. All these works are in the science of the laws, what the Scholastics were in the natural sciences before the time of experimental philosophy. Those who attribute their dryness and their obscurity to the very nature of the subject, are too indulgent.

In fact, what does that part of the law concern itself with? It treats of whatever is most interesting to men, of their safety, of their property, of their reciprocal and daily transactions, of their domestic condition in the relationship of the father, of the son, and of the husband. It is thence that *rights* and *obligations* proceed: for every object of the law may be reduced to these two terms, and there is nothing there of mystery.

The civil law is at the bottom, nothing but the penal law under another aspect: We cannot understand the one without understanding the other. For to establish *rights*, is to grant permissions; to give protection, is to create offences. To commit an offence, is to violate on one side an obligation; on the other, a right. To commit a private offence, is to violate an obligation owed to an individual, a right which he has over us. To commit a public offence is to violate an obligation owed to the public, a right which the public has over us. Civil right is therefore nothing but penal right considered under another aspect. If I contemplate the law at the moment, when it confers a right, or imposes an obligation, it is the civil point of view. If I contemplate the law in its sanction, in its effects with relation to this violated right, to these infringed obligations, it is the penal point of view.

What is understood by the PRINCIPLES OF THE CIVIL LAW? We are to understand the *motives* of the laws, a knowledge of the true *reasons* which ought to guide the legislator in the distribution of the rights which he confers on individuals, and the obligation that he imposes on them.

In that library of writings upon the civil law, we may look in vain for a single one, which has had for its object the founding of it upon reason. Philosophy has never passed that way. The *Theory of the Civil Law*, by Lirignet, which promises so much, is very far from fulfilling its promises. It is the production of a disorderly imagination in the service of a bad heart. Oriental despotism is the model to which he would lead all the governments of Europe, to correct their notions of liberty and humanity, which appear to torment him like lugubrious spectres.

The disputes of jurisprudence have given birth, even in the schools, to a sort of unbelievers, who have doubted whether there were any principles in it: According to them, it is altogether arbitrary: the law is good because it is the law, – because a decision, whatever it may be, produces great good to the country. There is in that opinion a little truth, and much error. It may be seen by this work that the principle of UTILITY is extended through that part of the laws as through every other; but its application is difficult; it requires an intimate knowledge of human nature.

The first flash of light which struck Mr. Bentham in the study of the law, was that the *natural right*, the *original compact*, the *moral sense*, the *notion of just and unjust*, which are made use of to explain every thing, were at the bottom but those innate ideas, the falsity of which

Locke had so well demonstrated. He saw that we revolved in a vicious circle. Familiar with the method of Bacon and of Newton, he resolved to apply it to legislation. He made of it, as I have explained more in detail, in the preliminary discourse, an experimental science. He discarded all the dogmatic words; he rejected whatever was not the expression of pain or pleasure; he would not admit, for example, that property was an inherent right, a natural right, because these terms explained nothing, and proved nothing. Those of *justice* and *injustice*, had to his eyes the inconvenience of prejudicing questions, instead of clearing them up. When he proposed to establish a law, he did not affect to find a correspondent one in the law of nature, nor by a common trick, to give as a thing done, the very thing which *is* to be done. When he explains *obligations*, he does not wrap himself up in mysterious reasons; he admits no supposition; he shows clearly that all obligation is founded upon previous service, received by the person on whom it is imposed, or that a superior want on the part of him in whose favour it is imposed, or upon a mutual compact which derives all its force from its utility. Thus always guided by experience and by observation, he considers in the laws nothing but the effects which they produce upon the faculties of man, as a sensitive being, and he always gives *pains to be avoided*, as the only argument[1] of real value.

The civilians never cease to argue about fictions; nor to give to these fictions the effect of reality. For example – they admit some *contracts* which have never existed; some *quasi-contracts* which have not even the appearance of a contract. In certain cases, they admit a *civil death*; in others, they deny the *natural death*. Here a dead man is not dead, – there a living man is not living. He who is absent is to be considered present – he who is present is to be considered as absent. A province is not where it is; a country does not belong to whom it does belong. Men are sometimes *things*, and in the quality of things they are not susceptible of rights. Things are sometimes beings who have rights, and who are subjected to obligations. They acknowledge unprescriptible rights, against which people have always prescribed: inalienable rights which have always been alienated; and *that which is not*, is always stronger in their eyes, than *that which is*. Take away their fictions, or rather their lies,[2] and they know not where they are; accustomed to such false supports, they are unable to hold themselves up without them. Mr. Bentham has rejected all these puerile arguments; he has not offered one gratuitous supposition, not one arbitrary definition, not one reason which may not be the expression of a fact, nor one fact which may not be drawn from an effect of the law, either good or evil.

4 John Neal

It is by this mode of reasoning, always referring to his principles, that he has made a new science of the civil law – new and even paradoxical for those who have been nourished in the opinions of the ancient schools; but simple, natural, and even familiar, for those who have not been misled by false systems. Thus a translation of this book would have the same sense and the same power, in all languages,[3] because he calls to his aid the universal experience of men; instead of technical reasons, reasons founded upon abstract terms, upon arbitrary definitions, having but a local value, and consisting only in words, disappearing whenever no synonymes are found for rendering them. It is thus that the African multitudes, who use shells for money, become sensible of their poverty the moment they have passed their frontiers, and wish to offer their conventional riches to strangers.

I ought to add, that on the subject of the English laws, Mr. Bentham had made frequent digressions, which I have suppressed; they had but a local interest. There are, however, some cases, where his observations would have wanted a groundwork, if I had omitted to mention the particular laws to which they referred. In trying to be more clear, by developing, what, in the original, was often but an allusion, I may have made some mistakes, which it would not be just to impute to the author.[4] These laws in general are so difficult to understand, that it is dangerous for any Englishman who is not a lawyer, to speak of them, and of course (for a much stronger reason), for every other than an Englishman to do so.

NOTES

[1] Or good to be obtained.

[2] Here we have the germ of Bentham's great work on *evidence*, just published in five octavo volumes; and reviewed in the Edinboro', 96.   N.

[3] How true! – and how –   N.

[4] Mr. B. has never read his works in French, nor indeed any part of them. Such confidence has he in the good faith and ability of M. Dumont.   N.

THE YANKEE;

AND

BOSTON LITERARY GAZETTE.

N°. 79.

UTILITY—The greatest happiness of the greatest number—BENTHAM.

NEW SERIES........NO. I.

JULY, 1829.

JEREMY BENTHAM.

For more than half a century the labours of JEREMY BENTHAM have been before the English, and the readers of English in every part of the world. And yet, up to this hour, though extraordinary changes have lately occurred, and though his avowed followers are now to be found in every part of Europe and throughout both Americas, and always among the more inquisitive, the more thoughtful, and the better-educated of their country, the views and objects of no man perhaps were ever so generally misunderstood, or so strangely or so safely misrepresented.

Things are said of him and of his works, every day, and by the first men of the age, who are believed by the multitude to be familiar with both, and whose judgments go abroad therefore with the solemnity of decrees, though full of mischief and error—things which have no foundation whatever in truth. Opinions that he never entertained in his life; theories that he has been waging war with for full fifty years, are attributed to him in works of authority, as the very foundation of that stupendous pile, which, after a long life of solitary labour, of discouraging, incessant, unassisted enquiry, he has now built up so high and spread out so far, and fortified with such magnificent proportions, that the rulers and lawgivers of the earth cannot overlook it, and will not be suffered to pass it by; for the eyes of the people are beginning to be turned upon it and upon them, throughout both hemispheres, with a holy determination to know the truth hereafter, and to enquire, each man for himself, into the great principles of legislation. They are growing weary of law, wherever law is not upon the very face of it, reason. They are no longer satisfied, they never will be satisfied again, it is to be hoped, with arbitrary usage, or avowed mystery in the business of rule. They are tired of making bricks without straw—of adopting faith after faith, in political as in religious life, at the bidding of authority. In a word, they are beginning to feel their strength, to interrogate the powers that be, to believe that they are worth reasoning with, and that however *we* may argue or philosophize, *they* are in fact the high court of appeal for the governing and the governed; for judges and for legislators; the ultimate sovereign power to which every other power must yield, whenever a matter comes fairly to issue before them, either in the trial-place of nations—the field of death; or at the bar of nations, the public-opinion tribunal.

But the perversity and error to which I have alluded, as now distinguishing those, who ought to be familiar with every work of their great countryman, will not be thought so very strange, perhaps, when we recollect that of what he has written, hardly a fourth part in bulk, and perhaps not a fiftieth part in value, has ever appeared in the native language of the author; that until within a very few years, the most valuable of his works were not only unknown to the great body of English every where, but actually unheard of by his next-door neighbours, and by most of the lawgivers of the British empire, except through an occasional newspaper paragraph, or a Quarterly sneer at the ballot-boxes, the unintelligible language, or the more unintelligible theory they were supposed to conceal. And this, while they were to be found in every public library of Europe, out of the author's own country,—and upon the table of every statesman, jurist, or philosopher of the continent; *this*, after nearly ten thousand copies of one work in three large octavo volumes, and nearly as many more of several other works by the same author, had been rescued by a foreigner, from a heap of neglected manuscripts—a treasury of wisdom—a store-house of wonderful thought—worked over into French, published at Paris—retranslated and republished into four or five other languages, and circulated in chapters throughout every quarter of the globe—the north striving with the south, the new world with the old, to give them simultaneous publicity; and the whole being regarded every where, except in the immediate neighbourhood of the author, among his fellow-countrymen, or among those who speak the same language, as by far the most profound, extraordinary, and useful work of the age.

It is very true that the style of Mr. Bentham now, is involved and peculiar; now, I say, because at an earlier period, when he wrote his Fragment on Government, in reply to Blackstone, and his celebrated work on Usury, it was thought remarkable for strength, purity, and ease. But the subjects now handled by Mr. Bentham, are as different from those then treated of, as are the problems of Euclid, or the doctrines of the Principiä, from the elements of arithmetic. Then, he might be allowed to *talk* on paper—to lay down what he had to say, without fear of being misunderstood or misquoted. But now, it would be neither safe nor wise for him to do so. His propositions are startling enough, though accompanied with all their neutralizing qualifications and exceptions. A period now is not a period merely, nor a paragraph, nor a page,—but a problem. Hence the difficulty of his language now. They who are not acquainted with his earlier works, who have not followed him, through abridgment after abridgment of the same views, till what was once a large book, has been reduced to a chapter and then to a table, or it may be a phrase, cannot well understand his English, and for that reason ought never to sit in judgment upon his works. But they may read him in French with safety. M. Dumont has made his chief mysteries intelligible; and it is to M. Dumont therefore that we should ascribe the growing popularity of Mr. Bentham among his own people. Compare the English quarto, entitled, "Introduction to the principles of Morals and Legislation," and published in 1789, with M. Dumont's abridgment of the same work. One is a severe and almost unprofitable study, except to the prepared and thoroughly-disciplined, while the other is a beautiful and eloquent work, which almost any body might read with pleasure.* But after you have gone through with the French author, and made yourself master of the outlines, if you go back to the English, it will be with a fervency and relish that in most cases, will keep you there. I never knew any body satisfied with Bentham till he had become acquainted with Dumont; nor any body that ever went back to the original, who could afterwards endure the translation. By this, I do not mean to speak lightly of the latter—for, after all, it is to the translator that the men of Europe are now indebted for all they know of Jeremy Bentham; and it is by the translator that posterity will be made familiar with him. No—not familiar. I should not say this—for M. Dumont had nothing to do with the *man*. It was the lawgiver and the philosopher that he dealt with; and if no other were to follow, and give society a portrait of Jeremy Bentham, *as he is*— with all his power and weakness, amazing wisdom and child-like simplicity—his breadth and his depth—in the every-day business of life, most of the errors that now prevail with regard to him and his views, would prevail forever.

But something more familiar must be had, something in the shape of a portrait; for his followers are multiplying at home now; a quarterly review has been established by him; several of his neglected manuscripts have appeared in pretty good English, though most of them were left to the editorship of inexperienced writers, or still more inexperienced thinkers; changes that he predicted years and years ago, have occurred in the political faith of his chief countrymen; the British parliament has felt and acknowledged his influence through her principal ministers, and ablest orators, and wisest lawgivers; and what more than any thing else, may have contributed to the removal of the ban of the empire, the men of the Edinburgh Review, and even those of the Quarterly, have had the courage to read here and there a chapter of his lighter works, and to pronounce judgment thereon, without much regard to the reputation of the author, as the head of a dangerous political party.

Notwithstanding all this, however, such is the retired life that Mr. Bentham has lived for nearly half a century, at what he calls the hermitage of Queen-square Place, never going abroad except for a walk in the fresh air, never seeing any body but his housekeeper and secretary till the business of the day is over; enduring no visits either of ceremony or curiosity, friendship or business, except when they refer to the subject-matter he is dealing with; encountering not so many as half a score of strangers in a twelvemonth, nor ever more than one at a time; that, as to the public of his country, they know nothing about him,—for his next-door neighbours hardly know him by sight; and as to the public men of his country, who are in the habit of telling, believing, and vouching for a thousand strange stories about the philosopher, as they call him—there are not forty, I do believe, that ever saw his face.

The truth is diverting enough to be sure; but the stories they tell are never true, nor ever much like the truth. It is believed by many, that he is the head of the Radicals; that they assemble together by deputation at his house from every part of the globe —holding a sort of congress, where all the turbulent and fiery spirits of Europe and the two Americas are literally represented. This idea grew out of the fact, perhaps, that young Mill, and a few more of Mr. Bentham's disciples, were in the habit, for a year or two, of meeting at his house every week for debate and consultation among themselves. But they never saw him at such times—nor had more than half their number ever interchanged a syllable with him. And as for the deputies from the disaffected of all Europe, I am sure that nobody was ever able to obtain a sight of him, for about two years that we were acquainted, without more delays and more difficulties than would have stood in the path of a presentation to half the crowned heads of Europe. I have known him refuse to see a Russian counsellor of state, who had come to London chiefly, if not altogether, for the purpose of seeing him, and I might mention a multitude more. Mr. Bowring the poet, who afterwards came to be the particular friend of Mr. Bentham, and is now preparing to write his life, told me himself, that he was trying for more than a twelvemonth to get a peep at the sage of Queen-square Place, before he succeeded; and for my part I can say that I was about a year in England, without knowing any body but Mr. Owen of Lanark, and a Mrs. Wheeler, the Mary Wolstencraft of our day, who had ever seen the face of that extraordinary man; that although, after reading his Theory of Punishments and Rewards, which I did, long before I left this country, and before I had learnt to prefer crude Benthamism to prepared or Frenchified Benthamism, I would have crossed the Atlantic but to spend an evening with the author; yet when I had arrived in England, I might say into the very neighbourhood of the hermitage, I could not find a guide that knew the way to his door; that while he knew nobody, nobody knew him; and that long after I had given up all idea of ever seeing the man, for I knew many persons who had been trying for years to be acquainted with him, we were brought together by the merest accident in the world; that I remained with him so long, and knew him so intimately, that—perhaps it would not be too much to say—probably no person alive knows more of the true character of Jeremy Bentham than I do. Mr. Bowring, and Mr. Mill, the author of British India, have known him longer; but never more intimately. They have seen him at intervals of a week or a month, year after year; but I have been with him every day for about eighteen months, and spent almost every evening with him, from six o'clock, the dinner hour, till about eleven or twelve at night, for the whole of that time. I have seen him therefore through all his changes; and I believe that I know him thoroughly and completely. May I not hope then, that what I say in contradiction to the idle stories I have already, or may hereafter refer to, will be received as something better than vague reports, or newspaper refutation?

· Another account of him I must give,—it came to me direct and on authority, after it was known that he had offered me an interview. Beware of Mr. Bentham, said my informer; I wonder you are not afraid of him—the queerest old man alive—one of his most intimate friends told me not long ago that he was undoubtedly deranged; that he keeps a number of young men in pay to follow him about and pick up what they call his sibylline leaves,—leaves upon which he had scribbled in characters that nobody but they who had gone through a long apprenticeship to the work, might ever hope to decypher.

I do not know, but I should suspect Mr. Bentham's old friend, Dr. Maculloch the geologist, of this story; so untrue is it, and yet so like the truth: For Mr. Bentham does keep two secretaries constantly employed in decyphering his abominable manuscript; and with one or the other, he is always seen when he goes to take his trot in the garden—the largest and most beautiful, by the way, that opens into St. James's Park.

At another time I was assured, also on authority, that not long before, one of the British cabinet having dropped a line to him to enquire about a provision recommended by sir Samuel Romilly, one of his disciples, he wrote a book in reply. This was a capital story, to be sure—but like the story told by Hazlitt, in his sketch of Bentham, about the miniature offered to him by Alexander of Russia; though there was some truth in it, there was so much untruth, as to spoil it. At the time alluded to, Mr. Bentham had never had any correspondence with the British ministry, except about his Panopticon, where the government were told in a few brief and powerful words, that they had broken their faith, and ruined a man for trusting to it; and to the value of a page or so with Mr. Canning, to obtain the release of a man who had literally insinuated himself into a French prison, by pretending to know more than he ever did know, or ever could know about the disorganized patriots of Europe. I allude to Mr. Bowring. But after this, Mr. Bentham had a somewhat lengthy—I like the word here—a somewhat lengthy correspondence with Mr. Peel, touching his celebrated reform and consolidation of the statutes.

And as for the writers of England who have attempted to give the public a notion of Mr. Bentham, there is not one—I say it seriously and advisedly—not one that ever knew him, and but one or two who had ever seen him. Parry dined with him but once; and Hazlitt hired a house of him, (the rent of which he never paid) overlooking the garden where Mr. Bentham used to jump about, with his white hair blowing in the wind. I mention the fact about the rent, because I do in my heart believe that Hazlitt, who values himself on being a good hater, would have loved Mr. Bentham, if he had been allowed to occupy the house rent-free. Yet were you to judge by the confident ease of the biographer, you would believe he had been familiar with Mr. Bentham almost from their boyhood up; yet he never spoke with him, I believe, and probably never saw him in his life except from a two-pair-of-stairs-window overlooking the garden alluded to. If I had Mr. Hazlitt here, I should borrow a page or two of what he had the audacity to give to the world, as a portraiture of Jeremy Bentham; but as I have not, I shall refer the reader to an extract from what he says, with great power and beauty of language, of his doctrines, of the colour of his eyes, and of the affair with the emperor of Russia—which, by the by, he misstates and misrepresents from beginning to end, while he affects either to set every body else right, or to tell the story from his own knowledge. He mistakes Bentham entirely—misunderstands the whole character of what he has done; for he says among other things that Mr. Bentham " has made *no discovery*," and is therefore only a sort of labour-saving machine, to " show what others had done before him, and how far human knowledge had advanced."

Perhaps one example of the correctness of Mr. Hazlitt, who has published two different portraits of Mr. Bentham within a year or two of each other, may give the reader a pretty good notion of their value, and of the impunity with which any thing may be said of him. One of the very first paragraphs in the biographical notice of Mr. Bentham, which appeared in the " Spirit of the Age," contains the following passage : " We believe that the empress Katherine corresponded with him; and *we know* that the emperor Alexander called upon him, and presented him with his miniature in a gold snuff box, which the philosopher to his eternal honour returned." Observe the language here. We *believe* this thing; but we *know* this. Now the fact is, that neither happens to be true. Mr. Bentham corresponded so far—not with Catherine—but with Alexander of Russia, as to receive a letter from him with a diamond-ring of great price, through the minister of that monarch at London,—the letter he kept, the ring he returned. One other fact—a trifle to be sure in itself,—but worth referring to, when regarded as the deliberate testimony of a man who professes to know the person he speaks of so familiarly. On the sixth page, he calls the eye of Mr. Bentham a lack-lustre-eye : on the very next page, however, the seventh—he speaks of it as a " quick and lively eye, and a restless eye"—all which is eminently characteristic of the showy, clever and spirited Magazine-writer, who made up the " Spirit of the Age" for the amusement of the public, and the profit of a publisher, without any regard to the great purposes of biography.

Were I called upon to give the character of Mr. Bentham, in a few words, without entering into detail, I should speak of him as the most child-like, and at the same time one of the wisest and best, and therefore one of the greatest of God's creatures ; a man whose errors—and with all his goodness and greatness, even he is not exempt either from errors of opinion or conduct—are no part of his philosophy, whatever they may be of his humanity. Having done this, I should try to run a parallel between him and Hobbes, for in the grander as well as the smaller features of both, in their strength as well as in their weakness, they are alike.

A few points of resemblance may be referred to now; but hereafter, when our readers are made acquainted with Mr. Bentham, as one man is with another about a supper-table, or at a lunch under the green trees in the open air—I do not say about a dinner-table; for two men will be better acquainted after spending five minutes together by the way-side, over a mug of beer and a bit of bread-and-cheese, than at half a dozen formal dinner-parties,—I may refer to a number more, quite as remarkable as the following.

Mr. Bentham is so afraid of death, that he will not allow the subject to be alluded to before him—he is afraid of being alone after dark; he is either read asleep every night, or left to fall asleep with a lamp burning; and he is a believer in what *he* calls ghosts; that is, in a something which makes him uneasy in solitude after dark.

So with Mr. Hobbes, the author of the Leviathan. He was subject to occasional terrors: he dreaded to be left alone, and a particular instance is told, says D'Israeli, in his Quarrels of Authors, ' that on the Earl of Devonshire's removal from Chatsworth, the philosopher, then in a dying state, insisted on being carried away, though on a feather bed. Various motives have been suggested to account for this extraordinary terror. Some declared he was afraid of spirits.' ' The terrible enemy of nature, death, is always before him.'

As a talker, though not often as a writer, Mr. Bentham is very dogmatic; and very much of an egotist; but still, it is an agreeable sort of dogmatism, and the pleasantest, the best-founded, and the most excusable egotism I ever met with.

So with Hobbes. ' His greatest imperfection was a monstrous egotism—the fate of those who concentrate all their observations into their own individual feelings. There are minds which think *too much, by conversing too little with books and men. Hobbes exulted he had read little, and was a solitary man*'—So does Mr. Bentham—" Hence he always *saw things in his own way.*"

' He *wrote against dogmas with a spirit perfectly dogmatic. He liked conversation—peevishly referring to his own works whenever contradicted;* and his friends *stipulated with strangers* that they should *not dispute with the old man.*' Mr. Bowring often does this; after having persuaded Mr. Bentham to see them; or if he does not *stipulate* to this effect, he himself is careful never to dispute with Mr. Bentham, and usually hints as much to others. 'Selden has often quitted the room of Hobbes' —'or Hobbes been driven from it in the fierceness of their battle.' The very same thing may be said of Mr. Mill, the author of British-India, and of some others—during their intercourse with Mr. Bentham. Yet no man is readier to forget and forgive—but he cannot *talk*, he says; and they who can, get the advantage of him.

Another resemblance may be found in their great age, and greater industry. ' Hobbes *delighted to show he was living by annual publications.*' 'His health and his studies were the sole object of his thoughts; and notwithstanding that panic which so often disturbed him, he wrote and published *beyond his ninetieth year.*' So with Mr. Bentham—he is now upwards of eighty; continually occupied with new works, in better health, and in a fuller enjoyment of life now than he was ten years ago.

P. S. The outline portrait which accompanies the preceding account of Mr. Bentham, is engraved from the copy of a very faithful and spirited sketch of him, by Mr. Robert M. Sully, a young Virginian of great promise, to whom Mr. Bentham sat in the year '27. It is altogether very striking and characteristic; and will be observed to bear a considerable resemblance to Dr. Franklin,—a bust of whom, by the way, is now in the possession of Mr. Mill, the father, which was sent to him by a friend at Paris, on account of its surprising resemblance to Mr. Bentham.

4

Thomas Cooper

Review

Rationale of Judicial Evidence specially applied to English Practice. From the Manuscripts of Jeremy Bentham, Esq. Bencher of Lincoln's-Inn. London. 1828

in

Southern Review
vol. V, no. X (May 1830), pp. 381–426

Thomas Cooper

Review

Rationale of Judicial Evidence specially applied to English Practice. From the Manuscripts of JEREMY BENTHAM, Esq. Bencher of Lincoln's-Inn. In 5 vols. 8vo. London. 1828.

Southern Review, vol. V, no. X (May 1830), pp. 381–426.

THIS is an extension of the *Traité des preuves judiciaires*, complied by M. Dumont in 1823, from the notes of Mr. Bentham. M. Dumont, with great propriety, left out of his book all of Mr. Bentham's applications to the English system of Law and of Practice. In the present edition, those applications and illustrations have been preserved and enlarged.

We could have wished the present editor had translated the work out of the obscure, involuted, Benthamee dialect in which it is written. A book, more disgustingly affected, and so nearly unintelligible, it is not possible to produce in the English language, with the exception of some of Mr. Bentham's former works, which equally exhibit specimens of what may, by the courtesy due to Mr. Bentham, be called English, but on no other score. Frequently, we have hunted with great care for some new and profound thought involved in a page of this mysterious dialect, and found only common-place notions arranged with pompous, needless accuracy.[2] Frequently, we have laboured on with tedious expectation that has, at length, been well rewarded, by the truth, the novelty, and the importance of Mr. Bentham's positions. Indeed, we have toiled through the five volumes, with frequent lamentations at the labour they required; but having so done, we can safely aver, that no book has so often unsettled, our long-cherished opinions, or convinced us more thoroughly than this, that the author understood his subject much better than we did on our first sitting down to the perusal. To an Englishman, it is, indeed, a most important publication: exhibiting in strong light, the manifold abuses of the principles and practice of English jurisprudence, and the dreadful curse the whole system of English law really is, in a national point of view. It proves this position with the most unsparing vituperation – in language of abuse unmeasured indeed, but, in our opinion, too often deserved: it attacks, and with a harshness that we cannot approve, the motives of men whom we have been accustomed to think of with high respect; nor will it be east to justify all the sweeping, indiscriminate accusation he has employed, notwithstanding his concession that the blame attaches to the system rather than to the persons: but we have risen from the perusal of the work, with a perfect conviction that the English system of Common Law and of Equity, is not the "perfection of reason," but needs the most radical, thorough-going reform. That it is a system of fraud, falsehood, absurdity, pretension, and deception, impossible to be defended honestly; and utterly undeserving the usual style of common-place panegyric applied to it by its ignorant or interested admirers. A thoroughbred common-law lawyer, whose maxim is, *neminem oportet esse legibus sapientiorem*, may abuse reform, may sneer at codification, may deny the possibility of converting judicial into statutory law: we attempt no impossibilities; we deem it hopeless to make any attack on such impracticable understandings: we hold up Bentham's volumes in our hands, and we appeal to the PUBLIC, in full confidence of the result.

Much light has been thrown on the defects of this system, by Mr. Ensor, Sir S. Romilly, Mr. Brougham, Mr. Peele, by the Parliamentary commissioners, and, more than all, by Mr. Humphereys, and Mr. Parkes, the editor of the Jurist. But their proposals, well-meant as they are, extend so partially – their reforms are so inadequate to the abuses of the system – their dread of the influence of the profession, of popular prejudice, of the imputation of rashness and radicalism – the cant terms of reproach applied to all proposals of effectual amendment – the fashionable demand for *gradual* reformation and moderation; all together, convert their expositions, however well-meant, into the blows of imbecility; *tela imbella sine ictu*: to be convinced how applicable to the system are the epithets we have applied to it, this work of Mr. Bentham's must be read, or rather studied; for without close attention, it will not be understood: and for this purpose, in particular, we recommend the fourth volume *in toto*. The design of the book is, to show much at length, and much in detail.

1. That in judiciary investigations, no kind of evidence whatever, capable of throwing light on the question agitated, ought to be rejected, unless its exclusion can be justified by avoiding vexation, expense or delay; amounting, if incurred, to a preponderant evil.

2. To point out the best means of securing the truth of evidence.

3. To point out the best means of judging of the value of evidence.

Hence it appears, that Mr. Bentham would annihilate at once, all objections to the competence or admissibility of a witness, and class them under objections to credibility: varying according to the circumstances under which the objectionable testimony is delivered.

As to the first point, he observes –

1. That the rules of evidence, under the legal system of England, are repugnant to the ends of justice.

2. That they are inconsistent with themselves: not a rule but what is violated by a multitude of exceptions or counter rules; which are observed in cases in which the reason of the rule so violated, applies with as much force, as the cases where it is observed.

3. That this inconsistency has place, not only as between rule and rule, but as between period and period: between the system observed in former periods, and the system observed in later periods: to which he might have added, as between judge and judge.

4. That, consequently, the objections drawn from the topics of innovation, subversion, &c. do not bear in the present case against the introduction of a rational and consistent system; inasmuch as it would suffice, in very many cases, for the purposes of reform, to adopt the exception in lieu of the rule.

5. That the proposed improvements would be better introduced by legislative provision, than in any other way.

6. But rather than to omit these improvements, they might be introduced by judicial authority; inasmuch as they form not the substantial part of law, but the adjective part – to wit, the means employed to carry into effect the substantive part. At present, these technical rules of evidence tend chiefly to frustrate the substantive part of the law itself, by causing decisions to depend, not on this substantive part of the law – not on the real merits of the question – but on the adjective, accessory, and minor parts; not on the end, but on the means technically adopted to arrive at that end – means, constituting a system known only to the profession, and unintelligible to the mass of the people.

Hitherto, the astuteness of the English Bench has been employed, in excluding, as far as possible, all the natural and obvious means of arriving at truth, and of doing justice between the parties, by excluding evidence instead of allowing for bias. This has been attended with the concomitant, so prolific of honour and of profit – *mystery*. Mystery, arising from conflicting doctrines, conflicting decisions, fluctuation and inconsistency of opinion, and uncertainty as to the state of the law on a given subject. All tending to mystification: all productive of business and of fees: all leaving open the doors of inquiry, and furnishing temptation to law-suits, and the materiel of subtle and plausible argument. For the profession, a delightful state of things – for the people, a most miserable servitude. Exemplifying Cicero's exclamation – *misera est servitus, ubi jus est vagum aut indiscriminatum*. But Greenleaf's volume of cases doubted and denied, forms but one item of the system.

Bentham's work may be divided substantially into five parts. Evidence available in a court of justice, is oral evidence or the testimony of witnesses; or it is written evidence. This latter is matter of record, or depositions and other pre-appointed writings meant to bear upon any part of a cause during its progress.

The FIRST division we make of his work then, considers oral testimony or witnesses; what is the actual state of their admissibility; and the defects of system in this respect.

The SECOND division comprehends his observations on written evidence.

The THRID division may be regarded as comprehending his grave but most bitter complaints of the management of the Judges during all times past in England, and connived at by every member of the present judicial corps of that country, to make the whole course of judicial proceedings subservient to their own emolument, and the emolument of the profession. This general accusation pervades the whole work: it occurs in places out of number, in the third volume, and the fourth volume is chiefly dedicated to its detail. We assert, without hesitation, that he has proved his point; and we shall be much surprised to find that any English lawyer of reputation has risked it on a reply to Bentham's charges.

A FOURTH division will comprehend his remarks on Courts of Equity.

And a FIFTH his proposals for altering throughout the principles on which oral testimony is rejected in a court of law; and a proposal for substituting what he calls the *natural* proceeding in judicial investigations, in lieu of the modern *technical* method of conducting a law-suit. Proposals in which, with few exceptions, we coincide.

Mr. Bentham's work now under review, consists of five thick octavo volumes, containing near 3500 pages. It is manifest, therefore, that the space usually allotted to a review, will permit us a very limited survey of the field he has traversed. We shall, therefore, confine ourselves to a brief notice of the spirit and substance of the first, the fourth and the fifth of the divisions we have precedently marked out. So many of his bitter objections to the fee-gathering system of England, being totally inapplicable in this country, where salaries are almost universally substituted for fees, we can only refer to his work for the piquant observations he has indulged in under the *third* division: rejoicing that the good sense of our own citizens has forestalled so many of his proposed alterations and improvements. One part of it only we shall take occasion to touch upon, the adoption of legal *fictions*.

First then, of oral testimony or witnesses. To be of value, it must be *Correct* in point of truth.

Accurate in its particulars.

Full and complete as to all its essential parts.

It must be given by a witness of competent faculties to observe.

By one who has had sufficient opportunities of observing.

And who has used them.

Who has no personal interest to serve by his testimony, either as to the event of the cause before the court, or the determination of the question involved in the cause.

Who has no bias from family interest.

Or from any *esprit de corps* of a political, a religious, or any other character.

It must be delivered orally and visibly, that hesitation or decision in the mode of the delivery may be observed.

In public. Publicity being the great friend and pledge of truth and justice.

As much as possible unpremeditatedly.

On examination by one party, and cross-examination by the other: and finally, by the Judge, whose duty it is to elicit truth equally on both sides. The bar would doubt this right of the Judge; the public will require it.

The testimony given, should, as to all essential points, be taken down in writing.

The witness should be liable to the questions suggested by each party to his own advocate; and by the jury to be put by the Judge.

The object being –

By the examination in chief by the party through his advocate, to obtain all the truth that it is the interest of that party to bring out.

By the cross-examination to obtain all the truth which it is the interest of the other and opposite party to bring out.

By the suggestions of the jury and the impartial examination of the Judge when the advocates have closed, to obtain all the truth on both sides which the just decision of the cause requires.

These rules hold good, whether in a civil or a criminal case. The Judge is not the advocate of the prisoner but of the public: and the public interest requires that the truth, the whole truth, and nothing but the truth, with equal impartiality, whether for or against a party, should be brought out.

Whenever circumstances appear to render it expedient, the witnesses should be examined out of the presence and hearing of each other.

A deficiency in any of these qualifications, will be a reasonable ground of defalcation from the credibility of a witness. In the English system of judicial regulation respecting evidence, many of these grounds of deficiency are held sufficient to exclude the testimony of the witness altogether; that is to go to his *competency*: in other cases they furnish (as they ought) objections to his *credibility*. Bentham's remarks on excluded testimony are contained chiefly in his fifth volume.

a. Danger of deception and misdecision not a proper ground of exclusion.
b. Of exclusion on the ground of interest.
c. Of exclusion on the ground of improbity.
d. Of exclusion on the ground of religious opinions.
e. Of exclusion on the ground of mental imbecility.
f. Of restoratives of competency under the English system.
g. Of testimony excluded on the ground of self-crimination.
h. Of testimony excluded on the ground of self-oneration.
i. Of testimony excluded on the ground of self-disgrace.
j. Of testimony excluded on the ground of self-discredit.
k. Of testimony excluded on the ground of prejudging a confidential trust.
l. Of testimony excluded on the ground of preserving family peace.
m. Of excluding the testimony of the plaintiff and defendant.
n. Of excluding testimony that does not apply directly to the points at issue.

Instructions for estimating the force of bias.

This division of the grounds of exclusion, with an analysis of Mr. Bentham's reasoning upon each, will afford the reader, a tolerable view of this part of his work, occupying upwards of 600 pages. If our analysis be brief and therefore imperfect, the reader will easily perceive that it is an offence pardonable, if we cannot succeed in condensing six hundred pages into a dozen; we shall endeavour to do our duty, whether we fail in it or not, and present the reader with the substance of Mr. Bentham's arguments, referring to the work itself for the able statement of them which the author has presented. Not always, indeed, in the pleasantest and easiest style that the English language admits of, but well worth the deliberate perusal and consideration of those who interest themselves in the improvement of our legal system. Much, indeed, most of his objections, will apply equally to American as to English law; so servilely have we trodden in the steps of the judges of that country: a class of men, by no means deserving the respect either for talent or integrity, which the comity of the profession, among ourselves, has been inclined to pay them

a. *Of exclusion of testimony, through fear of deception.*

This chapter of Bentham's work (vol. v. c. 1 and 2) should be read through. We shall endeavour to state the general turn of his argument.

The only real question is, has the witness, whoever he be, or whatever he may have been, a present motive to induce him to swear falsely? No man acts but by the impulse of some motive inciting him; and if a bad man has no reason to be a bad man on the present occasion, what has his past conduct to do with the present?

For what purpose does the Judge occupy the Bench? To decide rightly the cause before him. What then is the evil to be guarded against? Misdecision, produced by false testimony: for if the falsehood, however it may be a proper object of punishment, does not produce misdecision, it is of little moment, as to the subject-matter, it has no effect on the cause: while misdecision is an evil of the same magnitude, whether produced by falsehood and deception, or by any other cause.

The testimony offered and rejected, is either *necessary* to the party producing it, or it is *less* than necessary. Let it be necessary: then, for fear of possible misdecision from false testimony, you produce misdecision to a certainty be excluding it. As a panic-struck bird flies into the serpent's mouth; as a man jumps overboard for fear of being drowned. If the testimony be admitted, you may be on your guard, and correct the evil: if rejected, you have no alternative. Misdecision is inevitable if testimony, without which just decision cannot be had, be rejected.

You borrowed £20: you paid it in the presence of A.B. A.B. is convicted of perjury or other offence destroying his testimonial competency: his testimony is rejected. You *certainly* lose your cause. Could more injustice be done if he were admitted?

Not a day in any court of *nisi prius*, but false testimony is given in some cause or other. Is misdecision the certain consequence? No: every lawyer knows, that in nine cases out of ten, cross-examination or counter testimony correct it. The opposite party, the counsel, the judge, the jury are all on their guard: it is nearly impossible for perjury suspected before hand to succeed. But let the evidence excluded be *not absolutely necessary*, because the party offering it, has other testimony. Then, if the decision be given on that other testimony, the exclusion can produce, on the side of justice, no beneficial effect. It only puts the party to expense otherwise unnecessary, to procure evidence of a different description.

Again. A witness who *by law* ought to be rejected at once by the Judge, happens to be admitted on his credibility. The parties, the counsel, the judge, the jury, are all on the alert to detect his violation of truth. Nothing of the kind can be fixed upon him: after the cause is fully argued, the judge and the jury believe him. A very possible, not to say, a common case. Here then, the judge and the jury, after due investigation, believe a witness who the law says, ought not to be heard at all! Such is law: common sense would teach us, that a witness knowing the suspicions concerning him, and how much every one was on the alert to convict him of falsehood, would not commit perjury gratuitously; this is not in nature. If he have any specific motive for false swearing, then it is some motive extraneous to the legal reason for excluding him.

Even from a witness desirous of deceiving, examination and cross-examination will generally elicit useful truths.

Suppose you wish to examine a child, or a servant in your own family, who you know has been heretofore guilty of lying: do you therefore refuse to ask him any questions whatever? – No, indeed: you know the propensity, and judge whether it applies in the case before you, and allow for it.

This exclusionary system is not legislative law, but Bench-made law. Justice is said to be blind: is it necessary she should be deaf also? What is a judge placed on the bench for, if it be not that he has been all his life experienced in discriminating truth from falsehood?

But we shall see as we go on, that many of the legal reasons for excluding testimony, have no bearing whatever on the temptation to a witness, to utter either truth or falsehood.

b. *Of exclusion on the ground of interest*.

Interest is objected to as giving origin to motives of mendacity. Many persons, no doubt, are liable to the operation of such motives;

of which, positive gain, or the avoidance of loss or inconvenience, constitute the chief feature. This motive, however, is of very different force in different persons: a difference of force, dependent on the quantum of interest in question, the rank, station and society, the fortune, the education, the sensibility, and a variety of other circumstances belonging to, or connected with the witness. But the exclusion excludes all notice of these varieties. Of William Pitt or Charles Fox, would the loss or gain of £5, affect the testimony? Suppose, on the other hand, a working labourer, ill-educated, with a wife and children on the point of starving – is there any analogy between the cases? All men, whatever, are restrained from aberrations of veracity by, first, the difficulty of devising a falsehood that will pass examination in a court of justice; secondly, by fear of legal punishment; thirdly, by fear of disgrace, loss of station and character; fourthly, in most cases, the dread of future retribution. Whatever may be the amount of interest prompting to mendacity, before it be admitted as a ground of exclusion, it should be shown to preponderate on the minds of men in general, over the very powerful restraining motives enumerated. But the exclusion excludes also all such investigation.

By the English law, every man is presumed to be innocent until he be proved guilty: here we have a presumption of guilt perfectly gratuitous.

Who is the person suffering? the innocent suitor. Suppose the excluded testimony necessary to save the character or the life of the party offering it: one man is presumed to be a perjurer, and, therefore, another man is disgraced for life, or punished with death.

Where will you draw the line of pecuniary interest? Will you let it be one cent, one hundred, one thousand, one million, ten million? You cannot draw the line: hence, the manifest absurdity of the rule. We were present in a court in Pennsylvania, when a Judge refused to sit on an insurance cause, because he had three cents at hazard. All ratio between the sum in question and the pecuniary circumstances of the witness, is neglected under this wise rule of law which makes pecuniary interest a ground of exclusion. There are many secret and very strong motives that may operate to produce mendacity: friendship, *esprit de corps*, &c.; but who can be ignorant that money is a motive? Every one, therefore, who hears the witness, is on his guard where this temptation appears. Yet by the law of exclusion for pecuniary interest, a cent may render the President of the United States, a witness too suspicious to be credited on his oath! and this is law! The manifest inconveniences of this rule, in cases of forgery, are well known to the profession.

The exceptions partake of the character of the rule. Thus, a *certain* interest, to the amount of a dollar, excludes: a *contingent* interest, to the amount of a million, is unnoticed. A party, rich, keeping on high salary a concubine; the concubine is a good witness in his favour. A rich woman, on the point of being married; day fixed: all her property at stake: her betrothed lover a good witness.

We give the next exception in the words of Bentham, and the technical jargon of the case alluded to.

"Suppose a duke's daughter seduced; wanting a day of being of age. *Pier, porte action versus seducer.* Case: trespass *per quod servitium amisit.* Stockings remaining unmended, which *Fille* should have mended while in child-bed. Damages laid at £10,000. *Fille* good witness: why? Because she has no interest! What matters it to her, whether she be thought to have been defiled without consent, or to have delivered herself as Potiphar's wife would have done to Joseph? *Secus,* the day past, and *Fille* of age. *Action per Pier negist;* quia nul drot: because no right *pour faire Fille* mend stockings: *issuit* no damages *al Pier. Action per fille negist, quia nul seduction; fille ne esteant dans age: et encore fille* bad evidence; *quia nemo debet esse testis en son cause demesne.*"

For the other most absurd exceptions to this most absurd rule, we are reluctantly compelled to refer to vol. v. p. 66, 77.

c. *Of exclusion on the ground of Improbity.*

Take the strongest case – Perjury. A man has been guilt of falsehood when upon his oath, on a point material to the issue between the parties. With an absurdity that has many parallels in law, we do not punish his offence against society, viz. the falsehood; but we let that alone and punish his offence against religion.

Perjury admits many, very many degrees of delinquency: from that which puts it on a level with murder, to the falsehood under oath committed by the jury in half the trials that take place: a falsehood under oath, habitually practised by jurymen under the legal compulsion of unanimity, countenanced, approved, recommended, ordered by the grave judges on the bench: and complied with by the jury, because they are told to do so. Is there no scale of gradation in these different cases of guilt? Exclusion knows none.

Suppose a man once convicted of judicial mendacity, is it a fair conclusion that notwithstanding its consequences in the past case, he will be for ever after a sworn enemy to truth? Even when no motive can by possibility be alleged for his falsehood? Is a man to be abandoned for a single act of delinquency?

In this exclusion no account is taken of the motives and temptations that might in degree extenuate past delinquency: kindness, and honour may have intermingled with them. N'importe: the law imputes habitual delinquency from a single act: that may also have happened half a century ago, in the folly-tide of youth, and imputed in advanced years.

How can the law be so severe on perjury, when it supposes that interest to the amount of a dollar will induce any man whatever to perjure himself?

Suppose an attesting witness to title deeds: afterwards he becomes perjured: am I to lose my estate on that account? – All exclusions are punishments not on the persons excluded, but on the parties who need their testimony.

A perjured person may not be a witness in behalf of another, but he may in behalf of himself: for instance he may make an affidavit in his own cause.

As to exclusions on account of infamy attached to the judgment rendered in cases of treason, felony, &c. where an informer, a *particeps criminis*, is admitted and rewarded, provided the other party be convicted – of all this and the horrible absurdities connected with it, we must refer to the book for want of room.

Bentham proceeds (vol. v. p. 108.) to show that if habitual mendacity furnishes sufficient reason for exclusions, advocates and judges in England ought to be excluded as witnesses. We refer to the work for his reasons in support of the following conclusion of the chapter in his own words.

"No: it is not for the purpose of advocating but of reprobating exclusion of testimony, that these remarkable cases are spread upon the carpet; it is not for the purpose of proving that these ought to be excluded, but that none ought to be excluded: not only that the felon and the perjurer, nor even the mendacious advocate of any country, not even the constant arbiter, utterer, bespeaker, rewarder and compeller of mendacity, the English judge.

"No: let them not shut the door of the witness box against any human creature: but if nothing will satisfy them but that some body must be excluded – if the demon of exclusion must have victims – let judges and advocates be the first."

d. *Of exclusion on the ground of religious opinion.*

Heterodoxy always has been, and still is so unpopular, that a man must have no small portion of moral courage, and honesty, openly and publicly to profess it, rather than conceal it. Even in this country of religious freedom under the constitutions of the several States, but we cannot honestly say in this country of religious toleration, a man is sure to encounter much obloquy, and great practical inconvenience who has the courage to run counter to the religious persuasions of his fellow citizens.

Suppose a man produced as a witness in court: well known as a man of respectable station and character – of unimpeachable moral conduct in society: the advocate on the adverse side, says, "Sir, I ask you, do you believe in the existence of a God and a future state?" and the judge decides that such a question may be put, as in England, most undoubtedly it may. Let us suppose that by some strange aberration of judgment, the witness should in these respects be an unbeliever, and acknowledge in open court what no one before knew or reasonably suspected, that he is, in this case, an unbeliever: can a stronger proof of devotion to the cause of truth, to veracity in public as well as in private, be exhibited? Can more decided evidence of undoubted honesty be imagined? Yet in this case, his attachment to truth at all hazards, is the very reason assigned by the law, for regarding him as an habitual, determined liar! Language does not admit of expressing a case, or more detestable absurdity.

We have put this case, because we know that in many States of the Union where the court and bar are bigoted to the English code, such a question to a witness would be allowed. In South-Carolina, the constitution says, "that the free exercise and enjoyment of religious profession and worship, without discrimination and preference, shall for ever be allowed to all mankind." Now, this free exercise and enjoyment cannot take place, if every pert lawyer may convert a court of justice into a court of inquisition, and compel a witness to confess in public his religious creed, for the gratification of impertinent curiosity. To the witness, "James Maloney, did you see John Nokes pay 500 dollars to Thomas Stiles, on the 4th day of March, at 10 o'clock in the morning, at Thomas Stiles' store?" "Stop Sir," says the opposite counsel, "before you answer that question, answer mine: do you believe in the Divine Inspiration of the Old and New Testaments?" In the name of common sense, is John Nokes to be cheated out of 500 dollars, because James Maloney, the witness, may have doubts about Divine Inspiration? Is this the boast of common law? Is this the perfection of reason? Is this *Summa Ratio*? Truly *nemi nem oportet esse legibus sapientiorem!* is a most convenient maxim! However, let us proceed to Bentham's arguments.

The witness declares himself an Atheist, what should prevent him from affirming the contrary, and escaping the stigma which this confession will brand him with? What but a regard for his own character in society – his character in his own family – the habitual reverence for truth which exhibiting himself, he gives an example of to others. Are these sufficient grounds for disbelieving him? Doubtless they are, says the law.

A man is indicted for a crime: a witness, A.B. has been heard to declare he was present at the time, and knows all the circumstances. He is summoned: he wishes to screen the culprit. He suggests to the counsel for the prisoner, ask me if I am not an Atheist. The objection is taken: the witness dismissed: the culprit is set free. In this way any man whatever may get rid of the inconvenience of giving testimony: any knot of criminals may combine and secure impunity.

But an Atheist is not to be believed: indeed! How do you know an Atheist? What ear-mark has he? If he cannot be believed, then, when a man in open court professes himself an Atheist, he is by law a liar: then he is so in this instance: then he is not an Atheist.

In June, 1806, in England, the statute against Blasphemy (heterodoxy) was repealed. Yet did Lord Eldon persist in declaring that to deny the Trinity was still an offence at common law. That infamous falsehood and forgery of the English bench grounded on priests' supposed dictum, that Christianity is part and parcel of the common law, so decidedly, so irrefutably exposed by Mr. Jefferson, whose statement we have examined with the year-book before us, and know to be accurate, is still unblushingly advocated by judges even in this country!

Let us not be misunderstood: we are no advocates for Atheism, or any other kind of ism: we respect every man's honest convictions whatever they may be: we leave every reader to the free exercise of his own conscience. All we mean to say is, that the law ought to do so too: and when it refuses so to do, absurdities, inconsistencies, and inconveniences, are the necessary result of such intolerance. Whatever a man's theological creed may be, he will tell the truth between two of his neighbours, when he has no motive whatever to do otherwise.

Cacotheology an exclusion. – The law tolerates the God of the Jews, of the Hindoos, of the Chinese, of the Mohammedans: yet until recently, a Papist recusant was excluded: at this day, in England, a Quaker is so. Is it not so in this country too in criminal cases? Suppose a set of tipsy soldiers, were to enter a Quaker-meeting, bind the men and violate the women, how are the offenders to be convicted? not a witness present admissible in a court (of justice? – no, let us not be guilty of such misnomer) of law! Atheist, Papist, Cacotheist, all are good and legal witnesses, provided they have no scruples about swearing falsely. It is only when they show their uncompromising sense of their duty to society, and their obligation to tell the truth, that the law excludes them as untrustworthy witnesses! In Massachusetts, we presume a Socinian would be an admissible witness. We should doubt upon this point in New-York or Pennsylvania, where Christianity is part and parcel of the common law: by Christianity always meaning the faith, *fides carbonaria*, the convenient creed, of the presiding judge: orthodox of course.

e. *Of exclusion on the ground of mental Imbecility*.

In this as in all other cases, it is not suspicion, it is not caution we argue against: we allow all due objections to credibility. The question is competency – exclusion.

Infancy, superannuation, idiocy, lunacy, furnish reasonable ground for caution: but they are of such various degrees, that until the witness be examined, it is impossible to know whether and how far he may be trusted. Indeed, among these defects, infancy is the only legal ground of exclusion. Even here, a child of seven years of age has been examined, (2 Leach, 482, White's case.) In this case, a man who had committed violence of the last enormity on an infant of that age, was set free, because an oath had not been administered. In another case, (17th Sept. 1803) it was determined as to a girl of twelve years of age, that the witness must understand the nature of an oath, and what would be the religious consequences of telling a falsehood. Can any child answer these theological inquiries understandingly? Otherwise than as a parrot, by rote? The questions that common sense would put, are, what did you hear, or see, or feel? Not as it appears the case was, can you say your catechism? This puts the fate of the accused in the power of the parents or instructors of the child. Does the parent wish the testimony of the child to prevail, the catechism is taught with parental explanations, and the child goes up to the box an orthodox theologian. Does the parent wish the culprit to escape? The child has not been taught his catechism! Suppose the parents of Mary Ann Carney, in the last case, had been Universalists, the recorder at the Old Bailey would have set the culprit free. In one case, Mr. Justice Rooke, (Gwillim's Bacon, v. ii. p. 577) committed a young witness to the care of a clergyman of the established Church to be theologically drilled, before he would admit the infant (*i.e.* under adult age) as a witness. He was right: the duty of a judge is not to do justice, but to maintain law; and wofully ignorant must he be who confounds these two very different things.

The cases on Scotch marriages, are all in point in confirmance of the absurdity of this sweeping exclusion.

f. *Of the restoratives for Competency.*

Treason, felony, (except petit larceny) forgery, piracy, swindling and cheating, barratry, conspiracy, præmunire, bribing a witness, judgment on attaint for false verdict, winning money at unlawful games – render the offender incompetent as a witness in England; how far in this country is dubious from contrariant decisions. (See 2 Starkie, 716, and note by the American Editor.) Competency may be restored, by clerical purgation, so deemed at common law, (2 Starkie, 717) by proof of pardon, by reversal of the judgment.

Let us take Bentham's enumeration of specifics for this disease.

1. *The burning iron.* – Let the offender hold up his hand in open court, to which must be applied a red hot iron: let there be hissing and outcry on the part of the sufferer; the outcry to be performed by the sufferer or his deputy; the hissing by a piece of bacon applied to the hand; then will the virus of incompetency be burnt out by actual cautery, and the prisoner will then, and not before, be deemed a truth-teller, and trust-worthy ever after. Of late years, the judges have preferred sending the delinquent on his travels to Botany Bay. Whipping is not a restorative; burning is.

2. *The Great Seal* authenticating a pardon. The Privy Seal is held not to be a legal remedy in such case. Whether it be a pardon on the merits, or granted in consequence of some legal objection to the proceeding, no one inquires.

3. A *statute* pardoning several criminals comprehended in it.

4. A *record* containing some legal flaw in the process of conviction, or any subsequent part embraced by the record. But if there be no legal errors actually contained in it, what is to be done then? Never mind, the remedy is easy. Mr. Attorney-General comes into court with the record in his hand, and says, "I confess errors in this record;" whereupon, the errors are taken for granted, the record quashed, and incompetency cured. But here the toils are forcibly torn: cannot the captive beast be let out by the gnawing of the mouse? May not a copying-clerk commit real errors in writing out the record? Moreover, the judges have the absolute control over the record: they may allow it or not to be withdrawn; they may grant or not a copy of it; as when

intended to found an action for malicious prosecution. How well may all this discretionary power serve the purposes of political expediency!

g. *Of testimony excluded on the ground of self-crimination, or self-disserving – Nemo tenetur seipsum accusare.* – This is one of the wise laws of the profession. Doubtless, a man is not bound to go before a magistrate voluntarily, and accuse himself of highway robbery. The real question is, whether a witness, in a case in which the good of society requires the truth to be told, shall say to a judge, "I will not speak the truth, for it may criminate me. What is the good of society to me; my business is to take care of myself." We would hereon remark –

1. The best of all evidence is the acknowledgment of the party. *Habes consistentem reum.* What good reason is there that guilt should be privileged and exonerated?

2. It renders inferior evidence necessary: such as hearsay confessions; circumstantial evidence: written papers; common fame (by statute.)

3. All substitutes are dubious, difficult to procure, and expensive. The man is before you, why not put a question, which, if not put, enables him to set public justice at defiance? Is his interest, convenience and security every thing, and the public safety nothing?

4. Upon this principle it is (that no man shall be compelled to injure himself) that a plaintiff or defendant may not be asked questions of the highest moment to the justice of the cause in which they are litigants. A practice of the most outrageous absurdity, and which nothing but the pecuniary interests of the profession have sanctioned. In Chancery, indeed, the principle is broken in upon, but in a very imperfect manner. The parties may be put on their oaths, but not in the presence of each other, not with mutual power of examination and cross-examination. So in motions upon affidavit, a party is admitted as a witness in his own cause under the very worst possible circumstances; an affidavit, drawn up by his lawyer, and heard without cross-examination. Such are the very exceptionable exceptions, to this very exceptionable rule.

5. The rule of exclusion now under consideration, is not only calculated to screen guilt, to give impunity to crime, to cherish fraud, and counteract, in the most effectual way, the real ends of public justice, but it contravenes the great principle of legal evidence, that the best evidence the nature of the case can afford, should be adduced – for it rejects the best, and substitutes, in all cases, inferior evidence; at the certainly often, at the hazard always, of great delay, vexation and

expense; while the party exonerated laughs in his sleeve at the voluntary imbecility of rules of law! In no other civilized county but Great Britain and the United States, is this mischievous absurdity adopted and practised. The law has a right to say to a witness – "The public demands the truth: if it can do you no disservice to speak truth, speak it at once: if it be against your interest to speak truth, who has made it so but yourself?"

6. This rule is an infamous premium bestowed upon mendacity, by authority of law; which, indeed, as we shall soon see, deals in falsehoods by wholesale, either compelled, protected, or connived at by the court. "They have a letter of mine in their hands," says a party to his lawyer. "What then," says the lawyer, "you may deny it, or refuse to answer; let them prove it if they can; if not, we gain a victory."

Two young lawyers, members of a volunteer corps, were summoned to pay a fine of 17s. 6d. each: they were shown their names on the muster-roll in their own handwriting. "There are your own signatures, gentlemen: Is not this your own handwriting?" "That is your business to prove," said the delinquents: the proof was not ready; the fine was renounced, and the young lawyers saved 17s. 6d.[2] Is it a civilized and moral community that can permit this?

7. To save one malefactor from justice, the law bribes another malefactor to give evidence, by promising impunity for the crime. The one is hanged, the other goes off a whitewashed, trust-worthy member of society. *Ille Crucem pretium sceleris tulit, hic Diadema.*

But it is very hard upon a man to force him to criminate himself: it is so: it is very hard upon society too, that a man should be at liberty to play the rogue with impunity: it is very hard upon the rogue that he should be punished for his roguery. This is his opinion no doubt. What does the good of the community require? Why, that punishment should be inflicted, and roguery suppressed. The sympathy of honest men is with honesty – the sympathy of the law is in favour of all kinds of dishonesty: hence, whether in criminal or civil cases, law and lawyers protect it as far as they dare. The quibbles of the bench in favour of dishonesty, make honest men regard Judges upon the bench as enemies to the well-being of society: often, too often, indeed, they are so. Villains are let loose upon the public, by the pick-lock of legal quibble. Never mind, he is a bag-fox; he will return, and we shall have our sport. Impunity of this kind creates business.

Oh, but this is inquisition-practice and star-chamber practice. What then? Amid many bad, they had also some good practices. The question is, which practice best serves the interest of the public – that which detects crime, or that which conceals and rewards it. It does not follow because a man is compelled to tell truth, he is to be tortured into a falsehood against himself.

Judge to the witness: "You do not choose to answer that question; very well, we shall be compelled to take your delinquency as confessed. There is no other reason but conscious guilt that can prevent you. If there be any other give it: tell us the truth whatever it may be, but at your peril."

h. i. j. The other branches, self-onerating, self-disgracing, self-disserving testimony, being cases of inferior consequence, will follow the higher case of self-criminating testimony. No court will (ought to) permit a question to be put to a witness that does not tend to elicit necessary truth; and, in such case, the public interest is or ought to be the interest paramount. Suppose a man by telling truth, will, by collateral effect, render himself liable to the payment of a sum of money, what then? Is mendacity to be screened, or veracity to be thrown into the back ground, for fear a debtor may, in consequence, be compelled to pay a just debt, or become liable to an honest contract? It is the duty of justice to enforce truth, and in so doing, to afford no protection to any plan for avoiding the burthen which truth honestly imposes. This, I say, is the business of justice; unfortunately, not of law.

k. *Of testimony excluded on the ground of prejudicing a confidential trust.* – If the good of society requires that every witness in a court of justice should answer truly whatever question the Court thinks proper to be put, whether it criminates himself or not, *à fortiori*, he ought to be compelled to answer when it happens to affect another person.

Lawyer and Client. – The lawyer cannot be compelled to disclose the secrets confidentially intrusted to him by the client. (Bull. N.P. 284.) This is the privilege not of the lawyer, but the client.

If the client be not guilty of any offence, what is there to conceal?

If the client be guilty of any offence, the public good requires that he should be punished. Whether his guilt be discovered by himself, his lawyer, or by any other third person, is of little consequence: society requires that guilt be punished, in order that guilt be suppressed. This is of much more consequence, than protecting a lawyer who becomes the confidant of a guilty client.

If this be permitted, (it is said) no client will repose confidence in his lawyer. Well; what then? If the client retain the information, there is no danger of the lawyer revealing it. But suppose it necessary to the client's defence to reveal it. It then becomes the duty of the lawyer to say to the client, "Remember, if I am asked in court, I must tell all I know; conduct yourself with me accordingly." The only mischief will be, that the client will not derive so much aid in conducting his defence of a bad cause, as otherwise he might have done. At present, the lawyer and client join to cheat public justice. If the exclusion in question be abrogated, this worthy partnership may be in many cases broken up; and surely, this will be a prodigious misfortune to the public! A contract between a rogue and his lawyer, to avoid the punishment of roguery, is not such a contract as need be treated with much respect. Is not the misprision of a crime, a crime? No wonder the exclusion is defended by the legal profession; it is a fruitful source of causes and fees. The true question is, not what does the interest of the profession, but what does the interest of the public require?

Trustee and cestui que trust. – Upon the principles before laid down, if the supposed damage fell upon the trustee himself, he ought to bear the consequences of telling that truth which the public justice of the country (the public good) requires to be told: *à fortiori*, there ought to be no indulgence of scruples in relation to another person, if he has no right to have them indulged in favour of himself.

1. *Of exclusion on the ground of family-peace.*

Husband and wife. – Let us suppose they love each other as well as they love themselves: but when the public good requires truth to be divulged, we have shown that it ought to be so, even thought the consequences be self-crimination.

The objections against admitting husband and wife are –

The hardship upon the feelings of persons standing in this relation.

The implacable dissensions likely to be produced.

The danger of perjury.

As to the hardship upon their feelings is that to be put in competition with the demands of public justice? Is that a reason why criminality or dishonesty should be concealed, and rewarded with impunity? Is there nothing due to the feelings of honest people who are delivered over to plunder? Let it be remembered, that the rational rule – the only rule – is *salus populi* – the public good. To that rule every other consideration should give way; it is the basis of civil society. The contract of baron and feme, being voluntary on their part, they must submit patiently to all the evils attendant on it.

Implacable dissension consequent upon these disclosures. Is there any reason why the party affected by testimony compelled, should bear animosity against the other party for disclosing what he or she could not avoid disclosing? Had it been voluntary, there might be some reason for anger; not where the disclosure is compulsive. Is the public good to be sacrificed to a base, an unjust and unreasonable animosity? If the party-witness in this case be exposed to reproach, let it be, as it ought to be, set down as among the misfortunes of that connexion, so liable to concomitant evils. If the witness be the wife of a rogue, is that a reason why his roguery against me should be concealed and protected?

The danger of perjury. We acknowledge there may be temptations to that crime arising from the prejudices in favour of each other, so natural to the matrimonial connexion. Being foreseen, let the counsel, the judge and the jury be on their guard, and not much danger of deception need be apprehended. It is, like any other known bias, to be guarded against and allowed for, not excluded. If a substitute cannot be found, misdecision is the certain consequence of exclusion; while, if the evidence be admitted, it is a consequence of remote probability only.

None of these objections, however, are deemed of sufficient weight to support the exclusion, when a personal injury is inflicted by the husband on the wife, or by the wife on the husband; for this would destroy business. And yet, with a cruel absurdity, the exclusion is enjoyed by law, in that case, of all others, where the testimony ought to be admitted, viz. bigamy. Not one reason, supported by a scintilla of common sense, can be assigned for prohibiting the first wife to prove the fact of her marriage; a fact, which is neither disgraceful to the one or the other. The disgrace is not in the first, but in the second marriage. Yet, with an inconsistency no where found but in English bench-enacted law, the testimony of the first wife has lately (1817) been admitted to prove this fact in a collateral suit between third persons! Any body but the party injured – any body but the public, may be allowed the benefit of this testimony. Such is the pleasure of the learned judges.

A little further respecting family dissension. A man shall spend his wife's property, neglect her person, cheat her, beat her, behave morosely and cruelly to her. This does not preclude forgiveness; these are every day cases. So, on the other side, how much misbehaviour on the part of the wife do we see, that produces dissension indeed, but temporary dissension only. Shall we then say that irreconcilable hatred is to be the inevitable consequence of an act where legal compulsion takes away all blame? Where there is no injury but what could not be avoided? Where the will was repugnant to the voluntary act?

Let us view this case in another light. The more obstacles can be thrown in the way of criminality or dishonesty, the better. What greater obstacle to misdeed than a witness, that the misdoer cannot escape – a witness who, willingly or unwillingly, may be compelled to disclose the truth?

Again: It may be for the interest of the profession – is it for the interest of the public, that an evil-doer shall have a perpetual confidant and accomplice in the bosom of his family, from whom no law can wring the secret of his delinquency?

Suppose two married men guilty of a highway robbery. The one can be convicted by testimony without calling in the evidence of his wife. He is convicted, and suffers capitally. The other can be convicted, if his wife be compelled to give testimony, but not otherwise. The wife is excluded. He escapes with impunity. What kind of justice is this? I do not inquire what kind of law it is: we know that: it is English bench-made law; by the false courtesy of that country, called common law.

Husband and wife are privileged: they cannot be compelled to give evidence to the disservice of each other. Here then is every family converted into a nursery (so far as the law can effect it) of unpunishable crime. A constant temptation to criminality from impunity: a means and opportunity of debauching the morals of the innocent gradually, by the bold and secure criminality of the guilty. It intermingles hostility to the public with the marriage tie, and inculcates concealment and protection of crime and dishonesty, as a marriage duty. And who authorized this? The legislator? No: the judge, whose voluntary business it is, to manufacture new principles of decision, and dub them common law.

Suppose a man meditating a crime, to know and be aware that his wife, the friend of his bosom, however reluctant, will be compelled, in a court of justice, to disclose his delinquency – would it not be a powerful obstacle to his becoming guilty? Why, then, should we throw away such safeguard?

But how hard, say the lawyers, is this compulsion, considering that the converse and communication between man and wife, may be considered as one unreserved confession. What then? This only renders the evidence more trust-worthy and unexceptionable: it furnishes a stronger reason why it should not be rejected. It should seem that law has no sympathy but for rogues and roguery. What is gained to the cause of morality, by laying it down as an axiom, that however wicked and hateful in his conduct a man may be, it is still the duty of his wife to love, honour, cherish, obey, and protect him even in all his infamy? Surely, the proper ethics of the marriage contact are, that love, respect, confidence and attachment are due only where those qualities exist, which reasonably call for them. Is it for the benefit of society, that villainy, dishonesty, fraud and vice of all kinds shall be considered as equally entitled to affection and obedience, as every virtue under heaven? Enough of this.

m. *Of excluding the testimony of the parties in a civil cause.*

This question is discussed by Bentham in volume v. from pp. 350 to 463, with a detail of the numerous inconsistencies of the English practice, defensible upon no common principle, but that of multiplying suits, and producing delays, vexations, expense and injustice. This is an exclusion not adopted by the civil law, not adopted by chancery, not adopted in the ecclesiastical courts, not countenanced by the practice of foreign nations, not productive of good to society, but of emolument to the profession, and impunity to roguery. It is an exclusion of those witnesses who know most about the matter.

The pretences are – 1. The temptation to commit perjury. 2. Deception toward the judge and jury, producing misdecision. 3. The hardship and vexation to the party of compelling him to give evidence against himself.

As to perjury: the bias is known, foreseen, and all the correctives ready to be put in force against it. Cross-examination, counter-evidence of the opposite party, and other witnesses. There is not much danger. It can be believed so far as it is consistent with itself and other evidence, and no further.

As to deception from the bias in his own favour, the preceding remarks apply. Forewarned, forearmed; the skill of counsel, the experience of the Judge, the counter evidence, all are brought into play.

As to the hardship. We have no sympathy in favour of dishonesty or deception. Either the party has something sinister to conceal, or he has not. If not, he can have no objection to subject his testimony to examination. If he have, the truth ought to be elicited. The public good ought not to be sacrificed for the sake of the sympathy of the law with all kind of fraud.

The testimony of the party is admitted and without cross-examination, in the affidavit to hold to bail: in all motions by affidavit before the court: it is admitted in the justifying of bail: it is admitted in the worst possible form in all chancery proceedings; in the bill, the answer, the cross-bill and answer; in the various affidavits used in the progress of the cause; all without open cross-examination. It is admitted when a party is denominated prosecutor in a criminal proceeding; it is rejected when the same party is called plaintiff as to the same subject-matter in a civil proceeding: it is rejected in one criminal suit, but if an indictment for perjury be brought, it is then admitted. The rules of law, "nemo debet esse testis in propriâ causâ," and "nemo tenetur seipsum accusare," are practised only when injustice can be screened by the practice; but the exceptions (nearly all of them exceptions in defiance of common sense and justice) are so numerous, that the rules themselves serve only the purpose of deception, and are not true in fact. Nor is it true in fact, what the law takes for granted, that all men are liars, if there be the smallest pecuniary interest to tempt them.

When we come to propose a natural mode of proceeding in conducting lawsuits for the benefit of the public, instead of the unnatural, technical mode adopted by the law for the benefit of the profession, we shall say more in favour of admitting, or rather of compelling the evidence of the parties in all cases.

We omit the numerous objections that stare us in the face, as to the admission of subscribing, and the exclusion of all non-subscribing witnesses, as well as of the party himself: the construction of wills, by which the power of making a will is absolutely denied to every testator, who is doomed to have his own intentions perpetually frustrated by the technical rules of legal construction, which the lawyer himself employed to draw the will is never sure of, a nuisance in society most provoking and revolting: the exclusion of single witnesses where more than one is technically required, and the postponement of trustworthiness to number: the disgraceful quibbles on the omission or alteration of a letter, where no doubt about the real fact exists: the negative exclusions of testimony, really satisfactory to men of common understanding: the most wicked and absurd protection of a party, who is known to have a document in his pocket or in his hand, absolutely necessary to the right decision of the cause, setting the court at defiance, sure of their protection in refusing to answer a single question concerning it. These, and very many other objections noticed in this laborious and important work, for want of space, we must omit. We repeat, however, for the sake of the public, that no man can be aware of the gross absurdity and manifest iniquity of the English code of law, common and chancery, without a careful perusal of this book. No Englishman can approach with proper feelings and proper information the question of a reform in the law, till he becomes aware of the tyranny which the people are compelled to submit to, and the worse than folly of the class of men who have gradually built up this system of injustice, extortion, vexation, quibble, and protraction. Legislators and judges may, as they too often have done, deceive themselves from the prejudices of legal education and long habit of thinking and acting in a legal routine; they may, as they too often have done, consider law as synonimous with right, and confound the interest of the profession with that of the public. It is high time for the people to say, we will suffer these abuses no more. In this country, and in our own State of South-Carolina, many glaring evils have been remedied or avoided; much has been well, because honestly done; and the violent vituperations of Bentham do not apply with any thing like the force here, that they do in his own country. But look at the present state of the law and its practice in New-York, and who will say that reform is not required? Earnestly do we wish to impress upon our fellow-citizens that the bond and basis of all civil communities, the criterion of the propriety of every public law and every public measure is, the good of society – public utility.

To this rule and criterion, embracing as it does, whatever is honest and just, all human regulations ought to be brought. Whatever will not bear this test, is faulty, and ought to be rejected.

Having thus given a brief specimen of the mode of reasoning adopted by Bentham in one portion of his work, we proceed to another character of the English law; that stares on us on this side of the Atlantic also, with its hideous features: features the delight of the profession, who profess themselves enamoured of their beauty, and exclaim with incomprehensible flattery *in fictione juris consistit equitas:* a phrase which may be translated, *in fictione, juris consistit equitas*, the justice of the law is nothing but fiction.

n. *Of legal fictions.*

When we talk of fiction and falsehood, we apply the former expression to tales, stories, romances, to poetry, to works of imagination like Sir Walter Scott's novels, or Neale's Romance of History. When an untruth is thus used for the purpose of instruction or amusement, and is known to be so used, it carries with it no reprehensible idea; no notion of fraud or circumvention; no one is deceived, no one is injured, no one complains.

But when falsehood is gravely used, where truth is naturally expected – when legal transactions are carried on by fraudulent and false circumlocution, which might have been conducted briefly, honestly and truly – when it is employed to produce expenses, vexation, or delay in serious business – to pick the pocket of one man, in the form of fees improperly exacted, and paid over to another – when it appears as the handmaid and companion of mystery throwing her veil over extortion – this is a culpable use of untruth; it is a fraud and a crime most disgraceful to all concerned in it. But such is the practice, not merely connived at, not sanctioned only, but enjoined and directed by grave and reverend judges on the bench, who sit there under the false and fraudulent pretence of enforcing the precepts of morality by means of the rules of law. Fiction, as useful to justice as swindling is to trade, is the practice of every day in every cause in every court of English law; and I fear, though not to the same extent, perhaps, in most of the courts of the United States. Fiction, invented originally from motives not very justifiable by the judges of that country; and obstinately continued and connived at to the present day, without one justifiable or excusable end in view. In this country we are too apt to adopt without sufficient reflection or discrimination, the whole mass of English authorities good, bad, and indifferent.

To enumerate all the absurd and pocket-picking falsehoods of the English system, in full detail, would fill a volume. A few of them may suffice.

The first process in a civil action in the Court of the King's Bench; "in the custody of the marshal of the Marshalsea of the said court now being." A falsehood invented by the judges of that court to steal business from the others.

The *quo minus* clause in an exchequer writ, a falsehood of the same kind invented by the judges for the like purpose. King's Bench, (says Bentham) stole business from Common Pleas: Common Pleas stole it back from King's Bench. Avowed falsehood the common instrument. B.R. let off one lie: C.B. answered it by another: (exchequer, he might have added, another.) The battle is in all the books. Blacks. Comm: Sellon's Crompton: North's Life of Ld. Keeper Guilford. To the present day, these fraudulent falsehoods are at the very basis of the practice.

Sham bail, and pledges to prosecute John Doe and Richard Roe. Falsehoods. The test in common writs; a falsehood. So is the day of issuing the writ. "You are hereby required personally to be and appear before us on such a day at our court, at &c." The man summoned appears, and stays during every day of the court's session. Judgment goes against him by default for non-appearance. Why so? Because personal appearance does not mean personal appearance. It means that you shall employ an attorney to write a few words in the docket for you; your personal appearance so far from being required, is never noticed even if you are in court from morn till night.

The returns save the last in cases of *latitat:* falsehoods.

The *latitat* assertion never founded on ascertained fact, but assumed.

Fi. fa. frequently, knowingly, falsely returned *nulla bona.*

The nihils in case of *sci. fa.* against bail, falsehoods of regular practice.

The *non est inventus* return of the writ in that process; a regular falsehood.

The common *capias* of C.B. in England, a falsehood.

Declaration filed *de bene esse*: founded on falsehood.

Writ of *nisi prius,* a falsehood.

Record sent under close seal from the superior court to the *nisi prius* court, a swindling deception to enhance fees, as it is always made up, not by the clerk in court under the inspection of the judges, but by plaintiff's attorney.

Writ of trover, a falsehood. Declaration in trover, the same.

Suggestion of bailiff and receiver in account render, generally a fiction.

Declaration of eight courts in *assumpsit,* seven falsehoods.

Declaration in *quare clausum fregit,* laying the quantum of damage, alleged at *libitum,* a falsehood of indefinite exaggeration.

Action *per quod consortium amisit,* often a falsehood, always a mere form.

Action *per quod servitium amisit,* a falsehood.

Common ejectment, a congeries of the queerest and most laughable falsehoods.

Common recoveries and fines the same. To get rid of the statue *de donis* and cheat the legislature,

"The judges formed a plan for making business by enabling the proprietors of entailed estates to cheat their heirs. The King, as it is said, through policy, or perhaps through negligence, gave them their own way. A sham action was brought against the proprietor: the proprietor by direction of the judges, named a creature of theirs, the crier of the court, a man worth nothing, as the man of whom he had bought the land, and who stood bound to prove the title to it a good one, or on failure to give him another estate of equal value. The father lost the land; that is, obtained the power of doing with it what he pleased: but no injury was done to the children, because the father, and through him, they, his children, got the crier's land instead of it. This, the judges, receiving their fees, never failed to testify: it is entered upon the record. A record is the very tabernacle of truth: there is no such thing as averring against a record: let it say what it will, no man is permitted to dispute the truth of it or any part of it.

"Sham equivalent, as above to heirs: sham security to defendants: sham security to plaintiffs: sham notices to both, especially to defendants: sham pretences to one another for cheating one another of business. To give a list and explanation of all these shams, with the consequences drawn from them, would be to heap volume upon volume. – *Benth*. vol. iv. p. 300.

All this is detailed historically by Blackstone, as quite regular and right. Here then, the reverend judges enter into a combination to cheat the legislature; to superseded an act of Parliament; to cheat the heirs of the party praying their aid in this holy design; to cheat his creditors; and derange the policy of the government – why? to obtain for themselves and the profession down to the common crier, business, too complicated and mysterious to be understood out of the profession; too abominable to be suspected by the public; too lucrative not to be cherished; founded on a series of strange and out of the way falsehoods, to which the tales of Munchausen are gospels.

The process of conveyance by way of the fine, *hæc est finalis concordia*, is a fictitious and fraudulent invention of the same kind for the same purposes.

Luckily in this country, the abolition of primogeniture has, in most States, rendered acts of assembly necessary to bar entails: and these have mowed down as with a scythe all these swindling contrivances of the English bench. In Carolina, indeed, conditional fees are yet recognized at common law.

Writs of error, are not always, but generally false pretences to gain time, sold by the judges who know them to be so, and, who, for the sake of the fees and the business attendant on them, connive at and openly sell these fraudulent writs. For instance: The number of causes delayed by appeals on writs of error in two courts, viz. to the King's Bench from the Common Pleas, and from the King's Bench to the Exchequer Chamber, in three years ending in 1797, were 1809. Of these, 550 were brought to the King's Bench, and seven of them argued. To the Exchequer Chamber, 1259, of which twelve were argued. Of course 1790 writs out of 1809, were brought for the mere purpose of delay, without any further proceedings on them. The profit to the Chief Justice of the King's Bench, on the allowance of these writs of error in his court, £1434. The average delay gained by the debtor in fraud of the creditor about twelve months. The Lord Chief Justice of the King's Bench, and the Barons of the Exchequer Chamber, being the contrivers of and the connivers at this base scheme of swindling the debtor out of his money, and delaying the creditor of his just demand.

In the same class of falsehoods, connived at, may be reckoned all dilatory pleas. So, also, all dilatory returns to executions.

The process of outlawry abounds with fiction and absurdity.[3]

It is useless to extend this list: any lawyer can do it for himself. Clients may well view it with dismay: but old members of the profession cling to it as to pearls above all price. The wonder and contempt with which they regard the ignorant men called radicals and reformers – their horror at the modern insane proposals of codification – are all very natural and may be forgiven. They shew, however, that the people need not look to the profession to reform itself: whatever lawyers do, they will do it with such caution and deliberation, that a century will elapse before the effect be apparent: their motto is "festina lentè." To the people must the people look for effectual reform: whenever it shall be attempted, we may afford in this country to proceed with far more moderation than in England. But neither here nor there, ought reform to stop at the cheese-parings and the candle ends.

We omit the barefaced recommendations of the bench to the jury, to commit wilful and deliberate perjury in cases of larceny, to favour criminals, and to supersede and vacate the law of the land instead of recommending its alteration. We omit their offensive and disgraceful quibbles to save notorious and dangerous offenders: we omit the continual perjuries necessary to produce unanimity in the jury box: we refer to Humpherys, to Watkins, and to Parkes for the fruitful topics of frauds, delays, vexations and expenses in Chancery suits and conveyancing, hardly more than just noticed by Bentham; for of legal abuses in that country one may almost literally say, there is no end. Want of space also, compels us to leave untouched many other prolific sources of judicial misconduct; the deciding on the mistakes of technical procedure committed, not by the innocent parties, but by their attornies, the officers of the court, instead of deciding on the merits – the confusion and confliction of courts and jurisdictions – the chicaneries about notice – the jargon of special pleading – the total absence of intelligible simplicity throughout the system – the general mystery and obscurity of the language of the law for the common purpose of all mystery and obscurity, extortion upon the people – the habitual contempt shown to legislative law – the incessant changes made by the judges of laws and of principles by construction and exceptions, till the law and the principle are overwhelmed in the confusion, as in the statute of frauds, the statute of limitations, &c. – their innumerable conflicting decisions, cases overruled, doubted, denied, explained, ignota per ignotiora, until all is resolved into the glorious uncertainty of the law. Every good and honest lawyer will read this with inward acknowledgement of its truth, with lamentation for the existence of these evils, and peradventure with doubts whether the secrets of the craft ought to be thus exposed. Reform must come: but whenever it comes it will defalcate chiefly from the practice and the gains of ignorance and pettifogging; it will leave real knowledge and talent in full permanency of fame and profit.

The parliamentary commission of inquiry into legal actions and proceedings, appointed the 16th day of May, 1829, (9th of Geo. 4.) made a first report 1829, full of good sense so far as it goes, and suggesting some useful alterations. But it is a puny effort; telum imbelle sine ictu. It is the blow of a child against the body of a giant.

Speaking of legal fictions.

"They (the commissioners) take this early opportunity of expressing their opinions upon the general subject of legal *fictions*; to which in the progress of their inquiries, their attention has been much directed. Considered in its origin, it may be thus accounted for. Our ancient institutions having been adapted to a rude and simple state of society, the courts in later times gradually became sensible of defects of jurisdiction, and other inconveniences, to which the altered circumstances of the nation naturally gave rise. In some cases the remedy was applied by legislative regulation; but where this was wanting the judges were *apt to resort to fiction as an expedient for effecting indirectly, that which they had no authority to establish as law.* But to whatever causes the invention or encouragement of legal fiction may be assignable, there is no doubt but they have an injurious effect in the administration of justice, because they tend to bring the law itself into suspicion with the public, as an unsound and delusive system: while an impression of the ridiculous is occasionally excited by them, which must in some measure tend to degrade the science in popular estimation."

All this is very truly, and very leniently said. But what respect are those men entitled to, whose poverty of invention, and habitual propensity to falsehood, render them apt *on every occasion to resort to fiction as an expedient?* "for effecting indirectly that which they had no authority to establish by law." In the name of all that is veracious in legal history, when did these judges ever scruple to assume an authority of establishing by law, even in defiance of the legislature? Are not four parts out of five of the whole mass of the law, bench-made law? Is not all Chancery law of this description? The language employed by the commissioners befits the relative situation of themselves and the judges; but we do not hold it to be for the interests of society, that a system of falsehood built up for purposes of fraud, should be treated with the most circumspect mildness of expression, because the delinquents are or have been men in high station, from whom better things might reasonably have been expected. To us it seems a most degrading state of public institutions, when a court of law can be deliberately converted by its presiding officers into a Lyceum of mendacity.

Indeed these figments are far worse than useless, because they serve, and, indeed, (we are sorry to say) appear intended to put fees into the pockets of judges or their protegeés, barristers, attornies, solicitors, clerks in court, prothonotaries, sheriffs and law officers of all grades and descriptions; to take them out of the pockets of the suitors already harassed and worn down by expenses, delays and vexations, which make them often wish most unfeignedly for a summary proceeding and a Turkish Cadi, as far preferable in point of convenience, dispatch, and cheapness, to their present system. Fortunate, indeed, it is that these evils have given rise to courts of conscience in England: and courts of summary process here in South-Carolina; doors that open to a natural system.

In these United States, where our system is every where far preferable to the British, much yet remains to be reformed. The more our judges keep at a distance from the British code, and the British practice, in our opinion the better. We do not profess to know much of the detail of foreign codes. The Tuscan, the Belgic, the French, are pretty well understood among jurists. We strongly suspect the British is by very many degrees the worst in Europe. No man can read the preliminary debate (in 6 vols.) to the French code Napoleon, or the code itself, or the works of Pothier, without being wiser in the science of law. An English lawyer, does not study law as a branch of national ethics: it is an artificial technical system, to be taught and learnt as a trade, as a shoe-maker learns to make shoes: it has no tendency to enlarge the mind: hence of parliamentary debaters in England, the lawyers hold and ever have held but an inferior rank; and Mr.

Brougham is an acknowledged exception. If they are better in our own country, it is because every lawyer here is, *par metier*, also a politician, but he is not the better politician for being a lawyer: he is apt to look at great questions through a microscope.

In the United States, the judges, lawyers, prothonotaries, recorders, clerks of court, marshals, sheriffs, coroners, magistrates, constables, and juries forming the army of the law, do not amount to less than six thousand, and the expense of the system to not less than six millions of dollars annually, actually paid to these officers in one form or other, and another million is expended in loss of time and expenses to witnesses. The simplification of the law itself – the simplification of its forms of procedure, the saving of salaries, of fees, of time, might in our opinion amount to three millions of dollars annually. A saving, which added to the far more important saving of vexation of every kind suffered by a suitor, is an object not to be set at naught.

o. *Of the certainty of the English law.*

A division of the subject that will of course embrace the American law; for the servility of our adherence to the British precedents, is a feature among our judges and lawyers too well known to be controverted.

Sir Walter Scot, in his Life of Napoleon, speaking of the code of Napoleon, with "that humble prostration of the intellect" so well becoming a courtly writer, with that convenient time-serving deference to the superior wisdom of men in high station, and that profound ignorance of his subject which enables him coolly to state opinions, which his better informed readers cast their eyes on with astonishment – has entered into a laboured panegyric of the British system of law compared with the French code, from p. 54-60. We do not copy the passages. They will be found with most of the authorities we are about to cite in No. 3 of Parkes Jurist, p. 405. Little, indeed, can that man know of the subject in question, who, like Sir Walter Scott, considers English law and jurisprudence as synonymous, who deems a reported decision binding upon future judges *pari casu et in pari delictu*, and thinks it "stamps certainly upon legal principles, and stifles law suits in their birth." "The English law on the other hand (says Sir Walter,) is guarded as appears from Roper's Index, by no less than a thousand decided cases or precedents, each of which affords ground to rule any other case in similar circumstances. In this view, the certainty of the law of England, compared to that of France *bears the proportion of ten to one.* – pp. 58-69. Eng. edit.

Roper's thousand cases of precedents! Why, Greenleaf's collection of cases overruled, doubted or limited, amounted to very near a thousand nine years ago! So little did Sir Walter Scott know about the matter. But all the virtues under heaven may safely be taken for granted, when the object is convenient panegyric. All the lawyers in England profess the same opinion with Sir Walter, and, for centuries past, have persuaded the people of the same thing. What a lazy, creeping, terrapin-footed creature is truth! In the life time-serving, "*booing*," praise-bestowing spirit of disgusting flattery, utterly regardless of historical fact, has a late writer in Pennsylvania, on constitutional law, declared that *party spirit* NEVER *contaminates the judicial bench!* The grave Judges hung down their heads, and glanced at each other in silent confusion, on reading this outrageous specimen of satirical praise! while the gentlemen of the bar actually blushed at the unexpected, unexampled hardihood of assertion of their meek and modest brother!

Two hundred years ago, Lord Bacon declared that the laws were subject to great uncertainties, varieties of opinion, delays and evasions: that the multiplicity and length of suits is increased: that contentious persons are armed, and the honest subject wearied and oppressed: that the Judge is more absolute, who, in doubtful cases, hath a greater stroke and liberty: that the chancery court is more filled, the remedy of law being often obscured and doubtful: that doubts are so frequent and so many, that the ignorant lawyer can shroud his ignorance: that men's assurances of their lands and estates by patents, deeds and wills, are often subject to question, and hollow.

If such was the case two hundred years ago, has any alteration for the better, taken place since that time?

"The author," says Mr. Watkins, in his late treatise on *Copyholds*, "has been brief: and where the subject permitted him, he has endeavoured to extract consistency. This he found, however, not always even to be hoped for. He found reporter against reporter, and case against case. He found consequences continue when their causes had ceased. He found conclusions which justly followed from premises which once existed, applied to instances in which those premises could not exist. He found arbitrary assertion adopted by servility, cherished by prejudice, and at length matured into doctrines whose law could not be questioned, but whose absurdity was too apparent to be denied. It must not, therefore, be wondered at, if, when so situated, he has left the law in all its *glorious uncertainty*. To such uncertainty must it always be subject, while we consider common sense as subservient to precedent, and suffer the blunders of one age to be the criterion of right in another."

If this be true of the small, and purely technical branch of the law relating to copyholds – a division taken at random – how manifestly does Sir Walter betray his profound ignorance in thus panegyrizing the law *en masse?* But let us proceed with the aid of Mr. Parke. We vouch to warranty this gentleman to show that our author, Mr. Bentham, is not singular. Indeed, writers of this description may now say, our name is Legion, for we are many.

"The cases are so contradictory," says Mr. Serjeant Peake, (Law of Evid. p. 146) "that it is impossible to reconcile them."

"I have arranged all the cases, says Lord Mansfield, (Pugh *vs.* D. of Leeds, Cowp. 718) that have been determined in Westminster Hall, in order of time; and when I come to state them, you will be surprised to see how little they stand in the way as binding authorities against justice, reason and common sense. All they show is, the *great uncertainty of the meaning*, and the impossibility of putting an absolute sense to hold good in all cases: they are themselves so many *contradictions backwards and forwards.*" After marshalling the conflicting cases, he says, "thus stood all the authorities down to the year 1743, a period of two hundred years; not much to the honour of Westminster Hall, to embarrass a point which *a plain man of common sense and understanding would have had no difficulty in construing.*" (Pugh *vs.* D. of Leeds, Cowp. 718.) Yet does Mr. Powel, in his treatise on Powers, controvert this very decision of Lord Mansfield, through a hundred pages. It turned on the meaning to be given to the word "from."

"*There is so great contradiction in decisions* respecting the boundaries of evidence," says Mr. Justice Ashurst, in Bent *vs.* Baker, 3 T.R. 34.

"It seems to me," says Lord Eyre, in Barnes *vs.* Crowe, 1 Vez. jun. 495, that these two cases are in direct opposition to each other.

"These two decisions are in direct opposition to each other in principle," says Lord Ellenborough, Keen *vs.* Dormay, 15 East, 168. Again, the same Judge, in Leicester *vs.* Lockwood, 1 M. & S. 533, speaking of the Annuity Act, says, "We have not to struggle with the Act of Parliament, *but with decisions.* They are so many and so potent, that I feel it my duty to look into them, *in order to guide myself through the quicksands which they have opposed to the attainment of justice.*" On another occasion he remarks, (Rangers *vs.* E. of Chesterfield, 5 M. & S.5,) "so much ingenuity has been expended upon the construction of the act, that *doubts have been raised where otherwise they could not have arisen.*" (For "quicksands," read "bulwarks," *meo periculo*, says Sir W. Scott.)

"But, surely, (continues the Jurist,) it cannot be necessary to multiply authorities: (we say so too; if they be necessary, take up Greenleaf, and proceed, case by case, through his eighty-eight pages of about ten cases to the page, all bearing upon the point now before us.) How could it fall out otherwise? How is it possible that decisions should be uniform and consistent, when the very persons who pronounce them, are not agreed as to the nature and sources of the *Common Law*, upon which the greater part of the decisions profess to be founded? One declares the principles of private justice, moral fitness, and public convenience make *Common Law* without a precedent; another, that it is drawn from natural and moral philosophy, from the civil and canon law, from logic, from the use of custom and conversation among men, collected out of the general disposition, nature and condition of human kind: a third says, that immemorial usage alone constitutes it; a fourth, that it is what is agreeable to the principles of right and wrong, the fitness of things, convenience and policy." Millar *vs*. Taylor, 4 Burr. Rep. 2303, by the four judges, Willis, Aston, Yates, and Lord Mansfield. A fifth declares it is what is to be found in the opinions of lawyers, delivered as axioms, or to be collected from universal and immemorial usage; per Lord Kenyon, in Ball *vs*. Herbert, 3 T.R. 261. Blundell *vs*. Catterall, 5 B. and Ald. 268. A sixth says, that common error is its source; *communis error facit jus*; Holt, C.J. India Co. *vs*. Skinner. Comberbach, 342. Did not Lord Mansfield say, in derision of ancient common law decisions, "we do not sit here to take our law from Siderfin and Kebler?" Did he not also proscribe every case in Bernardiston? 2 Burr. Rep. 1142, note. We pray now, Mr. Jurist, do permit us to add another source of the common law; it is throughout bench-made, bench-enacted law. *Quod judicibus placuit, legis habeat vigorem*; and to this assigned source of that camelion, the common-law, we challenge denial.

"The practiques or adjudged cases, (says Sir Walter Scott, pp. 59, 60) in fact, form a breakwater, as it were, to protect the more formal bulwark of the statute law; and although they cannot be regularly jointed or dove-tailed together, (does he mean codified?) each independent decision fills its space in the mound, and offers a degree of resistance to innovation, and protection to the law, in proportion to its own weight and importance." What a pity it is, that this elegant collection of jointed and dove-tailed metaphors, should be so profound as to be unintelligible! How happy would Martinus Scriblerus have been to have dove-tailed this passage into his treatise περι βαθχς! These *bulwarks* of Sir Walter, Lord Ellenborough, as we have seen, terms *quicksands*.

"But we regard (says Sir Walter) the multitude of precedents in English law, as eminently favourable, not only to the certainty of the law, but to the liberty of the subject; and especially as a check upon any judge who might be disposed to innovate." See the rest of the passage to the same purpose, pp. 60-62. So then, all past judges are learned and wise; and checks upon the unlearned, unwise, and unconscientious judges of modern days! This may be true; but every sound lawyer, by the courtesy of the profession, takes for granted that all living judges are learned, wise, and upright, although he knows full well, with melancholy certainty, that this cannot truly be said of any given batch of past judges.

We shall borrow no more from this number (3) of the Jurist, but refer to it (p. 415) for instances of the contemptuous disregard shown to acts of the legislature, as well as to former decisions of their predecessors, by judges on the bench. To the list there given, we add all the changes made in the statute *de donis*, the statute of frauds, the statute of limitations, the annuity act, *cum multis aliis*. Let any lawyer examine the history of the rule in Shelley's case, the rule in Twines' case, the rule in Walton and Shelley, the infinite contrariety of decisions on the construction of wills, the admission of parol testimony in cases of written evidence, the history of the doctrine of notice, &c. &c. and he will be compelled to acknowledge, that decisions, *a parte ante*, are as chaff before the wind, whenever it suits a judge to get rid of them. Sir Thomas More is said to have puzzled a continental disputant ready to take up any thesis, *de omni scibile et de quolibet ente*, by the question, *an averia carucæ capta in witherno sint irreplegiabilia?* We too have a strong inclination to offer a puzzle-peg to Sir Walter Scott, who seems desirous, like the German logician, of passing himself off for a man of all kind of knowledge, and to know far more of the law than any good lawyer will dare to adopt on his authority; it is this – whence comes the toast never omitted at a circuit feast, *the glorious uncertainty of the law?*

We do not put much faith in prophecy, but we would venture a small wager, that the next edition of Greenleaf's book, including all the English and all the American cases doubted, denied, limited or explained away, will comprehend not fewer than twelve hundred.

We will close this part of the subject, by an extract from the "Times" newspaper of July 25, 1827. Lord Eldon, in defence of his proverbial habits of procrastination, was fond of recording such instances as the following: –

"The late Lord Thurlow, he used to say, once sent a question for the opinion of the Court of King's Bench, to which Lord Kenyon, then Lord Chief Justice, returned an answer so little satisfactory to the Chancellor, that he sent it back with a request that it might be reconsidered. Lord Kenyon was somewhat surprised at such a proceeding, but he did reconsider the subject; and the result was, he did give an opinion directly opposite to the first. I, myself, (Lord Eldon would add) at another time requested the Court of King's Bench to certify me their opinion as to the estate which a person took in some lands. The Court was unanimously of opinion that he took an estate in fee-simple. I was not satisfied with that opinion, and sent the case to the Common Pleas, the Judges of which Court were unanimously of opinion that he took no estate at all in the lands in question. Now, I was impertinent enough to think they were all wrong. I made an order at variance with the opinions of both courts, and my decision satisfied all the parties concerned."

Lloyd *vs.* Johnes, 9 Vez. 37. Lord Redesdale's book, says Lord Eldon, is a wonderful effort to collect what is to be deduced from authorities speaking so little what is clear, that the surprise is not from the difficulty of understanding all he has said, but that so much can be understood.

We extract the following from the "New-York Evening Post," of March 30, 1830:

Glorious uncertainty of the Law. – A writer in the 'National Intelligencer,' has had the curiosity to examine the Reports of the Supreme Court of the United States, for the purpose of ascertaining what proportion of causes have been affirmed and what reversed. He has stated, in a tabular form, the results of his examination of the Reports of Dallas, Cranch, Wheaton, and the first and second volume of Peters; and from his statement, it appears, that the whole number of cases in which the Supreme Court has either affirmed or reversed the judgments of the Courts below, including the cases of 1829, is 754. Of these, 425 have been affirmed, and the rest, 329, reversed. This gives an average of affirmances equal to 56⅛ per cent. The two states, the decision of whose courts seem to have fared the best, are New-Jersey and Maryland, from each of which, four cases were carried up, and all affirmed. On the other hand, Indiana and Missouri carried up but two, and they were both reversed. Of thirty-two from Rhode-Island, sixteen were affirmed, and as many reversed; and of forty-five from Georgia, twenty-five decisions, or 55 5-9ths per ct. were reversed. These things go far to show how great is what is termed 'the glorious uncertainty of the law;' and when this, the 'law's delay,' and the enormous expenses of litigation are added, it would really seem as if one might better decide a contested question by the turn of a copper, and learn the issue at once, than trust it to the tedious and uncertain ordeal of a trial before a court of law. There is one thing, however, to be taken into the account, which we should not omit to mention. The cases which are reversed or affirmed by the Supreme Court, are but a few of those on which judgments are pronounced by the Courts below; and as the parties, in a great majority of instances, concur in the decisions, it is to be presumed, that they are such as admit no hinge or loop to hang a doubt on. Though the expense and vexation attending appeals, may prevent litigation, and no doubt frequently does so."

Of Chancery. – 4 Benth. 324 et seq. Suits in Equity are in England commenced under one or other, generally, of two pretences: both of them in nine cases out of ten, notorious falsehoods.

And forasmuch as your orator is wholly without remedy at common law in respect to the premises, &c.

And forasmuch as your orator is unable to account with the receivers of our lord, the now king, by reason of the nonpayments and nonperformance aforesaid, &c.

After the king's courts of common law had been for some centuries in operation, the suitors began to find out that common law was one thing, and common justice a very different thing. The obstinacy of the common law judges refused to remedy this crying evil. Hence, gradually the Chancellor undertook the cognizance of causes, where in the courts of law, the suitors sowed money, and reaped nothing but feudal fictions, and Norman quibbles. By degrees the Court of Chancery proceeding on the same notices with the Courts of Law, namely, to institute modes of practice and procedure, having for their prime object extortion, vexation and delay, has become a far greater nuisance than any court of law whatever. No man who knows the history of Lord Eldon's administration as Chancellor, will venture to deny this.

Lord Thurlow alone, a very inefficient lawyer, and a most unprincipled politician, received from 1811 to 1826, as patentee of the bankrupt office, (one small department of chancery jurisdiction) £114,656 11*s*.1½*d*. to his own share out of £164,066 12*s*.11*d*.

sterling received at that office during that period: besides £434 70s.19d. and £23,298 on other pretences in that department, which we cannot explain. – See 2 *Jurist*, p. 320.

At this moment the property locked up in chancery belonging to suitors, may fairly be reckoned at forty millions of pounds sterling, or 170,600,000 dollars! According to Mr. Cooper's late account of the practice of the Court of Chancery (1828) a common suit by legatees or creditors cannot be terminated in less than five years, even supposing its duration be not prolonged by exceptions to the master's report, or appeals from interlocutory and final orders. But as generally happens, if these litigations take place, for five years, you may read fifteen or five and twenty. "Why Mr. Dramatist (says a reader of a manuscript tragedy) your hero and heroine are in such profound distress in the fourth act, that you have left no misery to inflict in the fifth." Pardon me, said the play writer, I will throw them into Chancery."

What is Chancery? a court where the complainant and defendant commence their litigation by bill and answer. For where the line of distinction between Chancery and Common Law is to be drawn who can tell?

The Chancellor claims, 1st, common law jurisdiction. 2nd, Equity jurisdiction. 3rd, Statutory jurisdiction. 4th, Especially delegated jurisdiction.

1st. Common Law Jurisdiction. For this, see Maddock's Treatise on the principles and practice of the High Court of Chancery, vol. i. ch. 1.

2nd. Equity Jurisdiction. Accident: account: fraud: infant: specific performance: trusts. In the three first of these, the Common Law courts claim jurisdiction also.

3rd. Statutory Jurisdiction. Bankruptcies: tythes: trusts, include public charities and corporations. Jews: infant trustees and mortgages. See several other enumerated in Parkes history of the Court of Chancery, 424.

4th. Specially Delegated Jurisdiction. Idiots and lunatics. Censor morum. Licenser of the press. (See the very acme of judicial folly in Lord Eldon's decision in the case of Lawrence's Lectures. Lawrence *v.* Smith, March 1822.)

The *Wellesley case*, and that of Blythe Shelley, establish the Chancellor's jurisdiction as censor morum, the arguments and sarcasms of the bar notwithstanding. As a sample of expense, Lord Wellesley before the termination of the cause relating to the abstraction of his children, had paid £5,500. To be sure this is nothing: the present Mr. Watt informed us that previous to the last decision of Watt *v.* Hornblower, and Hornblower *v.* Watt, for infringement of Mr. Watt's patent right in his steam engine, he had paid in fees and law expenses £11,000 sterling. The law is open to the rich and the poor said the judges: "so is the London Tavern, said Horne Tooke: but you must have gold in your pocket before you can venture in."

We have seen something of the glorious uncertainty of the law. How stands the Court of Chancery as to this point.

From 1 *Blackstone Comm, Intro.* § 2. & 3.

Equity thus depending essentially upon the particular circumstances of each individual case, there can be no established rules and fixed principles of Equity laid down, without destroying its very essence, and reducing it to positive law.

What equity is, and how impossible in its very essence to be reduced to stated rules hath been shown in the preceding section.

From 3 *Blackstone, Comm. ch.* 27.

Once more, it hath been said that a Court of Equity is not bound by rules and precedents, but acts from the opinion of the judge, founded on the circumstances of every particular case. Whereas the system of our Courts of Equity is a laboured connected system governed by established rules, and bound down by precedents, from which they do not depart, although the reason of some of them may perhaps be liable to objection.

So far Blackstone. But what say other sages of Chancery law?

Per Lord Keeper Bridgeman. Parkes, 459.

Certainly precedents are very necessary and useful to us, for in them we may find the reason of the equity to guide us: and besides, the authority of those that made them is much to be regarded: we should suppose they did it on great consideration and weighing of the matter: and it would be very strange and very ill if we should disturb and set aside what hath been the course for a long series of time and ages.

By Lord Chief Justice Vaughan. – Argument on the case in Chancery Term Pasch. 22. ch. 2. Parkes 459.

I wonder to hear of citing of precedents in matters of Equity: for if there be equity in a case, that equity is an universal truth and there can be no Precedent in it: so that in any precedent that can be produced, if it be the same with this case, the reason and equity is the same in itself; and if the precedent be not the same case with this, it is not to be cited, as being nothing to the purpose.

In Bochm and De Tastet, 1 Vez. and Beames, 326, Lord Eldon admits that even the orders of the court may be nullified and reversed by long continued dissonant practice.

For the gross and manifold abuses that the Equity practice allows suitors to put in force against each other, (see Mr Vizard's letter to W. Courtenay, Esq. London, 1824.)

This bungling intermixture of common law jurisdiction and equity jurisdiction, of Saxon law, and feudal law, and Roman law, and anomalous bench-made law, and statutory law is a system of ignorance and incongruity unknown elsewhere in Europe. It is in part gotten rid of in some among the United States, as in Massachusetts, in Pennsylvania, and far better than all, put together in the simple and natural code and practice of Louisiana; thanks to Edward Livingston.

Why should we have one set of courts for quibbles, and another for common sense? Why should we try cases by jury in one set of courts, and without jury in another? Why should we have *viva voce* testimony in one court, and affidavit testimony in another? Why when a suit is nearly terminated in a court of law, shall a party be permitted to renew it for half a dozen years more in a court of equity? Why shall better testimony (by examination and cross-examination) in a court of law, be overthrown by worse testimony in a court of equity? Why shall the evidence of the parties be excluded in a court of law, and admitted in a court of equity? And if admitted, why admitted under circumstances that nullify is value, and give every temptation, and every latitude to mendacity and perjury? without *viva voce* inquiry, without cross-examination, or confrontation, and with leisure to suit the evidence to the interest of the party it is intended to serve.

If lawyers find reason to be enamoured of that incredible mass of contradiction and of barbarism called English law, and of a judiciary establishment, consisting, "of equity judges common law judges, civil law judges, ecclesiastical judges, criminal judges, judges with juries, judges without juries, grand jurymen, common jurymen, special jurymen, sheriffs and sheriff's jurymen, coroners and their jurymen, justices of the peace for criminal matters, justices of the peace for civil matters, the peers in parliament who are a court of appeals, the court of exchequer a court of appeals, the court of the king's bench a court of appeal, courts of bankruptcy before commissioners, courts for insolvent debtors, courts of conscience, courts of requests, courts leet, courts baron, county courts." (no. 4, Jurist 36) – if lawyers are in love with this complication of remedies, almost all of them diseases of an intolerable character, there is no good reason why the public should be in love with it, even in England. In these United States, much has been remedied, curtailed and improved; much, very much remains to be so, existing at present a curse upon the community. But does it not work well, said a lawyer to us, with whom we were arguing the point – Yes; well enough for the profession, ill enough for the people.

Judge (Chancellor) Kent of New-York, a very good lawyer of the old school, says somewhere, that it will require the labour of a long life to qualify a man to become a common law judge: and the labour of a long life to qualify a man to become an equity judge. This, however, can be gotten over, on Cicero's definition of persona – *Ego unus gero tres personas.* So the barons of the Exchequer, are animals *bipartiti;* one half of each of them is an equity judge, the other half a common law judge. So in our Federal Courts, Judge Marshall, Judge Story, and their brethren, are of the same description: common law judges one morning, equity judges the next. Heaven knows how they contrive as to Chancellor Kent's objection. They become suddenly, we suppose, and intuitively, ex-officio vested with a long life's worth of knowledge, which they never spent an hour in acquiring before. There are some questions, however, relating neither to common law nor to equity, which they would fain get hold of if the people were idiots enough to permit them. But the sovereign people of each State, must reserve their own sovereignty to themselves, undegraded by this all-grasping tribunal.

Speculations on Reform. – Hints only, suggestions, and those very brief are alone in our power. But they are not suggestions hit off at random and on the spur of the occasion: they are the result with us of much observation, much conversation, and much reflection.

The hateful word codification has been employed. It is a word taken from the civil law, expressing that what has been done with that law, may with like reason be done with our law. The French have adopted it: the code Napoleon, so much calumniated by the bigots of the profession, is considered in France as a blessing to the nation, and is the basis of the modern codes of the most enlightened portion of Europe. We say without hesitation, that the sneers and sarcasms with which it has been treated, the assertions and prophecies of its uselessness, are the offspring of gross and impudent ignorance, silenced in England, by more accurate information of Continental facts; and uttered here in hopes of finding abettors more ignorant than those who abuse that code: a discovery not easy to be made.

We have already the excellent digest of Comyns; we have already, half a hundred treatises on separate branches of the law, of which the pith and marrow might be comprized in one tenth of the compass, because the illustrative cases need not be copied. Why might not a committee divide the whole law into separate heads and branches, and collect under each the actual decisions of the courts, and no more? beginning with statute law. When this is done, why not enact this collection by legislative authority? Why is one law to consist chiefly of judge-made law – alterable according to the talents or the want of talents, the knowledge or the ignorance of a presiding judge? Oh! but doubts and decisions and cases upon cases will still arise in never ending profusion as heretofore. Will they? appoint then a decennial committee of revision, and you cure the evil. Let that committee suggest what alterations appear to them desirable.

But the great reform is that adopted in Louisiana. Substitute a national system in lieu of a technical system. Let the one sole bearing of the system be the search after the real merits of the question. Extend, therefore, the principle of the imperfect statutes of Jeofail, till nullification for a technical mistake shall be heard of no more.

Let the first process in every suit, be a distinct and accurate statement of the plaintiff's claim filed in the office as a ground for a summons, and a copy served on the defendant, requiring him in his own proper person to meet the plaintiff in court on a given day. Let each be heard and examined before the judge on his oath, and their respective admissions and denials put down in writing. Let the judge say, when they shall again appear to have their cause tried; before a jury if facts be denied, before himself if law be in question. Let the expense of proving a point denied, fall upon that party who is in the wrong. Let all costs be *real* costs, not *taxed* costs: this of itself would wring the truth out of the parties; and would be no more than justice. Let the parties, themselves, the very best of all witnesses, because they know most of the transaction, and all other witnesses who can throw light on the case, be admitted, under the observations of counsel and the charge of the judge as to the probable effect of bias. Let them be examined and cross-examined on oath.

I have said on oath. I recant. Punish mendacity committed in court, as you now punish perjury: not perjury. The crime against society, is not the offence against the Deity: who without our impious intermeddling, will punish or not punish as to his infinite justice and mercy may seem fit. The evil is, injustice from misdecision: the crime is, mendacity in open court, producing or meant to produce, misdecision and injustice. This is the only offence against society; let society punish it *eo nomine*, and leave perjury to the cognizance of that tribunal with which society has no right to interfere.

Abolish your Court of Chancery: give chancery powers to common law courts, and make a court of law what it ought to be, a court of justice. Why may not a court of law direct a bill of discovery, a bill to perpetuate testimony, specific performance of contracts, writs of estrepement of waste, ne exeats, and process to call parties into court, where, under the *viva voce* system we now propose, as many minutes would suffice in most instances to settle the justice of the case, as it now takes months or years.

Let your *civil* causes be the exclusive business of one description of courts: your *criminal* causes of another: extend the principle of arbitration, and the powers of arbitrators, and enable this mode of trial (as by the act of William and Mary) to take place under rule of court in all cases where the parties are agreed to arbitrate. Let two decisions by jury out of three, be a final settlement of the cause. If civil causes should occasion too great a press of business, questions relating to marriage-contract and marriage-rights, wills, minors and orphans, executors, administrators and guardians, idiots and lunatics, insolvents, and other straggling portions of chancery powers might make a third set of courts. Let your judges sit, *de die in diem*, during nine months of the year, and make every writ returnable at as short an interval as convenience will permit, a week for instance: for under a preliminary *viva voce* examination of the parties, the time for trial might be fixed by the judge as the circumstances of the case required.

Under a reformed system, it might be worth while to inquire, whether a fewer number than twelve might not constitute a jury. We are aware of the cogent arguments from their being twelve signs of the zodiac, twelve months in the year, twelve apostles, &c. but we doubt whether these ought to be considered as conclusive. Nor is it quite certain that the jury ought to be driven to tossing up, calculating averages, and such other devices to get over the objection of unanimity, so often the parent of perjury. Nor are we satisfied of the indispensable necessity of a grand jury. The system of law is at best sufficiently onerous to the community, without increasing the burthen unnecessarily by this very imperfect, and as it seems to us, useless tribunal.

Oh! but all this is the wild dream of a reformer! Is it so? Have you been in a court in Louisiana lately? If not, keep your assertion to yourself, till you have seen how much of all this can be beneficially accomplished, how easily, and to the people how satisfactorily.

NOTES

1 Take the following as a specimen of Mr. Bentham's language and mode of treating a subject: – "Facts at large, whether considered as principal or as evidentiary, may be divided into classes, according to several different modes of division.

"If, on the occasion of judicial procedure in general, and the evidence elicited for the purpose of it, no practical benefit were derivable from the considering facts in this point of view, and under these distinctions, the mention of them would not have found its place in this work. But the conception entertained respecting the nature of the facts, in relation to which evidence will come to be elicited, and the nature of the evidence so applied, and the application made of it, would, without close attention to these distinctions, be inadequate, and, in practice, delusive.

"Applying, as they will be seen to do, to every part of the field of thought and action, including that of art and science, the instruction, if any, which may be found derivable from them, will not be the less useful in practice.

"Applying, as they will be seen to do, to judicial procedure, sometimes directly, sometimes through the medium of the correspondent substantive branch of law; the utility of the mention here made of them, will not be diminished by any application which may be capable of being made of it to any other portion of the field of art and science.

"I. *Distinction the first.* – Facts physical, facts psychological.

"The source of the division here is, the sort of beings in which the fact is considered as having its seat.

"A physical fact is a fact considered to have its seat in some inanimate being; or, if in an animate being, by virtue not of the qualities by which it is constituted animate, but of those which it has in common with the class of inanimate beings.

"A psychological fact is a fact considered to have its seat in some animate being; and that, by virtue of the qualities by which it is constituted animate.

"Thus, motion, considered simply as such, when predicated of any being, is a physical fact; true, it is an attribute of animate beings, but not in virtue of those qualities which constitute them animate, since it is equally an attribute of inanimate ones.

"But if, to the word motion, we add the word voluntary, we then introduce, over and above the physical fact of the motion, another fact, viz. an exertion of the *will*, considered as preceding and causing the motion. This last fact is a psychological fact; since it is not capable of having its seat in any other than animate beings; nor in them, by virtue of any other qualities, than those by which they are considered animate.

"Of these two simple facts – one a physical, the other a psychological fact – is composed the complex fact, *voluntary motion;* a fact of a mixed character, partly physical, partly psychological.

"The classification and arrangement of physical facts must be left to natural philosophers. The classification and arrangement of psychological facts must, in like manner, be left to metaphysicians. It may not be improper, however, to give in this place, a short indication of some of the principal classes of psychological facts.

"1. Sensations. – Feelings having their seat in some one or more of the five senses; sight, hearing, smell, taste and touch.

"Sensations again may be subdivided into those which are pleasurable, those which are painful, and those which, not being attended with any considerable degree of pleasure or pain, may be called indifferent.

"2. Recollections: the recollections or remembrances of past sensations.

"3. Judgments: that sort of psychological fact which has place when we are said to assent to, or dissent from a proposition.

"4. Desires: which, when to a certain degree strong, are termed passions.

"5. Volitions, or acts of the will, &c.

"II. *Distinction the second.* – Events and states of things. Source of the division in this case, the distinction between a state of motion and a state of rest.

"By a fact is meant the existence of a portion of matter inanimate or animate, either in a state of motion, or in s state of rest.

"Take any two objects whatever, consider them at any two successive points of time; they have, during these two portions of time, been either at rest with relation to each other, or one of them has, with relation to the other, been in motion; has, in the course of that length of time, changed its place.

"The truth is, that as far as we are able to judge, all portions of matter, great and small together, are at all times in motion; for in this case is the orb on which we exist, and as far as we can judge, all others which come under the cognizance of our senses. When, therefore, in speaking of any portion of matter, rest is attributed to it, the rest ascribed to it, cannot be understood in any other sense than a relative one.

"Whether they or one of them, be in motion, or whether both of them be at rest, any two portions of matter may be considered, and spoken of, in relation to one another; and in this case, the most obvious and simple relation, is the relation of distance.

"Thus it is then, that considered in the most simple state in which it can be a subject or object of consideration, a fact may be either a state of things or a motion, and under one or other of these descriptions it cannot but come.

"By an event is meant some motion, considered as having actually come about, in the course of nature. Thus, whatever be the occasion, the ordinary subjects of consideration and discourse come under the general denomination of states of things, or events, or both.

"The fall of a tree is an event, the existence of the tree is a state of things; both are alike facts.

"An act or action is a name given to an event in so far as it comes to be considered as having had the human will for the immediate cause of it.

"A fact then, or a matter of fact, is either the existence of two or more beings, considered in relation to one another, as being in a state of rest during successive portions of time, or an event; in the idea of which event is uniformly included that of motion on the part of some portion of matter, *i.e.* a change in its relative position to, and distance from, some other portion of matter.

"An act or action, a human act, a human action, is either external or purely internal. In the instance of an external act, there must of necessity be something of complictaion; for to the external action of the body, or some part of it, must have been added an antecedent act of the will; an internal act, but for which it would have been on the footing of those motions which are exhibited by the unanimated, and even by the unorganized ingredients in the composition of such parts of the world as are perceptible to us.

"An internal act may, on the other hand, be of the simplest kind, unattended by any motion on the part of any portion of matter exterior to the individual whose act it is.

"It being understood that it is to the mind that it is ascribed and attributed, the term motion may still be employed in the designation of it, although in what happens in the mind upon the occasion in question, no change of place can be observed: for, in speaking of what passes in the mind, we must be content, for the most part, to employ the same language as that which we employ in speaking of what passes in and about the body, or we could not in any way make it the subject of discourse.

"III. *Distinction the third.* – Facts positive and negative.

"In this may be seen a distinction which belongs not, as in the former cases, to the nature of the facts themselves, but to that of the discourse which we are under the necessity of employing in speaking of them.

"In the existence of this or that state of things, designated by a certain denomination, we have a positive, or say, an affirmative fact; in the non-existence of it, a negative fact.

But the non-existence of a negative fact is equivalent to the existence of the correspondent and opposite positive fact, and unless this sort of relation be well noted and remembered, great is the confusion that may be the consequence.

"The only really existing facts are positive facts; a negative fact is the non-existence of a positive one, and nothing more; though in many instances, according to the mode of expression commonly employed in the speaking of it, the real nature of it is disguised. Thus, by *health*, is meant nothing more than the absence, the non-existence of disease; by *minority*, the individual's non-arrival at a certain age; by *darkness*, the absence of light; and so on.

"For satisfying himself whether in the case of a certain fact, it is the existence or the non-existence, the presence or the absence of it, the course a man may take, is to figure to himself the corresponding image; he will then perceive whether, by the expression in question it is the presence or the absence of that same image, that is indicated, and brought to view."

This is, indeed, following to a letter the advice of the Frenchman: Enfin mon ami, il faut tonjours commencer par le commencement.

One other passage of mystification and we have done. – V. 4. p. 256. "Idea of a system of pleading adapted to the ends of justice."

"He who has a right to any subject of property – immoveable or moveable, sum of money to be paid him by some one else, service of any other sort to be rendered by a determinate individual – is he in whose favour some one in the list of *events or states of things*, having, with reference to that right, the effect of *collative* (or say *investitive*) events, or states of things, has taken place: no article in the list of those to which with reference to the same right, the law has given the effect of *ablative* (or say *divestitive*) events or states of things, having subsequently taken place in his case."

Mr. Bentham complains with equal justice and severity of the language of the English law, the system of jargonizing, as he calls it. If such specimens as we have presented, do not fall under the head of mystification or jargonizing, we are wonderfully mistaken.

2 Morning Post and Morning Chronicle, Nov. 18, 1803.

3 At the late governor M'Kean's table, we heard his son-in-law, the Marquis D'Yrajo relate this story.

"About the time when the excitement in London occasioned by John Wilkes and the Middlesex election took place, that gentleman having left the kingdom, a writ of outlawry was issued and pursued to the extent of outlawry. His friends thought it best that he should return and endeavour to get the proceedings reversed. He did so. The question of the validity of the proceedings came on in the Court of King's Bench, on a day appointed, and Mr. Serjeant Glynn argued the case as counsel for Mr. Wilkes, who sat by his side. The bench was crowded with nobility, and distinguished foreigners, among whom was our ambassador from the court of Spain, who, on his return to his house wrote to the Spanish Government an account of this transaction. "I was in court (says he): I sat near Lord Mansfield, the chief judge of the kingdom: the whole Court was crowded by characters of rank and eminence. Mr. Wilkes was in court: he sat by his counsel opposite to Lord Mansfield. When Mr. Wilkes' counsel had finished his argument, Mr. Wilkes stood up with a design of addressing the judges. Lord Mansfield said to him, Mr. Wilkes, sit down: Mr. Wilkes, however, persisted, when the chief judge told him, Mr. Wilkes, you ought to know better, Sir, you are not in court."

No wonder, said the Ambassador, in his despatches, that these people are heretics, and deny the holy mystery of the real presence, when the chief justice of England can say to a man standing before him, Sir, you are not here!

5

[Hugh Swinton Legaré]

'Jeremy Bentham and the Utilitarians'

Southern Review, vol. VII, no. XIV (August 1831), pp. 261–96

in

Writings of Hugh Swinton Legaré,
2 vols. (Charleston, S.C. 1846), II. 449–81

JEREMY BENTHAM AND THE UTILITARIANS.

Principles of Legislation; from the MS. of Jeremy Bentham, Bencher of Lincoln's Inn. By M. DUMONT. Member of the Representative and Sovereign Council of Geneva. Translated from the second corrected and enlarged edition; with Notes and a Biographical Notice of Jeremy Bentham and of M. Dumont. *By John Neal. Boston.* 1831.

WE do not know whether the publication of this book is to be considered as any proof of the growing popularity of Bentham and Utilitarianism in the United States. But sure we are—if we know any thing of the state of public opinion in this country—that it will do nothing to increase that popularity. The author professes himself, every where, a devoted admirer of his "guide, philosopher and friend," yet it is difficult to conceive a more ridiculous figure than he makes him cut in his pages. It is just such a portrait as a very wicked or very simple *valet de chambre* might be expected to paint of a very absurd hero. If Sancho Panza, for instance, had written the Life of Don Quixote, with that odd indescribable mixture of reverence and suspicion which runs through his conversations with the knight, it would have been much of a-piece with the biographical sketch before us. Mr. John Neal, indeed, prostrates himself devoutly before his idol—exalts and magnifies him above all Greek and Roman fame—pronounces him, as Lucretius does Epicurus, the great light of the world, and its redeemer from spiritual bondage—yet, when we survey the whole picture together, it is hard to believe that there is not a good deal of waggery in these lofty expressions of homage. We do not think there is a Life in Diogenes Laertius—and that is saying much—which makes philosophy, in the person of one of her most renowned votaries, so despicable and repulsive.

The style in which the author tells his story is full of a quaint pedantic affectation of simplicity. He is as confiding and communicative as "downright Shippen or as old Montaigne." He talks to his reader as if he were writing an epistle to one of Jeremy's private secretaries, and as if the world had nothing to think of but the "High Priest of Legislation and the Lord Bacon of the age." The excessive importance which he attaches to every thing connected with the Reformer and his dogmas redounds, of course, upon his humble self. But he

does not trust to distant inference for his share in the honours of the school. His self-conceit is fully commensurate with his admiration of his betters, and he takes care to garnish his panegyric upon his master with an abundance of garrulous egotism. Nobody understands Bentham but Mr. John Neal—"the readers (and the *writers*) of the Edinburgh, Quarterly, Westminster and North-American Reviews, will *now* have, what they never had before—an opportunity of knowing the truth and the whole truth, about the character and opinions, the philosophy and the faith of a man," &c. His object, as he announces it in his preface, is twofold. By the first part of his work, "which is nothing more than a familiar biographical sketch," his readers are to be "brought acquainted with the *man* Jeremy Bentham, and by the *last*, which may be regarded as an abridgment of his whole system of philosophy, with the philanthropist, the lawgiver and the statesman." We hope he knows more about "the *man* Jeremy," than he seems to understand of his translator's language. At page 271, we observe the following *naïve* confession of ignorance, accompanied by, what appears to us, a very sufficient exemplification of it:—"Thus every act of cruelty produced by a passion, the principle of which is in every heart and from which every body may suffer, may cause an alarm which will continue until the punishment of the offender *has removed the danger from the side of injustice.* * * * * * * * *"
Upon which we have the following note:—"The meaning of this I have not been able to make out, with any sort of satisfaction to myself. It reads thus in the original, 'fera éprouver une alarme qui continuera jusqu' à ce que la punition du coupable ait transporté le *danger du côté de l'injustice, de l'inimitié cruelle.*'" Whatever we may think of the style, the meaning of this passage is clear enough from the context. Jeremy, or rather Dumont, is speaking of the terror which the unrestrained indulgence of certain passions would inspire. This alarm, he says, will continue until the punishment of one who has sinned through the influence of such passions, has inspired him, and those like him, with fear, in their turn—until "injustice and malignant hatred" are made, by the law, to feel some of the terror they occasion; literally, "until the punishment of the guilty has transferred the danger *to* the side of injustice," &c. It is strange that any one should set up for an interpreter of French who does not know the effect of the *du* in the phrase, *du côté de*, and it is lamentable to reflect that we, the *uninitiated*, have no other means of understanding the inestimable Benthamee, but the translation of a translation by such a druggerman as Mr. John Neal.

The drift of this attempt upon the Life of Jeremy Bentham, is thus explained by the biographer himself.

"Such a portrait is now to be attempted for the lovers of such biography. It will be for them to say whether a magnificent picture, which, by resembling every body, would be a *portrait* of nobody, is worthier of admiration. It may be wanting in dignity—*I hope it may*—but of this the reader may be sure: whatever it wants in dignity shall be made up in truth; and in such truth too as will soon be sought after with deep solicitude, not only here, and in the country of our philosopher, but throughout the whole earth.

"After a few preliminary observations, I shall take up a body of memoranda, now lying before me, which were made every night, and before I slept, after we had passed the evening together, and transferred them, with as little change as possible, directly to these pages. They, therefore, who wish to be acquainted with the lawgiver and the philosopher, and with him only, need not throw away one single hour upon this part of the book, which is intended for such, and for such only as care to be acquainted with the man, but proceed forthwith to the second part, where Bentham and Dumont are occupied with the great business of morals and legislation." pp. 14, 15.

We shall follow the author in the course he has marked out—first, saying a few words about the character of Jeremy Bentham, and then discussing, with all possible brevity, his pretensions to the admiration which is challenged for him by his biographer.

This great luminary of the age was born, it seems, in the year 1747-8. He was the son of an attorney who was, according to Jeremy himself, "a weak man," and to whose mechanical predilection for his own profession, we owe the light which his son has been able to shed upon the philosophy of jurisprudence. To be sure, misfortune—which has ever been the best nurse of genius—had its share in this result; for the man, who was destined to reform the whole body of the law, does not seem to have been fitted to excel in the most important part of it, viz. the application of its principles to practice. "On a particular occasion, (said he to Mr. Neal,) I gave a legal opinion which turned out not to be law, because the law had been altered without my knowledge or consent. I refused to give an opinion after this." p. 61. Whereupon, his biographer remarks, with great simplicity, that "he could not help imagining, as he went through the history of this early error, how *much* of his subsequent *views* of the law, the lawyers, and the judges of England, might be owing to this very incident. * * * * * * * * *

Most of Mr. Bentham's peculiar views, peculiar habits and peculiar figures; I believe I might say all, may be traced in the same way to incidents connected with his youth—his hatred of English law and of English lawyers, of Blackstone, of Mansfield and of Eldon—to his *fortunate* [qu.] failure in his profession. Other facts of the same nature will appear in the further development of his character." p. 61.

His first work was an expression of his very natural, if not very reasonable grudge against these odious objects. He made, it seems, while yet a very young man (he was in his 28th year) "a masterly attack" on Blackstone's Commentaries. Lord Mansfield, if we are to believe Mr. Neal, or rather Bentham himself, used to speak of this diatribe in the highest terms, though, on Blackstone's being asked if he intended to reply to it, *his* answer was "no, not if it were better written." His dislike for the author of the Commentaries discovered itself at a very early period. He related to his biographer the following story, "to be repeated in Yankee-land."

"*April* 4. Mr. B. relates a story of Blackstone, to be repeated in Yankeeland. 'As early as sixteen,' said he, 'I began to *query* Blackstone, my Gamaliel, while I was sitting at his feet. He was a stiff, pompous, proud quiz—Mansfield couldn't bear him. I told you, I believe, that he, M., had the whole of the Fragment read to him, and liked it mightily. When Blackstone was Vinerian professor at Queen's College, Oxford, he sent to Dr. Brown, provost of the College, to know what distinction should be awarded to him, or how he should be ranked. Tell him, said Brown, who was a shrewd fellow, tell him he may walk before my beadle,—the beadle that preceded him with a mace, when he walked out. Mr. Eden (the writer on penal law,) afterwards Lord Ackland, and Blackstone did something together once, which Bentham approved. Out of this grew something of Mr. Bentham's, about which Blackstone wrote him, complimenting him rather highly." pp. 133, 114.

In 1788, he published his "Views of the Hard-Labor Bill, with observations relative to Penal Jurisprudence in general," and nine years after his celebrated "Defence of Usury." In 1789 appeared the original quarto edition of MORALS and LEGISLATION, "the ground work of the author's whole fame with Dr. Parr and others of like amplitude and strength of mind." Mr. Neal pronounces it, oracularly, "the *novum organum* of Morals and Legislation'" and he makes the celebrated scholar just mentioned say of it that, since Lord Bacon's great work, there had been nothing in the history of the human mind to compare with it. It is this same treatise, be it remembered, in its most approved form, or rather its quintessence, that constitutes the second part of the volume before us.

After this publication, he favored the world with an immense catalogue of lucubrations of greater or less importance—the *Panopticon* or Inspection-house—or new plan for the construction of penitentiary-houses, prisons, work-houses, lazarettos, hospitals and schools. "These are," it seems, "the celebrated letters on the subject of *Prisons and Prison-Discipline*, to which Europe and America are chiefly indebted for the improvement, made during the last half century in the structure of prisons and treatment of prisoners, and all this without any acknowledgement in favor of the author"—a charge we regret to add, which lies against "our Prison-Discipline Society of Boston, among the rest." This excellent scheme, however, like many of equal promise in the island of Laputa, was, for some reason or other, never put into practice. Then came A Draft of a Code for the Organization of the Judicial Establishment of France, 1790—An Essay on Political Tactics, afterwards embodied in a long work, in two volumes, by M. Dumont—Chrestomathia—Plan of Parliamentary Reform—Papers relative to Codification and Public Instruction—Church of Englandism—The Book of Fallacies—Analysis of the Influence of Natural Religion, published by *Richard Carlisle*, in 1822—an able book, saith Mr. Neal, of which the object was to prove that all religions are equally unworthy of regard. In this connection, our biographer holds the following emphatic language:

"From what I know of Mr. Bentham, I have no doubt of his being an atheist. I have been told so, by those who knew him; a good many of his more youthful followers are so—if they themselves may be credited; and, though we had never had any conversation together that satisfied me, still, as I have said before, I have no doubt of his being an atheist. And I mention this here, that I may not be charged with blindness to what I look upon as not only the greatest, but as the only great error of that man's faith. Not that he *believes* there is no God—I do not say so: but he is not thoroughly satisfied, I believe, that there *is* a God. If he would inquire, and it is not even yet too late, he would perceive what he must delight in hoping, even if it were not proved, the existence of One who is emphatically the Father of such men as he is. Peradventure, it is not so much atheism after all, as it is a mistake with him. He mistakes the uncertainty of one fact, or rather a want of mathematical certainty in one fact, for the certainty of another fact: the *want* of such kind of mathematical proof, as he is habituated to, that there *is* a God, for conclusive demonstration that there is *not*. I know well the nature of his mind; and I do not scruple to say that I believe this. Not being satisfied as other men are, and not being at leisure, in his old age and just on the shadowy and shifting threshold of another world, to investigate the subject in his own way; and being imbued with the pestiferous, and most unreasonable doubts of a Frenchman, who was a believer in Voltaire, and the first teacher of Mr. Bentham; and withal having translated Le Taureau Blanc of Voltaire, without acknowledging it,—nor does he know to this day, probably, that he was ever suspected of it; and having produced the work on Natural Religion, above-mentioned, which was edited by one atheist, and published by another, (the infamous Richard Carlisle,) it cannot be expected of him that he should now inquire very diligently or wisely, nor that his disciples, whatever *he* might do or say now, would be satisfied. We may be sorry for such things, but, if they are otherwise good men, our sorrow will lead us rather to pity than to rage or hatred for them. As well might we rebuke those who are troubled with fever, as them that require to be convinced by touch, or taste, or ciphering, of the existence of a Deity. Why may not men be suffered to believe what they please, or what they *can* rather, about God and a future state, and all the mysteries of theology, as about any other subject of dispute or inquiry. We do not quarrel with men now about their belief touching wizards, or the motion of the planets, or the origin of the blacks. Why should we, about their belief respecting their Father above? What I say, I believe. I am no atheist—If I were, I should avow it in the face of heaven and earth, and abide the consequences." pp. 33, 35.

Besides many other works, of which we have not space

enough to repeat the names, some MSS. of Bentham passed through the hands of a clever Frenchman, Dumont, who, (as Mr. Neal affirms upon the authority of Mr. Gallatin,) used to write the very speeches that Mirabeau delivered! We strongly suspect there is some mistake about this part of the story. But, be that as it may, it is admitted that the best, if not the only means of understanding many of the great Reformer's speculations is to read them in a foreign language. It is difficult to conceive by what species of divination M. Dumont is able to decypher the strange gibberish of his author. According to Mr. Neal's account of the *Benthamee*, no mystagogue ever earned his wages more fairly. The progress, which the philosopher has been gradually making in this corruption of style, is rather a singular phenomenon in itself, but it is not more strange than his biographer's notion that it is to be explained by the tenderness of Mr. Bentham's conscience.

"But to conclude this part of our subject. As Mr. Bentham grew older, he grew more and more dissatisfied with the *inadequacy* of language, with the want of exactness in it; and he therefore began to prepare a new system of logic for himself—a few chapters of which have lately been booked into a readable shape, by his nephew, Mr. George Bentham, one of the most promising men of the age, both for acuteness and for strength. From this, he went on, growing less and less elegant, and to the careless reader, the novel-reader, or the newspaper-reader, less and less perspicuous every year; for he went on abridging volumes into chapters, and chapters into tabular views, till it was impossible for any body to understand him, who had not gone step by step through his preliminary demonstrations; till at last he came to a style, which cannot be defended—such as that of the article he wrote for the Westminster Review. And yet, though all this may be said of that particular paper, it is due to him and to the public to add, that as he has grown older he has grown wiser; *that the style referred to grows out of his exceeding honesty*,—for he does not allow himself to separate his assertions from their qualifications—so that his periods are encumbered on every subject of interest; that in ordinary matters where a newspaper style would do, no man alive writes a more off-hand, free or natural style than Jeremy Bentham; and that—after all—the very difficulties we complain of are attributable more to the *subject* handled by him, than to the style in which they are handled; more to the nature of the science treated of, than to any thing else; and that for people, who are not acquainted with his early works, to complain of *all* his late works for not being clear, is about as absurd as it would be for a man, who had never studied his multiplication table, to find fault with a treatise on fluxions for not being as intelligible, straight-forward and agreeable as a newspaper-essay upon the private character of a political adversary."—pp. 38, 39.

It would be exacting too much of a biographer to require him to write the life of another, without occasionally alluding to his own, and Mr. Neal has, therefore, taken the liberty of detailing, (p. 41,) with the greatest precision, all the circumstances which led to his acquaintance with Jeremy. It was about twelve years ago that he first heard that illustrious name. He was, at that time, "a student at law in Baltimore, Maryland," when it so happened that Mr. Hoffman published his "Course of Legal Study." In this "Course," the works of Bentham were to be studied by the novice, who, in common, he says, with most of the literati of the United States, did not know who or of what country this same Bentham was. But as some of the works alluded to were written in French, our author naturally concluded that the author was a Frenchman; which, as "he was not very easy with French at the time," must have been rather a discouraging inference. After "many years had gone by," however, and he had attained to his present *proficiency* in that language, "on hearing Mr. Hoffman express a desire that somebody would undertake to render the two volumes referred to, into English," he very readily offered to do so, "if he could find"— that only Mecenas of aspiring genius in these mechanical days— "a publisher." He accordingly wrote to a Mr. Riley, at New-York, "one of the largest law-publishers in the country," undertaking to translate two volumes, 8vo. with notes, and so forth, for *three hundred dollars*, one half payable in law-books. But Mr. Riley knew his business, and nobody, knew Bentham. And so, moderate as these terms were, the overture was unceremoniously rejected, and there the matter rested until 1825, when Mr. Neal and Mr. Bentham "were accidentally thrown together in the native country" of the latter. The biographer's account of his first approaches to the awful presence-chamber of the reformer, is too curious and characteristic to be omitted. He began with one of the outposts of the school, the debating-club of the young Utilitarians at the philosopher's house. His picture of this notable scene and assembly is what might be expected from the *dramatis personæ* who figure in it. We beg our readers to remark, in this living instance, the practical tendency of that cynical narrow-minded and degrading philosphy, which professes to do more, than any other, to advance the real happiness of life, by indiscriminately proscribing its highest graces and accomplishments.

"But, although I would have crossed the Atlantic, as I have said before, to enjoy his company for a single evening, had I been able to afford it; still, after I *had* crossed the Atlantic—nay, after I had arrived in the very neighborhood of his house, I could not find a person that knew him, or had ever seen him; and I was there above a twelvemonth, before I knew where he lived, though his habitation was hardly a pistol-shot from my own lodgings, in Warwick-street, Pall-Mall. At last, however, when I had given up all idea of ever seeing the man, for I knew several native Englishmen of high character, who had been trying for years to find the way to his door, as they acknowledged without scruple.—we were brought together by the merest accident in the world; and I remained with him so long, and knew him so intimately, that, perhaps, it would not be too much to say—probably no person alive knows more of the true character of Jeremy Bentham than I do. Mr. Bowring, and Mr. Mill, the author of British-India, may have known him longer; but never more intimately. They have seen him at intervals of a week or a month, year after year: but I have been with him every day for about eighteen months, and spent almost every evening with him, from six o'clock, the dinner-hour, till about eleven or twelve at night, for the whole of that time. I have seen him through his changes therefore; and I believe that I know him thoroughly and completely.

On Friday evening, Oct. 22d 1825—I have the very day before me—I was invited to meet with the Utilitarians at his house, for debate,—a body of youthful conspirators against government, order and morality; the fine arts, and all the charities and sympathies and elegancies of life, you would suppose, were you to judge of all by two or three; or even by what is said of all, by those who occupy the high-places in the commonwealth of literature. This formidable band, however, consisted of but seven persons, most of them young men, mere boys in age and experience, and the others below the middle age. They were all, without one exception, I believe, atheists—fixed and irretrievable atheists *in their own opinion*, though of the whole, no one had ever read much, or thought much, or written much, even for a youth. Nor were they otherwise remarkable. As debaters, they were unspeakably wretched; as writers they were nearly as bad, with one or two exceptions; but they were good reasoners; and one of their number was certainly the closest and clearest I ever knew under the age of thirty-five. Yet he was hardly eighteen I believe; certainly not over nineteen. They had a young gentleman to preside, of whom all that I can remember is, that he had very black hair, very bright eyes, and very large teeth; that he was clever, but saucy, and a great lover of paradox. After the business of the society was over, young Mr. Mill, the editor of Mr. Bentham's Rationale of Evidence, then going through the press, read a portion of the manuscript, with two or three of his own notes, which were certainly very surprising for such a youth. Having already learnt to prefer crude Benthamism to prepared Benthamism, I detected the original of much that Mr. Mill, the father, had furnished for the supplement to the Encyclopedia Britannica here. We had almost the whole of his renowned essay on Jurisprudence, in a colloquial form. After this, they had what they called a debate—and such a debate! No wonder the Utilitarians are at daggers drawn with oratory. Of the leaders, not one was ever able to express himself, with power and beauty, even about his own faith; not one converses well, not one is there that speaks with energy, clearness and fluency, at the same time, nor one that may ever hope, under any circumstances, to be distinguished as a speaker. I know them all, and I know what I say to be true. Mr. Bentham is very unhappy in conversation, the moment he leaves preaching and begins to argue; and Mr. Mill, the father, never attempted a speech but once, they say, and then he failed so utterly and so hopelessly that he has been at war with oratory ever since. However, as I have said before, they are almost to a man powerful and acute reasoners, though much addicted to questioning the most obvious truth when it stands in their way. This evening the subject was the poor-laws, and the policy of their introduction into Ireland. It was opened by a Mr. P., a good-natured, large, agreeable man, who, like two others in this society of seven, was afflicted with an impediment of speech, and used to stop and breathe between every two or three words. No wonder they sneer at oratory! He was replied to by young Mill, in a very modest, firm, unprepared speech. The reasoning and the language of Mr. M. were both good, though he appeared somewhat anxious; and a part of his pronunciation was that of the North country, waound, raound, &c., for wound, round, &c. He was followed by another, who got up with a sort of fling, and began with a loud, free voice, which died away after a moment or two; when he lost himself entirely, having said this, and this only: Sir, I rise to make a few observations,—and *but* a few. My opinion is decided, and *very* decided. Here he began to talk lower and lower, and soon ran himself out, courage, waggery and all." pp. 43–47.

The school was so very prepossessing, that our young countryman was more curious than ever to be introduced to its visible head on earth. The memorable day at length arrived—the doors of "Q. S. P." (p.55.), which seldom turned upon their hinges to admit the mighty ones of the earth, were thrown open to a friendless foreigner—and it would be difficult to match the quaint and pompous *niaiserie* of the following description:

"After this brief sketch of the Utilitarians I saw gathered together at the hermitage of Mr. Bentham, in Queen-Square Place,—and whom, by the way, it was my lot to oppose, whenever they touched upon theology,—the reader will be prepared to feel as I did, when at the end of another week, as I was sitting by my-self in my landlady's little parlour, a young man whom I knew for the private secretary of Mr. Bentham, and whom I supposed to be one of the two keepers mentioned by the trust-worthy Parry, entered the room, and, after interchanging a word or two about the weather, dropped his voice, and communicated a verbal invitation to me from Jeremy Bentham, as if it were the pass-word for something, which it were a matter of life and death for any body to over-hear. So—I was to dine with the philosopher; and the day fixed upon was the 2d of November (1825); the hour six. But query, said I to myself, as the day drew near—must I go punctually or not? If I go punctually, who knows but I may be charged with affectation or ignorance; a disregard or want of acquaintance with the usages of the country, not to be pardoned. I knew very well that 'fashion's six is half-past six or seven,' just as 'not at home' is,—I have no time to throw away on you. But then the philosopher, they say, is not a man to be trifled with: he is, moreover, somewhat whimsical, and he cares nothing about fashion. Perhaps, therefore, if I do not arrive punctually, I may be reproached for my want of republican virtue, and put off without my dinner. This determined me, and I started in good season; but, owing to the difficulty of finding the way without a guide through Queen-Square Place, the secretary had been obliging enough to say that he would leave the iron gate open for me, which enters on the park. The gate I missed; and I did not arrive therefore till a quarter after the time. But, after I had arrived, there seemed to be little or no prospect of my seeing the interior. I could find nothing that resembled what in our country is denominated a front-door—nothing in the shape or size of a principal entrance. A door I saw, and I marched up to it; but there was no knocker, and, after feeling about in the dark for awhile, I discovered the steps, and circumnavigated the whole premises, including the coach-house, and a part occupied by Mr. Coulson, editor of the Globe. At last I found myself just where I started from. So, for the want of any thing better, I began to pound away at the door with my knuckles. After a minute or two spent in this way, the door opened, and the secretary appeared in a room on the left of the passage-way, seated at a piano—as vile a thing, by the by, as I ever saw, though he had a decided taste for music, and played the organ with a masterly touch for an amateur. We entered into conversation immediately, and were beginning to understand each other, when I stopped to listen to a cheerful trembling voice that appeared to be approaching. The next moment I heard my name pronounced and somebody talking very fast and not very intelligibly at the door, which opened with a nervous, hurried shake, and a middling-sized, fresh-looking old man, with very white hair, a good-humored, though strongly marked face, a true quaker-coat, and a stoop in his gait, entered and began talking to me as if we had known each other for years. A—a welcome to the hermitage—I can't see here (turning away from the light)—a—a—there's my hand—a—a—we must form—a—a—I've heard of you a—a—anti-holy alliance together. I made the best reply in my power, delighted with his cordial strange way, though sorely puzzled to make out what he said. "Just time enough to look at my garden—a—a—" clapping on a large straw hat as he spoke, with a green ribbon to it (the reader will not forget the season of the year,) and grasping a cane. I thought of Parry here, the veracious Parry; but on the whole, as it was very dark, I did not feel much afraid of being mistaken for the keeper of a gray-haired lunatic. Yet I was half afraid to offer my arm at first; and when I did, he threw it aside with a laugh, and I began to prepare for a trot, as described by that facetious gentleman, up one street and down another. Away we went as fast as we could go, he keeping a little ahead, and talking away as fast as ever, though with a slight hesitation of speech hardly perceptible at first. N. B. He is the founder of the Utilitarian school of oratory. This way, this way, said he, as we drew near another part of his large garden, this way now, taking my arm as he spoke; I'll show you—this is classical ground—a—a—much to *classicalize* it. I had no time to bow, nor would he have seen me if I had. Rush was here, a—a—down on your marrow-bones,—a—a—I gave him a piece of the balustrade of Milton's house—a—a there it is (pointing to the back side of a two-story brick house) that belongs to me—a—a—large garden—the largest here that looks upon the park, except the royal-gardens—a—a—now it is dinner-time." pp. 47-49.

Then comes the dinner.

"This over, he led me up to what he called his work-shop: a small crowded room, with a false floor occupying two-thirds of it; a sort of raised platform, with a table on it, just large enough for himself, his two secretaries, and one guest—he never had more. I had what he called the seat of honor opposite the sage, with Mr. Secretary Doane at my right, and the other at my left. I had been told, I know not how many queer stories about the household economy of the philosopher; but they were all very far from the truth. He began with removing a cover—judge of my amazement to see one potato in the dish, and but one. It was large and mealy, to be sure; but hardly a mouthful for a hungry man, who had long passed his regular dinner-hour. But, while I was wondering at the simplicity and straight-forwardness of the philosopher, who fell upon the potato, broke it up, and began peeling it with his fingers, a tureen of capital soup was served; and I was directed to a bottle of Burgundy that stood on my right, and a bottle of Maderia on my left, which, as the philosopher himself never tasted wine, were probably intended for his two secretaries and myself. To the soup succeeded oyster-paties, a very savoury dish, under the management of his cook. Then we had plum-pudding, apple-pie, and beef; and, while he ate of the two former as a first course,* such being the fashion of his youth, we were served with the beef; and, while we partook of the plum-pudding and apple-pie, he *took* beef, as we say here. I mention the courses, and the very dishes, and the order in which they appeared, thus particularly, because of the strange stories that are

* As the old-fashioned of our country still do. You know the law, reader—he that eats most pudding shall have most meat.

abroad on the subject, all of which are not only untrue, but ridiculously untrue. He talked a good deal after the heavy work of the dinner was through; and his conversation was delightful, not so much on account of the subject or the language, though the former was full of interest, and the latter good enough to satisfy me, as on account of the general, unaffected pleasantry of his manner, with here a dash of good-natured sarcasm, and there a sprinkle of downright roguishness. I should not say of Mr. Bentham that he had much of the manner of the old school, or any thing of a high-bred air; but he had what I cannot help revering and loving much more, a playful and easy manner, like that of one who is tired of being upon his good behaviour, and is glad to let a stranger see the inside of that which all but a very few are only permitted to judge of by the outside—his real character." pp. 50, 51.

As it would be unreasonable to expect that many of our readers should buy this whole book, while it must be owned that some of the anecdotes which it contains are amusing enough, we shall make pretty copious extracts from the biographical sketch.

Every body, we suppose, has laughed as heartily as Lord Byron over Capt. Parry's account of what his lordship facetiously called "Jerry Bentham's cruise." On that subject Mr. Neal mentions what follows:—

"I watched my opportunity this evening, and alluded to Parry—Captain Parry, the authority of the North-American Review, for January, 1828. Captain Parry—*Major Parry* he calls *himself*, said Mr. Bentham, with decided emphasis, and a little anger. He lied—he dined with me, and went away drunk; we dined at six, my usual hour, instead of eight or nine. The secretary on his right and the secretary on his left, appeared rather blank too, at the mention of Parry." p. 58.

It may be true that Parry threw a *little* exaggeration into his amusing sketch—but, if Mr. Neal is not himself a caricaturist, it *could* have been *very* little. Compare with that picture, the anecdotes and sketches in this book. An old man—an octogenarian—five feet high, bent down under the weight of years, with a plentiful head of white hair streaming like the tail of the pale-horse in the Apocalypse*—hallooing in the heart of a great city as loudly as a man-of-war's boatswain in a storm—"hurrying away in a *respectable* trot," (what *can* that mean?)—the straw hat, the woollen stockings rolled over the drab cloth trowsers, &c. How is it possible to add any thing to the effect of an image so ridiculous and *outré*?

"21st. Calls me every day to walk in the garden with him before dinner. Halloos like a man-of-war's boatswain in a storm; good practice for the lungs—thinks they are strengthened by it, as they undoubtedly are. When he began to halloo, he could not make himself heard in the library; now the whole neighborhood may hear him. I observe to-day that his real stature, before he began to stoop, must have been about five feet six. I do not know that I ever saw a finer picture than this old man, *hurrying away on a respectable trot*, with a cane that he calls *dapple*, after the

* Manfred.

favourite mule of Sancho Panza; a plain, single-breasted coat of a dark greenish olive; white hair, as white and plentiful, and curved about as much as the mane of a horse; a straw hat, edged and banded with a bright green ribbon; thick wollen stockings, rolled up over his knees outside of a pair of drab cloth trowsers, (he hates breeches—never could look at himself in breeches without laughing he says;) a waistcoat of thin striped calico, all open at the bosom—a dress, take it altogether, which he wears, not only in the depth of winter, but in the heat of summer." p. 64.

* * * * * * * * *

"This very day, (Aug. 24,) after going out to receive a small annuity, he trotted all the way from Fleet-street to Queen-Square Place, Westminster, a part of the way very fast—not at all tired, though warm. Perhaps he did so to re-assure himself—on the way back from a life-annuity office, of which he was the only surviving annuitant of a particular age." p. 95.

His habits are cynical throughout. His bed, especially, is a fit receptacle for such a body. One would suppose that, like Diogenes of Sinope, he had taken the first hint of his manner of living from a rat.*

"25. Sunday. Mr. B. sleeps standing after dinner; fell once he says, and hurt himself on the elbows; the approaches of sleep are extremely delightful, he adds, being half asleep at the time. He sits up in bed in the morning to enjoy the approaches of sleep—not to sleep. And here it may not be amiss to describe the bed. *The philosopher sleeps in a bag, and sometimes with his coat on; the bed not being made up for a month together.* p. 66."

* * * * * * * *

"He shuts the flap of the book-case to hide the hole in the floor, which is occupied by the player at the organ; the darkness being rather unpleasant to the philosopher, he affects to believe it full of ghosts—not seriously to be sure, but more than half-seriously. He sleeps in his coat now—having ordered the flaps to be cut off, which are too warm for the night, and bring on the heat and itching of the skin, with which he is afflicted after dinner—the *devil* he calls it. Having drawn a line down each side of the middle-seam, with a bit of chalk, he has ordered a strip of the cloth to be cut out, and a cord to be let in, like the lacing of stays, to keep his backbone cool: D.—the mischievous dog he employed for this purpose—having cut off the flaps of the coat and ripped it up in the back, now added the initials of the philosopher's name, as if to provide against his going astray,—putting them in large white letters in the very middle of the back. When I mentioned it, saying—If you escape now, sir, you will be brought home; instead of being offended, he laughed, said it was a foolish joke, and made the secretary rub it off. Such a figure no mortal ever saw before out of a mad-house. I cannot think of it to this day without laughing. I can see him now, it is the fourteenth of June, thermometer 76°;—There he goes with a pair of thick leather gloves on, woollen stockings rolled up over his knees outside, his coat-tail shaved away like a sailor's round-about, and stooping, with his reverend rump, pushed out like that of a young chicken. I made a sketch of his figure, but am half afraid to publish it. He sleeps now with his feet in a bag. On some occasion, wanting an improvement in the shape of his bed, he told the carpenter to jump in, so that he could judge for himself what was wanted. In the fellow jumped, shoes and all covered with mud,—No idea I could sleep in such a place, added our

* Diog. Laert. in Diog. Sinop.

philosopher, with the most diverting simplicity. On hearing the fact mentioned, I could not help thinking of his regular ablutions every night, and of the cleanliness insisted upon in the Panopticon." pp. 81, 82.

* * * * * * *

"I am told to-day that he has his bed made only when he changes the sheets, that is, about once a month—sometimes not for six weeks; that coffee has been spilt on those he now sleeps in—that it is all spotted and discoloured with his fleecy hosiery, which he wears to bed with him, though wet and muddy; and that sometimes other droll accidents occur, which, added to his peculiar night-dress, the truncated cloth-coat, and the bag for his feet, are indeed examples of idiosyncracy not often to be met with." pp. 83, 84.*

The language of "Q. S. P." is in keeping with the rest of the establishment.

"I must now give two or three specimens of the peculiar phraseology at Q. S. P. Instead of saying to the secretary, on my left, please to touch the bell, or please to ring it, he says *make-ringtion*; and this not merely for the joke, but in sober earnest, though intended for a caricature of his own theory. But he, and the secretary on my left, who has lately betaken himself to the church, are in the habit of substituting words, which, though synonymous at law, are not so in practice. Instead of saying a *rich* paste, they say an *opulent* paste; for *shortness*, they say *brevity*; for veal-pie, the *basis* of that pie is veal; for *good* mutton, *virtuous* mutton; for pretty-good, or apparently good, *plausible*; and so with I know not how many more words; all which from the mouth of Mr. B. the philosopher and the humourist, the great and good, though whimsical old man, is rather diverting than otherwise. But, when repeated by a youth, and with imperturbable gravity, as if a new mode of speech were to be learned by those who had the honour of eating at the table of his preceptor, it was infinitely diverting." pp. 67, 68.

The uncouth jargon is particularly well adapted to the vulgar blasphemy of which it is every moment the vehicle. We have already seen a flat avowal by Mr. Neal, that "this great and good, though whimsical man," is an atheist. But it is not every atheist who is fortunate enough to be able to clothe his doctrines in such an appropriate guise as Mr. Bentham. We could not read the passage which we are about to cite, and which presents so lively an instance of the indecent wantonness and license of this old man's conversation, without being strongly reminded of the lines—

<blockquote>
"Nullos esse Deos, inane cœlum
Affirmat Cœlius; probatque
Quòd se videt, dum negat hæc, beatum."
</blockquote>

* It is impossible to read these passages, without thinking of Socrates, as he appears even in what may be considered as the flattering representations of Plato and Xenophon. See the beginning of the *Convivium*, where Aristodemus, meeting Socrates in a clean dress and with shoes on, asks him on what extraordinary errand he is bound. So, in the *Memorabilia*, (c. 6,) Antiphon says to him—"You live as no slave could bear to live. Your meat and drink are the worst possible, and your raiment is not only mean and shabby, but the same winter and summer, ἀνυπόδητός τε χιδχιτων διατελεῖς."

"*June* 12, 1826. Ever hear of a bargain I propose—a—a—a bargain for the future, said he. Some comfort for my death-bed; first year of my death will be the first year of my reign; if you have not, you are the only one of my intimates that has not. I know very well how long I have a right to live at my age; I look at the tables—four years now; the longer I live the harder the bargain God Almighty will drive with me. Now I say—here God Almighty; here are four years: Now I'll give up two of the four, if you'll let me take the other two at such intervals as I like; one hundred, two hundred years hence; I should like to see the effect. Had no answer to the purpose yet—perhaps there may be. Wilberforce or ———— or————, naming several more, they might have one, or others in a more advanced stage of human discovery.

"His health instead of growing worse, would appear to be growing decidedly better. He used to have the tooth-ache, the ear-ache, the head-ache, and always winter-coughs, till within the last two years—now he is entirely free from all these troublesome and wearing ailments. I see no reason why he should not live to a century." p. 85.

* * * * * *

"*July* 7th. A favourite expression of the lawgiver, when he hears any thing new, is, Lord God, only think o' that! accompanied with a shake of his white hair, and a look of eager surprise, with the forehead thrown back, and the whole head thrust forward." p. 87.

It is worth while to extract another passage, which shews that this philosophical Mezentius stands in sufficient awe of the Infernal gods, at least.

"Mr. Bentham is so afraid of death, that he will not allow the subject to be discussed before him—he is afraid of being alone after dark; he is either read to sleep every night, or left to fall asleep with a lamp burning; and he is a believer in what *he* calls ghosts; that is, in a something which makes him uneasy in solitude after dark." p. 114.

In this respect, the reformer of "Q. S. P." resembles Hobbes, and Mr. Neal takes occasion to run a formal parallel between them, much after the manner of Fluellin. His comparison does not strike us very forcibly. The point in which Hobbes and Bentham approach each other nearest, in our opinion, is the perfect contempt for other men's understandings, and the proportionate confidence in their own, which contributes so much to the air of originality and vigor that pervades their respective works. But in reference to this very originality (of which it is our purpose to say much) they differ as widely as any two writers can. Of all men, the philosopher of Malmesbury most detested verbal disputes, technical phraseology, and the mystical and unmeaning jargon of the schools. He thought that the universities, for which he has no great respect at best, were particularly obnoxious to censure on this score. They had substituted words for things, and persuaded mankind that they had learned philosophy, when they had only acquired a strange, perhaps a barbarous nomenclature.* Nothing can be more

*Leviathan, p. i. c. 1. He is speaking of "sensible species," &c., which he denounced as unmeaning and deceptive phrases—"I say not this as disapproving

just than this charge. It is really astonishing to reflect, how much of what was considered knowledge and philosophy once, is utterly passed away, never to be revived or even remembered more. How little, for instance, how very little of the whole stock of learning, (the erudite ignorance, as Voltaire calls it,) that made Thomas Aquinas and Albertus Magnus so famous in their times, is any thing more than the jargon of the schools, very ingeniously (no doubt) and skilfully put together, and requiring as much thought and time to acquire it, as the science of Newton and La Place, but absolutely good for nothing either in practice or in speculation. To go up to the fountain head of all that learning; who that has ever read through Aristotle's logical works can have failed to make the same remark? The amount of intellect expended upon those compositions, is stupendous. Take the Categories for example. It shows wonderful comprehensiveness and acumen, as well as originality of mind, merely to have been able to reduce all affirmation to these ten predicaments. It was considered as a clever thing of Hume to point out the few principles which govern the association of ideas—cause and effect, proximity of time and place, &c.—and Coleridge has thought it worth his while to claim the honor of so great a discovery for the "angelical doctor" just mentioned. But the Categories are a much more complicated and difficult matter, in themselves, and Aristotle could not, at that early period, have had any aid from his predecessors. He was himself the inventor, the creator of this body of philosophy. Nor is it only the original conception that strikes his reader. He is still more astonished at the completeness and harmony in all its parts, and the perfection even in its minutest details, of the system that is built upon it. The boundless copiousness of the Greek language seems exhausted, its utmost capability of refined distinction is tasked, by the philosopher in developing his doctrines through all their shades and ramifications. Yet after all, for any one *substantial* purpose in literature or in life, of what use is all the logic of Aristotle? It is a question we have asked ourselves over and over again, after toiling for three or four hours together over his Analytics, and taking immense pains to possess ourselves of his whole train of thought. Every thing is admirable to look at—but *materiam superabat opus.* The wonderful skill of the artificer strikes us as much as if the work he has erected were destined to answer some of the great ends of society, but science has gone on improving and a day is come, when all his ingenuity, except as matter of philosophical curio-

the use of universities; but, because I am to speak hereafter of their office in a commonwealth, I must let you see, on all occasions by the way, what things should be amended in them, amongst which the frequency of unmeaning speech is one."

sity, is absolutely thrown away. For is there a man on the face of the globe, or has there ever been one, who was wiser or abler either in speculation, or in affairs, for having made himself master of the Analytics, the Topics, or the Metaphysics of Aristotle? Or of the thousands and tens of thousands of wise and able men, who have directed the studies, or managed the affairs of mankind, without giving themselves the trouble once to think of topic or category, would any one have been the better of a thorough acquaintance with these speculations? "How much of many young men's time (says Locke,) is thrown away in purely *logical* inquiries, I need not mention. This is no better than if a man who was to be a painter, should spend all his time in examining the threads of the several cloths he is to paint, &c."* There never was a more just and pregnant observation.

So of the rhetoric of the Stagirite—considered merely *as rhetoric* and not with a view to literary history—and so of all rhetorical and grammatical studies. All that one learns from them is *language*—the names of his tools—that what one speaks every day is *prose*—that this or that deviation from the *sermo pedestris*, is a trope or figure, with this or that sounding name. We do not deny that every scholar would do well to learn these names; but he will sadly deceive himself, if, after having done so, he mistake them for things, and set that down as an acquisition of science which is only the accomplishment of a linguist. In these studies, however, as in logic and metaphysics, great ingenuity and even originality and comprehensiveness of thought, may be, and have been displayed by celebrated writers—but it is all comparatively thrown away because the results of such inquiries never can be any substantial addition to the stock of human knowledge. They resemble the pleadings (as they are technically called) of the common lawyers. Nothing can be more subtle, systematic and logical—nothing looks more like exact science. But their merit is simply dialectical. They are only an organum or instrument to be used for some purpose, for their adaption to which and for that alone, they are valuable—and the remark just cited from Locke strictly applies to them.

That Jeremy Bentham is a most vigorous and original thinker cannot be denied. We do not pretend to be familiar with all, or even the greater part of his works, but we have seen enough of what he has done, to be satisfied, that, like Hobbes, he may justly boast of being very little indebted to his predecessors, either for the conclusions he comes to, or for his manner of deducing and illustrating them. Whether these conclusions be discoveries or not for other people, they are so for himself. Whether it be difficult or not to establish them, in the usual way of treating such subjects, it always costs him great

* On the Conduct of the Understanding, 87.

pains to arrive at them. He has no idea of any intellectual labor-saving contrivance—he carefully eschews the shortest distance between any two points—he hates simplicity, as if it were not the great end of all philosophers to simplify. We have seen what a jargon is used at his fireside—he adopts a similar one in his ethical and juridical speculations. His nomenclature or terminology is a study of itself—as complicated, if not quite so systematic, as that of the chemists. This wrapping up of plain matters in the mysteries of artificial language, which Hobbes detested so much, is Jeremy's great title to the admiration of the world. He is the Heracleitus of the age. We cited, in a former number,* a very long passage from the book on Judicial Evidence as a specimen of this truly *original* language. A great deal of ingenuity may doubtless be displayed in such things, inelegant, unphilosophical and worthless as they are in themselves. But it is all a wasteful expenditure of intellect—it is dialectical trifling—it is darkening counsel with words without understanding—and puffing up the unhappy *adepts* in the pretended science, with a self-conceit as unbounded, as it is absurd and pernicious.

It may be worth while to add that this same charge was made by the ancient philosophers against Zeno and the Stoics. The originality of which these latter boasted so much was said to consist only in their arbitrary neology. "Of all philosophers, (says Cicero in the Dialogue de Finibus) the Stoics innovated most in this respect: and Zeno, their head, was an inventor not of things, so much as of words."† And, in another part of the dialogue, he makes a Peripatetic say of the same school—"They have stolen from us, not one or two dogmas merely, but the whole body of our philosophy—and, as thieves alter the marks of the things they take, so these men have attempted to pass off our doctrines as their own, under the disguise of new words."‡

In moral philosophy, more than in any other department of knowledge, the field of discovery (properly so called) is, at once, excessively confined and completely preoccupied. What can you tell a man of himself, which he has not over and over again experienced? Mechanical philosophy, with the double advantage of experiment and demonstration, may go on improving to the end of time—astronomy may reveal unknown worlds, or make us better acquainted with those already known—and there is manifestly no assignable limit to the analytical researches of the chemist. But what discovery is to be made in human nature, at this time of day? What nook has been left unexplored in the heart?—what *terra incognita* in the mind of man? Accordingly, it is here, if any where, that Hume's pointed observation applies, that "nothing is more usual than for philosophers to en-

* So. Review, No. 10, Art. V. p. 382. † De Finib. l. iii. c. 1. ‡ Ib. l. v. c. 25.

croach upon the province of grammarians, and to engage in disputes of words, while they imagine they are handling controversies of the deepest importance and concern." The truth of this observation is, we venture to say, more and more felt every day that a man lives, whose time is at all given to such studies, and the great and almost peculiar merit of the incomparable writer, from whom we quote, consists in his clear perception of it, exemplified by his own practice. His essays contained, in a condensed, simple and intelligible form, the substance of as many volumes, loaded as such volumes usually are, with wire-drawn verbiage, dull truism or startling paradox.

We do not mean to say that all ethical compositions are superfluous and uninstructive. Far from it. We beg leave to distinguish. Ethical *literature* is as delightful and as useful as ever. *Paintings* of the passions and affections and manners of men—*precepts* of morality—whether in prose or in verse, can never be multiplied to excess. There is always room for eloquence and poetry—for the drama, the novel, or the essay—for vivid descriptions of life, and impressive exhortations to duty. Addison and La Rochefoucault, Johnson and Fenelon cannot be superseded—they please as much, and instruct as well now as they ever did. Our observations apply to ethical *science*, strictly so called—to inquiries into the *principles* of morals—to such dissertations, in short, as that which constitutes the second part of the volume before us. We maintain that to talk of Jeremy Bentham as a great *discoverer*, "a Columbus," as he is pronounced by Mr. Neal, because he teaches that *utility* is the only true ground of moral approbation, is just as absurd as it would be to vaunt that sublime doctrine revealed by Shaftesbury to a world lying in darkness, that ridicule is the test of truth—with this difference, by the by, that there really is some smartness and novelty, in the latter proposition, and that there is not a particle of either in the former. The following is a specimen of the language in which the admirers of Jeremy Bentham express their belief in his extraordinary powers :—

"This magnificent rule of conduct, which may be regarded as the greatest discovery in morals that ever was made, did not originate with Bentham. Ages ago, people talked about the *fitness of things;* and Helvetius, that extraordinary Frenchman, had got his foot upon the shadow of the pyramid, and was preparing to measure its altitude for the benefit of all who were at sea, in the vast ocean of morality, when Mr. Archdeacon Paley appeared, and brought forth a new instrument, under the name of UTILITY, and gave us what we required—a name for that, which will hereafter be a guide for the nations, a pillar of light, for the journeying ages that are to follow in the footsteps of this.

"And after Paley came Bentham, who looking abroad with the eye of one that is able to read the universe of thought like a map and fixing upon two or three first principles, in Morals and Legislation, as clear and as satisfactory, as the law of gravitation in physics, laid the foundation of a new science, which, for the want of a better, we may call by the name of Utility." pp. 120, 121.

As to the wonderful merit of this discovery, it is curious to compare what Paley himself says of his own originality, with what Mr. Neal says for him. The most sensible writer excuses himself for frequently omitting the names of the authors whose sentiments he makes use of, on the ground that "in an argumentative treatise and upon a subject which allows no place for discovery or invention, properly so called, and in which all that can belong to a writer is his mode of reasoning or his judgment of probabilities," he thought it superfluous.* Yet Paley's doctrine of obligation really had some novelty (and we think just so much error) in it—whereas Bentham's, so far as we are able to perceive, has none at all—except, perhaps, in its spirit and tendency, of which we shall speak by and by. A great philosopher—and that neither Helvetius nor Paley—who has, we venture to affirm, exhausted the subject of utility, and put it in the justest and the clearest point of view—appears to regard "the greatest happiness principle" as any thing but a mystery. "It seems (he says) so natural a thought to ascribe to their utility the praise which we bestow on the social virtues, that one would expect to meet with this principle every where in moral writers, as the chief foundation of their reasoning and inquiry. In common life, we may observe that the circumstance of utility is always appealed to," &c.† This position we are persuaded, could be fully made out by any one learned enough to gather up, like Grotius, the expressions of the common sense and feeling of mankind, which are to be found scattered through the literary monuments of all ages. Thus, when Horace tells the Stoics that their great paradox—the equality of crimes—is repugnant alike to the common sense of mankind and to *utility*, which is (almost) the mother of justice and equity, &c.

Sensus moresque repugnant
Atque ipse utilitas, justi *propè* mater et æqui. *Sat. li.* 3. 97.

he enunciates, in a single line, the proposition which Hume establishes. "Whatever is expedient is right," says Paley, and so Socrates, in Plato's Meno, affirms that "whatever is right is expedient." παντα τ'αγαϑα οφελιμα· ουχι ;‡ Nor is this an accidental inconsiderate *dictum*, thrown out without any view to consequences; for the question discussed throughout the whole dialogue is whether virtue be an affair of the head or of the heart—whether a good man is or ought to be guided in the discharge of his duties by enlightened reason, rather than by the in-

* Pref. to his Philosophy, p. 13.
† Hume's Essays, v. ii. c. ix. p. 20; and cf. his Essay on "Justice," "Civil Society." ‡ 87, &c.

stincts of a generous nature, or the inspiration of heaven itself—by a comprehensive view of consequences, rather than a spontaneous, but infallible impulse of the soul. So there is a discussion of great length in that admirable dialogue, "Protagoras or the Sophists," of which the very end is to prove that all moral virtue is *prudence*, and consists in balancing, with judgment, good against evil or a greater against a lesser good, and bestowing the preference where it is deserved. In like manner Polybius traces the origin and growth of the sense of justice and the το' καλον from the selfish feelings of the heart,* and there never has existed a code of laws in which the greatest happiness principle" (under proper limitations however,) was not implied, nor a language of civilized man, in which it has not been mentioned with assent and approbation.

It is really curious to see how all the artificial arrangement and elaborate dialectics of Bentham lead to results, of which no man, in his senses, ever entertained any doubt. Let the reader turn to the book before us at p. 247, and he will find the author of the Principles of Legislation treating at great length of the "secondary circumstances which influence our sensibility"—sex, age, rank, education, habitual occupations, climate, race, government. He then proceeds to the practical application of his theory. It consists in making due allowance for the effect of such things upon our sensibilities—is a mere *rifacimento* of Aristotle's distributive justice and may be all summed up in two lines of Tasso.

"Vario è l'intesso error ne'gradi vari
E sol l'igualità giusta è co'pari."

The same observation, it seems to us, applies to the whole treatise. We have searched in vain for any substantial addition which it has made to the previous stock of knowledge upon the subject—whether for theoretical or practical purposes. The form is novel and peculiar—the substance is quite *banal*. If *specificatio* or the giving a new shape to an old thing, be a legitimate source of property in literature as the civilians allow it to be in law, this theory is all Mr. Bentham's. It is the very thing Horace meant in the disputed passage, communia proprié dicere. But otherwise, we see nothing *new but the quackery*—the absurd affectation of mathematical exactness, in a matter which does not admit of it. "To multiply pleasures and diminish pains," he tells us, is the whole business of the legislator—and this he is taught by the Utilitarians to do according to Cocker!

"It is proper to observe that the *principle of sympathy and antipathy* may often coincide with that of *utility*. To feel affection for those who

* Lib. vi. c. 4.

benefit us, and aversion for those who injure us, is the universal disposition of the human heart. Thus, from one end of the earth to the other, the common sentiment of approbation for benevolent acts, and of disapprobation for hateful acts. Morals and jurisprudence, guided by this instinct, have therefore most frequently reached the great object of utility, without having any clear idea of the principle. But these sympathies are not sure and invariable guides. Let a man refer his blessings and his evils to an imaginary cause; and he is subject to groundless affection and to groundless hatred. Superstition, quackery, the sectarian spirit of party, depend almost entirely upon blind sympathy or antipathy." p. 205.

* * * * * * * *

"According to this principle, legislation is a matter of study and of calculation: according to the ascetics, it is a matter of fanaticism: according to the principle of sympathy and antipathy, it is an affair of caprice, of imagination or of taste. The first ought to please the philosophers, the second the monks, the third the people, the wit, vulgar moralist, and men of the world." pp. 206, 207.

* * * * * * *

"Would one estimate the value of action? He must follow in detail the operations that have just been described. They are the elements of the moral calculation, and legislation becomes a matter of arithmetic. The *evil* caused is the expense: the *good* that one produces is the profit. The rules for this calculation are the same as in every other." p. 238.

* * * * * * *

"This theory of moral calculation has never been fully explained; but it has always been followed in practice; at least, wherever men have had a clear idea of their own interest. What constitutes the value of a lot of ground? Is it not the amount of pleasure to be drawn from it? And does not that value vary according to the greater or less duration that we are able to promise ourselves in the enjoyment of it? according to the proximity or distance of the period, when we are to enter into the enjoyment? According to the certainty or uncertainty of the possession?" p. 238.

Merely speculative, philosophical principles have seldom had any sensible effect upon the conduct of educated men. Yet they *may* do much harm in practice. When, for instance, they are promulgated in times of trouble and excitement, and are preached to the mob in a popular and plausible style, as in the first French revolution—they shake all the institutions of society to their foundation. So in the case of an individual—if his taste be perverted, if his temper be bad, if his natural propensities be base and grovelling—a theory of morals, which is at all Jesuitical, may lead to the worst crimes. Much depends, too, upon the *spirit* in which a doctrine is preached and the purposes and the character of those who inculcate it. Take this very principle of utility for an example. In the hands of Paley, it is quite harmless—it is even, in one point of view, a beneficent and consoling principle. It presupposes the perfect goodness and wisdom of God; for the rule of moral conduct, according to that Divine, is His will, collected from expediency. This—whatever we may think of its philosophical correctness—is a truly christian doctrine, christian in its spirit and its influences, no less than in its origin and theory. There is nothing in it to harden the heart, to pervert the understanding, to inspire a wilful domineering self-conceit or a jacobinical fanaticism. It merely affirms a proposition—which we believe to be, by the great fundamental laws of nature, both in the moral and material world, strictly true—that virtue and happiness are synonimous terms, that our interest and our duty are identical, and that whatever promotes the prosperity of all, in the long-run, is right, because it were a solecism and a contradiction, on the supposition of God's benevolence, to believe that any thing wrong or vicious could promote the prosperity of all.

We need not say that "the greatest happiness principle," in the teachings of Jeremy Bentham and his school, differs, in its origin and spirit, from the utility of Paley, as widely as atheism and christianity. But, in their tendency and pretensions, they differ, at least, as much. The object of Paley is merely to explain the sense of obligation in a manner more satisfactory to himself, than by referring it to an original principle of human nature. Perhaps, it was to furnish an additional topic in favor of christianity. It was not enough, in his opinion, to say that men *feel* the beauty or deformity of character and behaviour, just as they feel the beauty or deformity of natural objects, and that this susceptibility of moral impressions—this inborn love of virtue—is one of the essential attributes and the most glorious privileges of a rational being. He thought the "moral sense" too variable a criterion to depend upon in matters of so much importance, and that a spontaneous compliance with the impulses of the heart was inconsistent with the very idea of *obligation*. "A man," according to him, "is said to be obliged when he is urged by a violent motive, resulting from the *command of another.*" That violent motive was the expectation of being rewarded or punished after this life, and that command was the voice of God himself. We think this doctrine, as we have already observed, and shall presently show, radically erroneous; but it is, at best, in Paley's system a speculative, rather than a practical one. When he proposes utility as the test of duty, he is explaining a phenomenon of nature, not laying down a rule of conduct. He plainly regards it as a mere abstraction, and accordingly touches upon it, as Mr. Neal observes, very slightly and briefly. The *practical* rule which this philosopher proposed was the decalogue and the gospels. His followers were not left to their own shallow and fallible understandings, to deduce, by refined argument and nice calculation, by a comparison of distant contingencies and possible effects, inferences utterly unsafe to depend on, which were to guide them in their most important duties, and to supply the place of the unerring and eternal instincts of the heart. They had a written text and a settled law to go by. But that law, text, gloss and commentary, is exploded by the Benthamites—together with that other law engraved upon the heart of man—quam non didicimus, accepimus, legimus, verum ex naturâ ipsâ arripuimus, hausimus, expressimus—ad quam non docti, sed facti; non instituti sed imbuti, sumus.* In this new system of "mental pathology and intellectual dynamics," every thing, as we have seen, is reduced to mathematical precision. A sin, a vice, a crime, is only an error in arithmetic—not, perhaps, a very venial one, because it were a foul reproach not to know, what it is so easy to learn, the multiplication-table of this infallible school!

The presumptuous and reckless confidence, which such views must needs inspire, is not the least pernicious of their effects. A thorough bred Utilitarian, or rather Benthamite, is never wrong; for he goes by "arithmetic," and figures cannot lie. He is absolutely sure, in every imaginable situation, what the greatest happiness of the greatest number requires at his hands. Propose to him the most puzzling problem in casuistry; he solves it in a moment—the most difficult and momentous question of public policy, he feels not the smallest hesitation. Let the life of his father or the existence of his country be at stake—he has no scruple about sacrificing them to what he *knows* to be the interest of the majority. It is vain to speak to him of the fallibility of the human understanding—he has never been conscious of it himself. Talk to him of the voice of nature or the instincts of the heart, he laughs outright at such childish and ridiculous superstition. To say that his sensibilities have been extirpated by the stern discipline of his school, is only to say that he is an Utilitarian—but a worse effect, if possible, of this discipline, is the inevitable extinction of that chastity of moral feeling, which has never sinned even in thought—that "pious awe and fear to have offended," though but in a dream—that PUDOR, as Hume expresses it, which is the proper guardian of every kind of virtue and a sure preservative against vice and corruption. The whole system of the Utilitarian, when reduced to practice, is a system of Jesuitical sophistry and compromise; and it appears to us next to impossible that a mind, accustomed to consider every thing that should be sacred as subject to controversy, and to entertain, with complacency, ideas that are, and ought to be revolting to every unsophisticated heart, can long retain a very lively sense of moral distinctions.

When we speak thus of the system of the Utilitarians, we would be understood to address ourselves especially to that system, which Mr. John Neal applauds so highly in the volume before us—the system of Jeremy Bentham, and the "horrid crew" of Q. S. P. It is not because they attach great importance to the principle of utility, that we hold them and their doctrines in

* Cic. pro Milon.

utter detestation—for in that respect, as we have seen, they are not peculiar. It is because they attach importance to nothing else—because they make war upon the highest graces of the human character, and the most generous and ennobling sympathies of the heart—because, in short, their whole philosophy is "of the earth, earthy," leading directly to a sordid and calculating (and what is worse, miscalculating,) selfishness and drawing off its votaries from the contemplation of the τὸ Καλον— of the sublime and beautiful in morals—of all that is best fitted to elevate the soul of man, and fill it with the enthusiasm of virtue. Nil generosum sapit atque magnificum, as was long ago said of the Epicurean philosophy.*

Indeed, the doctrine of the Utilitarians is precisely the same as that of Epicurus—with this difference, however, that Bentham has deformed and debased it with an infusion of his own cynical coarseness and vulgarity. The agreeable, if not elegant, philosophy of the Gardens becomes, in his hands, so sordid and ungainly, that a reader of Lucretius might wonder how it could inspire poetry at all—much less *such* poetry. The soothing images of retired leisure and philosophical repose of mind, which enter into our idea of a blissful Epicurean life, and which have been wrought up into an enchanting fiction in Thompson's Castle of Indolence, are certainly not awakened by the mention of Q. S. P. Bentham is a compound of Antisthenes or Crates and Epicurus. But with this qualification, there is a perfect coincidence between his philosophy and that of the sect just alluded to. In both, pleasure and pain are the *end*—the τέλος— of all human action; and the test of virtue is its tendency to increase or secure the former, to diminish or exclude the latter. In both, the pleasures of the imagination and the arts, which minister to them, are proscribed, and all the poetry, the grace and the elegance of life.† Atheism is an ingredient in both— more essential, indeed, to the system of Epicurus, of which the very foundation is a knowledge of physical causes and perfect freedom from all superstition—but flowing naturally enough from the sheer worldliness, and the grovelling *égoisme* of the Benthamites. *Utility* plays the same part in the Epicurean philosophy as "the greatest happiness principle" in the "Morals and Legislation" of the new school. *Prudence*, of which the very end and office is to take care of the interests of life—is the first of the cardinal virtues—the prime good of Epicurus.‡ *Temperance* and *fortitude* are subordinate to it, and formed by its discipline and controlled by its dictates. *Justice* is, for our pur-

---
*Cicero.   †Cic. de Finib. l. i. cc. 5. 7. 20.

‡ Τούτων δὲ πάντων ἀρχὴ χ̓ τὸ μέγιςον ἀγαθόν φρόνησις. See the tenth book of Diogenes Laertius and the Commentary of Gassendi. Philosoph. Epicur. l. iii.

poses, a better illustration still. Gassendi, in his laborious work on the "Philosophy of Epicurus"—to which we refer those of our readers, who have any curiosity on these subjects, for a full exposition of its doctrines—has a very interesting dissertation to shew that utility is what Epicurus affirms it to be, the origin and test of all justice and law.* We wish Mr. Neal would read this dissertation, and then tell us what he thinks of the wonderful discoveries of "the philosopher" in this unexplored region of morals!

It is certain that the philosophy of Epicurus was the most widely diffused of all the ancient systems and that the succession of its school was kept up, long after the others were fallen into decay.† The eloquent Lactantius, adverting to this fact, attempts to account for it by shewing that that philosophy addressed itself, by turns, to every vice of man's nature. "The slothful it forbids to cultivate letters—the avaricious it exempts from the expenses of the popular largess—it tells the unambitious that they must abstain from public affairs—the lazy, from athletic exercises—the timid, from war. The irreligious man is taught to despise the gods—the unfeeling and the selfish, to do nothing for the benefit of others, since a truly wise man acts with a view exclusively to his own interests. To one who shuns the crowd, the charms of retirement are painted in fascinating colours—a stingy fellow learns that he may get through life perfectly well upon bread and water. If you hate your wife, you hear of the advantages of celibacy—if you have bad children, you are told what a blessing it is to be, without them—if your parents be not affectionate as they ought to be, you are absolved from the obligations of nature," &c. Lactantius speaks in this passage the universal sentiment of antiquity in respect to the tendency of the Epicurean doctrine. Torquatus, in the Dialogue de Finibus,‡ affirms that Cicero is singular in not detesting the head of their school, however much he disapproved of its dogmas. This general odium could not exist without a sufficient cause—nor do we think that such a cause has been assigned by Gassendi, and after him by Bayle,§ in the active hostility and great influence of the Stoics—"the Pharisees of paganism". The truth is, that the doctrine of *utility* is found to be essentially selfish and licentious, the moment it is attempted *to reduce it to practice*. No matter what may be its form

* The expression of Epicurus is somewhat different and more just. "Natural justice is the symbol or test of the useful," If just, then useful. Τό τῆς φύσεως δικαιόν ἐςι σύμβολον του συμφέροντος. See infra.
† Diog. Laert. ub. sup—Cic. de Fin. l. i. c. 5. l. ii. c. 15.—Lactant. (apud Gassendi) l. iii. c. 17,
‡ De Fin. l. i. c. 5. quod Epicurum nostrum, non tu quidem oderis, ut fere faciunt qui ab eo dissentiunt, sed certe non probes.
§ Bayle Dict. Art. Epicure.

and complexion—whether it allure us by the charms of Epicurean ease and voluptuousness—or take the coarse, cynical and, if we may so express it, ruffian shape of the "greatest happiness principle" of Q. S. P.—no man, it appears to us, can act systematically upon calculation and compromise—can regard the principles of morality as a subject for perpetual cavil and controversy—can treat the holiest feelings of nature, as so many rank superstitions, and violate them without scruple upon any presumptuous notion of expediency—in a word, no man can be a *practical Utilitarian* without imminent risk of falling into a loose casuistry, and forfeiting, in a greater or less degree, as by eating of the fruit of some forbidden tree, the primeval loveliness and innocence of his character.* And, although in persons very happily born and carefully educated in other respects, the effects of such a doctrine may not always be very visible, yet the propagation of it among the great mass of mankind can scarcely fail of being extremely pernicious. Even were it philosophically just in the abstract (which it is not) it is so liable to be at once misunderstood in theory and abused in practice! "Your encomiums upon pleasure, (says Seneca to the Epicureans,) are dangerous, because what is good in your precepts, is hidden—what corrupts, obtrudes itself upon the view."† The observation is strictly applicable to the Utilitarianism of our own day—the worst, because the most exaggerated and extravagant form of it.

But *every* theory which affects to resolve all obligation into the single principle of utility—that is to say, utility existing and *perceived* in each particular instance—is radically wrong, as being either insufficient to account for the phenomena, or something worse. "Why am I obliged to keep my word," asks Dr. Paley. His answer is "because it is the will of God." But why am I *obliged* to conform to the will of God? Because you will be eternally punished if you do not, replies the same philosopher. We see very clearly, that it is our *interest* to avoid this consequence, and there can be no doubt that a rule of conduct, enforced by such a sanction, is more apt to prevail among the bulk of mankind than any other. But how is the *feeling* of *moral* obligation explained in this way? How am I made to love the "beauty of holiness" by such a motive? It were just as accurate to affirm that a hungry man is *morally* bound to eat his dinner, when we only mean that he cannot chose but yield to the natural appetite. In vulgar parlance, indeed, one is said to be *obliged*, whenever he is *compelled* to act: but surely this confusion of terms—which, so long as it is confined to common discourse, is very excusable—is quite shocking when it creeps

---

*See a disgusting instance of this in the volume before us, p. 146.
† Hoc est, cur ista voluptatis laudatio perniciosa sit, quia honesta præcepa intra latent; quod corrumpit, apparet,—De Vita. Beat. c. 13.

into a philosophical system. According to Paley's doctrine, there is no morality at all without religion, and a Manichean, we suppose, is *bound in conscience* to worship one of his gods as much as the other, and, of course, to conform his actions to this divided empire of good and evil in those whose will may determine the reward, and so must give the rule of his conduct.

Now, to suppose that man—whose chief end and highest attribute are *moral* responsibility—is not prepared for that responsibility by the very frame and constitution of his nature—by some original, inherent principle—which, however reason may enlighten and education control or modify it, is still quite independent of either and inseparable from the idea of such a being—is, as it seems to us, to doubt that very wisdom and goodness of God assumed by Paley for the foundation of his whole doctrine. Such a creature would be an anomaly in the universe. If, for instance, instead of the instinctive love which springs up in a mother's bosom, as soon as she has an infant to press it for nourishment—a love pervading all animated nature and necessary to its preservation—she had to settle a previous question—to work an algebraical equation of utility—miserable, indeed, would be the boasted privilege of reason! But it is not so, and a woman that should have to argue herself into the performance of that holiest of duties, would justly be regarded as a monster deserving the execration and horror of all mankind. It is true, that some philosophers affect to explain these, apparently, instinctive determinations of nature by the force of habit and the association of ideas. They resolve the principles of all actions ultimately into utility and self-love; but they admit that a virtuous man becomes, at length, quite unconscious of any such connection. The later Epicureans introduced this improvement, as they considered it, into their system.* This sort of "philosophical chemistry" is, in its very nature, entirely speculative and therefore harmless and immaterial. We have no great objection to Utilitarianism, until it is reduced to *practice*—until it becomes the professed object of its teachers to *awaken* the mind to the consciousness of its self-love and to make a calculation of interests, with arithmetical precision, the rule of conduct in all cases. This is the odious boast and peculiarity of the Benthamites. We shall not quarrel with any body because he imagines that what he admits to be, in practice. social affections, are in their origin or *genesis*, selfish. This may be so, just as the Rev. Mr. Allison has endeavored to resolve the emotions of sublimity and beauty into the associations of ideas. In either case, the origin of the *sentiment* is within, and its ope-

* *Cic. de Fin.* l. ii. c. 26. Attulisti aliud humanius *horum recentiorum, nunquam dictum ab ipso illo,* quod sciam; primo utilitatis causâ amicum expeti, cum autem usus accessit, tum ipsum amari propter se, etiam omissâ spe voluptatis, etc.

ration is what is commonly called instinctive or mechanical—and therefore not liable to the objection of explaining that by *reason*, (or by "a violent motive resulting from the command of another" as Paley has it)—which must be resolved into an original law of nature. We beg leave, in this connection, to quote a passage from Hume. "Though reason, when fully assisted and improved, be sufficient to instruct us in the pernicious or useful tendency of qualities and actions; it is not alone sufficient to produce any moral blame or approbation. Utility is only a tendency to a certain end; and were the end totally indifferent to us, we should feel the same indifference towards the means. It is requisite a *sentiment* should here display itself, in order to give a preference to the useful above the pernicious tendencies. This sentiment can be no other than a feeling for the happiness of mankind and a resentment of their misery; since these are the different ends which virtue and vice have a tendency to promote. Here, therefore, *reason* instructs us in the several tendencies of actions, and *humanity* makes a distinction in favor of those which are useful and beneficial." To deliver precepts of morality to men, if they had no original perception of moral distinctions, whould be neither more nor less absurd, than to lecture to the blind about the colours of the rainbow. A moral sense—an innate sensibility to the beauty and deformity of conduct—is quite as much presupposed in the one case, as the use of the bodily organ in the other.

It is to this division of the offices, which *reason* and *sentiment* perform in morals, that we owe the discussion of a question, which (as we have seen) frequently arose, at Athens, between Socrates and the Sophists; whether virtue were an art or science, capable of being reduced to exact rules and principles, or an impulse of the soul, an inspiration from above. The sublime, though visionary, genius of Plato leans obviously to the latter opinion. His sages have that wisdom which is from above, and are all θεῖοι—divinely inspired. It is certainly not the object of that great writer to underrate the importance of an enlightened understanding, in all matters of moral conduct or opinion. He argues that side of the question too strongly to be supposed not to have very fully considered it. But Plato, as we should conclude from the general scope and spirit of his speculations, thought that the great desideratum of moral discipline was, not to shew what are the duties of life, but to dispose men to perform them, and rather to make them enthusiasts in the love of virtue, than casuists and cavillers about the subtleties of doctrine. He seems to have thought it easy enough, in these matters, to convince the mind by argument, but hard to persuade the heart, to win over the affections, to fortify the soul against the temptations of the world, and to raise it above the grovelling influences of sense and selfishness. His philosophy, therefore, has a poetical colouring. It is delivered in a lofty and glowing strain, and addresses itself to the imagination, which it inflames and elevates with visions of perfection and hopes of bliss. He is persuaded that such are the attractions of virtue—so ravishing is moral beauty—that, if mankind could but be persuaided to lift up their eyes from the meaner objects which too constantly engross them, and fix them upon the only one that is really worthy of their aspirations, they could not fail to be smitten with the deepest love. When we read the writings of St. Paul, we are struck with the resemblance they bear, in this respect, to the dialogues of Plato. The faith, hope and love (commonly translated *charity*), which good christians are exhorted to cultivate and cherish, are dwelt upon in a strain as rapturous as any in which Socrates pours out his eloquent admiration of the First Good and the First Fair. Indeed, to inspire a certain degree of enthusiasm, a divine fervour of feeling, a holy intenseness of purpose, is the very end of all christian discipline, and it is because that discipline abounds in the means of accomplishing this end, far more than any scheme of philosophical teaching, that its moral effects are so conspiciously beneficial. What, indeed, is the love of God, the great pervading principle of christianity, but a new motive—a sublime and solemn enthusiasm—counteracting the downward tendencies of self-love—the evidence of a regenerated nature purified from the contaminations of the world and the body, acting under the influence of grander views, and reasserting its original glory and perfection?

The aims of Utilitarianism are the very reverse of all this. It seems to be taken for granted, in that discipline, that *sentiment* has no share in moral approbation, and ought to have no influence upon moral conduct. Its inevitable tendency, if not its avowed object, is to chill enthusiasm, to extinguish sensibility, to substitute wary, and even crafty calculation, for the native goodness of an uncorrupted heart. They are not satisfied with laying down general principles of conduct or forming habits of virtue. An account-current of consequences is always open before them and their love and their hatred, their approbation and censure, vary with every appearent change in the balance-sheet. Their sage never forgets his arithmetic for a moment—the most sublime instances of heroic self-devotion, the most touching pictures of benevolence and charity, are examined with the same *sang-froid* with which a beautiful body is cut up in the dissecting-room. A cockney tradesman associating the recollections of Cheapside with the scenery of Switzerland—a rude hind, noting the vicissitudes of the seasons, the rising and setting of the heavenly bodies, and all the glorious phenomena of nature only as they are connected with his vulgar occupations,—such is the image of an Utilitarian contemplating the sublime and beautiful in morals. Like Mammon, he is

"—— The least erected spirit,
That fell from heaven: for, even in heaven,
His looks were always downward bent, admiring more
The riches of heaven's pavement, trodden gold,
Than aught divine or holy else enjoyed
In vision beatific."

The whole complexion and character of Utilitarianism, as a practical system of discipline, is determined by its fundamental maxim, that whatever is expedient is right. We certainly do not deny the truth of this proposition—but we do object to the form in which it is enunciated, and the emphasis that is laid upon it. Whether we arrive at the conclusion, with Paley, by reasoning *à priori* from the assumed or established attributes of Deity, or by experience and observation, we have no doubt but that utility (properly understood) and virtue are one and the same thing, or—to express it in a more familiar way—that honesty is, and must forever be, in the long run, the best policy. It is, in this respect, that the utility of Paley differs from that inculcated by Lysimachus, in Plato's Republic, and by Carneades, in his famous discourses or prælections at Rome, so often alluded to in the dialogues of Cicero. The *utile* thus considered is always opposed to the *honestum* or to fitness and propriety. But that is a short-sighted Machiavelian policy—the utility of the footpad and the usurper, of Jonathan Wild, and Borgia or Bonaparte. We admit that Jeremy Bentham has not gone so far as openly to profess *this* science, but we contend that, however he may affect to distinguish his doctrines from those of the true Newgate school, they have, in practice, an awful squinting the same way. If he had only affirmed that whatever is right is expedient, we should have found no fault at all with the dogma. But this proposition would not have suited his purposes. It is entirely too consonant to truth and nature. It would be only repeating what every body has said for, at least, three thousand years, and would leave mankind as much under the influence of those superstitions, miscalled natural feelings, as if no "Bacon of the age" had ever been vouchsafed to them. Those ingenious gentlemen, who are disposed to moot questions, which, according to Aristotle, ought to be answered by a jack-ketch instead of a dialectician,* would have had no room

* This passage of the Stagirite is remarkable enough to be quoted. It is to be found in the Topics, l. i. c. 11. "It is not every problem or thesis that deserves consideration: but such only as are matters of doubt to men, who want to be enlightened by argument, not to those who are worthy of punishment, or without some of the senses. For they who doubt, for instance, whether they ought to honor the gods, or love their parents, deserve to be punished—they who doubt

at all for their innocent paradoxes, or been confined in their discussion of them to a plea at the Old Bailey. It is the boast of Jeremy that, by his version of the maxim just cited, he has exploded altogether what he calls the system of sympathy and antipathy—that his disciples can very coolly argue propositions, of which the bare idea is revolting to people whose consciences are more nice than wise—and that, if his sect spread, civilized nations may not long have to envy savages the right of destroying their sickly children and superannuated parents, or Mr. Mill, jr. or Mr. Francis Place, or any other good Malthusian, boggle about teaching and practising infanticide as "the sovereign'st remedy on earth" for a glut in population.

True philosophy, we repeat it, is studious to inculcate not that whatever is expedient is right—but that whatever is right is expedient.* The rules of morality are few and simple. Follow nature, as the oracle said to Cicero. Love your neighbour, and indulge, without fear of consequences, the promptings of an honest heart. The duties of life are, generally speaking, plain and obvious to any man of common capacity, and woe to those who consider them as problems, as matters of recondite and perplexing science, which all the powers of algebra are required to settle! The true seat of intelligence and wisdom, in morality, is (where the ancients placed it in all things) the heart. It does not occur in one case out of a thousand, perhaps ten thousand, that the advice of a casuist is wanted even in the weightiest concerns of life. To talk of a system of ethics, built upon the everlasting feelings of nature, as "arbitrary," or "mutable," appears to us to be abusing language. The differences in the morality of civilized nations, in spite of all the causes that seem to conspire to aggravate them, are very slight, and those (be it remembered) occasioned not by the *feelings* of men, but by what is called their *reason*—by *policy*—by positive legislation and instituted rule. These, indeed, continually fluctuate and vary infinitely—as every thing founded upon the conclusions of Utilitarian logic will ever be found to do. But the great bulk and body, if we may so express it, of the morality of nations—the *jus gentium* of civilized people—springing, as it does, out of feelings which are inherent in the heart wherever it beats—is perpetual and uniform. The same taste in literature, which pronounced Homer the first of poets in his own times, has survived all the vicissitudes of empire and manners. Nature does homage to his genius still, because his genius is always true to nature.

whether snow be white or not, are destitute of a sense." This reminds us of Cyril, who said, that a man must be a Jew to insist upon reasons, and ask *how* upon mysterious subjects, and that this same *how* would bring him to the gallows. Bibliot. Univers. vii. 54.

[* Jambl. Ch. Vita Pythag. No. 204-5. Porphyry Id. No. 39.]

His pictures of virtue and vice are as just and as pleasing now as they ever were, and time has made far greater changes in the spot where his heroes fought—the face of the great globe itself— than in the sentiments which their achievements and their sufferings are fitted to awaken. School-boys are still taught to repeat the heroic exhortation of Sarpedon, and to study, in Hector, the model of every public and private excellence.

The intellectual discipline of the Utilitarians is of a-piece with the moral. Its professed object is the same, and so are its effects. It aims at cultivating the understanding alone, at the expense of the imagination and sensibility. It proscribes poetry and eloquence, and we have Mr. Neal's authority for saying that this part of the system, at least, has been completely successful. Here, too, they are at war with nature, and their "vast Typhœan rage" vents itself indiscriminately upon whatever most embellishes society and refines and exalts the spirit of man. Why is there so much about us to inspire genius, and to make the heart "o'erflow with fragrance and with joy?" Why is nature vocal with sweet music, and clothed all over in beauty, as with a bridal garment, so that the most useful objects in creation are still the most distinguished for grandeur and loveliness, and there is one glory of the sun, and another glory of the moon, and yet another glory of the stars, and "great and innumerable fruit, and many and divers pleasures for the taste, and flowers of unchangeable colour, and odours of wonderful smell?"* Why, we ask, is this; and what is still more, why was a being placed in the midst of all this magnificence and deliciousness, with a moral and intellectual constitution in perfect harmony with the external world thus adorned and pleasant, and with every capacity for enjoying it, if his whole duty was to be self-denial, and his highest perfection, insensibility? The truth is, that poetry is a part, and an essential part, of human nature; and he who can look out upon the material world, as it lies before him in its grandeur and beauty, or read of the heroic doings of the mighty dead, without feeling his bosom warmed with that enthusiasm which is the soul of poetry, falls, so far, short of what man ought to be. The ordinary relations and duties of life are surrounded with associations which have a like effect upon the imagination and the heart. "Honor thy father and thy mother" is a precept of universal morality, and even an Utilitarian, we suppose, would *generally* assent to its reasonableness—but what a difference is there between a cold compliance with the letter of the law,—between such conformity as "the greatest happiness principle" exacts of a politic "arithmetician"—and the religious veneration, the fervid and holy love, the entire devotedness of soul which Sophocles has consecrated

* Esdr. ii. 6, 44.

in the person of Antigone! It is this *poetry* of the affections—thus protecting and cherishing the virtue which it adorns—that is seared and blighted by this churlish and cynical doctrine. "All the decent drapery of life," to borrow the felicitous language of Burke, "is rudely torn off," and the beauty which gives to moral excellence its highest attraction, and the love which makes duty happiness, and the endearing sensibilities, without which the most scrupulous propriety of conduct is cold and ungainly, wither away beneath its influence. If, by some sudden change in our own constitution, or in that of the material world, whatever, in sensible objects, now charms the eye and the ear, and, through them, the imagination and the heart, were to become indifferent to us—so that all music and beauty should cease to be, and sight and hearing should inform us merely of the existence of nature, without filling us with such transports of pleasure and admiration as her works are fitted to inspire—how deformed and desolate would this magnificent universe become! Such is precisely the effect of the discipline in question—such is the havoc which it makes in the soul of man.

But enough of Utilitarianism—a philosophy, the very reverse of that so justly, as well as beautifully described in Milton's Comus:

"How charming is divine philosophy—
Not harsh and crabbed as dull fools suppose,
But musical as is Apollo's lute
And a perpetual round of nectared sweets."

6

[Caleb S. Henry]

Review

Morals and Legislation. By Jeremy Bentham.
Translated into French by M. Dumont, *with notes; and from the French* (2d. ed. corrected and enlarged) *with Notes, and a Biographical Notice of Jeremy Bentham and of M. Dumont,* by John Neal. Boston, Wells & Lilly. 1836.
Bentham's *Deontology.*
Westminster Review. No. XLI. Art. I. *The Principles of Moral and Political Philosophy.* By Willam Paley, D.D.'
in

New York Review
vol. I (March 1837), pp. 58–75

ART. II.—*Morals and Legislation.* By JEREMY BENTHAM. Translated into French by M. DUMONT, *with notes ; and from the French,* (2d. ed. corrected and enlarged) *with Notes, and a Biographical Notice of Jeremy Bentham and of M. Dumont, by* JOHN NEAL. Boston, Wells & Lilly. 1836.
BENTHAM's *Deontology.* Westminster Review, No. XLI. ART. 1.
The Principles of Moral and Political Philosophy. By WILLIAM PALEY, D. D.

THE name of Mr. Bentham is every day gaining increased celebrity as the rallying-point of a new school in morals, and the very "loadstar of reformation" in politics. His political principles will become the subject of discussion hereafter. It is our purpose now to offer some strictures on his principles in morals; and as those principles are held substantially by the other author, whose well-known and favorite name we have placed at the head of this article, we shall take this opportunity of making some remarks upon the nature and tendency of his ethical speculations also.

What is duty? and whence our obligation to perform it? are questions which have been long agitated, but in regard to which, especially the latter, there is still much difference of opinion. At the sight of certain actions we are all conscious of a movement of mind by which we *approve* or *disapprove;* and if the actions are proposed to ourselves, we experience still further an impulse, either to perform or to avoid them. What then is this moral movement so different from mere physical force, and yet so obvious to all—and by what quality in actions is it awakened? Whence that broad distinction—that gulph which no power of education or self-deception can annihilate—which is recognised in all languages, seen by all minds which appears forever to separate vice from virtue? Does this difference result from the very nature of things, and remain therefore through all changes of law and policy immutably the same; or is it created by the mere authority of some law, human or divine—by the mere fact that the one has been forbidden and the other required; so that were the mandate of the law reversed, what we now call *virtue* might in one moment be transformed into *vice*, and the blackest crimes become the greatest virtues?* Or, do we feel that there is an original and essential difference between actions, which, springing from the relations of things, must not only be antecedent to Law, but must itself be the basis of all Law?

If such original difference be admitted, what is its nature? Does it respect merely the *tendency* of actions—their fitness to injure or to benefit; or has it an independent character of its own? In other words, are truth, integrity, charity, virtues, merely because they contribute to private or general happiness, because they open the way to enjoyment in life, or to never ending blessedness after death; or are they virtues in consequence of some inherent and indestructible quality—a quality which depends not on circumstances or effects—which would impart to actions its own sacred impress, even though they were the occasion only of misery, and which, through all the revolutions of

---

* "If God," says Ockham, "had commanded his creatures to hate himself, hatred of God would have been praiseworthy."

polity and time will ever hold them up, as objects of the same commanding reverence?

These are questions equally interesting to the scholar and to practical man. At first view they may seem to present only a subject for curious speculation. But in reality they are entertained, and not only entertained,—in effect they are decided by every mind; and that decision has a serious influence on its character and conduct. In life, each one has his leading principles of action—his ultimate reasons into which he resolves all duty; and those principles must impart their hue to his whole deportment as a citizen—as a man of business—as a neighbor and even as a Christian. In preferring one course of conduct to another, we must do so, either because we consider it to be our interest, or because while we *think* it to be our interest, we also *feel* it to be our duty—feel at our hearts the promptings of some impulse higher and holier than mere self-love, urging us to virtue and to the perfection of goodness as an end of our being no less than as the means of our welfare. We are fair in our dealings—exemplary in our families—patriotic in our public labors—and Christian in our creed and worship, either, because we see HAPPINESS in the distance alluring us forward, and because we think the pursuit of happiness, is the one only end and object of our existence; or we are all these, because side by side with happiness there is another and more venerable form—it is HOLINESS, VIRTUE, demanding of us yet higher homage—worthy to be followed, not simply as a guide to conduct us to bowers of pleasure, but as a mistress, having intrinsic and surpassing worth.

We have thus indicated two leading *systems of duty* which have divided the suffrages of the learned, and the affections of the multitude. In the present age, so remarkable for the ardor of its pursuit after what are called *practical* and *popular* interests, it is easy to discover a marked tendency towards one rather than the other of these systems. Among the young, especially, who enter life amidst such an intense and universal strife for wealth and distinction; and who are made to feel so quickly and sensibly, every movement of public opinion, there is an unusual disposition (natural indeed, but not therefore the less to be lamented) to view happiness as the one thing needful, and the attainment of happiness as the single end of all their labors. Ours is an age, moreover, when men tired of venerable abuses, are inclined to bring every thing to the stern test of utility—and it is not strange that being in such a frame, and solicited on every side by physical means of enjoyment, they should think too exclusively of a gross and palpable utility which attaches only to the outward man, while they overlook that nobler excellence which belongs to the mind and the heart. At such an era, philosophy and literature catch the prevailing spirit. Reacting upon it, they give that spirit new impulse, which in its turn again flows back upon the speculations of the sage; and thus men venerable for learning and even for piety, are brought to lend their sanction in lessons of surpassing talent, to the maxims of a sordid philosophy which would confound virtue with prudence, and place the self-devotion of the patriot and philanthropist, upon a level with the calculations of the trader, or the schemes of the demagogue.

It is a fact which ought to be known and pondered, that the selfish morality, which was first taught by Epicurus, and which extended itself till it contributed to unnerve the stern virtue of the Romans, and to overthrow, at one blow, their patriotism and their liberty; which was revived in France during the reign of a licentious court, and helped to prepare the nation for all the guilt and atrocities of the Revolution; which reappeared again in England about fifty years since, and was the means of producing, says Robert Hall,* an entirely new cast of character, equally remote from the licentious gaiety of high life, and the low profligacy which falls under the lash of the law; a race of men distinguished by a calm and terrible ferocity, resembling Cæsar in this only, that they went with sobriety to the ruin of their country;—it deserves to be known, that this philosophy is revived in our own day, and is taught with indefatigable zeal by some of the ablest writers in our language. It comes to us, at present,† under the auspices of Bentham, and is the presiding spirit in all his powerful but singular works. It has succeeded in establishing one of the ablest of the British reviews, (the Westminster,) and may be met in publications of every size and rank, from the quarto volumes of Mr. Mill and Dr. Bowring, down to the humblest effusions of a daily press. Nor these

* See sermon on Infidelity.

† It is a singular fact, that Mr. Bentham and his followers should claim for him the glory of having discovered this philosophy. His first principles, i. e. that men always act, and were made to act, from a primary regard to their own interest, has been proclaimed in almost every age and country of the civilized world, not excepting Hindoostan and China. The Epicureans of Greece had their predecessors in one of the moral sects of India. Like their antagonists the Stoics, they illustrate the excessive tendency to simplicity, which has always characterized moral speculations, especially in their earlier stages. The other great principle of Mr. Bentham, and in which he takes specia pride, viz.: that we are to find our own interest in contributing *to the greatest happiness of the greatest number*, was held in substance by Epicurus, and has been taught in form by many of the moderns. E. g. Hume and Godwin.

alone. Hume and Godwin,* and we must add Paley, still live, in their works, to plead its cause; while it numbers, as allies, mightier than all, the spirit of the age, the sordid inclinations of the heart. Thus addressing us under the sanction of honored names; thus clothed in all the grace and brilliancy that the highest genius can bestow—taught us perhaps as one of our youthful studies—reiterated now in the literature of our libraries and our drawing rooms, it becomes us to weigh well its claims. It approaches us when least we suspect it, in the worldly-wise maxim—in the levity and banter of conversation—in the flexible politics of private as well as public life—in the countless influences of a busy and a worldly age. If, then we would not imbibe it as thousands do imbibe it, unconsciously—if we would recognise it in all its disguises and be prepared deliberately to accept or withstand its influence, we should make it the subject of study. We should weigh its principles—consider its tendency, and try it by that unfailing ordeal—the ordeal of history.

What then is this system usually called the selfish system of morals?—For an answer to this question we go to its most esteemed advocate, Dr. Paley, and we find it stated by him in few and explicit words. "Virtue," says Paley, "is the doing good to mankind, in obedience to the will of God and FOR THE SAKE *of everlasting happiness!*" The motive then from which all duty or virtue must proceed is the hope of everlasting happiness. It must be in accordance with the will of God, because he alone has everlasting happiness at his disposal, and it must consist in doing good to mankind, because it is by that means alone that he will permit us to attain eternal happiness! The same principle is laid down in another form. "Why," says Paley, "am I obliged to keep my word?"—and we may add, to relieve the poor or perform any other duty. The simple and only answer given, is, " because I am urged to do so by a *violent motive*," (viz. the fear of everlasting misery and the hope of everlasting happiness) "resulting from the command of God." Paley, it must be remembered, was a Christian and a divine—

* It may surprise those who are acquainted with the writings of Hume and Godwin, to hear them quoted as advocates of the selfish theory. It is true that they formally maintain the capacity of man for disinterested affections; and one of them seems, at times, even disposed to regard benevolence as the only proper spring of action. Their language on this point, however, is vague and contradictory; while they hold fully with Paley and Bentham in estimating actions by their consequences, and in making utility the only ground of moral distinctions. Doing so, they deny in effect, that there is in actions any such thing as an independent moral quality; abolish the distinction between natural and moral science, and open a way for most of the evils of the selfish theory.

and it was of course needful that he should bring into view the precepts and sanctions of his religion.—Not so with Bentham: who, as we learn from Mr. Neal, was an Atheist. Translated into his language and into the language of most modern and ancient Utilitarians, Paley's definition would read more simply thus,—" Virtue is the doing good to mankind for the sake of my own happiness."—I am obliged to keep my word, and feed the hungry and clothe the naked, not because I am touched by a noble impulse,* which finds delight in acts of justice and charity—not because I am urged by a sense of duty, which, though it speaks with still small voice, yet speaks in tones of rightful and supreme authority—but, simply, because I am urged by a violent desire to secure my own happiness, which (alas!) can be secured on no other terms. Nature or necessity has so bound up my own welfare with that of others, that I am not at liberty to attain the one without promoting the other, and therefore I must needs be just and charitable. Still my own happiness is the only thing for which I am required, or was ever destined to care. In laboring for the benefit of others, I am to do it simply because I am myself to be the gainer, and not because I need feel any sincere interest in it. When performing the highest offices of philanthropy, I fully acquit myself of all the claims of duty, though intent only on my own good, and utterly careless of their welfare for whom I labor. Nay more. If I could indeed lose sight of my own interest, if utterly unmindful of the reward which was to follow, I were capable of an act of kindness to my fellow men, simply from good will to them, or from a sense of gratitude and veneration towards that Supreme Being in whose image they were made, I ought not to regard such an act as virtue. I ought rather to repress such an impulse from within, as factitious and foolish; and consider that it is not by feeling, but by a cool calculation of interest— by a nice computation of profit and loss, that I am to deter-

---

* Paley repudiates altogether the notion of such impulses. (B. III. P. I. ch. v. P. II. ch. v.) Bentham and his followers seem disposed, at times, to recognise some of the benevolent affections as part of the original constitution of man; and recently a writer of the sect, (West. Rev. No. 41. Art. Deontology) for *the sake of argument*, admits a moral impulse or conscience. Such admissions, however, are effectually neutralised by the doctrine, that in yielding to these impulses, we do it, not instinctively, nor because they are superior in authority, but on a deliberate calculation that it is only by such obedience that we can secure the greatest amount of happiness. This is a new rendering of Pope's verse—

" Modes of self-love, the Passions we may call."

The fatal objection to such a doctrine is that it subordinates conscience to self-love, and makes no distinction between instinctive and deliberative principles.

mine the preference of truth to falsehood, of piety to blasphemy, of humanity and justice to cruelty and blood.

This, we believe, is an impartial exhibition of the grounding principle of that philosophy, which can be distilled from almost every page of Dr. Paley's celebrated work on morals, and which forms the glory of the plan by which Bentham and his disciples would regenerate the world. We do not propose now to call in question the specific rules, which this system may prescribe for the regulation of our conduct. He might even admit that these rules, so far as they respect the outward conduct, are identical with those furnished in the Scriptures, or in any other moral code. What we object to here, is the *spirit* of the system—the motive on which it makes virtue dependent. We contend, that in resolving all duty or virtue into self-love, it strips it of its dignity—debases our moral sentiments, and offers violence to fundamental notions of the human mind. And we propose farther to show, that the system has never prevailed in any country or at any age without tending to the subversion of morality and order. Man is sufficiently sordid from the impulse of his passions. He needs no aid from philosophy to render him sordid on principle and selfish by rule.

Our *first* remark on this system is, that it *confounds virtue with prudence*. This is virtually acknowledged by Paley, who states that the only difference between an act of prudence, and an act of virtue is, that in the one case we have respect to the happiness of this life alone, whereas in the other, we consider also, what we shall gain or lose in the world to come—a difference, be it observed, for which there is no place in the minds of those who do not admit that there is a world to come ; and which disappears in practice, we apprehend, from the minds of most, if not of all, who adopt the system. In truth, it is simply a verbal difference. If the mere fact, that an action is useful to the agent, be sufficient to constitute it a virtuous action, it can matter little whether the benefit be of shorter or of longer duration. It follows then, in effect, that prudence is virtue, and that the highest virtue is but the highest prudence. If a capitalist makes a wise investment, or a merchant projects a judicious and successful voyage, we may term these respectively a *virtuous* voyage, and a *virtuous* investment ; just as Bentham was wont when he spoke of good mutton, to call it *virtuous mutton*, and when he petted his favorite animal (a deer) to style it his *virtuous deer*.* If on the other hand, the same man performs some noble deed of

* See Neal's Biog. Notice of J. Bentham.

patriotism or philanthropy—some act in which seeming to forget himself, he toils and sacrifices only for the benefit of others—why, he is merely a *prudent man*, who uses the means of happiness entrusted to him.

For example, Sir Thomas More, after a year's imprisonment, and when enfeebled by suffering, is offered permission to return to his wife and children whom he loved so tenderly—to the intellectual pursuits in which he took such delight—to the summit of greatness from which he had been plucked down, if he will but sacrifice a scruple of conscience. He indignantly refuses and prefers rather to perish on a scaffold; and he, on this system, is but a prudent man, who has a proper understanding of his interest! Lafayette, a husband and a father—with every thing in certain prospect or in actual possession that the highest ambition could crave or the warmest sympathies desire, surrenders all—hurries to the aid of a distant and almost hopeless cause, and offers, not only without regret, but with exultation, the endearments of domestic life and the favors of his prince in exchange for toil and danger in behalf of suffering strangers—and he too, is but a prudent man! The great Washington tears himself from the peaceful and honored shades of Mount Vernon, assumes reluctantly a command more fearful perhaps than was ever before entrusted to man—a command which puts at peril his fame, his fortune and his head. Campaign after campaign he toils almost without resources, loaded down with responsibility, the object of machinations at home, and of deadly hostility abroad;—and at length, when victory is achieved—his country independent—his name on every tongue, hastening to lay down his command, he escapes from the thanksgivings and honors of his grateful country to the silence of his home; and this is but *prudence!* and through all this career of seeming glory there has been but the shrewd calculations of an exclusive self-love!

It would be easy to multiply such examples. What shall we say of Howard, leaving a home of opulence and ease that he might dwell "in the depths of dungeons and amidst the infection of hospitals." What of the soldier of the cross as bidding farewell to the scenes of his childhood and the land of his fathers—rupturing the ties of affection—counting not his life dear unto himself, he goes out to gather amidst malignant gales and in savage wildernesses a harvest for his Lord? What of that Lord himself, as he comes forth from the glory of universal empire, and clothes himself in human form, and becomes a man of sorrows and consents at last to die in agony for the rescue of the guilty and the vile? Is there nothing here but prudence?

Is it all self-seeking? Has there been no principle—no patriotism—no philanthropy—no love of liberty—no disinterested zeal for God and man? Then we say, let history be rewritten, that it may strip these pretenders of their factitious greatness. Let the Evangelists and the Acts of the Apostles, too, be revised, that they may no longer tell of benovolence and zeal—that they may record of Peter and James and John,—when they appear before us rejoicing that they are reckoned worthy to suffer for the name of Jesus—when they resolve that, in spite of the decrees of councils and the madness of mobs, they will still publish the things that they have seen and heard—when they go from city to city smiling on the rage of persecutors, lifting their warning voice in the presence of rulers, and making the very prison-house vocal with their songs;—let the historian, amended and corrected by the Utilitarian, tell us that, after all, these were but men who had a keen eye to their own interest and were in quest of honor and reward! In quest of honor and reward they doubtless were. That they had no thought of these, or that they were not, in truth, advancing their highest happiness by this very self-devotion, is not pretended. But was this all? Their happiness, they had a right to think of! To neglect, or madly trifle with it is alike folly and guilt. But did they think of nothing else? Was it by dwelling exclusively and intently on their own interest, that they were moved to tears and sympathy—that they were nerved to deeds of self-sacrifice—that their hearts were made to bleed for the sins and sufferings of distant strangers and benighted heathen? Or is it in man, when engrossed with himself and thinking not of others, to rise to the stature of such deeds, and write his name high and bright among the benefactors of his race. Surely this life must be delusion—history a romance—the Holy Evangelists but a tissue of fables, or else the philosophy in question is false.

And yet further.—This philosophy not only confounds virtue with prudence. It goes so far as to *confound it even with vice* to abolish all intelligible distinction between right and wrong, and place them before us on the same moral level. For what, according to the Utilitarian, is *virtue?* It is a wise forecast and calculation respecting our own happiness. And what is *vice?* It is an *unwise* calculation and forecast in regard to the very same thing. To both the virtuous and vicious man is presented the same object to be pursued from the same motive, and the only conceivable difference is one of degree, not of kind. The one looking for happiness rises to justice and beneficence—the other in quest of the same end descends to deeds of infamy and guilt. Where is there room for that vast and radical distinction which we are accustomed to make, for that deep and heartfelt reverence on the one hand, or for that intense disapprobation and displeasure on the other? Is a mere "error in arithmetic"—a mere mistake in the computation of gain and loss such an enormous crime that it ought to kindle indignation; or is simple "expertness in posting and balancing the moral ledger," in anticipating the chances of a given adventure, an achievement so lofty, that it ought to bow down our souls in admiration? On the supposition that this system is true, where is there room for the exercise of moral esteem and reverence, or for those sentiments of contempt and reprobation which we feel at the sight of the seducer and oppressor? And the guilty man himself, when he takes a review of his life and finds that he has been an extortioner, a sensualist, a blasphemer, what occasion has he for that remorse with which he is wont to goad himself? At the worst he has but calculated badly—made an unwise speculation for which he may well feel regret—but should suffer no remorse. Once admit the principle that man acts and ought to act only from a regard to his own happiness, be it in this or in a future world, and it must be followed out till there remains no place for moral distinctions. Duty sinks till it becomes synonimous with prudence, virtue with skill, vice with error, remorse with regret, and indignation with pity.

There is yet another objection. Dr. Paley, as we have seen, admits the Divine will to be our rule of duty, and inculcates implicit obedience. But on what ground does he do so? Is it on the ground that God has a *moral right* to our obedience—that as our creator and best benefactor—as the source and centre of all excellence, he merits and should receive the deepest homage of our gratitude and esteem? Far from it. We are not obliged, on his principles, to cherish one sentiment of gratitude, or of reverence. "Love the Lord thy God with all thy heart," merely means, in this school, "be very careful not to incur his displeasure? He has at his disposal, your eternal well-being—be extremely cautious lest you provoke him to make it a sacrifice!" Such caution is doubtless proper. It is enjoined in one sense by all the sacred writers and by Christ himself. It shows the expediency of consulting the Divine will. But is it the *ground* on which they rest the *duty* of obedience. Is it the great informing principle of their morality—the source whence they deduce the authority and the obligations of religion? In other words, is the government of God built on the mere basis of power, and not of right, so that we are called to submit, not because we ought, but because we must? Such is indeed the view which these speculations seem to take; and it may assist us in forming a proper estimate of the system, when we thus find it blotting from the divine character all moral attributes, such as justice and holiness—holding up his Omnipotence as the only proper object of regard—representing his commands as merely arbitrary decrees, and our own moral notions as little better than fictions of law.

We have thus considered the violence which this theory offers, as well to language as to our moral notions, and the debasing views which it takes of the whole subject of duty and religion. We proceed to speak of its *history*.

To ascertain its legitimate influence, we should look, not at its first teachers and masters, but at its disciples. Paley, a philanthropist and a Christian—reared under the wholesome morality of the Bible, might adopt such a theory in after life, might inculcate and apply it throughout a volume, and yet feel little of its influence in practice. And it is a fact worthy of remark, that the same writer, who in his Moral Philosophy, comes to the conclusion that there is in man no conscience or moral sense which can be distinguished from prejudice and habit, declares, when he turns from his speculations to the practical labors of the ministry, and addresses his hearers in regard to their eternal concerns, that "conscience, our own conscience, is to be our guide in all things," and that it is "through its whisperings that the Spirit speaks to man."* So Bentham, Rochefocault, Epicurus, might embrace this philosophy in the regions of speculation, and yet hold it with many saving clauses, and in private life commend themselves as honest, amiable and philanthropic. But what has been its effect on those who have imbibed it early in life; who have carried it forth, not as a system to be defended, but as a principle to be acted upon—who in adopting its leading doctrines have lost sight of conditions that modify, refine, and spiritualise it—who have been accustomed to appeal to it in the hour of temptation, and amidst the tumults of a corrupt and corrupting world? What indeed must be the influence and tendency of that system which teaches, that regard for our own happiness embraces the whole duty of man? We answer by adducing facts, and the authority of some of the best and wisest men.

The severe and upright Romans first heard of this philosophy through ambassadors whom they had sent to Greece, or received from there. They listened to it with aversion and disgust. We are told that Fabricius† on his return from Epirus, whither he had been to treat for an exchange of prisoners, announced that he had heard, during his absence, of a new doctrine which was

---

* See Paley's Sermons.   † Cic. de Senec.

rapidly gaining converts at Athens; and that this doctrine represented the love of pleasure as universally the leading motive of men's actions. Cicero adds that the friends of Fabricius who had been intimate with the immortal Decius, and who felt convinced by his example, as well as by their own emotions, that there was an intrinsic rectitude and virtue, independent of mere pleasure, and which the noble and generous mind would ever keep in view—these friends, when they heard the intelligence, declared at once that the people who embraced such a doctrine, would soon forfeit their liberties, and fall an easy conquest to their enemies.

At a later period an Athenian philosopher of this school (Carneades) visited Rome on an embassy. While waiting for the answer of the Senate he amused himself, we are told, in an attempt to demonstrate to the people, and especially the youth, that justice and injustice derived their origin from expediency, or from positive institutions, and that there was no foundation for a distinction between them in the nature of man. This gave great alarm to the fathers of the Republic;—Cato, the Censor, was so disturbed at the thought of having the opinions of his countrymen unsettled on points so sacred and important, that he never rested till the ambassadors received their final answer and were dismissed from Rome.* And were these great men mistaken in their estimate of the consequences of this philosophy?

Let him who thinks so, trace its history among the Grecian disciples of Epicurus, who, disregarding the severer maxims of their master and acting upon his great principle as they understood it, sunk from one degree of degeneracy to another till the very title of their sect became synonymous with indolence and sensuality. Let him follow it, as migrating to Rome, it trained up a Cæsar to overthrow the liberties of his country; and there extended itself among all classes till the entire nation became one scene of effeminacy, venality, and corruption.—Let him observe its later history in France. First put forth in the celebrated maxims of Rochefocault, its influence was soon felt in every department of literature and through every circle of society. It contributed in no slight degree to create that levity of principle and that heartless frivolity of manners which was so long the reproach of the French people. How many writers has it sent forth whose business, to use the language of Addison, the first English critic by whom it is noticed, "seems to have been to depreciate human nature, and consider it under its

---

* Stewart on the Active and Moral Powers, p. 143. Cambridge, 1829.

worst appearances—giving mean interpretations and ascribing base motives to the worthiest actions—laboring to do away all distinction between man and man, or between the human species and the brute." As an illustration of the spirit of this philosophy, let the following extracts from a comedy composed previous to the Revolution be taken, and let it be considered whether it was strange that in a nation where such sentiments prevailed, the whole fabric of society was convulsed and overthrown :—" As for my own part (says Cleon in the *Méchant* of Gresset) to speak impartially, I am not one of those who believe in the existence of the wicked," "a phantom conjured up by the low prejudices of the vulgar. I consider every body as bad, and nobody as bad. As for the duplicity and intrigues with which you are offended, I see nothing in them when examined to the bottom but a fund of amusement for myself. We all take and give so as to balance our accounts pretty well with each other. The only crime now known is *ennui*, and as this would soon make its way into the best society if there were any serious attachments among friends, we must have only prejudices, calumnies and absurdities. Hence every body should speak and act according to his own humor; believing that all is wrong—all right, and that all the world is equally happy."

Our limits have not allowed us to enter as minutely as we proposed into the history of this philosophy. We conclude this branch of the subject with a remark or two respecting our own country. The perpetuity of the blessings which we enjoy as Americans, depends, as is well known, on the virtue and integrity of the people. Education is at present doing much for their intelligence; but it should never be forgotten that mere intellectual education unaided by moral influence can train up no people to a stern and incorruptible virtue. The "Schoolmaster may be abroad." He may carry down his lessons to the humblest hovel, and yet those lessons be only the means of perverting and demoralizing.—Are they addressed chiefly or entirely to the sordid desires of our nature? Are the rising generation appealed to only, or principally, by their regard to their own interest, when we would incite them to knowledge and virtue? Is it our hope that when the people are thus enlightened in respect to their true welfare, such knowledge will be sufficient to exalt and save them? We could not devise a more fatal expedient for leading them to ruin.—All history proclaims that where public morality rests on the basis of expediency rather than of duty, it is as shortlived as spurious, and that when it expires it carries with it all the vigor and glory of a people. Such a morality never builds up a great and glorious public spirit; and without such a spirit, no nation endures long in honor and prosperity. Let the day come when among us that spirit is discarded as obsolete and old fashioned;—when virtue, which ought to be the prompt impulse of the heart, gets to be the creature of the brain; when questions of duty are adjourned from the bar of conscience to the noisy tribunal of expediency—when we determine how far we shall discharge duty only by ascertaining how far it will subserve our advantage, and at that day the name of liberty may remain to us, but the reality will have fled. Better infinitely in such case that no schools had been opened, nor schoolmasters sent abroad. When a shrewd, enlightened, calculating people once become devoid of moral and religious principle, they must present a spectacle sufficient to fill every friend of humanity with sorrow and dismay.—A nation ignorant as well as depraved—imbecile in mind as well as corrupt at heart, may be governed, and in some sense saved. But a nation composed of strong and unprincipled minds, endowed with a thousand-fold energy, but restrained by nothing but self-interest— ready whenever passion indicates its expediency for wrong or outrage—such a nation contains within its bosom elements of woe and discord which must soon explode; and with a shock too that will convulse the world.

Thus far, we have spoken only of the motive, or *principle* on which, according to the utilitarian, all duty must ultimately rest. There is another feature of his system, equally obnoxious to censure. To obviate the objection, that whoever acts merely from regard to his own interest will be ready to sacrifice the interest of others, he proposes a method by which self-love, (or, as Bentham calls it, *self-regarding interest*) can be pressed into the service of the public, and private and general utility became coincident. "God," says Paley, "wills and wishes the happiness of his creatures," and therefore any action, the general tendency of which is to promote that happiness, must be agreeable to Him, and conduce of course to our own final welfare. When, then, in any instance, we would know our duty, i. e., our highest interest, we must inquire into the general tendency of the contemplated action, in respect to the welfare of others, and so act as in the language of Bentham, "to promote the *greatest happiness of the greatest numbers.*" Bentham himself, inasmuch as he believed in neither natural nor revealed religion, had to reach this result by a somewhat different course. Accordingly he maintained after the example of Hume, that even in this life he is most likely to enjoy personal happiness, who consults most assiduously the general good. It would extend this discussion to an unpardonable length, to enter at large into the grave exceptions which may be taken at every step, in this train of reasoning. It rests, (we for the present confine ourselves to Paley's) as we conceive, on more than one false assumption—it establishes a rule often impracticable, and always dangerous, and it proceeds in practice on principles wholly at variance with some of the most obvious laws of our nature.

For example, it assumes that the great and only design of the Divine Government, is the *promotion of human happiness;* for if besides happiness, that government has any other great moral design, such as the promotion of virtue and holiness; or, if aiming only at happiness, it still comprehends in its plans the happiness of other worlds, and of higher intelligences with whose well-being, perhaps, the happiness of this insignificant planet may not always be in unison, then it follows that acts may be according to His will, which on the whole do not subserve human happiness. Waiving this, however, and admitting that to advance man's happiness alone, is the object of the Divine administration, does it follow that what *appears to us,* conducive to that end is therefore acceptable to God? Be it so, that the end is clear and definite; are the means equally so? God may "will and wish" the happiness of mankind; but may he not also "will and wish" the particular *way* in which he will have it compassed? And when we sit down to meditate, is it certain that the way which commends itself to our preference, is that on which, in his boundless wisdom and sovereignty, He has fixed? The President of the United States sends his minister to the court of France, to negociate a matter of great and delicate concern. Doubtless he would have him keep his eye intently fixed on the honor and interests of his country. But is that all? Does he leave him to exercise his own private discretion, as to the manner in which that honor, and those interests shall be maintained? Or, does he not rather say "the responsibility of these measures must devolve ultimately on me." For me it is to see, that they be so conducted as to accord, not with your views of public utility, but with my own ulterior plans, and with facts not yet made known. I must, therefore, be permitted to prescribe the *method* of your procedure—and where the letter of your instructions does not suffice for this purpose, be governed by their spirit, by what you have seen of my measures in analogous cases, and by the dictates of honor and conscience, as well as by any views which you may have of public utility.

Passing however, these assumptions, there is to this rule, the still more formidable objection, that it is often unavailable, and more often, dangerous. It is unavailable, because it calls us frequently on the verge, or in all the hurry of action, to decide a problem among the most difficult ever presented to the human mind, viz: the ultimate tendency and bearing of a measure—supposing said measure to become general. This is the very question which legislators are called to decide—and they do it—often how imperfectly! On many subjects which come before them, considerations of general expediency are their only guide, and do they find it easy with no other guide to reach the truth? Is there no difference of opinion among them when they deliberate on the bearings of a proposed measure? Even among the most gifted and enlightened minds, united in one with to advance the public weal, is there no discordance of views?—And when after weeks or months of deliberation, it has passed into a law—when it goes out and meets the countless currents of prejudice, and passion, and business-life—its purpose counteracted here, and promoted there—how different a thing does it often appear, from that which even the most sagacious apprehended. Here, then, are questions which cannot be decided aright, even by the wisest men after months of united counsel. How, then, shall the humble and unlettered man—of contracted views—who has rarely loooked at remote consequences—who knows little of the countless interests to be affected, how shall he hope to decide such questions, with even the most distant prospect of being right? How certain that, appalled with the magnitude of the inquiry, he will abandon it in despair, or else catching up the principle, that "whatever is expedient, is right" he will construe it to his own taste, and make it the pretext for self-indulgence and sin!

Even when carried out to its application in solitude, and by men anxious to show its excellence, this rule has sometimes taught lessons which send a chill through the heart. Look at Paley, the Christian moralist—the consecrated servant of the altar. He expressly teaches, in his work on Moral Philosophy, that, "falsehoods are not criminal if they do not happen to deceive" or if the person to whom they are spoken, "has no right to know the truth"—that there are no moral maxims, or rules, which may not innocently be made "to bend to circumstances"—and that the direction, "not to do evil that good may come" is for the most part a salutary caution, but is not always to be obeyed. Look at Hume. Guided by the principle of utility or general expediency he arrives at the conclusion, that moral, intellectual, and corporeal virtues, are nearly of the same kind—or in other words, and to use the paraphrase of Bishop Horne, that "to want honesty, to want understanding, and *to want a leg*, are equally objects of moral disapprobation—that adultery must be practised if a man would acquire all the advantages of life—that if generally practised, it would in time cease to be scandalous, and that if practised secretly and frequently, it would by degrees come to be no crime at all." Look at Godwin. In his Political Justice, he walks by the light of expediency; and where does it conduct him ? "The maxim," says he, "that we should love our neighbor as ourselves, though possessing considerable merit as a popular principle, is not modelled with the strictness of philosophical accuracy." He maintains, that, if our neighbor is more worthy, or useful than ourselves, we ought to love him better—ought to prefer, for example, his life before our own, and that on the same principle, if we had to choose between saving the life of a Fenelon, or the life of our own mother, we should prefer the former, if his life were of the most importance to the world ! He insists further, that gratitude, "a principle, which has been so often the theme of the moralist, and the poet, is no part either of justice or virtue"—that "men have no rights"—"that promises, absolutely considered, are an evil, and stand in opposition to the wholesome exercise of an intellectual nature"—that "oaths of allegiance being surperfluous promises, their imposition is atrociously unjust, and the breach of them, peculiarly susceptible of apology"—and that "treaties of alliance, are, in all cases wrong." In fine, as if to sum up the glories of expediency in a single proposition he declares, that " all human laws are unjust, and tyrannical." "Who," he asks, " has authority to make laws —to exercise that tremendous faculty of prescribing to the rest of the community, what they are to perform, and what avoid." The answers to these questions he adds, " are exceedingly simple. Legislation, as it has been usually understood, is not an affair of human competency." "Law tends no less than creeds and catechisms, to fix the mind in a stagnant condition, and to substitute a principle of permanence in the room of that increasing perfection which is the only salubrious element of mind." On this subject " the language of reason is plain. Give us equality and justice, but no constitution." And anticipating a time when such constitutions shall be for ever done away, he breaks out in the exclamation : " With what delight must every well-informed friend of mankind look forward to that auspicious period, the dissolution of political government—that brute engine which has been the perennial cause of the vices of mankind, and which has mischiefs of various sorts incorporated with its very substance, and not otherwise to be removed than by its utter annihilation !"

Such then is the doctrine of expediency; or in the language of our own day and of a large and growing school of writers, such is Utilitarianism, the philosophy which resolves all actions into self-interest as the motive, making public utility our *rule* of life. We have spoken of it as furnishing a *ground* of duty; and also as affording a *criterion* or standard by which we are to estimate all actions. We have endeavored to test its truth by comparing its principles with the native dictates of the human heart and with the unalterable truths of history. In tracing its consequences on the speculations of its defenders, and on the state of ancient and modern society we have submitted it to its own ordeal, the ordeal of *utility*. We have followed it out to its bold results in the writings of a Godwin and a Hume, as well as to its timid developments in the equivocal suggestions and partial licenses of the Christian divine.—Such as it is we commend it to the study of our readers. Before they adopt it in form or in substance, let them as they would cherish in their hearts a pure and lofty morality, weigh well the principles of this system. Let them guard alike against its more plausible and its more odious developments. In this age of utility, when we are so frequently measured only by our success or our popularity, the approaches of such a philosophy are equally insidious and constant. It is at such a time then, that we ought to cling most closely to the good, though old-fashioned, philosophy of our Bibles—the philosophy, which builds its authority on the moral constitution that God has given us, and on the essential and immutable difference between right and wrong. Instead of sending us abroad over the earth to calculate tendencies and possibilities, this philosophy bids us turn our eye homeward, and consult, with reverence, the dictates of the monitor within. In order to enlighten, and strengthen, and quicken these dictates, it offers us the aid of divine teaching and divine influence. It demonstrates, too, that while duty and happiness are distinct and independent, they are still perfectly coincident; and that we are never so sure of the latter as when thinking little of it, and intent chiefly, if not wholly, on the former, we give ourselves to the service of our race and of our God.

> *Love thyself last*—cherish those hearts that hate thee;
> Corruption wins not more than honesty.
> Still in thy right hand carry gentle peace
> To silence envious tongues. *Be just and fear not;*
> *Let all the ends thou aim'st at be thy country's,*
> *Thy God's and truth's.* Then if thou fall'st—
> Thou fall'st a blessed martyr.

7

[Anon.]

Review

*Theory of Legislation, by Jeremy Bentham,
translated from the French of Etienne Dumont.*
By Richard Hildreth, author of Banks, Banking and Paper
Currencies, etc., etc. Vol. I. *Principles of Legislation – Principles of
the Civil Code.* Vol. II. *Principles of the Penal Code.*
Boston: 1840. Weeks, Jordan, & Co.

in

New York Review
vol. VII (July 1840), pp. 263–7

9. *Theory of Legislation*, by Jeremy Bentham, translated from the French of Etienne Dumont. By R. HILDRETH, author of Banks, Banking, and Paper Currencies, etc., etc. Vol. I. *Principles of Legislation—Principles of the Civil Code.* Vol. II. *Principles of the Penal Code.* Boston: 1840. Weeks, Jordan, & Co. 12mo. pp. 276–268.

To need double translation — first into a foreign language, and then back into his own — before he could be read or understood by his fellow countrymen, is, we suspect, the singular fate among authors of Jeremy Bentham, *substantia singularis*. Yet such, with him and his writings, has been the simple fact. His own original speculations were unread, if not unreadable, in English; translated into French, by his household friend and admirer, Dumont, they became a familiar theme to the continental public, while yet a mystery at home — again to be re-translated into their original tongue, with all the advantages of double distillation — under ordinary circumstances, the eventual product would not be likely to have gained much from such compound process. With Bentham, however, it has been otherwise; and to his first translator his speculations are indebted for much of their popularity, and the whole, it would seem, of their intelligibility and scientific order. Such dubious parentage, however, naturally awakens some interest as to the circumstances that led to it. Dumont, it seems, was a political refugee from his native city, Geneva; driven from his own country by persecution, he first sought a genial home in St. Petersburg, but eventually in London, under the patronage of the Lansdowne family. There he first made Bentham's acquaintance, soon became his friend and disciple, and eventually the domesticated guardian of his fame, at least, and his papers. He was thus permitted to examine Bentham's manuscript treatises *rudis indigestaque moles*, and discovering the value of the hidden treasure in spite of the uncouth casket, proceeded zealously to the task — upon extorted leave of arranging, condensing, filling out, compiling, and eventually translating it into the French language, these scattered leaves of his Sybilline oracle. Such was the origin of the successive French works, of which the present was the earliest, which spread through continental Europe the fame of Bentham as a master mind in political science, and which, re-translated, have awakened the question in his own country, under the more bitter form of personal and party politics. Of this result, in our country, there can be no danger; and therefore we hail this translation of Mr. Hildreth with a pleasure unqualified by any fear of consequences. We, who have nothing among us, whether of good or evil, that stands on the ground of ancient reverence — neither cherished abuses nor antiquated errors — in which a doubtful balance must be struck between the evil of innovation and the good of reformation — we Americans can have nothing to dread from a voice like the present, that summons them in the name of reason to the bar of utility. Whatever reverence our laws have, they have upon this showing; so that the reasoner who becomes their accuser, is but enabling them to produce, upon their trial, the title-deeds by which alone they pretend to hold possession. Were we, indeed, Englishmen, on the other hand, we should scruple at such summary process, and be inclined to hold on to many an ancient buttress built in the olden time, and take for granted that it propped up some material part of the edifice, rather than permit this modern Archimedes to undermine in order that he might try its strength, or pull it down in order that he might re-construct it on more scientific principles. An old government, it is true, like an old mansion, will be apt to accumulate in it what may rightly be termed lumber, and to have here and there a dark hole or corner in which dirt accumulates — notwithstanding all which, it is, we think, apt to be a more quiet and comfortable residence, especially to those long accustomed to it, than a more tasteful building — and even a new occupant will, if he be wise, think twice before he tumble all things "topsy-turvy" for the sake of untried alterations. These scruples, however, belong not, as already said, to America. As for us, we have lashed our political rudder on that "tack," and must bide the billows it brings upon us of popular expediency. We give up to the question, therefore, every arraigned culprit among our civil institutions — only let him have fair trial, and stand or fall according as "the greatest good of the greatest number," the modern Minos, shall determine. But there is another point on which we do not yield, but are and must be at open war with Bentham and the Benthamese philosophy, whether sheltered under the name of its first or second parent, or any of their prolific offspring — we mean the application of his principle of "utility" to moral reasoning and ethical duties. As a political reasoner, Bentham is as sharp-sighted and sagacious as he is bold; this we acknowledge — carrying out fearlessly, and in general soundly, the infinite ramifications of the branches of man's civil life, as they spring from the one sole root of political society — EXPEDIENCY. But when, stepping beyond this line, he appears as the moral teacher of our race, and proceeds to demonstrate the present expediency of an action as the sole ground of duty to the individual himself, or to measure the line of that duty by man's microscopic vision of its visible results, then we must confess we hold Bentham and his opinions alike in high disdain, and declare against them war, irreconcilable war. Moral science and Benthamism cannot both stand — one or other to the block. If duty be but another name for expediency, then may we shut up our ethical works, and even the precepts of the Gospel may be dispensed with — there is then no other virtue than prudence — no other test of it than its visible consequences — and the good man and the profitable machine are placed on the same level of merit and desert — or rather there is no such thing as "merit." This word "*merit*," says Bentham, " can only lead to passion and error. It is *effects* good or bad, which we alone ought to consider." So much for Bentham's one-sided philosophy of man's nature — so much for the man with the leathern apron applying his rude "last," which sufficed well enough for the lower parts of the structure, to measure the God-like lineaments which speak for the man as originally made in the "image of Him who created him," and who even now, in this work-day world of expediency, has not yet lost "all his original brightness." But we must take ampler space and a more appropriate time for this braving of Bentham and his opinions on moral science; suffice it for the present to say, that it stands wholly apart from our judgment of him in legislation, though even here his conclusions are often false, through the imperfection of his philosophy of human nature. Laws fitted for man without a conscience, will not always suit the man who has a conscience. Among the marked instances of this, is Section II. of Chapter V. upon Divorces—under the question, *For what time* the marriage contract is to be formed. Bentham's decision here flies in the face of both law and gospel. It is, that the marriage contract should be "dissoluble at the pleasure of the parties." Now we hold him to be not only a bold, but a most unwise reasoner, who thus ventures to shake, that he may try the strength of this fundamental pillar of society — the inviolability of the marriage contract — and we trust that, on this point, at least, we Americans shall not learn the Benthamese language, nor ever hear it spoken in our halls of legislation. Amid all our attacks on monopoly, let us reverence at least that

" Sole propriety in paradise,
Of all things common else;"

nor be willing to take from the lips of a Jacobin and a celibate, the rules by which the happiness of married life is to be secured for us and for our children.

But to pass from the author to his American translator. Mr. H., in this work, establishes at least his own reputation. The translation appears faithful, and is unquestionably ably done. It has, indeed, much of the freedom and force of an original composition, and that, too, without departing from the precise and condensed style of the original. The following passage may be taken as a sample of the best parts, not only of the translator's talent, but of Bentham's mind, showing wisdom as well as acuteness in his bold questionings into the established order of things. In this passage, however, we rather think we have the comments of Dumont, and not the reflections of Bentham. Into his mind " of one idea," there entered no such wise scruples of his own principles as are exhibited in the following closing paragraph of the chapter on the civil code: " But, however bad existing laws may be, let us distrust the declamations of chagrin and the exaggerations of complaint. He who is so passionate in his ideas of reform as to desire a revolt, or to bring the established system into general contempt, is unworthy to be heard at the tribunal of an enlightened public. Who can enumerate the benefits of law, I do not say under the best governments, but under the worst? Are we not indebted to it for all we have of security, property, industry, and abundance? Are we not indebted to it for peace between citizens, for the sanctity of marriage, and the sweet perpetuity of families? The good which the law produces is universal; it is enjoyed every day and every moment. Its evils are transient accidents. But the good is not perceived: we enjoy it without referring it to its true cause, as if it appertained to the ordinary course of nature; while its evils are vividly felt, and in the description of them, the suffering which is spread over equal space and a long series of years, is accumulated by the imagination upon a single moment. How many reasons we have to love the laws, in spite of their imperfections!" This we hold to be eloquent wisdom, and with all our spirit of " conservatism," to which charge we plead guilty, we shall never quarrel with the innovator who proceeds to question *human* laws, under the guidance of such feelings.

We now take leave of Bentham for the present, and but for the present too, we hope, of his translator; since both for his sentiments as given in his preface, as well as for the ability displayed by him in the translation, we feel sincere respect. We are pleased, also, to see that he holds himself aloof from the " Principle of Utility," as the foundation of morals, and is content to advocate it but as "the only safe rule of legislation." This distinction is an all important one; and we trust that in a future edition of this work, or in some subsequent translation of others of Bentham's treatises, more especially his " Deontologie," should he be inclined to take it up, he will exhibit more fully than he has here done, the baselessness of a moral system built upon such shifting sands. Of his "Deontology," however, it is well for Mr. H. to be aware that an English translation, or rather a direct compendium from Bentham's own papers, has already been made in England, the proof sheets of which are now in our possession, sent out to us by Dr. Bowring, Bentham's literary executor, with a view to their republication here. To this request, however, we have returned a respectful negative, being neither willing to appear as foster-father to such a theory of ethics, nor to put forth a work written in such pure Benthamese as that, from hasty examination, appeared to us to be.

8

[John O'Sullivan?]

'Jeremy Bentham'

The United States Magazine and Democratic Review
vol. VIII, no. XXXIII (September 1840), pp. 251–71

JEREMY BENTHAM.*

A WRITER in the Westminster Review remarks, that the two men of the present age, who have most strongly influenced the minds of their countrymen, are Samuel Taylor Coleridge and Jeremy Bentham. Without questioning the accuracy of the observation, as it respects Coleridge, we think there can be no doubt of the truth of so much of it as applies to Bentham. Whatever may have been the influence of the former, whose researches were mostly in the region of abstract thought, and whose sympathies were altogether with the past, it must have been of that occult and delicate nature which only a few learn to appreciate. But the influence of Bentham, with his practical cast of mind, with his rugged sense, with his contemptuous disregard of authority, with his bold onsets upon cherished modes of faith, and with the immediate interest attached to all his inquiries, must have made itself felt speedily, and that in a shape which might be easily recognised. He addressed himself to affairs connected with the every-day business of men; and if the results of his investigations had not arrested attention, it would have been owing, not to those investigations themselves, but to his peculiar manner of treating them.

* Theory of Legislation, By Jeremy Bentham. Boston: Weeks, Jordan & Co. 1840.

He was, however, equally successful in the selection and in the treatment of his subject. Few men ever lived that have infused their convictions more deeply into the minds of their contemporaries. During his life, his works, though not without reputation, were hardly estimated at their real value; and it was only after they had founded a distinct and independent school of thinkers, when the worth of his conclusions had been brought to a practical test, when a host of accomplished and persevering disciples had forced them upon the consideration of the British Parliament, when discussion had proved their validity, and hostility and denunciation had revealed their strength, that Bentham was acknowledged as the great luminary of his era, the leader and teacher of the vast, ever-expanding, and all-conquering party of Reform. Since then, his place as the nucleus of that party, into whose folds all who are not wedded to things as they are must be gathered, has been admitted. It is an undeniable fact. Jeremy Bentham is the father of law reform, the founder of legislative science, the powerful advocate of political emancipation, and a distinguished friend of the moral advancement of the human race.

In this capacity we propose briefly to consider his merits, accompanying our comments only, with such personal notices, as are necessary to enable the reader more thoroughly to comprehend the man.

First, then, a few words of Bentham himself. He was born in London, in the year 1747, and was remarkable in childhood for the quickness of his parts, and the solidity of his judgment. At three years of age he read for amusement Rapin's History of England; at eight was a skilful performer on the violin; and at thirteen commenced his collegiate studies in Oxford. It was at this early period that his inquiring and conscientious turn of mind manifested itself; for being required to sign the Thirty-Nine Articles of the established church, he did so reluctantly, and the act ever afterward proved to him an occasion of deep regret. He looked upon it as deliberately setting his seal to what he thought to be false, as a species of self-degradation which disturbed the clearness of his moral convictions and broke the integrity of his spirit. His father, who was an attorney of some note, gave him the opportunity of becoming a profound and skilful lawyer. Nor did he fail to prosecute his studies with immense labor and research; not, however, in the spirit of those who ordinarily pursue that profession, but with the discrimination of a philosopher and the zeal of a philanthropist. He was soon disgusted with the technical falsehood he found pervading every branch of the law, which, in connexion with the repugnance excited by its indirectness, inconsistencies, unjust arrangements and barbarous phraseology, inspired him with the ambition of devoting his life to its reform. The first fruits of his purpose appeared in a short essay, called a Fragment on Government, published anonymously in 1776. It was the criticism of an episode in Blackstone's Commentaries, written with singular clearness and vigor, but hypercritical in its tone, though distinguished in many passages by astute observation, and reasoning at once logical and profound. It is some sign of the estimation in which this work was held on its first appearance, both as a literary and philosophical performance, that it was successively ascribed to Lord Camden, Lord Mansfield, and to Mr. Dunning, one of the most accomplished lawyers of the day. It was followed by the publication, two years afterward, of a review of the "Hard Labor Bill," with observations relative to jurisprudence in general, which contained the germ of several sagacious doctrines unfolded at length in later and more detailed works. Then came the "Defence of Usury," a tract of remarkable force, and one of the best specimens of the exhaustive mode of reasoning ever printed. In less than two years, the "Introduction to the principles of Morals and Legislation" appeared, being the first extended and methodical exposition of his peculiar notions that had been given. This work gave him a place at once among the thinkers of the day. The originality of its arrangement and expression, together with the boldness of its views and the pertinacity with which they were pressed, arrested the attention of the leading minds of that period. Some few hailed the new teaching as the harbinger of more liberal and consistent methods of treating the great questions of government and moral science, but more looked upon it as an extravagant reproduction of exploded theories, better adapted to excite merriment, than to awaken inquiry, or to become the occasion of a radical and comprehensive reformation of the laws. Many, however, confessed the peculiar vigor and acuteness of the author's intellect, although few were inspired with confidence in his judgment. Yet the book worked its way. One after another, distinguished men were compelled to admit, if not the soundness of his conclusions in detail, the general necessity of subjecting law to a thorough revision. Meanwhile, the author himself, apparently content to allow his theories to bide the test of rigid scrutiny, busied himself in sending forth pamphlets upon the various minor and collateral branches of the great subject to which he had given his life. Draughts of codes, essays on political tactics, on colonial emancipation, on pauper management, on parliamentary reform, on church abuses, on the art of instruction, on the liberty of the press, on codification, and a hundred other matters, followed each other in rapid succession. But a treatise on the "Rationale of Judicial Evidence" was the largest and most elaborate of the works then published. It was filled with profound thoughts and instructive suggestions, and soon became the foundation of important changes in the law of procedure. No one read it without acquiring a deep conviction of the reach, strength, astuteness and integrity of the intellect from which it sprung. It detected the absurdity of the old practice with so much skill, exposed it with so much point and vivacity, and unfolded a better scheme with so much judgment and tact, that it readily obtained for the author the reputation and rank of a master-mind.

Three of Bentham's treatises, and those not among the least important, were published in French, and possessed a wide continental influence before they were generally known to his countrymen. This arose from the careless habit of writing into which, in the latter part of his life, he suffered himself to fall. Abandoning that clear and nervous style which marked his earlier works, he indulged in loose, irregular, and unintelligible modes of expression. His thoughts were not written out, but dotted down, sometimes in briefest outline, and at others, in an uncouth and perplexing jargon. Catalogues, synoptical tables, summaries, references, brief hints, interspersed with long dissertations, composed the bulk of his manuscripts. Fortunately, these fell into the hands of an ardent and accomplished disciple, in the person of Dumont, a citizen of Geneva, for some time an eloquent preacher at St. Petersburg, but who had come to London at the request of the Lansdowne family. There he formed the acquaintance of Bentham, and entered at once with zeal and activity into all his speculations and plans. Never was a literary friendship formed under happier auspices. To a thorough appreciation of, and profound reverence for, Bentham's genius, he united great patience of labor, a quickness of apprehension, indefatigable public spirit, and a felicitous style of writing. "His manners," says Lord Brougham, "were as gentle as they were polished and refined. His conversation was a model of excellence; it was truly delightful. Abounding in the most agreeable and harmless wit, fully instinct with various knowledge, diversified with anecdotes of rare interest, enriched with all the stores of modern literature, seasoned with an arch and racy humor, and occasionally a spice of mimicry, or rather of acting, but subdued, as to be palatable it must always be, and giving rather the portraiture of classes than of individuals, marked by the purest taste, enlivened by a gayety of disposition still unclouded, sweetened by a temper that nothing could ruffle, presenting especially perhaps the single instance of one distinguished for colloquial powers, never occupying above a few moments at a time of any one's attention, and never ceasing to speak that all his hearers did not wish him to go on, it may fairly be said, that his conversation was the highest which the refined society of London and of Paris afforded. No man accordingly was more courted by all classes; no loss was ever felt more severely than his decease; and no place in the most choice circles of literary and political commerce is so likely long to remain vacant." To this man was committed the task of compiling, arranging, condensing, filling out and translating several of the best of Bentham's manuscripts. The services which he rendered in this way were an invaluable assistance to his master, but not so great as has sometimes been represented. Says Mr. Macauley, himself one of the most eloquent and accomplished living writers of English—" If M. Dumont had never been born, Mr. Bentham would still have been a very great man. But he would have been great to himself alone. The fertility of his mind would have resembled the fertility of those vast American wildernesses in which blossoms and decays a rich but unprofitable vegetation, 'wherewith the reaper filled not his hand, neither he that bindeth up the sheaves his bosom.' It would have been with his discoveries as it had been with the 'Century of Inventions.' His speculations on law would have been of no more practical use, than Lord Worcester's speculations on steam-engines." But this is a mistake which does great injustice to Bentham. As much as he was indebted to Dumont, it was only for a small part of his fame. To say nothing of those works in which the latter had no hand, works that under any circumstances would have raised the author to eminence, it must be admitted that as Bentham had the power to be perfect, it is probable, had there been no overtures of friendly assistance, he would have undertaken the task which another accomplished for him. Dumont was at all times solicitous to decline the merit of having been the author of the works published under his editorship. "I declare," said he, "I have no share, no claim of association in the composition of these works. They belong entirely to the author and to him alone. The more I esteem them, the more desirous I am to disavow an honor which would be an usurpation as contrary to the faith of friendship, as it is repugnant to my personal character." Again, he observes: "My labor, subaltern in its kind, has been limited to details. It was necessary to make a choice among various observations on the same subject; to suppress repetitions; to throw light upon obscurities; to bring together all that appertained to the same subject; and to fill up those gaps which in the hurry of composition the author had left. I have had more to retrench than to add; more to abridge than to expand. The mass of manuscripts put into my hands was considerable. I have had much to do in attaining correctness, and preserving uniformity of style; little or nothing as it respects fundamental ideas. A profusion of riches left me only the care of economy." This, while it explains the nature of Dumont's labors, acquits Bentham of the debt with which in Mr. Macaulay's essay he is charged.

The work at the head of this paper presents, in a portable form, the best summary of his doctrines that has been published. It is a translation, by Richard Hildreth, of Boston, from the French edition of Etienne Dumont, originally printed in Paris in 1802, with a supplementary essay upon "the influence of time and place on laws," which does not appear in this edition. If any person would obtain a correct general idea of Bentham's system, without wading through the ponderous and often repulsive tomes over which the details of it are scattered, he will find all that he wishes in this succinct yet comprehensive collection of Dumont. It is distributed into three parts, the first giving the general principles of legislation; the second, the principles of the civil code; and the third, the principles of the penal code. As a manual of political and legal ethics it is an inestimable offering, and the thanks of the community are due the translator for his attempt to render its doctrines more widely known to the American public. He has introduced it seasonably; at a time when the subject of law reform is beginning to be agitated in the legislatures of several of the States, and when the young men of the nation, as we fondly believe, are attaching themselves to sentiments of democratic freedom and progress. It will aid the efforts of the latter in their researches after truth, and the former, should they resolve to be guided by its tenets, would find it a treasury of important instruction.

We should augur the happiest results as well to our habits of thinking as to the moral condition of society, from a profound study of its contents. The legislator who should go forth armed with the weapons of this magazine of thought would prove an invincible champion in the cause of justice and truth.

Let us, then, proceed to give some account of Bentham's general doctrine. As the fairest, as well as completest method of stating it, we shall confine ourselves, as near as may be, to the expressions and reasonings of his own treatises. His fundamental principle, supposed to be present to the mind of the reader in all his works, is, that the public good ought to be the object of the legislator, or, in other words, that 'general utility,' sometimes designated as 'the greatest good of the greatest number' is the only legitimate foundation of legislative science. This utility, to which a clear and distinct meaning is to be ever attached, is exclusive of every other principle, and is to be faithfully applied to all cases of legislation, by the most rigid processes of a moral arithmetic. Nature has placed man under the dominion of pleasure and pain. His only object in life is to seek pleasure and avoid pain, even when he imagines himself most free from the empire of these eternal and irresistible sentiments. Utility expresses the property or tendency of a thing to procure some pleasure or prevent some pain; and that which is conformable to the utility or the interest of a community is what tends to augment the total sum of the happiness of the individuals of which it is composed. Virtue is esteemed by the disciple of the principle of utility as a good only because of the pleasure that it produces, and vice is regarded as an evil only on account of the pains which result from it. If he finds, therefore, in the ordinary lists of virtue an action from which there follows more pain than pleasure, he instantly classifies it among the number of vices; and so, on the other hand, if there is found in the common lists of offences some indifferent action, some innocent pleasure, he will not hesitate to transport this pretended offence into the class of lawful actions.

To arrive at a correct notion of utility, in any given case, it is necessary to have a full and accurate knowledge of the different kinds of pleasures and pains. The variety of sensations which we momentarily experience must be minutely analyzed, dividing the simple from the complex, and arranging the whole in catalogues, which will assist the memory, while it renders the judgment more precise. Not only the number but the value or power of pleasures and pains, both as they relate to individuals and as they relate to communities, must be learned; and this we shall find to depend upon their intensity, their duration, their certainty, their proximity, their productiveness, their purity, and their extent. But inasmuch as all causes of pleasure do not give the same pleasure to all persons, nor all causes of pain produce the same pain, that difference in human sensibility from which that difference of pleasure and pain proceeds must be investigated. This difference of sensibility is either in degree or kind; in degree, when the impression of a given cause upon many individuals is uniform but unequal; in kind, when the same cause produces opposite sensations in different individuals; and in both cases depends primarily upon temperament, health, strength, corporeal imperfections, knowledge, intellectual faculties, firmness of soul, perseverance, the bent of inclination, notions of honor, notions of religion, sentiments of sympathy, antipathies, disorder of mind, and pecuniary circumstances. As, however, these causes of different sensibilities cannot be easily appreciated, there are in certain secondary circumstances, viz.: sex, age, rank, race, climate, government, education, and religious profession, palpable and satisfactory indications of interior dispositions. These secondary circumstances are easily seized, few in number, readily combine into general classes, and furnish the grounds, in the contrivance of any law, for extenuation or aggravation.

Possessed of a knowledge of the true nature of the various kinds of pleasures and pains, we may then take up the analysis of political good and evil, and of the manner in which they are diffused through society. It is with government as with medicine, that its main business is a choice of evils. Law, being an infraction of liberty, is an evil, and hence the legislator, in devising any scheme, is to consider, first, whether the acts which he undertakes to prevent are really evils; and secondly, whether, if evils, they are greater evils than the means he employs to suppress them. In other language, is the evil of the disease or the evil of the remedy the greater? He is to remember that evil seldom comes alone, but takes different forms, and spreads on every side as from a centre. It first affects the persons immediately concerned in it, and then, by arousing the idea of danger and alarm, affects the whole community. For the protection and welfare of society, therefore, certain acts are to be erected into offences, by which is meant that they deserve punishment. But some evil acts are not of this sort, and had better be left to the punishments attached to them by the natural or social sanctions, than included in the number of those which are touched by the political sanctions. In making the discrimination, between those which belong to the domain of politics, and those which belong to morals exclusively, resort must be had to the great doctrine of utility, which accompanies this whole inquiry.

Here is the sum of his theory. The first thing that occurs to us to say of it is, that Bentham does not seem to have had a deep penetration into the metaphysics of that part of it relating to morals. He appears to have taken his general doctrine for granted, without investigating very profoundly into the grounds of it, and without giving due weight to the elaborate researches of other philosophers. More of a thinker than a reader, though by no means deficient, as some have alleged, in the latter respect, he fell into a contemptuous mode of treating the subtle inquiries of older metaphysicians. He everywhere regards the results of their speculations (those, we mean, which respect a moral sense, and the grounds of moral obligation) as the mere expression of their individual prejudices and sentiments. They were excuses for dogmatizing, indirect modes of asserting peculiar biases, or adroit contrivances to avoid the appeal to anything like an external standard. He regarded them as quite unintelligible, or intelligible only so far as they inclined toward his own favorite doctrine. In no instance does he make a full and candid statement of what they are, or assign in detail the reasons why they are rejected. He simply enumerates them under one name or another, and then, by a fell stroke of the pen, sweeps them all from the board, as unworthy of farther notice. Nor is he any more explicit in establishing the theory which he sets up in their place. He asserts it boldly, frequently, without compromise, but never demonstrates it; scarcely, indeed, makes an attempt to demonstrate it. His readers must receive it on his dictum, or seek elsewhere for a satisfactory exposition.

This logic, summary as it is, might be retorted upon Bentham. If his great doctrine were dismissed in the same way without examination, neither he nor his disciples could justly complain of discourtesy. But the question, lying as it does at the foundation of all subsequent reasoning, is too important to be passed over thus cavalierly. It must be looked into with no loose nor divided attention. The neglect of it would lead to the same errors into which Bentham fell—to wit, a confusion of certain palpable and necessary distinctions, a disregard of some of the most important facts of the human constitution, and a too rigid and sometimes fantastic application of his main principle.

The truth is, that Bentham was a man in many respects qualified, and in others disqualified, for the career he had chosen. He was fitted for it, by the peculiar practical structure of his intellect, by his questioning spirit, by his keenness of sensibility, and by his moral independence of judgment. The sphere selected for his exertions involved details which only the most patient and practical mind could endure to investigate; it was surrounded by so many associations connected with the past, that no one who deferred to ancient wisdom would dare to attack its outworks, much less the citadel; the spirit of injustice lurking through it, and covered by innumerable subtle and plausible pretexts, could only be detected by one possessing the quickest sense of wrong; and so thoroughly had it been interwoven with the habits and notions of society, that to make an onslaught upon its weaknesses was to sever the assailant from all the sympathies of his fellows. Bentham was adapted to meet the difficulty at every point. He was inquisitive, persevering, and fearless. He had the sagacity to perceive defects, the wisdom to suggest the remedy, and the fortitude to expose the one and defend the other, in spite of all hostility. But his very excellencies led him into the weakness of excess. His readiness to question degenerated into scepticism, his ability to reconstruct begat a vain desire of superfluous and fantastic theorizing, and his firmness and self-reliance betrayed itself into a contemptuous disregard of the opinions of former thinkers. This last became his besetting sin. From doubting the conclusion of others, he soon grew to despising them; he took nothing for granted; he proved by formal demonstrations the simplest truisms; and addressed his readers as a pedagogue would his pupils, as so many abecedarians to be instructed in the rudiments of knowledge.

Bentham's moral theory is, that men are universally under the dominion of pleasure and pain, that happiness being the great and sole object of human life, all things are desirable only as they contribute to that end, and that consequently virtue consists in the production of happiness, or in other words, that we can have no idea of the moral quality of actions apart from their power of producing either pleasure or pain. We have only a few words to say on this head. It will be perceived that there are several questions, more or less distinct, and each requiring an independent consideration, mingled in the statement which has just been given. They may all, however, be resolved into these two: first, are pleasure and pain the sole governing motives of men?—and secondly, is the tendency of an act to produce the greatest amount of happiness the only reason why it is binding upon the conscience?—or to state the same thing in another form, is there no method of testing the morality of an act except by applying to it the standard of general utility?

We have no desire of going into a formal investigation of questions of so abstract a nature, or we might take issue with Bentham on each of these points. His first proposition revives the old bone of metaphysics, as to the disinterestedness of human virtue. The doctrine of most philosophers, and, we believe, of all men of the world, is, that whatever a man does has relation to his own good; if he is virtuous, it is because it is more agreeable for him to be so than otherwise; and should he be vicious, it is because he finds his greatest pleasure in that. All conduct, in this view, is only a balancing of interests; and benevolence itself, or what is sometimes called a generous sacrifice, is a mere prudential calculation as to the pleasure and pain of one course or the other. When a missionary, for instance, leaves the comforts of a civilized home, for the miseries of a savage wilderness, he pursues his pleasure merely ; he is driven by his fear of remorse and of hell on one side, to brave the perils of want and death on the other, and in this way barely selects the more agreeable alternative. There is a higher pleasure in his view in preaching to the savages, than in sharing the luxuries of refined society ; and in preferring the former he acts upon the same principle of self-love, as the chimney sweeper would in giving up his sooty rags for the purple linen of a prince. He adds to the number of his agreeable sensations, and on that account, and that account alone, changes his one condition for another. Now, in reply to such reasoners, we say, there is no doubt that a lofty pleasure attends the exercise of any form of benevolence'; but is that pleasure—and here is the point—is that pleasure the immediate *object* of the benevolence ? Bishop Butler, the profoundest and acutest of the English metaphysicians, set this matter at rest when he first urged this distinction. The direct object of any human affection is altogether distinct from the pleasure which may accompany its exercise ; and, though virtue is pleasant and vice painful, the object of the mind in pursuing a virtuous or vicious course, is not the pleasure or pain that attends it, but something entirely different, such as the conferring a benefit or inflicting an injury. The motive, therefore, may be separated from all considerations of a self-regarding nature.

Again, as to Bentham's second doctrine, that a moral act is obligatory only because of its tendency to produce the greatest amount of happiness, is that true ? Before we can answer this question, it must be understood what is meant here by the word 'because.' It means, either a stated antecedence and sequence, that is, that the idea of producing the greatest amount of happiness is invariably followed by the sense of moral obligation ; or it means, that the idea of right and wrong is comprehended in the idea of producing the greatest amount of happiness. As to the former, we venture to say, that not a man in the world is conscious of the connexion implied in it, and that no parent, teacher, orator, or writer, when he would awaken the moral feelings of the persons to whom he addresses himself, ever commenced his appeal by descanting upon the greatest amount of happiness. And as to the latter, the two ideas must either be coextensive, in which case it would be difficult to say which was the cause of the other, or they must not be coextensive, in which case there must be some actions producing the greatest amount of happiness that would not be binding, or some actions binding upon the conscience which would not produce the greatest amount of happiness ; and it is incumbent on those who maintain the theory, to detect the element which marks the difference. In neither way can it be proved that there is this relation of cause and effect existing between the two ideas. Let us see, then, in what method we get at the notion of moral obligation.

We find, upon analyzing our consciousness, and tracing the feeling that some things ought to be done and others ought not to be done, impressed indelibly upon it, that certain dispositions and affections are contemplated with a sense of moral complacency, and others with sentiments of aversion. We find, we say, the following circumstances, which seem to us to be facts :* 1st. That all sentient beings stand in various and dissimilar relations to each other, such as the relation of man to man, parent to child, brother to brother, citizen to citizen, subject to magistrate, recipient to giver, &c. 2d. That as soon as these relations are apprehended by the mind, there spontaneously springs up in the consciousness a feeling of moral obligation connected with the very conception of these relations, or that certain dispositions are to be manifested toward the beings to whom we are thus related ; and 3d. That the nature of these dispositions varies with the nature of these relations, but that they are all pervaded by the same generic feeling of obligation, or *ought to do*, which on all occasions asserts its supremacy as the guiding and controlling feeling in the healthy mind. According to this statement, the sense of obligation is a part of the human constitution, not to be traced beyond it, and having for its authority the simple fact that we are so made. It is evidently not derived from the idea of the greatest amount of happiness, for whoever contemplates actions simply as useful, or as right, is conscious of a very dissimilar feeling in regard to them. No one that has noticed the interior workings of his own mind could fail to have marked the difference, and to have formed as distinct a conception of it as he has of the distinct sensations of hunger and of thirst.

This feeling, then, having a real existence, is capable of becoming a motive, and a motive acting independently of all notions of pain or pleasure. Whoever has experienced how often it sets itself in opposition to his most cherished notions of pleasure will testify to the power of its workings. It acts as the great antagonist of the inferior forces of the soul. An intense and dubious struggle is incessantly waged between it and the swarms of our grosser appetites. If it be allowed to be overcome, it is turned into an avenging monitor, shooting arrows of keen remorse : but when it conquers, it is the angel of peace, shedding its soft influences over and irradiating by its genial smiles the depths of the inmost soul. There are now, and there have been in all ages of the world, men in whom the sentiments of benevolence, the love of friends, devotion to country, have been never-failing springs of action, invincible by all the motives of self-interest which could be brought to bear against them ; men who in the accomplishment of a lofty purpose would pass days and nights of pain and labor, who would

---

*See Wayland's Moral Science, page 26.

sacrifice without regret the most cherished gratifications, to bring aid to the needy, or balm to the distressed; men who would recoil from the thought of meanness or wrong with as much quickness as the instinct of a pure woman shrinks from the approach of contamination; men who in a contest for principles would spurn the suggestions of self-interest with an instant scorn, and who would relinquish property, comforts, rank, children, and friends, with joyful alacrity, before they would surrender one jot of their faith, or compromise in a single point the integrity of their aims. There are now, and there have been in all ages of the world, and in every nation, men who have kept loyal to duty in the midst of the frightfulest tortures which human ingenuity whetted by malice could inflict: men who, when nailed to the stake, while around them the faggots have crackled in the flames, when the devouring jaws of wild beasts have been opened for their destruction, when their limbs, by a cruel variety of infernal mechanism, have been torn piecemeal one from the other, have preferred the serenity of rectitude to an escape from the most terrible sufferings, crowned with the plaudits of a surrounding world. They have willingly confronted death rather than lose honor, or tarnish their innocent consciousness by the indelible stains of injustice or untruth.

Here is the leading and radical defect of Bentham's moral teachings. He takes no account of this deep-seated sense of right, so wide and irresistible in its influences over the volitions of human will. Utility, as the mere standard and test of morality, in some degree serviceable in general reasonings, is confounded with the feeling of moral approbation, which should be the immediate and direct incentive to all moral action. That all good acts have a beneficent tendency, that temperance, fortitude, generosity, justice, truth, produce the happiest consequences both to the agent and to society—that whatever we feel to be virtuous would be beneficial if performed by all men under the same conditions—that the disposition to confer happiness is accompanied by a feeling of moral complacency—in short, that the production of the greatest amount of good is an inseparable quality of virtue—we might admit to be among the established facts of moral science. But that this ulterior happiness is to be the motive with which virtuous acts are to be performed, and not for the sake of the virtues in themselves, we cannot admit. It strips virtue of its very character as virtue, and sinks it from an end into a means. No man who is bold because it is more dangerous to be cowardly, is a brave man. No man is benevolent who distributes pleasure, not because it is virtuous, but because it is reputable. No man is just, who acts impartially, not because it is right, but because it is safe or commanded by the laws. Virtue is an imperious goddess exacting service for her own sake, and not permitting it when performed for more remote objects. The moment the motive is divided, the worship is no longer acceptable, and, innocent as it may apparently be, is in her sight impure. She must be loved, reverenced, and pursued with a single aim, or her advantages cannot be realized, nor her blessings merited. To substitute any other motive, that of producing happiness, for instance, is accompanied by the worst effects on the cultivation of moral character. It is to diminish that intrinsic pleasure which always attends the performance of a virtuous act. It weakens the force of those habitual feelings which are the best promoters of rectitude and probity. It supplants a strong present motive by a more distant, and consequently weaker, inducement. It renders moral judgments uncertain, fluctuating, and difficult. It opens the heart to the more easy approaches of self-delusion. It shifts the attention from the interior impulse to the bare outward act. It enables the selfish and unamiable passions to mingle themselves with less probability of detection among nobler impulses—tends to justify wrong actions under the disguise of expediency—allows too broad a discretion in the application of moral rules—and admits too readily of the passage from the consideration of general, to that of particular and specific, consequences. No man who makes pleasure his chief aim can give a full developement to his character, or form an adequate notion of the great purposes of human existence, or of the destinies of society.

But these objections do not apply in all their force to the principle of utility as it operates in the province of the legislator. It is true, the legislator, like the moralist, must place himself under the guidance of the immutable principles of justice. He must obey the instinctive dictates of that moral faculty in which are laid the foundations of all righteous law. Justice, eternal and unchangeable justice, is to be his supreme aim, in establishing the relations of the state. For he legislates, not for himself, but for a community, and a community which presupposes, in the very meaning of the term, a collection of conflicting interests and of equal claims. He adjudicates between a host of widely various rights; is to neglect none, infringe upon none, and favor none; yet is to distribute the advantages of law over a wide space, and among a multitude of competitors. How can he discharge his duties impartially? How is he to ascertain what is just in all circumstances? How is he to separate that which is permanently right from that which is for the time only expedient? Here is the difficulty. Here the necessity for some general rule of legislation begins—the necessity for some external invariable standard, some test, some guide to direct him in his perplexities, and to preserve him from shifting, uncertain, and confused decision. Now we know of no better rule, than that which insists upon producing the highest good to the greatest number of people. Government is an instrument for executing the purposes of society. Society is composed of an aggregate of individuals, each having his distinct objects and solicitous about his own welfare. In consenting to any government, each man wishes it to accomplish the highest good for himself; if, therefore, it secures the greatest good of the largest number, it comes nearest to the perfection of its design. It legitimates itself when in all its action, in all its arrangements of even the minor details of law, it keeps true to the fundamental idea of its institution. By rigidly adhering to this notion, Bentham has achieved his noblest triumphs. He has carried it with him into all his inquiries, has resolved by it all his difficulties, and has made, as Macauley remarks, a science out of what was before a jargon.

It were difficult to describe at length the extent and value of what he has done. Unless we should follow him through all his researches, and in that way compose a volume instead of penning an article, no adequate notion could be given of the research, profundity, variety, and usefulness of his labors. To enumerate all the inconsistencies he has detected, all the errors he exposed, all the crudities he destroyed, all the false maxims he rectified, and all the truths he established, would be a herculean task quite equal to his own capacity, and certainly too much either for our ability or our space. We should say, however, that his services might be summed up in general terms, under the following heads :

1. The attempt at a thorough reform of legal science was in itself no small service. He found the English law what blind usage, occasionally altered by hasty legislation, and from time to time corrected by fettered judicial decisions, with such improvements as professional writers added, had made it. It had come to be what it was piecemeal, irregularly, without order or system. Founded in the first place on the feudal relation, it retained the feudal spirit long after society had outgrown its barbarisms. One stage of civilization succeeded another, but the law had not kept pace with the change. A warlike people had become an industrious and commercial people, but there was no introduction of laws fitted to their new relations and new modes of existence. Whatever alterations took place, were made by forced applications of old rules, or by new rules brought to square with the old, though a process of violent adjustment. As opinion and social customs advanced, its structure became constantly more heterogeneous and confused. Here a part would fall into disuse, and make a huge hiatus in its theory. There a portion would be knocked off, in the struggles of society to enlarge itself, and the place supplied by some strange and uncongenial substitute. The courts would strain a point one day, to adapt themselves to the growing wants of a more active and refined state of human intercourse, and the legislature would strain another point another day, either to rebuke or justify the courts. Thus, construction was heaped upon construction, evasion followed evasion, one fantastic fiction became the excuse of a fiction still more fantastic, amendment trod upon the heels of amendment, until the whole mass seemed like a vast pile of rubbish, or rather like some

of those ancient structures which are seen in Italy, with here a broken column, there a shattered portico, in the third place a crumbling roof, but the whole grotesquely stuck together with plaster and wood, to make a modern habitation. In the entire course of its existence, there had been no attempt to remodel it, or bring its parts into more perfect symmetry and shape. Of the thousands that in every age devoted their lives to the study of it, no one cared to investigate its corruptions or undertake the labor of improvement.* Those who read it, read it to learn what it was, and not to inquire what it ought to be. Those who wrote about it, wrote as expositors and not as critics. All the publications put forth concerning it aspired to no higher character than that of digests, abridgments, commentaries, synopses, or didactic essays. Not that its defects were unperceived, nor that its cumbrous and illogical reasonings had not forced themselves into notice, nor that its injustice had not often been felt; for there had been solitary and distant complaints uttered from time to time on all these points. Sometimes a judge in the course of a decision would diffidently suggest an improvement, and sometimes a general writer would speak in harsh terms of certain of its details. But generally the system was revered in proportion as it was absurd. Elegant dissertations, like those of Blackstone, had persuaded men that it was 'the perfection of reason;' and as few were disposed to question with any earnestness the dicta of profound and skilful lawyers, there was an unbroken acquiescence where there should have been an uncompromising opposition. It was in this state that Bentham found it, when he ventured upon the opinion that it was all wrong. It was in this state he found it, when he began to ridicule its pretensions, and lash its absurdities. It was in this state he found it, when he commenced an investigation, with a view to root up its very foundations, and build the entire structure anew. He was not satisfied with the examination of a single title, nor an isolated branch, but he applied an unsparing analysis to each and every part, picking to pieces, demolishing, tearing down, and building up, until scarcely a particle of the original fabric was left, and a beautiful fair-proportioned edifice rose on its ruins. Even if his efforts had been less successful, the attempt would not have been without its use. It would have broken the charm which had been thrown around the subject, it would have attracted attention from thinking minds, and it would have prepared the way for subsequent exertions more pertinent and beneficial than his own. Honor, therefore, to him, who could tear himself from the fetters of a prescriptive servitude, and familiarize the public mind to the contemplation of a formidable and gigantic reform.

2. A more essential service rendered by Bentham was his mode of setting about his work. He began, not in a hap-hazard way, destroy-

---

* The attempts of Bacon and Hale are no exceptions.

ing wantonly whatever seemed to him unworthy, but in obedience to a regular and consistent design. His method was not novel in itself, although it was original in its application. It was essentially the same method which for more than a century had been the glory of physical science. It was in another form the observation and induction of Bacon, the method which rejected authority, which dismissed sophism, which labored for precision, which investigated facts, which put questions, in Bacon's own expressive phrase, to nature. He settled in the outset his guiding principle, and then made use of it unflinchingly in the treatment of the minutest parts of his subject. One of his profoundest chapters is that in which he expounds the false methods of reasoning used in legislation. He showed that there is but one right reason, and that the authorities on which jurists commonly relied were an improper dependence. He showed that antiquity, though it might create a prejudice in favor of a law, was not a reason for it; that the sanctions of religion, such as those cited from the Old Testament in the famous work of Algernon Sidney, were not reasons; that an arbitrary definition, such, for instance, as that with which Montesquieu opened his great treatise, was not a reason; that metaphors, like that of the English jurists as to a man's house being his castle—that a fiction, that certain offences, for instance, work a corruption of blood—that a fancy, such as Cocceiji's as to the right of a father over his children, because they were a part of his body—that antipathies and sympathies arising in the breast of the legislator—and that imaginary laws, such as the thousand-and-one laws of nature that were spoken of—were not reasons, but mere pretences put forth to escape the obligation of deciding upon measures according to their good or evil tendency. In rejecting the pretexts by which the law, as well the good portions of it as the bad, were defended, and enforcing against himself with rigor the strict rules he had prescribed, it became necessary for him to take the whole body of the law in parts, to dissect its vessels, articulations, and muscles; to penetrate the mysticism which had all along enveloped its logic; to examine its generalities in detail; to uncover its secrets; to inspect the maxims which had grown gray in its service; to probe the fictions interwoven through its entire texture; to compare piece with piece; and to prove the whole by reducing it without mercy to the test of impartial reason. He found it encumbered with useless forms, fettered by arbitrary precedents, abounding in flagrant absurdities, and pervaded by an unwise and pernicious spirit. He found it a confusion of obsolete terms; of silly affectations; of intricate and conflicting provisions; of defective and artificial arrangements; of capricious rules; of quibbles, subtleties, refinements, and tyrannical technicalities. These he fearlessly exposed, and left them to the taste and judgment of his readers.

3. But not content with pulling down so conglomerous a mass, he went to work with indomitable energy to the task of putting up something in its stead. In the process he taught mankind several invalu-

able truths. He demonstrated that the framing of laws was a matter of practical business, to be conducted with the same good sense, and on the same principles, which plain men use in their most ordinary affairs. He took the law from the number of those objects of human study which have their roots and defences in authority, and gave it a place among real sciences—by the side of mathematics, chemistry, and general physics. He did more; he brought discredit upon all mere technical systems, by setting before us, in great beauty of arrangement and considerable completeness of detail, a system founded upon a natural characteristic of those actions which are the subjects of law. He practically exhibited the advantages of that system, showing how it was equally applicable in all nations and at all times; how it detected bad laws by the mere force of its arrangement, giving them no place in its nomenclature; how it effectually excluded all barely technical offences; how it closed the door upon technical reasonings, reasonings which only the lawyer can understand; and how it simplified and illustrated the institutions and combinations of institutions that compose the matter of legal science. The superiority of the natural system is one which the philosophical jurist must instantly recognise. It has the same advantages over others that the botanical arrangement of Jussieu has over that of Linnæus, substituting the unity, simplicity, and beauty of nature for the inexact and often bungling contrivances of art. A lawyer merely, one educated to the intricacies of his profession, whose knowledge of law has no reference to it as a complete and harmonious code of rules for the conduct of society, will prefer the detached and scattered fragments to be found in the complicated decisions of the courts, but minds accustomed to just and philosophical modes of thinking will find their attachments fastened to more consistent and symmetrical arrangements. Nor will they esteem the labors of Bentham in this department of trivial importance.

4. Had he done no more than demonstrate the possibility of LEGAL CODES, he would have accomplished a great good. His views in this respect are peculiarly original and just. He has shown how it was practicable to make a code which should reduce all the laws of a country into a body of written enactments, coming directly from the legislator, and adapted to the immediate guidance of the judge in the decision of all the various cases falling under his cognizance. This, of course, embraced much more than had been included in the codes suggested by the eminent jurists of either ancient or modern times. The code of Justinian, admirable as it proved as a digest, was nothing more than an attempt to bring into a more manageable shape the existing laws of the empire. Tribonian, and those who were engaged with him, merely undertook to make a more compendious arrangement of what was found in the Rescripta Principium, the Edicta Prætorum, the Leges et Plebiscita, which they regarded as the established rules of the State. Nor did the code of Frederic, designed for the

Prussian monarchy, nor even that of Napoleon, aspire to a much higher character. The latter, which is the most perfect of all, and a vast improvement upon the old French law, fails, in leaving its meaning in many instances to be determined by the decisions of the judges, which in time accumulate precedents, and make the study of the science a matter of as immense labor as that of the common law of England. It did not contain within itself a definition of its own terms, nor an accurate and appropriate classification of its parts. Bentham's idea went farther than this. A code in the true sense, he thought, should be one comprehending whatever was necessary to enable the judge to put in force, without extraneous or adventitious aid, the will of the legislator; which should possess, if we may so term it, the power of self-interpretation; and which should make provision for its own improvement and correction. In his plans for the codes of Russia and the United States, he endeavored to realize this general theory, by showing of what parts a code should consist, and the relation of the parts. But the nearest actual approach to his own notion is effected in the Penal Code, prepared by the Law Commissioners of Great Britian for the government of India, published in 1837. Whoever will consult it, will discover, if not a thoroughly unexceptionable code, one that proves the practicability of codification, and the beauty of an orderly and systematic arrangement. How it has operated practically we are not informed, but have no doubt of its success from the fact that it combines, as the framers of it state, the advantages of a statute book and of a collection of decided cases. It is at any rate, an approximation to something better than the miserable jumble of rules called law, to be found in most nations of the civilized world.

5. Be the opinion, however, what it may in respect to the practicability of codification—and we know that many, even among law reformers, are dubious—it must be conceded that Bentham, by the enthusiasm with which he prosecuted his task, if not by any actual success, kindled a spirit of active inquiry on this subject, which is working in the bosom of society with more and more power to this day. Commencing with the private student and the philosopher, it has gradually stolen its way into houses of legislation. At first Dumont, then Mill, then Romilly, then Brougham, and then less conspicuous men, caught the genial fire of the great master, and by a series of unsurpassed exertions, in the midst of scorn and opposition, directed public attention to the mighty truths which he proclaimed. The progress of opinion, it is true, has been slow, but when we contemplate the obstacles it has met, in the general worship of authority, in the pride and indifference of the legal profession, and in the stubborn habits of society, we are somewhat surprised at that which has been already accomplished. We were struck, in reading a late English work,* at the

---

* Miller on the Unsettled Condition of the Law.

number of changes which had been almost imperceptibly effected. Of these may be enumerated the alterations of laws, materially improving the relation of debtor and creditor, diminishing the number of oaths, softening the penalties, and ameliorating the spirit, of criminal law, simplifying the proceedings and forms of pleading at common law, defining more distinctly the rights, duties, and revenues of ecclesiastical persons, consolidating statutes, and harmonizing and modernizing the barbarous provisions of the law of real property. All these we attribute indirectly to Bentham, because his was the seminal mind from which the movement sprang. What may be the result in after ages, the progress of time will reveal. Our confidence is that his genius is destined to still nobler and vaster triumphs.

6. Nor should it be forgotten, in an enumeration of the services of the same great mind, what ought to have been insisted on before, that he has done much toward establishing the true functions of government. He has stated with more clearness than any preceding writer the real objects of civil law, and the best methods of attaining them. If he has not carried his ideas to the extent to which American statesmen are disposed to push their theories of government, he has made a near approximation to it. Indeed, the most radical of American statesmen can find much instruction in what he has uttered on this head. Law of any kind he regards as a retrenchment of liberty, and is consequently never to be imposed without a sufficient and specific reason. For there is always a reason against every coercive law in the fact that it is an attack upon the liberty of the citizen. Unless, therefore, he who proposes a law can prove that there is not only a specific reason in favor of it, but a reason stronger than the general reason against it, he transcends his province and invades the rights of the individual. Again, he says, the single aim of the legislator should be to promote the greatest possible happiness of the community. But happiness is increased as our sufferings are lighter and fewer, and our enjoyments greater and more numerous. As the care of his enjoyments ought, however, to be left entirely to the individual, it becomes the principal duty of government to guard against pains. If it protects the rights of personal security, if it defends property, if it watches over honor, if it succors the needy, it accomplishes its main purposes. Government approaches perfection in proportion as the sacrifice of liberty on the part of the subject is diminished, and his acquisition of rights is increased. Can the most rigid democrat carry his own theory much farther? Adopt these principles in legislation, and would they not lead to all those results for which he contends? Would they not simplify government until it became what it ought to be, a mere instrument for the protection of person and property? Would they not abolish all partial legislation, root out exclusive privileges, destroy monopolies, prevent the granting of acts of special incorporation, do away with unequal laws, and leave society to its own energies and

resources, in the conduct of its business and the prosecution of its enterprises? And this is all for which the great democratic party, the party of progress, is striving. It seeks to direct government to its true ends, to restore its action from the partial direction that has been given it, and urge it on to the accomplishment of those general objects, for which alone it was instituted, and which alone are compatible with the rights, the interests, and the improvement of man. Bentham himself, it must be admitted, has sometimes departed from these objects, but only when he violated unconsciously his own fundamental principles.

We have dwelt longer upon these topics than it was our intention when we begun, and longer we fear than the patience of the reader will excuse. We have done so, because we have been enamored of the theme, and have endeavored, in our own feeble way, to kindle the interest of others. If we have quickened the purposes of any to engage in the great study of law-reform, the time has not been unredeemed. It is a great subject, connected with the best interests of society and men, and worthy of the patient labor of the noblest minds. We know of no way in which the intellect could be more profitably tasked, or the purest sympathies more suitably indulged, or the firmest moral purpose more honorably tried, or greater good conferred on men, or a richer harvest of reputation reaped, than in prosecuting and applying the lofty inquiries which Bentham so auspiciously commenced. The law is yet a fallow field, covered with stubble, thorns, and weeds. There are many briars to be rooted out, many excrescences to be pruned, many decayed branches to be lopped, and many vigorous and wholesome shoots to be ingrafted upon its more ancient and withered trunks. What obscurities perplex its theory, what inconsistencies confuse its details, what vexations attend its practice! How numberless the absurdities which disfigure the statute-books! How aristocratic the spirit of much of its reasonings! How expensive, wearisome, and disastrous the greater part of its proceedings! Would any one confer a blessing on the poor, let him shorten its delays, and diminish its costs. Would any one spread peace among men, let him simplify its rules and make certain its decisions. The law is a science of mighty influence and vast extent. It is the prolific source of evil or of good. It is the instrument of the oppressor or the defender of the oppressed. It is the handmaid of virtue or the pander of vice. It mingles with all our business, with our pleasures, with our solitary studies, and with our social intercourse. When righteously administered, it is the great guardian spirit that guides the most important earthly relations of man. It watches over society when it slumbers, and protects it when it wakes. It confirms order, secures peace, encourages virtue, and assists freedom in developing and perfecting the social destinies of the human race. How important, therefore, that it should at the same time establish justice! A worthier name could not be achieved than by taking part in the effort to correct its abuses, to remedy its defects, to symmetrize and beautify its whole structure, to conform it to the image of immutable justice, and to enshrine it in the centre of the Temple of Truth, where it is now permitted, we fear, to occupy only the outer courts. There may be more dazzling, but there are no more honorable or useful spheres of exertion than in the department of LAW REFORM.

9

[W. Phillips?]

Review

Theory of Legislation; by Jeremy Bentham. *Translated from the French of* Etienne Dumont, by R. Hildreth, Author of "Banks, Banking, and Paper Currencies," "Despotism in America," "Archy Moore," &c. Boston: Weeks, Jordan, & Co. 1840

in

The North American Review
vol. LI, no. 109 (October 1840), pp. 384–96

Art. VI. — *Theory of Legislation;* by Jeremy Bentham. *Translated from the French of* Etienne Dumont, by R. Hildreth, Author of "Banks, Banking, and Paper Currencies," "Despotism in America," "Archy Moore," &c. Boston: Weeks, Jordan, & Co. 1840. In Two Volumes. 12mo.

Mr. Dumont's office in respect to Jeremy Bentham's fragments, was the same as that of the comparative anatomists in respect to extinct species of animals, who, digging into the earth, the great magazine of animal *exuviæ* and *débris*, and finding a tooth or a claw, a shell or a bone, here and there, construct therefrom the entire skeleton, and clothe it with flesh and a skin; and give, in due systematic order, the genera and species that have been extinct some thousands of years. So M. Dumont has ransacked the inexhaustible magazine of Bentham's fragments, and brought together the scattered parts, as it seemed to him, of systems of ethics and legislation, in which, however, he has himself supplied many deficiencies. Mr. Bowring, as executor to Mr. Bentham, has succeeded M. Dumont in the business of giving symmetry to the specimens of his testator; but his task is more arduous, for, instead of having finished and half-finished parts to piece out and fit together, he has little more than mere outlines, rudiments, and hints, of which he is to make entire systems, such as Bentham might perhaps have constructed if he had lived long enough.

The mass of works thus produced by M. Dumont by translating Bentham's manuscripts, and filling up the gaps, and adding something by way of ornament and illustration, has had an immense circulation on the continent of Europe. The effect of such speculations as those of Bentham, working in the minds of the busy political philosophers, must doubtless have been very considerable. The force of his ethical writings is almost spent; the principle of utility as the sole foundation and criterion of morals is about passing into the limbo of vanities. The effect, while it was in vogue, was no doubt beneficial in fixing the attention of mankind more steadily on utility as a landmark and guide to moral sentiments and philanthropy; but, on the other hand, it was injurious in making men overlook and forget the intuitive moral perceptions, and the spontaneous instinctive promptings and aspirations of the human mind, as being the basis and revealed principle of systems of ethics. The utility theory teaches us, that we learn the distinction of right and wrong, and virtue and vice, as we do geometry, whereas it is born with us, like hunger and thirst; and as there is a vast deal of art and science involved in the gratification of the appetites, so there is in giving direction and scope to the sentiment of goodness; but we must start with the *postulatum* of the sentiment, the innate feeling of right, and of the obligation of right, as an ultimate fact, the existence and verity of which cannot be proved; any more than that of taste and smell, being a mere matter of individual experience. Moral sentiment and obligation being conceded, it is then easy to perceive a difference between a good man and a useful machine. We must inquire what is most useful, and pursue it, say the utilitarians. Why? what is the obligation? This question they do not answer. They do not point out the distinction, in ethics, between the useful machine and the useful man who works it. The word *duty* seems to have no meaning in their philosophy.

Mr. Bentham's political speculations are also not without theoretical distortions; but he is not very Utopian, he does not write of perfect commonwealths, founded upon a state of manners, morals, and intelligence of rights and obligations, that have been out of vogue ever since the golden age. He takes mankind as he finds them, with their passions, views, depravity, and blind prejudices; and sometimes reminds his readers of Solon's modification of theories and principles, by the rule, that you are only to give a people as good a code as they will bear. Still he keeps the political *beau idéal* in view, as the central point which legislation is always to seek, but from which it is always driven off by the centrifugal perversity and inaptitude of men, or the untowardness of circumstances. He is a downright, sturdy, hardworking man, of great power and no grace, and utterly free from all offences of the imagination; but he is frequently commonplace and utterly sterile, with, at the same time, great parade of science and analysis, making formal divisions in due order of first, second, and so on, in so long a series that the reader often can hardly but forget where he began, long before he comes to the end. And then he has a way, in the beginning of his chapters and sections, of using a word in a singular and often in an uncouth sense, and then solemnly defining it, with the oracular air, all the while, of revealing momentous truths; whereas the whole of this analytical pageant is only an awkward shift to disguise the want of clear and precise thinking, and mastery of language. After faring on a tiresome length in some of these sandy tracts, the reader is ready to faint and give up the pursuit, but by and by, all by surprise, he finds himself on a firmer footing, in the midst of rich products. And from time to time he is recreated by a chivalrous emprise of the stout old knight, in battering down the moss grown fortress of some venerable prejudice ; opening to the day the lurking-place of some monstrous error ; or piercing, by his sarcasm, some empty form of conventional mummery. He becomes, all of a sudden, original, strong, fervent, and poignant. The greatest merit of Bentham's writings lies in his occasional heats and intellectual paroxysms, where he does not indulge in his cynical skepticism. It is hard and tiresome to read through his works, or rather the tomes that come out in his name, so much of which consists of mere rude masses ; but then, again, one would not willingly forego his masterly passages. It would be a great service to the science of legislation and of ethics, and to his own memory, to collect his good things. A volume or two of excerpts might be made from his works, which posterity would gladly take along with them.

Bentham begins the present treatise on the "Theory of Legislation," by announcing with much solemnity, that he is the partisan and standard-bearer of utility. "The public good ought to be the object of the legislator ; GENERAL UTILITY ought to be the foundation of his reasonings." And what is utility ? It is "the fixed point to which the first link of a chain is attached"; it is the beginning, the end, and the middle of his system, the alpha, the omega, and all the rest of his political alphabet. It is the talisman that charms away all ill, and attracts all good. There is no end of his eulogies of utility. Its sovereign virtues surpass those of all quack medicines, and he speaks of it as the advertisers and venders of these same do of their elixirs and balsams, as something of his own discovery, to which, by his manner of speaking, you would suppose him to be entitled to a patent right. He tells us, "Utility is an abstract term. It expresses the property or tendency of a thing to prevent some evil, or to procure some good." This is utility. We understand it quite well if we know what *evil* and *good* are, but, lest we should not, he defines these also. "*Evil*," he says, "is pain, or the cause of pain ; *good* is pleasure, or the cause of pleasure. *Moral good* is good only by its tendency to produce physical good. *Moral evil* is evil only by its tendency to produce physical evil; but, when I say *physical*, I mean the pains and pleasures of the soul, as well as the pains and pleasures of sense." So we understand what utility is. We are at the same time instructed that to give to this principle all its efficacy, three conditions are necessary; 1. "To attach clear and precise ideas to the word utility;" 2. "To establish the unity and sovereignty of this principle;" 3. "To find the processes of a moral arithmetic by which uniform results may be arrived at." The first condition is complied with, the meaning of utility is understood; the second may be conceded, viz. its unity (whatever this may mean) and sovereignty; the third is not so easy; these "processes of moral arithmetic, by which uniform results may be arrived at," are not readily discovered. Mr. Bentham beats about for them in vain, leading his readers into darkness and perplexity, beclouded with misty phraseology and definitions upon definitions, and divisions and distinctions infinite, but no light, no consequences, no "uniform results," only a vast vacuity of jargon and charlatanry. Perhaps there was more meaning and wisdom in this scientific parade and solemn marshalling of forces, thirty years ago, when this treatise was originally written; but, at this day, it certainly appears to be mere mummery, the "uniform result" of which, to the reader, is, that Mr. Bentham cannot think and express himself with scientific simplicity, and clearness, and precision. He mistakes obscurity for profoundness. It is this scientific parade without definite meaning, or meaning worth expression, that renders him so insupportably tedious; insomuch that his most docile and confiding disciple, most happily endued with patience and long-suffering fortitude, cannot choose but give over, and pass by the scientific flummery, and choose out the passages where he talks with plain straightforwardness upon a practical, interesting question, where he heaves out masses of sense, with frequent felicity of phrase, illustration, and historical and classical references, though often with too bitter antipathy to creeds and hierarchies.

Take any one of the topics treated of in these volumes upon legislation, as for instance, whether a man who has with his own labor raised a crop of wheat, and stored it, shall, on his being overtaken by a fatal disease in the autumn, have the right by law to leave it to his family, for their support after his decease, or shall leave it to be confiscated by the public, and his family to go to the alms-house. This is the topic of one of the chapters, which is treated very well; and the conclusion is, that the law, which gives the bread to the children, is the better one. Here is a question, readily understood by everybody; and all that can be said upon it, expressed in common English words, used in their ordinary acceptation, is level to the comprehension of any reader of ordinary intelligence. What possible assistance can be derived to the discussion, from the "unity and supremacy" of utility, and the "moral arithmetic," and the definitions and axioms and vague generalities, with which the reader has been afflicted through one half or two thirds of the preceding parts of the treatise? Mr. Bentham would say, that he conducted the whole discussion, and came to his conclusion, upon the consideration of the greater utility, that is, the greater aggregate of good or pleasure, as he has it, or the greater alleviation or prevention of evil or pain, arising from one or the other law; just as if he were the first philosophico-political writer, who has treated the question in this manner. This is really a notable instance of self-conceit, for he seems honestly to suppose, that he has made utility better understood, by saying, that it involves the comparison of good and evil, and pleasure and pain; and that mental pain is physical pain, which last is mere nonsense. It is plain, that after reading all this analysis and speculation, which occupy much space in all Mr. Bentham's philosophical writings, we have no more knowledge of pleasure and pain, and good and evil, and utility, than we began with; and it is only the author's own overweening self-esteem, that can make him imagine that he has enlightened us.

From the time when the first man first breathed, down to this present, all mankind have been in active quest of this same utility, of good, pleasure, ease, content; and the same motive has influenced them in legislation as well as in war, hunting, agriculture, commerce, and the arts. To enjoin this motive on men, is as superfluous as to exhort them not to expose themselves to fire and frost.

The introduction of the doctrine of materialism into the definition and estimate of good and evil, and defining mental enjoyments and sufferings to be merely physical, does not strengthen this motive, nor throw the slightest light upon its operation. The difficulty is, to discriminate good and ill, the useful and the harmful; and a still greater difficulty, to reinforce and give predominance to the motives for pursuing the one, and eschewing the other.

Mr. Benthan has done something in the great and still beginning and never ending labor of demonstrating what is pernicious, and he sometimes points out the proper alternative, the useful. In this search, he is not, however, always successful; and still less is he in the work of reinforcing and multiplying the motives to the right in preference to the wrong. This, indeed, he rarely undertakes at all. And the effect of his exertions is all the less, by reason of his uncouth, empirical phraseology, affectation of profoundness, and other impediments already mentioned.

Mr. Hildreth remarks, in his Preface to this translation,

" Public attention in America is every day more and more attracted to the subject of Legal Reform ; and the translator flatters himself that he will have performed a useful and acceptable service, in restoring to its native English tongue, the following treatise.

" It includes a vast field, never before surveyed upon any regular plan, and least of all according to such principles as Bentham has laid down. In the application of those principles, he has doubtless made some mistakes ; for mistakes are of necessity incident to a first attempt. But he has himself furnished us with the means of detecting those mistakes and of correcting them. He asks us to receive nothing on his mere authority. He subjects every thing to the test of *General Utility.*" — p. viii.

From his speaking of *restoring* the treatise to its native English tongue, we infer that he was not aware that the same treatise, or something substantially the same, and bearing the same title, was published in English some ten years ago by Mr. John Neal.

It is very true, that the treatise " includes a vast field," but the assertion that it has never before been surveyed upon a regular plan, must be limited to the qualification of " regular plan," at least, if not to that of its not having been surveyed " upon the same principles " ; for at the date of the composition, and long before, the continent of Europe teemed with similar speculations.

In 1830 the writings and character of Bentham came under the animadversion of the author of some ably written letters, under the signature of *Eunomus*, addressed to Sir Robert Peel, on the occasion of the discussions respecting the revision and consolidation of the English statutes on various titles. He says of Mr. Bentham,

"Taking advantage of the peculiar condition of ignorance, in which the English alone among modern nations exist, of the real truths of judicial and jurisprudential science, one of the most singular, and, in some respects, the most talented writers of the day conceived the design, which he has at length, to a very considerable extent, achieved, of founding an individual fame upon the means which his prolific and scorching pen conferred upon him of abusing that ignorance. The circumstances of this case, Sir, in all points of view, place it among the most curious incidents of modern literature. A future generation, fully informed by intermediate discussion in the principles of jurisprudential economy, will review it with an interest, and perhaps with an indignation, which we can scarcely yet realize. They will say, — *This writer* was not one of those who could justly shelter himself under the general ignorance which then prevailed of the principles of jurisprudence, or of the practical results of the tests to which those principles had been submitting on the continent of Europe for a long series of years. He was a man to whom neither the languages nor the literature of the continent were unfamiliar; he was a man who contrasted, by a long life of uninterrupted literary leisure, those engrossing pursuits of routine which excluded almost all other men from investigations which did not immediately belong to the business of established departments. He was a *citizen of the world*, in a degree which did not ordinarily belong to Englishmen. He was a citizen of France by a decree of the National Assembly, — he was a member of the French Institute, — he spent several years of his life upon the continent, — his personal connexions were principally continental, — and his name was of sufficient occurrence both in French, in German, in Russian, and in Polish literature, to compel a person of his very acute sensibility to fame and notoriety to keep a frequent eye to the journals and literature of the continent. All these circumstances, they will say, appertained to that individual; and, despite of them all, he either shut his eyes to that which he might have learnt from those peculiar sources of information, or he trusted to their remaining enshrouded in that obscurity which had hitherto been interposed between them and the English nation. For a long course of years, he continued, unweariedly, to inoculate the public mind with a series of mendacious and ignorant assertions and theories, in regard to their existing jurisprudence, and the causes of its defects, one and all of which would have been dispelled, and scattered to the winds, by only a moderate acquaintance with the experience and the wisdom of that continent with which he was, or might be, so familiar. The doctrine which he most strenuously accumulated his efforts to disciple the English nation to, was, that all the faults, all the abominations of their jurisprudence, arose from law having been made by judges instead of by legislators ; — that it was the business of judges only to *pronounce* the law which legislatures concocted ; — that a text-law might and should be framed, in which, ' saving the necessary allowance for human weakness,' ' no case that could present itself should find itself unnoticed or unprovided for.' He *did not tell them* that seventy years before, a man who, like himself, ' had just and profound views on all sorts of subjects,' * — FREDERIC THE GREAT, — had made the same discovery of the cause of the ill condition of the law ; that he not only *projected* but *executed* the same remedy ; — that with the same antipathy to judge-made law, and belief in the all-sufficiency of legislator-made law, the express directions of the King were that the Code might be simple, popular, and so complete, *that the judge might find in a precise text of law the decision of each individual case ;* and that he *prohibited all analogical interpretation of the rules it contained by the judges*, and ordained that, in every case for which the code did not provide, application should be made to the legislative authority. He *did not tell them* that the absurdity of the project, though backed with all the *éclat* of the *great monarch's* reign, terminated its existence in less than thirty years ; and that the first step that accompanied the publication of the *new* code was the restoration of the right of interpreting the laws to the judges. He *did not tell them* that the talented jurists who composed the *projet* of the Code Napoléon had, in their *Discours préliminaire*, exposed, in the most eloquent and profound manner, the vulgar absurdity of supposing ' that a body of laws could be framed which would provide for all possible cases, and at the same time be understood by the lowest citizen ; ' and had boldly declared that the *details* of law ' must necessarily be abandoned to the empire of usage, to the discussions of the learned, and to the decision of the judges.' He *did not tell them* that the most talented, experienced, and philosophical jurists of Germany, of Holland, of Belgium, of Italy, of Switzerland, of Russia, had been engaged almost unceasingly in some or other of those countries for half a century, in

---

" * This was Frederic's own description of himself, in his *Plan pour réformer la Justice*, ' Ce prince, qui a des vues justes et profondes sur toute sorte de sujets,' &c."

the construction, discussion, and re-construction of CODES; that one of the greatest difficulties they had had to encounter had been to draw the line between the respective functions of LEGISLATION on the one hand, and JUDICIAL JURISPRUDENCE on the other; and that, in the result of all that discussion and experience, *those* codes had ultimately fallen into most disesteem which attempted most to supplant the functions of the judge, and to anticipate the details of *application*. Availing himself of a distinction which had originated in the laws of ancient Rome, centuries before the introduction of printing, and which had been absurdly enough continued by habit to the present time, — the now nominal distinction of *written* and *unwritten* law, — he represented to the community in the most mendacious terms, that the common law of the country was *unwritten*, and therefore *unknown* and *uncognoscible* law. He *did not tell them* that the *unwritten common law* was PRINTED four times as often in every year, — and in four times the number, — of the printed copies of the *written* or statute law. He argued upon *that unwritten* common law of which three thousand printed copies were distributed annually over the British Empire, as if it had been the same thing as the common law of Russia before the time of the Empress Catherine, which existed only in the Ukases of the judges; Ukases which were accessible and known only to those few persons who in that country corresponded to counsel or advocates in Britain, and to which persons they *were* accessible and known, only by the circumstance of their having been judges' servants, or having had other such private opportunities of learning the forms of courts, and of being acquainted with precedents and Ukases.

"Taking advantage of the same ignorance, he put forth claims to be the first of created excellences, who had conceived and had carried into execution, the project, which he represented as hitherto unknown and unattempted, of promulgating *the reason* along with each rule of law; — that reason which should be at once the sanction and the commentary. He *did not tell them* that the very distinction which constituted the superior excellence of the unwritten or common over the written or statute law, — the very ground on which its preference was awarded to it by professors, — was that the common or judge-made law existed, and existed alone, in the shape of a series of *rules deduced from reason*; that the rule was, with certain anomalous exceptions, never to be found unaccompanied by the reason; that it was often to be deduced *only* from the reasoning itself, the subject-matter of law being often too subtile and too complicated to admit of the very *form* of proposition. He *did not tell them* that that body of written or promulgated law which had obtained so great a celebrity under the title of the CODE NAPOLÉON, though unaccompanied, in its official and portable shape, by the *motifs* of the compilers, was scarcely ever consulted by the jurisconsults of those countries where it was received without the accompaniment of those motives, either in the same or in a separate volume. He *did not tell them* that those '*motifs*' and the '*discussion*' constituted, practically, a part of the French legislation. He *did not tell them* that under the title of '*La législation civile, commerciale, et criminelle de la France*,' the text of the five codes, that text of which the brevity has so much been admired, was then in a course of publication in twenty-four thick octavo volumes, the product of the additions to that text of the *motifs*, the *discussion*, and the suppletory laws; — that publication emanating from the chief Secretary of the *Conseil d'État*, compiled from the official documents, and being therefore, in every substantial sense, itself official.

"All these things he either himself refused to notice, although going on under his eye, and within the immediate range of those vibrations which converged into the literary hermitage of Queen Square Place; and although he visited Paris personally so lately as 1825, was received with honors by the French advocates, and promised them to write a work upon the legislation and jurisprudence of France; — or, if he did notice them, he trusted to chance, and to the well-known Confucian ignorance of his countrymen, for a season of undetection sufficiently extended for all the calculable purposes of his own fame."

But at the same time, another English writer on jurisprudence, Mr. E. Sinclair Cullen, gave a very exalted character of Mr. Bentham. He says;

"When I read the criticisms of those who
'Bounded by nature, narrowed still by art,
A trifling head, and a contracted heart,'
attack the opinions and deride the style of Mr. Bentham, I am the more struck with his stupendous superiority of mind, and his enviable superiority of feeling. Men of ordinary capacities fancy there cannot be any great wisdom beyond their own narrow ken, — that there can be no altitudes above their reach, — no depths which they cannot fathom, — no world which they cannot hold in their dirty little hands. Such men are yet more shrunken in their capacities by the worldly interests and feelings which continually absorb and degrade their

contemplations and faculties. The venerable Bentham has preserved the purity of his soul and the lucidness of his judgment by a hermit life, — having early withdrawn himself from the sullying and corrupting assaults and seductions of that self-interest which a worldly life presents to other men at every turn and at every moment; and, emancipated from their power and exempted from their taint, has calmly and almost superhumanly contemplated and judged the motives, and duties, and powers of men, — dwelling with peace, and wisdom, and virtue, in the shrine of his renowned and noble seclusion. But I let my pen drop with humility; — suddenly ashamed at my presumption in fancying that I can offer any worthy homage to a person so celebrated in all quarters of the world as a benefactor to mankind."

So opposite are the opinions entertained of Jeremy Bentham and his labors.

The circulation of this translation, or any work on the same subject in the United States, will have a good effect as far as it may have any influence to invoke attention to the science of legislation, a science which has come to be much more studied, and better understood, on the continent of Europe, than in either England or this country. It is now but a short time, since the introduction of a code of laws was with us considered to be nothing less than a revolution. The United States, and the several States, had their statute books, which they were constantly enlarging, and never a year passed without some material change in the laws. And yet a code, which is nothing more than a systematic arrangement of the laws, supplying chasms and changing such as appear to be defective, was considered to be some terrific innovation. Of late, however, this horror has subsided, and the construction of a code, most usually under the name of *revised statutes*, is quite a usual occurrence. It is true, that formerly some of the speculative philosophers were too fiercely bent upon upturning the whole mass of laws, and introducing many new ones, as foreign to the habits, and business, and wants of the times, as many of the old ones necessarily had become by changes in the social and economical condition. Men thought it better to "bear the ills they had, than fly to others that they knew not of." But the alarm has passed, and men are not now afraid to arrange under appropriate heads, the laws they have, and to supply obvious defects, and to change what is palpably wrong, by the revision of the laws from time to time, whenever the statute book has grown to be of unwieldy bulk, and the law has become perplexed by detached and piecemeal legislation. The science of legislation is, therefore, an eminently practical one with us ; in other words, we do a vast deal of legislation, and shall continue to do a vast deal as long as the course of things continues to be onward instead of becoming backward ; and this activity in law-making cannot be repressed, notwithstanding that some of our grave and respected seniors may shake their heads ominously. The tides are moving, the winds are blowing, and the sails are spread, and the ship's company will not be induced by ever so loud warnings to come to anchor. If then an inactive, stationary security is wholly out of the question, as it undoubtedly is, we must seek safety in skill and science, in the pursuit of which a glorious career is opened to both ambition and philanthropy ; to ambition, for it is most honorable to point out the way of improving the laws ; to philanthropy, for in no pursuit can greater service be rendered to society.

10

[John L. O'Sullivan?]
'Edward Livingston and his Code'

The United States Magazine and Democratic Review
New Series, vol. I, no. 1 (July 1841), pp. 3–20

THE UNITED STATES MAGAZINE

AND

DEMOCRATIC REVIEW.

New Series.   JULY, 1841.   Vol. I. No. I.

EDWARD LIVINGSTON AND HIS CODE.*

We endeavored in a late number of this Review to make our readers better acquainted with one of the great intellects of England. It was a labor of love to speak of Jeremy Bentham; for from our earliest youth he had been an especial favorite. We remember how violently he had been traduced by the writers of the day, when he first began his attacks upon the rotten system of English law, and how nobly, by the dint of persevering industry and superior genius, he had triumphed over his adversaries. We saw his strange doctrines gradually making their way into thinking minds, until a school of mighty and disinterested spirits gathered round him as their chief; and such men, both great and good, as Romilly, Mackintosh, and Brougham, made it their highest aim to carry into effect the benevolent theories which in silence and loneliness his master-mind had conceived. With all his whimsies and odd conceits, in spite of his hard and cold system of morals, we delighted to dwell upon that high enthusiasm which could relinquish a lucrative profession for the prosecution of a toilsome and unprofitable reform; upon that intrepid valor which assailed without quailing a citadel fortified by the habits and opinions of ages; upon that severe and patient diligence which, through long years of cruel abuse, kept right on its way, and upon that noble

---

* Eloge Historique de M. Livingston, par M. Mignet, Secretaire Perpétuel de l'Académie des Sciences Morales et Politiques. Lu à la Séance Publique, du 30 juin, 1838. Paris, 1838.

A System of Penal Law for the State of Louisiana, prepared under the authority of a law of said State, by Edward Livingston. To which are prefixed a Preliminary Report on the plan of a Penal Code, and introductory reports to the several codes embraced in the system of Penal Law. Philadelphia, 1833.

love of truth which gave no rest to its possessor till every lurking-place of sophistry had been explored, and every abuse of legislation corrected.

It is with still greater pleasure that we turn to a kindred genius of our own country, who in many respects reduced to practice what Bentham had only suggested; who, taking up the subject of law-reform where the master had left it, pursued important parts of it to a complete consummation; and who, not satisfied with the speculations of the closet, succeeded in inducing the legislative power of a magnificent state to request him to make law of that which had before been only theory. Edward Livingston, in the code now known as the Code of Louisiana, a code at once simple and comprehensive, raised himself to the first rank among jurists as well as among public benefactors; and had it been adopted, would have conferred a distinction upon his chosen State more glorious and lasting than ever warrior gave to the land his blood had defended. He would have achieved a mightier emancipation than was ever won by the sword. As it is, his reward will be an enduring fame and the perennial gratitude of a great people.

We desire to acquaint those of our readers, who are not already informed, with the nature and extent of his services. It is a high duty to keep the remembrance of those men who have done good things perpetually fresh. But it is a higher duty never to permit the great principles of truth, no matter in what department of inquiry they may have been started, to fall into the neglect to which the busy pursuits and frivolous pleasures of life would consign them. They are the guiding stars that God has set along the heaven to conduct society in its slow and uncertain advances.

First, a few words as to the man. Livingston was born in the colony of New York, in the year 1764. His family, which had formerly been one of the most powerful and illustrious clans in Scotland, driven away by religious persecution, were among the earliest settlers of America. They brought with them to the place of their exile, along with lofty tastes and generous manners, an indestructible love of liberty. When the infant colonies, oppressed by the mother-country, began to stir with the aspirations of independence, their sentiments and principles had already prepared them to take part with those who struck for freedom. Edward Livingston, the youngest of eleven children, was a witness of many of the exciting scenes of the Revolutionary war. His brother Robert was a member of that magnanimous Congress which, for seven years during the vicissitudes of a bloody contest did not despair of their country; and had, with Jefferson, Franklin, Adams, and Sherman, drawn up a Declaration of Independence that was the "birth-act" of a nation. His brother-in-law, the chivalrous Montgomery, in the young vigor of his hopes and faculties, perished gloriously in the assault upon Quebec. And his hearth was ever the hospitable home of La Fayette, and those other noble auxiliaries of the American cause who so gallantly battled for the rights of humanity, in sustaining the feeble but spirited arms of the small band of American patriots.

Under the influence of such examples, the foundation of his character was laid. When he afterward came to act for himself, a long life of public usefulness and unspotted purity testified that early impressions were durable. He never forgot the love of justice, nor the disinterested patriotism that had always marked the characters of his ancestors and friends.

He devoted himself to the profession of the law. In his preparatory studies, which were alike thorough and discursive, he made himself familiar with the doctrines of the common law, which had been adopted from the mother-country, and with the principles of the civil law, as they were found in the old writers, and as they were illustrated on the continent of Europe. His practice in the courts was followed by all the success that a distinguished and wealthy connexion could give a young man of extraordinary industry and talent. He rose rapidly into fame; and in 1794, he was chosen a representative of New York in Congress.

It was an important epoch. The American people had just emerged from a fierce and protracted struggle for independence; they had formed a government before then unknown to the legislation of the world; Washington had been selected as the first to administer it; and around him were gathered the tried spirits who, either in the counsel or the field, had assisted him in the mighty work of revolution. The constitution, binding free and sovereign states in an indissoluble league, after long anxiety and deliberation, was about to be tried. Its strength and its weaknesses, its tendencies, whether for good or for evil, were soon to develop themselves in practical operation. Parties, taking their principles from the bent of their dispositions toward a stronger government or a stronger people, were already formed. At the head of one division stood Thomas Jefferson, the ardent friend of liberty, from his youth a champion of the people on the broadest grounds, a philosopher of the French school, sanguine, far-sighted, sagacious. At the head of the other was Alexander Hamilton, also a friend of liberty, but distrustful of the people, skilled in the politics of England, accomplished, ambitious, and eloquent. Livingston lost no time in ranging himself among the disciples of the former. He entered with enthusiasm into the defence of the popular measures of his day. He opposed the British treaty of '94; he fought resolutely against the sedition law; and to this day, in many of the log huts of the western frontiers, his able speech against the atrocious provisions of the alien acts constitutes a part of the household furniture. Here it was, too, that he formed the acquaintance of a delegate from the distant and obscure territory of Tennessee, with whom he was afterward destined to perform so conspicuous a part, both in war and peace. The delegate was Andrew Jackson.

Livingston continued in Congress till the end of the administration of Adams. He was then selected by his fellow-citizens to discharge the duties of chief municipal magistrate of New York. In this office, he had occasion to manifest other traits of character than those which had given him political prominence. Soon after his return, the yellow fever began to rage with unusual violence. Livingston gave himself up entirely to the care and protection of the sick; and, by personal visitation, by the gratuitous distribution of his fortune, by a wise direction of the city government, he contributed greatly to the restoration of the general health. When seized himself with the fever, as it began to abate, the spontaneous gratitude of the whole population, manifested by anxious visits, by expressions of sympathy, and by gifts, told how deeply his noble generosity had fastened him to the affections of all classes. But that freedom from selfish feeling which had saved others, sacrificed himself; and, in the fortieth year of his age, when he fondly thought that leisure would be afforded him to resume those elevated studies which had been the charm of his life, he found himself stripped of his wealth, and compelled a second time to commence his professional career.* To a man of less energy, this would have been no ordinary trial; to Livingston it was only an occasion for manifesting his lofty virtues. He speedily arranged his affairs, and in a few months found himself an emigrant in the new territory of Louisiana, recently purchased by the United States from the French. That territory was then a new and uncultivated country, but beautifully placed by Providence in one of the largest and richest valleys of the world, watered by the grandest rivers, and at the head of a magnificent gulf, communicating with the main ocean. The mighty stream of population, so long hemmed in by the range of the Allegenies, had burst its barriers, and was already spreading over

---

* We would dwell more minutely upon these incidents of Mr. Livingston's life, had not the elegant pen of an admiring friend, Mr. Auguste Davezac, already anticipated us. See Democratic Review, First Series, Vol. viii. No. xxxiv.

the almost boundless prairies of the west. In a few years the forests had disappeared, fertile plantations and growing towns covered their sites; a fine city at the mouth of the Mississippi served as an outlet to its productions, and wealth, order, and civilization, rewarded the toils of the enterprising settlers.

Livingston engaged in the practice of the law, and fortune followed his exertions. Not satisfied, however, with the mere accumulation of property, he suggested and accomplished, in connexion with others, important reforms of his favorite science. The various fortunes of Louisiana, as a dependancy, first of Spain and then of France, under a territorial government and as an independent state, had introduced a world of confusion into its law. It was a vast miscellany of Spanish customs, French decrees, English precedents, and conflicting legislative enactments. In its forms of procedure, particularly, it was defective and inconsistent. Livingston set about correcting its evils. Rejecting alike the interminable proceedings of the French, and the absurd fictions of English practice, he formed a short and simple code of procedure, which combined the advantages of the various systems that prevailed, and was at the same time free from their vices. He digested and methodized also the more ancient civil laws that were recognised as authoritative. Nor was it the least of the benefits flowing from those preparatory labors, that his mind was directed to that grand and comprehensive scheme of law-reform which he subsequently carried into effect, with such honor to himself and to the legislature which had the wisdom to engage his talents.

The war of 1812 interrupted his plans. Ready as he was to do good to his country with his pen, he was no less ready to take up the sword in her defence. During the siege of New Orleans, he seconded the efforts of the patriotic Jackson. He shared in the dangers and in the glory of the battle; and when the strife had ceased, he was employed in the benevolent task of negotiating an exchange of prisoners.

With the return of peace, the great purpose of his life was renewed. The legal studies that had been relinquished again absorbed his thoughts; he completed a plan of penal reform; he procured himself to be elected to the Legislature of the State; he unfolded his enterprise to that body; and in February, 1820, to the immortal distinction of its members, he was appointed to prepare at length a report of all that he proposed to accomplish. Livingston undertook the task with avidity, making himself acquainted with whatever had been done in his own country and abroad in relation to the subject, corresponding with distinguished jurisconsults of all nations, comparing the principles of every theory — and before the end of four years had the satisfaction to see his plan approved.

It is of that plan we design to give some account. His system is so important, so original and comprehensive in its provisions, so rich in suggestions, that it cannot be too profoundly studied. It were worth whole years of toil, to bring it into a more general adoption.

We shall advert, for a moment, however, to what had been done for a reformation of penal laws at the time Livingston began his labors. In the earlier stages of modern civilization, those who made the laws for the trial and punishment of criminals seem to have been moved solely by a spirit of blind and unmitigated ferocity. Society, in departing from many of the barbarous usages of the feudal age, retained much of its savageness of manners and disposition. The discipline of force under which it had been educated continued long after to exert an influence upon the habits and opinions of the people. An increasing intercourse among states and men, the consequence of the growth of commerce, while it liberalized the pursuits and refined the exterior courtesies of life, did not impress its effect so deeply upon the general mind, as to efface the traces of former selfishness and brutality, nor to remove from existing institutions those fierce and vindictive provisions which a ruder condition had originated. Mistaking severity for justice, supposing vengeance to be the single object of public, as it had been of private, punishment, excluding those who had infringed upon the law from the common sympathies of their race, criminals were treated by it (unless protected by rank or interest) as outcasts, were arrested with   ise, condemned without trial, and punished with the most excruciating tortures and the most infamous deaths. Under the cruelest laws, they were arraigned before the most unfeeling judges; they were denied the right of being heard in their own defence, subjected to insult and caprice, and often compelled, on the rack or by the flame, to confess crimes of which they had never been guilty, or to purchase immunity by the grossest falsehoods and most degrading infidelity. Secret tribunals, inquisitions, lettres-de-cachet, mutilations, and indiscriminate butchery, were the instruments with which the law executed its purposes, alike upon offenders of every age and sex, and of every degree of guilt. Even in England, distinguished from other nations by the institution of the trial by jury, by the habeas-corpus act, and by the sturdy and independent spirit of the people, these harsher features of criminal jurisprudence were relieved, but not obliterated. "Prisoners were deprived the assistance of counsel; men were executed because they could not read; those who refused to answer were compelled to die under the most cruel torture. Executions for some crimes were attended with butchery that would have disgusted a savage. The life and honor of the accused were made to depend on the uncertain issue of a judicial combat. A wretched sophistry introduced the doctrine of corrupted blood. Heretics and witches were committed to the flames. No proportion was preserved between crimes and punishments. The cutting of a twig and the assassination of a parent; breaking a fish-pond and poisoning a whole family or murdering them in their sleep, all incurred the same penalties; and between two and three hundred different actions, many not deserving the name of offences, were punishable by death. This dreadful list was increased by the legislation of the judges, who declared acts that were not criminal under the letter of the law, to be punishable by its spirit. The statute gave the text and the tribunals wrote the commentary in letters of blood; and expanded its penalties by the creation of constructive offences. The vague and sometimes unintelligible language employed in the penal statutes, and the discordant opinions of elementary writers, gave a color of necessity to this assumption of power; and the nation submitted to the legislation of their courts, and saw their fellow-subjects hung for constructive felonies, quartered for constructive treasons, roasted alive for constructive heresies, with a patience that would have been astonishing, even if their written laws had sanctioned the butchery."

Society was slow in emancipating itself from the capricious despotism of its criminal laws. Nothing is changed with more difficulty than practices which have received the sanction of antiquity and habit. Even political evils, falling upon large classes of the community, and thus arraying against themselves a combined opposition, are long permitted to develop their effects in misery before the inert mass are aroused to demand their removal. How much greater the delay in those laws which inflict their curses only at intervals and upon single and friendless persons! Criminal legislation, more than all other kinds of legislation, has been marked by the slowness of its progress. Now and then, when the public sense of justice was offended by some extraordinary instance of severity, slight modifications were made in the existing arrangements; but the great body of them were suffered to remain in all their original deformity and rigor. The bench and the bar, apparently infatuated with the love of a system which had neither beauty nor truth, nor any charms save the equivocal charms of age to recommend it, applied themselves diligently to its study, but did not give a thought to its improvement. The meliorating influences of a growing civilization, that seems to have touched with a quicker movement every other sort of human activity, did not reach the secluded and stationary forms of the law. And had it not been for the liberal spirit of popular writers, penal law would have continued what barbarism had made it.* But the advent of Montesquieu and his disciples wrought a gradual change. Montesquieu, by the spirit of justice that pervaded his great work, Beccaria, by his solemn protests against the punishment of death, Filangieri, by his wise and noble sentiments, prepared the way for the great English luminary, Bentham, destined to shed a flood of light upon every department of legal reform. Nor are the services of Howard, who penetrated the prisons of Europe to lay open their horrid iniquities, to be forgotten in this commemoration; nor yet, that exalted band of auxiliaries, the advocates of "prison discipline," who, in every nation of the world, had devoted their time and substance to the good of a class whom society had long rejected as its refuse. Among these the Quakers ever took a distinguished part. "Abstracted by their tenets," says Livingston, "from the pleasures that occupy so large a portion of life among other sects; equally excluded from other pursuits in which so many find occupation; freed from the vexations of mutual litigation, by submitting every difference to the umpirage of the elders, and from the tyranny of fashion by an independent contempt for its rules, the Quakers devoted all that time which others waste in dissipation, or employ in intriguing for public office, to the direction of charitable institutions, and that surplus wealth, which others scatter in frivolous pursuits, to the cause of humanity. In every society for promoting education, for instructing or supporting the poor, for relieving the distresses of prisoners, for suppressing vice and immorality, they were active and zealous members; and they indemnified themselves for the loss of the honors and pleasures of the world, by the highest of all honors, the purest of all pleasures — that of DOING GOOD."

It would be hard to put together a more heterogeneous and (but for the importance of the subject) a more amusing mass than was formed by the criminal laws of Louisiana, when Mr. Livingston commenced his task. The province had been successively under the government of Spain, France, and the United States, from each of which it had received peculiar traditions, customs, and statutes. These had been variously modified in the various stages of its progress, by the local enactments which a gradual change from barbarism to civilization had rendered necessary. But the most glaring defects arose from a combined recognition of the authority of the English common law and of the equally old institutions of Spain. The common law of England, much as it has been extolled, is, at best, a rude, uncertain, inconsistent, and dangerous jumble of precedents and customs. In the first place, it is confessedly founded upon general and local customs, the origin of many of which are lost in antiquity; then, it is unwritten, and liable to be determined by the variable and arbitrary decisions of the courts; twenty years of laborious study are insufficient to acquire a knowledge of what it declares; and, finally, when it is once learned, it abounds in the absurdest fictions, in the most disgusting technicalities, in wild and extravagant doctrines, and the most pernicious errors. It is an unseemly piece of patchwork, a residuum of the conceit and insolence of uncultivated centuries, a depository of all the *débris* of society, crumbled off under the influence of advancing intelligence and refinement. It was, however, outdone in atrocity by the relics of the ancient Spanish laws. For in these the most ludicrous and the most horrid offences were conjoined; the legislation of the fifteenth century was considered law for the people of the nineteenth; and offences that could only be committed in the days of witchcraft and judicial astrology, were ranged side by side with invasions of property or attacks on the person. Infamous punishments could be inflicted at the option of any choleric magistrate; political disabilities were attached to the most innocent acts under the name of crimes; gamblers, buffoons, usurers, recreant knights, forsworn promise-breakers, comedians, and procurers, were classed as persons equally dishonorable; a child born out of wedlock could never serve as a witness; a lawyer who should cite the law falsely was indictable; incantations, love-powders, and wax-images, were specially inveighed against; divination was a capital offence, except when done by astronomy, which was "one of the seven liberal arts, taken from the books of Ptolemy and other sages;" sorcerers, fortune-tellers of every description, and enchanters who raised the spirits of the dead, except it was done to exorcize the devil, or to preserve the crops from hail, lightning, and insects, were punished with death; blaspheming the Virgin Mary, heresy against the Catholic church, crucifying young children at Jewish festivals, were all enumerated offences; and for a thousand frivolous things, as well as for more important matters, a man was liable to lose his head or his limbs. It was doubtful, also, whether the torture, in its most excruciating application, could not be legitimately used at the discretion of the judges. Surely, vagaries of this kind were as disgraceful as they were dangerous to the people by whom they were endured. Laws so absurd, so conflicting, so pernicious, called for a reform; nor was the task of accomplishing it an easy labor.

Mr. Livingston, aware of the high responsibility he assumed, gave to the discharge of his duty his best faculties and most profound consideration. He set out under the guidance of judicious but decided principles. While he determined that no dread of mere innovation should restrain him from proposing the most radical changes, he was yet fully conscious of the importance of consulting the habits and feeling of the people. A simple repeal of the laws that had become offensive would not be enough; the arrangement and modification of existing statutes would in a short time have led to the same evils that were then deplored; and the introduction of a body of laws before unknown, might be viewed with prejudice and alarm. He resolved, therefore, upon the construction of a code, at once simple and congruous, retaining whatever of the old laws might be pertinent, but the whole to be conformed to principles deduced from just and enlightened reason. In this, he evinces his sagacity and wisdom. A code is the best form in which the supreme rules of the state can be presented, particularly in the rules relating to criminal matters. It imbodies in a brief compass, accurately defined, methodically classified, complete as a whole and in its parts, all that it concerns the public to know of their legal rights and duties. The judge it enables, in a moment, to ascertain his own powers, to detect what is an offence, to discover how it is to be proved, to administer the punishment; the citizen is informed, with no less ease, when his rights have been infringed or when his interests have been protected; and the legislature, without legal acquirement or experience, is made competent to repeal, supply, or amend, any incongruity or defect developed in the course of its practical working. By its brevity, its arrangement, its accuracy, and its comprehensiveness, a code must ever be superior to every other form of instituting and publishing the supreme will of the state. Let it contain within itself a provision for its self-rectification, and the acts of subsequent legislatures, which have now the effect of multiplying and confusing laws, would bring them at each step nearer to perfection.

Four codes (comprised in one general code) were matured by Mr. Livingston. They were (1) the code of Crimes and Punishments; (2) the code of Procedure; (3) the code of Evidence; and (4) the code of Reform and Prison Discipline. To each there was prefixed a preliminary title, declaring its fundamental principles, followed by a book of definitions. We shall speak, of these codes, as briefly as we can, in their order.

I. The general provisions of the first book embrace the common rules for the protection of criminals from injustice, which prevail in the jurisdiction of most modern and enlightened nations. But these in some instances have been very much modified and extended. Among those which have appeared to us the most novel, is one excluding all that class of offences known to the English law as constructive offences. The will of the legislator is made the only rule; by which means a host of acts which the vague notions of the judges as to the laws of nature, morality, and religion, have erected into offences, are protected from punishment; as well as all others which are not forbidden, not only by the spirit, but by the letter of the law. Another peculiarity is in the distribution of the degree of guilt between the persons concerned in the crime. An accomplice is one who instigates a crime, and an accessary one who becomes privy to it afterward; but no relative of the principal offender, either in the ascending or descending line, or in the collateral as far as the first degree, nor any person united to him by marriage, or subjected to him in the capacity of a servant, can be punished as an accessary. A third provision asserts the right to publish without restraint the proceedings of all criminal courts, and to discuss with perfect freedom the conduct of every officer engaged in administering the law. And that this may be done the more effectually the judge is required to furnish, at the instance of either the accused or the prosecutor, a record of his decision, and of the reasons upon which it is founded; while it is further provided, that a full and accurate publication shall be made, by a competent officer, of all trials remarkable for the importance of the principles they may involve. But the most original among these general provisions, is one declaring that in no criminal prosecution can the trial by jury be renounced. It is not enough, Mr. Livingston reasons, that the mode of trial should be left to the choice of the accused; for there is a higher interest to be consulted than that of the culprit, namely, that which the state may have in his conviction, or rather in the certainty that he has had an impartial trial, before judges inaccessible to influence, and unbiased by mistaken views of official duty. "Another advantage," he says, "of rendering this mode of trial obligatory, is, that it diffuses the most valuable information among every rank of citizens; it is a school of which every jury that is empannelled is a separate class; where the dictates of the laws and the consequences of disobedience to them are practically taught. The frequent exercise of these important functions, moreover, gives a sense of dignity and self-respect, not only becoming the character of a free citizen, but which adds to his private happiness. Neither party-spirit, nor intrigue, nor power, can deprive him of this share in the administration of justice, though they can humble the pride of every other office, and vacate every other place. Every time he is called to act in this capacity, he must feel that, though perhaps placed in the humblest station, he is yet the guardian of the life, the liberty, and reputation of his fellow-citizens, against injustice and oppression; and that, while his plain understanding has been found the best refuge for innocence, his incorruptible integrity is pronounced a sure pledge that guilt will not escape. A state where most obscure citizens are thus individually elevated to perform those most august functions; who are alternately, the defenders of the injured, the dread of the guilty, the vigilant guardians of the constitution; without whose consent no punishment can be inflicted, no disgrace incurred; who can by their voice arrest the blow of oppression, and direct the hand of justice where to strike. Such a state can never sink into slavery or easily submit to oppression. Corrupt rulers may pervert the constitution; ambitious demagogues may violate its precepts; foreign influence may control its operations; but while the people enjoy the trial by jury, they cannot cease to be free."

The second book, with remarkable precision and brevity, enumerates, classes, and defines all offences. Any contravention of the penal law is deemed an offence, and, according to the object it affects, is either public or private. Public offences are those which affect the sovereignty of the state, in its executive, legislative, or judiciary departments; the public peace; the revenue; the elective franchise; the public records; the current coin; the commerce, manufactures, and trade of the country; the freedom of the press; the public health; the public property; the public roads, and navigable waters; and whatever restrains the free exercise of religion, or corrupts the morals of the people. Private offences are such as injure individuals in their reputation, persons, civil rights, political privileges, profession, or trade, their property, and means of acquiring or preserving it. Suicide being an offence against one's own person, for which the friends alone, and not the perpetrator himself, can be punished, is not recognised as an offence. Nor are other acts of self-infliction or debasement, too gross to be mentioned in words, suffered to pollute the pages of the public law.

All these offences are minutely and accurately defined, particularly those against the legislative and judicial powers, and the punishment of each is affixed, so as to repress the abuses that have grown up under the general right of punishing for contempts.

Having thus settled the prohibitory and mandatory part of the law, the author considers the means of securing obedience, and the securities necessary to be annexed to its infringement. The punishments he proposes are these: pecuniary fines, imprisonment, degradation from office, deprivation of civil rights, imprisonment at hard labor and solitary confinement during certain intervals of imprisonment. It will be seen, that this list is free from several of those barbarous modes of punishment which are the disgrace of older codes. Neither banishment, deportation, confiscation of property, public exposure, mutilation of the person, stripes, nor death, is reckoned among the legitimate sanctions of penal law. Banishment, were it an efficient remedy, inflicts a great wrong upon the foreign nations to which criminals are sent; deportation has no effect as an example to the community, and in many cases is deemed a benefaction rather than a punishment; confiscation of property often involves the innocent with the guilty, and makes it the interest of the government to multiply convictions; and exposure on the pillory, or stocks, or public works, imprints marks of indelible disgrace which destroy the sensibility of offenders, and consequently compel them when the punishment expires, either to repeat their crimes, or die of idleness and want. As to the punishment of death, Mr. Livingston was led to abolish it after the most solemn and deliberate consideration. The reasons that acted upon his mind were these: he felt that the great end of punishment is not to retaliate upon the offender, but to prevent the commission of crime. This prevention is to be effected in two ways; by the reformation of the criminal, and by impressing a salutary restraint upon the mind of the community. Death is inadequate, as a punishment, in either view. It has been found an ineffectual penalty in those nations in which it is imposed for slight offences; how much more ineffectual then must it be in those more atrocious crimes, only, committed by the most hardened and brutalized delinquents, or by persons under the influence of the most strong and ungovernable passions! That it is not absolutely necessary, is proved by the history of those nations in which it has been adopted, where crimes have increased in proportion as the severity of punishment was ameliorated, and by a mass of statistics showing that milder forms of infliction have been followed by a decreased frequency in the commission of acts of gross violence and outrage. Add to these proofs of its inefficacy, that the punishment of death, though an impressive and horrible spectacle at first, loses its effect at every repetition, until a ferocious taste is created to behold its infliction; that it inexorably reduces every shade of guilt to the same complexion; that it offends the convictions of many who are compelled to sit as jurors, and therefore either to violate their feelings or their oaths, so that the guilty are permitted to escape; and above all, that being irrevocable, no place is given for the correction of those errors to which, in the heat of prejudice or passion, from the uncertain nature of human evidence, and the fallibility of the best men, all judicial tribunals are liable,—add all this, we say, to the confessed inefficacy of the punishment, and the conviction becomes irresistible, that death is a punishment both injudicious and dangerous.

Mr. Livingston very wisely, therefore, discarded death from the list of his penalties. Had he retained it, his code of punishments would have lost one of its highest advantages, as it now stands— its capability of being infinitely divided, so that there is no offence however small, for which it does not supply an appropriate corrective, and none however great, for which, by cumulating its degrees, an adequate punishment cannot be found. It also admits of accurate apportionment, not only to every species of offence, but to every kind of offender, sex, age, habit, constitution, and every circumstance that ought to modify the infliction of suffering, having its due weight. Add to this, that under such kinds of punishment, it is not unreasonable to expect the reformation of the criminal; that he is restrained from the repetition of his offences; that a permanent and striking example is constantly operating to deter the rest of the community; that the mildness of the infliction will prevent the passions and sympathies of the public from taking part with the offender in opposition of the law; that the same cause will influence public officers to a rigid execution of their duties; that juries will not be led by compassion to acquit the guilty; and that, if by chance or prejudice the innocent are convicted, the error is not, as in the case of the infliction of stripes, stigmas, or death, beyond the reach of redress; and the perfect wisdom of Mr. Livingston's schemes becomes vividly apparent.

But our limits compel us to pass to the subsequent and no less important codes.

II. The Code of Procedure. This code is divided into three books, preceded by a prefatory title, containing general provisions. In the introduction, the objects of the code are formally and explicitly declared. These are stated to be, the prevention of intended offences; the protection of the innocent against unjust charges; to take away from the guilty all hope of escape by a resort to formal or technical objections; to give to the criminal proceedings the greatest degree of despatch that is consistent with the prosecution of justice, on the one side, and the defence of private rights on the other; to subject the innocent to no expense and to impose none on the guilty but such as may be apportioned to their offence; to abolish all forms that produce vexation to the prosecutor, to the accused, or to the witnesses; and to render the whole form of proceeding simple and perfectly intelligible to all.

The first book relates to the means of preventing offences and of putting an end to such as continue, designating the cases in which the military force may be employed and the rules by which it shall be governed while in service.

The second book prescribes the mode of bringing offenders to punishment, and the whole process, from the initiatory steps of arrest to the rendition of final judgment.

The third book give the forms that are to be used in all the judicial proceedings authorized by the code.

Under each head, the directions are minute and complete, omitting nothing that may be necessary to guide the officers of justice in the discharge of their duties, and in maintaining the just rights of the individual citizen who may be accused. Our limits will not permit us to go into an examination of details. We must remark, however, that we regard his provisions amending the great writ of *habeas corpus*, as it exists in the common law, his giving the privilege of the final speech to the defendant, his confining the charge of the judge strictly to the point of the law, and his prohibition of those presentments by juries which recommend candidates to office, express political opinions, or eulogize the virtues of men in power, as immense improvements in the forms of criminal procedure. Indeed, it is hardly possible to read a page of this code, without being struck with the immense learning and judicious spirit of the writer.

III. The Code of Evidence, like the other, begins with an introductory title, designed to establish certain general principles necessary to the complete elucidation of the subsequent parts. It is then divided into two books, the first, treating of the nature and different kinds of evidence, and the second, of the rules applicable to the several kinds. Evidence, defined to be that which brings or contributes to bring the mind to a just conviction of the truth or falsehood of facts asserted or denied, is divided into testimonial, scriptory, and substantive. And this evidence, in proportion to the degree of effect it produces, is either presumptive, direct, or conclusive. It can be derived from the personal knowledge of the judge, or from extraneous sources, or from personal communication, written documents or natural objects. Testimonial evidence is exhibited by affidavit, by oral examination, and by deposition; scriptory evidence, by authentic acts, as notarial acts, judicial records, and legislative enactments, or by unauthenticated acts, as acts under private signature and all other kinds of writing, as books, maps, almanacs, &c., &c. And substantive evidence, by natural objects which throw light upon the matter in dispute, as a bloody weapon in a case of murder, or marks on a tree in questions of disputed boundary.

As to witnesses, those only are excluded, at all times, from giving evidence who are, 1st, of an insane mind at the time of examination, and 2d, children under fourteen years of age whose faculties are not sufficiently developed either to receive correct impressions, or to relate them intelligently. Other persons are included in particular cases, as a slave, who is not suffered to testify in any case but one in which another slave is prosecuted for some offence; a counsellor-at-law, as to any fact communicated by his client; and a priest of the Catholic religion, who comes by his knowledge through the religious confession of a penitent. Exclusion of witnesses on the ground of infamy, or of disbelief in certain religious truths, as a state of future rewards and punishments, is not admitted.

In regard to the method of receiving evidence, all questions pertinent to the case, except such as suggest facts, may be put and must be answered, and in written examinations, the same rules apply, as in oral.

The law relating to each of these points, and to all the subsidiary topics, is minutely laid down in the code, so that scarcely a question can arise, which cannot be determined by a reference to its provision. Should such a question, however, occur, it is made the duty of the judges to report it to the Legislature, that the omission or defect may be supplied.

IV. THE CODE OF REFORM AND PRISON DISCIPLINE regulates the manner in which prisoners of different descriptions are to be confined and treated as well before as after judgment. The places of confinement, are two; first, the house of detention, appropriated to persons charged with offences; second, the penitentiary, devoted to the punishment of convicted offenders. In the former, there are four divisions designed for prisoners of the following classes: males detained as witnesses; persons confined for misdemeanors, disturbance of courts, forfeiture of recognizances, and non-payment of fines; females, of the same character; males regularly committed on the accusation of crime; and females of the same description. In the latter, there is to be a cell, in an enclosed court, for every convict, with a hydraulic or other machine for manual labor, so disposed that a convenient number of persons may work at it separated from each other by a wall; school-rooms sufficient for the instruction of a class of persons; an infirmary, and all other buildings necessary for the safe-keeping, support, and health of the prisoners. These houses are to be under the direction of wardens and keepers, assisted by mailons, physicians, chaplains, and teachers, whose duties are prescribed at length. The manner of keeping each class of prisoners is also prescribed, with particular attention to the nature of their offence or the cause of their incarceration. Careful isolation, in most cases, and solitude in all, are regarded as the fundamental principles of discipline. The labors to be performed are distributed according to the age, sex, and crimes of the classes. Nothing is left to the discretion of keepers, so that they cannot be treated either with unnecessary severity or with caprice.

To these Codes are added a book of definitions, giving accurate and invariable meanings to all the important words that are used in them.

It was our intention, when we commenced this article, to have furnished more full and satisfactory analyses of the different parts of the Codes. But finding that it would encroach upon the limits assigned to the papers of this Review, we are compelled to defer to a subsequent number the more detailed examination we had proposed. Sufficient, however, is given, to enable the reader to form an idea of the extent of Mr. Livingston's labors, and of the wisdom he has manifested in their performance. No man could have been better qualified than he, for the work he had undertaken. A combination of dissimilar and almost conflicting qualities, conferred upon him peculiar fitness for carrying out a reform. He was a lawyer equally skilled in the technicalities of practice, and the abstrusest principles of legal science. Yet he had not become so enamored of the profession as to look upon it as perfect, or close his eyes to its defects. He saw at once its excellence and its weakness, and was as willing to acknowledge the one as he was to extol the other. A profound and patient thinker, he still saved himself from the abstraction and impracticableness of the mere student. For his mind, both acute and vigorous, was no less correct than comprehensive. The command of a clear and forcible style enabled him to impart to others the conclusions that had been matured in secret. Practical habits of business had trained him to bold and decided action; and daily business intercourse with men, had had the double effect of creating tact and sympathy,—tact to discover the laws best adapted to the actual relations of men, and sympathy to infuse into them the sentiment of a broad benevolence. If he investigated as a philosopher, he recommended as a man of the world; if he felt as a philanthropist, he acted with the spirit of the hero. Thus he was prepared for every kind of opposition, as well from the criticisms of the learned, as from the assaults of the ignorant and interested. Superior knowledge availed him in answering the first, and logic, eloquence, and enthusiasm, in discomfiting the second. Fearless but prudent, theoretical and yet practical, indefatigable in vindication as well as in pursuit, there was no hostility he could not encounter, and no assailants he might not in open contest, vanquish. And had he lived to a later period, the State for which he labored, long ere this, would have retrieved the disgrace which the neglect of his excellent system now inflicts upon her fame.

11

[John L O'Sullivan?]

'Early Life of Jeremy Bentham'

The United States Magazine and Democratic Review
vol. X, issue 48 (June 1842), pp. 545–60

[John L. O'Sullivan?]

Early Life of Jeremy Bentham[1]

The United States Magazine and Democratic Review,
vol. X, issue 48 (June 1842), pp. 545–60.

IN a former number of this Magazine,[2] we took occasion to express our views of the philosophical merits – in the departments both of morals and legislation – of the great founder of the Utilitarians. We are happy to be able, by the receipt of an early number of the first part of Mr. Bowring's Memoir of him, to furnish our readers with some traits of his personal character. This might have been done before from the "Recollections" of Dumont, and from the various sketches and notices of the English Reviewers, but not with so much satisfaction and detail as it is now in our power to do it, from the more authentic materials gathered by his friend and literary executor, Mr. Bowring.

There is a part of the life of all distinguished men which is generally the most interesting, but with which the public, notwithstanding all their curiosity, are seldom made acquainted. We mean their youth and early education. Nothing can be more agreeable than to know how those who have come to exert an important influence over the minds of mankind, or on the destinies of society, comported themselves before they began to attract the attention of the world – when, free from the consciousness of observation, they acted freely, and gave a loose rein to the native bent of their dispositions, unawed and untrammelled by the conventionalities and restraints of our forced social existence. How eagerly we catch at all the traits of the childhood of great men, which either tradition or history has preserved! How we pore over the lessons given by his mother to the infant Washington! With what a strange feeling of delight do we read of the fierce independence and inflexible energy of the military student of Brienne! And what treasures would we have given, had some school-companion, or brother playwright of Shakespeare, seen fit to let us know somewhat of his sports on the merry banks of the Avon, or his madcap pranks in the midnight streets of London! "Can we not," asks D'Israeli, speaking of the youth of genius, "in the faint lines of his youth, trace an unsteady outline of the man? In the temperament of genius, may we not reasonably look for certain indications or predispositions announcing the permanent character? Is not great sensibility born with its irritable fibres? And the unalterable being of intrepidity and fortitude, will be not, commanding even amid his sports, lead on his equals?"

In the case of Bentham, we should be compelled to answer the question in the affirmative. As soon as he began to think, he was very much the same being he was when, forty years afterwards, he projected the grand scheme of Panopticon, or when, eighty years of age, he devoted days and nights to the development of his benevolent principles of legislation. The same originality and ardor of mind, the same disinterested love of truth and of his species, the same eccentric methods of thinking and speaking, characterized him at either period; the only difference being, that in the one he was Bentham the young philosopher, and in the other, Bentham the old philosopher.

Mr. Bowring, fortunately, has collected the memorials of his early years; and as these are full of interest, as well as little known, we shall occupy ourselves briefly with a few of their more striking or entertaining incidents.

Bentham was born in Houndsditch, London, in the year 1748. His father was a prosperous scrivener, once a Jacobite, but who transferred his allegiance subsequently from the Stuarts to the Guelphs, without, as Bentham himself says, "much cost in conveyancing." His mother, whose maiden name was Alicia Grove, belonged to the family of an honest shopkeeper. Their residence, at the time of his boyhood, was in a retired spot, called Browning Hill, where, in the company of the grandmother Grove, a widow Mulford, and an unmarried great aunt, Deborah, their lives passed with great uniformity and comparative comfort. The father, rather a worldly, ambitious turn, not having succeeded to the best of his wishes in securing a distinguished place in the world's regard, conceived great hopes of his son. At first, the diminutive size and feeble health of that son led him to fear that these hopes might be disappointed, but the astonishing precocity which the child soon manifested only heightened and inflamed his ambition. Many examples of this unusual forwardness are furnished us by his biographer. Bentham knew his letters before he was able to speak. The Latin Grammar and the Greek alphabet he learned on his father's knee. As soon as he was well able to read, he began to write; and before the sixth year of his age, he was tolerably skilful in music.

His earliest recollections of infancy were, as he expressed it, of being "starved" for want of books. No opportunity for enlarging his knowledge was allowed to pass without being seized upon with the utmost eagerness. One or two pleasant instances of the avidity with which he read whatever he could lay hold of, are recorded in the present volume. It happened one day, before he was "breeched, and he was breeched at three and a half years old," he had gone with his father and mother, and some of their acquaintances, to take a walk. Their talk, which was about Mr. This and Miss That, soon became wearisome to the child; he managed to slip away from them unperceived, and scampered home. The house was far off, but he reached it some considerable time in advance of the pedestrians. When they came in they found him seated at table – a reading desk upon the table, and a huge folio upon the reading desk – a lighted candle upon each side, and the boy most intensely engaged in study. The work was Rapin's History of England; nor was this the first time that he had hung enamored over its pages.

In the year 1751, Bentham being then in his fourth year, there is in his father's book of accounts an entry for "Ward's Grammar, 1s. 6d. – Fani Colloquendi Formulæ, 6d. – Nomenclator Classicus Trilinguis, 8d. – being two and eight-pence for Jeremy junior," showing at what age his classical studies began; and in the year 1753, a nicely written scrap of Latin is preserved among his father's memoranda, with this notice: "Mem. the line pasted hereon was written by my son Jeremy," and a few days after this is the following entry: "Paid to Mr. Robert Hartely, for double allepine for Jeremy's coat and breeches, to his pink waistcoat, £0. 12s. 3d."

Bentham's parents united in keeping out of his way, as far as they were able, all books of amusement. They were possessed of a strange conceit, that there was a sort of moral contagion in works of that kind, which would bend his mind from more profitable and elevating studies. Knowing, too, his passion for reading, and that he contrived to get hold of all books that were accessible, they laid an absolute prohibition upon fictions and poetry. The list of these, therefore, to which he was restricted is rather curious, particularly as connected with the impression they made on his young mind. He has himself given this account of the matter: –

"There was first, said he, 'Burnett's Theory of the Earth,' in folio, by which I was informed of the prospect I had of being burned alive; 'Cave's Lives of the Apostles,' in a thin quarto, with cuts, in which the said Apostles were represented playing each of them, (as a child with a doll,) with that particular instrument of torture by which he was predestined to be consigned to martyrdom. Another quarto was an old edition of Stow's [Chronicle], in black letter. This Chronicle had stories in it which acted upon me with a fascination similar to that which certain animals are said to be subjected to by the serpent, to which they become, in consequence, a prey. Several pages there were, by every one of which I was filled with horror as soon as ever I ventured to risk a glance at them. Yet never could I venture into the little closet, in which almost the only sources of my amusement were contained, without opening the book at one, or two, or more, of the terrific pages, and receiving the accustomed shock. The book concluded with a description of a variety of monstrous births. I thought the world was coming to an end. My sensibility to all sources of sentiment was extreme, and to sources of terror more particularly so; and these volumes teemed with them. There was also a 'History of England,' in question and answer, by a Mr. Lockman, with a quantity of cuts: but my father's caution had not gone so far as to divest the book of its embellishments, though better it would have been for my peace of mind if it had; for there it was that I saw the blessed martyr, Charles, with his head on the accursed block – there it was I saw the holy bishops burning as fuel at Smithfield – there it was I saw the Danish Coldbrand, with a Saxon's sword in the act of finding its way into his body. Not long after, to this 'History of England,' was added a 'History of Rome,' in like form and demeanor, by the same author. Lockman was secretary to some associated company, into which my father had contrived to introduce himself; which incident was perhaps the cause of the instruction I was destined to derive from these two sources. Lockman was of the number of my father's protegés. He may have given these books to my father. My father had some books: I knew it well; for they sometimes escaped from the receptacle in which he destined them to be buried; the being allowed access to which would have been indeed a pleasure and a privilege to me. Such was 'Churchill's Voyages,' in several volumes folio. I saw them once or twice by accident, but never knew whence they came nor whither they went. In these I should have found instruction, and most useful instruction: but then the instruction would have had amusement to sweeten it; and that idea was not to be endured. My father gave me once 'Phædrus' Fables;' but fables, inasmuch as they are stories in which inferior animals are represented as talking together like men and women, never had any charm for me. One of my tribulations at this time was the learning Church collects: they used to give me the colic;

but my father insisted on my getting them by heart. When living at Aldgate, a volume of Swift's works was left about. There was the poisoning of Curl. I did not know what to make of it, whether it was true or false, serious or jocular. It excited my sympathy, however; a sort of provisional sympathy.

"'Rapin's History of England,' which I often read, whatever benefit it might have been of in other respects, was of little advantage in a moral point of view. Rapin was a soldier by trade, and his history is a history of throat-cutting on the largest scale, for the sake of plunder; and such throat-cuttings and plunderings he places at the summit of virtue. Edward the Third's claim to the throne of France was, in my view, an indisputable one. I followed his conquests in their progress with eager sympathy. My delight grew with the number of provinces given up to him against the will of their inhabitants, and with the number of Frenchmen left dead in the field of battle. Yet do I remember how great was my mortification when, after so many victories gained, he had, at the head of one hundred thousand men, advanced to the gates of Paris, which I thereupon expected to find given up to him without a struggle, and all France following its example; instead of that, the termination of his career – of this part of it, at any rate – was the same as that of a certain king of France of whom it is narrated, that he,

> 'With forty thousand men,
> Marched up the hill, and then
> Marched down again.'

On Calais, too, I could not help thinking that he had bestowed more time than it was worth. Our conquerors, I observed, had, according to the account given of them by the historian, two main instruments by which their conquests were effected: One of these instruments was the sword, – a brilliant instrument, never beheld by me without delight, as it glittered in my eyes; the other instrument was negotiation, – a word which met my eyes too often, and never without annoyance. Having consigned the sword for a time to the scabbard, Edward betook himself to negotiations; and how it was that so much was to be got by negotiation, and so little, in comparison, by the sword, I could by no means explain to myself, nor find explained. At the sight of the word negotiation, my spirits began to droop; at the sight of the sword, when once more drawn from the sheath, they revived again. In a victorious king, merit was in the direct ratio of the number of armed men slaughtered by him, and in the inverse ratio of those employed in slaughtering them. With this impure alloy, during a great part of my boyhood, was mixed up the pure, virtue which the moral part of my frame had imbibed from reading 'Telemachus.' Such were the contents of my library; a library that was no otherwise my own than by the door being left unlocked of the small room in which the books were deposited; a room on the first floor at the head of the principal staircase, situated over the principal door into the house. At this house, in which my father scarcely ever made a longer stay than from Saturday evening to Monday morning, he had no library of his own. My mother was too much occupied by her children, and other family concerns, to have a moment's time for books.

"As to my grandmother; she had her own library. It was composed, besides the Bible, of two or three books of devotion, so much in use as nearly to have fallen in pieces. These books, not containing any of them the poison of amusement, there could be no objection to my studying them as much as I pleased. One of them was the book of sacred poetry, by Bishop Ken. It began –

'Awake, my soul! and with the sun,
Thy daily course of duty run;

the first lines of the first hymn; and to render them the more intelligible, the sun was represented in a vignette as beginning his daily course, and making himself a pattern for me. I feel even now the sort of melancholy which the sight of it was to infuse into me. Another book which was imported for my use, did not contribute to lessen my melancholy: it was 'Dodsley's Preceptor,' with the Vision of Phedora, and the Hermit of Teneriffe, found in his cell: the production of the gloomy moralist, Samuel Johnson – of one of the last of whose clubs I became, in process of time, a member. Like Godwin, this man infused a tinge of melancholy, though of a different hue, into every book he touched. There was the poor ideal traveller, toiling up the hill, with Reason and Religion for his guides, his lacerated corpse; as it actually did those of the greatest part of the travelling population whom I saw toiling toward that summit which so few of them were destined to reach. Every now and then, after reading a page in this history, or another page in that system of cosmogony which taught me to look out for that too probable day in which I should be burnt alive, it occurred to me that I had better not have been born: but, as the misfortune had actually happened to me, all I could do was, of a bad bargain to make the best, and leave the rest to chance or Providence. Had I had children of my own age to associate with, these gloomy ideas would not have filled so large a portion as they did of my time. Except once or twice, no such solace was I destined to experience."

Bentham appears to have been remarkable also in early life for his extreme susceptibility of the emotions of pleasure and pain; a lively sensitiveness to the beauties of external nature; strong feelings of humanity for animals, and an invincible love of truth. His boyhood was generally a very happy one. There were many sources of enjoyment within himself, and the tenor of his existence was in the broad way of felicity. In this, perhaps, we perceive the secret of that serenity which marked his old age. No strong passions nor disquiets, arising from internal difficulties, filled his young mind with the bitterness which is apt ever afterward to tinge the intellectual perceptions of its victims. Another thing, which it is important to observe, hinted at in the above extract, is the want of associates which he felt for the greater part of his juvenile life. It had a strong influence, no doubt, in habituating his mind to the self-reliance, the complete and even prejudicial independence of the deductions of other intellects, for which he was distinguished beyond all other men that we can call to mind. Had his playmates been more numerous and more congenial, their companionship would have created a deference for the opinions of others; the absence of which we think a defect in his mental constitution. Not that he was ever intolerant, although sometimes unjust; his impatience of theories and sentiments different from his own, not permitting to give due weight and authority to whatever of excellence or merit they may have contained.

From the year 1754 to 1763, or from the sixth to the fifteenth year of his age, he was at school and college. The purposes that were the employment of his life, seem to have been formed in his mind at a very early period. He related once to Mr. Bowring that he had a distinct recollection of the time when the conviction impressed itself upon his heart, with the strength of an instinct, that he should devote himself to legislation. It was on an occasion when several friends of his father were engaged in discussing the subject of *genius*. Having perplexed themselves, as people generally do, we have observed, who attempt definition, they called in the boy to settle the dispute. What is genius? asked the father; but the poor timid, trembling child, although celebrated as a prodigy, knew no more about it than did the three grave and learned doctors of divinity who composed part of the company. Yet he did not, like them, give up the question in despair. He was puzzled by it, and whatever puzzled him could not be dismissed until some solution was found for it. For a long time he was haunted by the topic, until it occurred to him that *genius* must mean invention. Quick as thought, he asked himself, "Have I a genius for anything? What can I produce?" Then came another question, "What of all earthly pursuits is the most important?" Helvétius had said Legislation. "Have I genius for legislation?" Again and again was the question put to himself; he turned it over in his thoughts; he sought every symptom he could discover in his natural disposition and acquired habits. "And have I indeed a genius for legislation! I gave myself, fearfully and tremblingly, the answer – YES!"

Is there a man living who has read the works of Bentham, who will say that there was anything of vanity in the reply?

At school, the Westminster school, Bentham obtained considerable reputation as a maker of Greek and Latin verse. A great many specimens of these, mostly written in his tenth year, are given by his biographer. They are interesting, not as showing any prodigious powers for language or versification – although not without great merit as schoolboy exercises – but as indicative of the peculiar structure and turn of his mind. Formed, as they are, after the ancient models, they are yet in idiom, thought, and association, thoroughly English, and that an English after Bentham's own sort. Verse-making, however, was not the subject to which he most inclined. Indeed, all the exercises of the school appear to have been irksome to him, on account of the stupidity and despotism of the teachers. Like all sprightly youth, he felt that its time-consuming and logic-chopping methods were anything but useful or agreeable.

On the 27th June, 1760, Bentham's father set out with his son to place him at Oxford. He was thus made a gowned collegian when he was only twelve and a half years old: "An extraordinary age, or youth rather," says his biographer, "for University education, but the precocity of Bentham's talents was the cause. He was not only very young, but very short – quite a dwarf – so that he was stared at in the streets wherever he went." On account of his tender age, he was not at first required to take the oaths – a ceremony for which, even then, he felt the greatest repugnance. But he was called on to subscribe the Thirty-Nine Articles of the Established Church, and the necessity threw him into the greatest distress. We cannot but regard it as a singular degree of conscientiousness in one so young, that he should object to going through a process which ninety-nine persons out of a hundred look upon as a mere unmeaning form. But he viewed the matter in a higher and more serious light. Understanding that the sole object of such a signature was the declaring, after reflection, with solemnity and upon record, his concurrence in the truth of the propositions to which his name was to be attached, it seemed to him that he was bound to examine them in that aspect. He accordingly did so, but with an unfortunate result. In some of their doctrines he could discover no meaning at all, and in others no meaning that he could reconcile either to reason or Scripture. He found that some of his fellow-collegiates were sharers in his distress; on inquiry, they learned that one of the Fellows of the college was set apart, by virtue of his office, to remove all scruples of the kind we are speaking of; and they immediately repaired to him. But his answers were cold and unsatisfactory; the substance of them being, that it was not for uninformed youths, such as they, to presume to place their private judgment against a public one, formed by some of the holiest as well as best and wisest men that ever lived. Bentham reluctantly acquiesced in the decision, but through the whole of his after-life he regretted the hypocrisy that he was forced to practise, and protested vehemently against the despotism which thus applied the discipline of Procrustes to the dictates of the conscience.

The tutors and professors at Oxford, according to his biographer, offered nothing to win the affections of Bentham. Some of them were profligate, and he was shocked with their profligacy; others were morose, and their moroseness alienated him; but the greater part were insipid, and he had no taste for insipidity. Yet he seems to have discharged his duties with commendable diligence.

Nor were the students any more agreeable than the instructers. All sorts of oppressions were exercised by the older upon the younger classes. "They were all either stupid or dissipated," says Bentham. "I learned nothing. I played at tennis once or twice. I took to reading Greek of my own fancy; but there was no encouragement; we just went to the foolish lectures of our tutors to be taught something of logical jargon." We refer to this as evidence of the condition of the English Universities, on the testimony of a good judge, less than a century ago.

In 1765 Bentham was entered as a student of the Court of King's Bench, Westminster Hall. He was an attendant upon the lectures of Blackstone, whom he describes as a formal, precise, and affected lecturer, just what might be expected from the character of his writings, cold, reserved, and wary – exhibiting a frigid pride. But the lectures were popular, and many of Bentham's companions took notes of them, although he was unable to do so himself, because his "thoughts were occupied in reflecting upon what he had heard." His first brief, after he had begun the practice of law, was got from a Mr. Clarke; it was a suit in equity, on which £50 depended; and the counsel he gave, with a most unlawyerlike disinterestedness, was, that the suit had better be put an end to, and the money that would he wasted in the contest saved. His own remarks upon his entrance to the practice of his profession are amusing. "On my being called to the bar," he says, "I found a cause or two at nurse for me; my first thought was, how to put them to death: and the endeavors were not altogether without success. Not long after, a case was brought to me for my opinion. I ransacked all the codes; my opinion was right according to the codes; but it was wrong according to a manuscript unseen by me, and inaccessible to me – a manuscript containing the report of I know not what opinion, said to have been delivered before I was born, and locked up, as usual, for the purpose of being kept back or produced, as occasion served." It may be expected that, under these circumstances, an ingenious and original mind as his was would not be the most favorably disposed to the practice of law. He very soon contracted a disgust for it. "I went to the bar," he says, "as a bear to the stake." In a short time he relinquished the practice entirely – but he did not relinquish the study of the law. On the other hand, he prosecuted the study with increasing zeal and activity. He had become filled with a great notion of the reform of legislation, and applied all his powers to the preparing and fitting himself for the task. An extract from his common-place book will show how various, comprehensive, and benevolent were the schemes that at this time occupied his thoughts:–

Subjects for Premiums.

1. "Essay on the Measures to be kept in Legislation, in all cases between Private and Public Interest.":

2. "Essay on the best method of reducing the burden upon the Nation from sinecures and unnecessary offices, consistently with a due attention to the rights of the present patrons and possessors; with a due examination of the question how far, and whether to bad or good effect, the balance of power would be affected by such a scheme. None but a good minister will have the courage to endure such a discussion as this."

3. "The best collection of examples of virtue adapted to the different classes of mankind."

4. "The best Moral Catechism for the use of Schools."
5. "The best Legal Catechism for the use of Schools."
6. "History of Criminal Law in this Country, divided according to the several crimes. A compilation, or rather, as the degrees of merit in the execution of it could not be very various, and the compilation would be too voluminous to engage a number of writers upon hazard, – An Essay delineating the plan, and indicating the sources from whence the materials are to be obtained."
7. "A new Treatise on a new species of Brachygraphy, or a System of Rules for the Conversion of Long Sentences into Short Ones, for the Legislatorial Style."

Title for a Book.
"The Homage of Foreigners to the British Constitution."

Education.
1. *Moral Department.* – "Inspire a hatred for conquerors, and a contempt for their admirers. Show the difference between conquest by an individual, and conquest by a nation. Conquest by an individual, especially made in the ancient or modern Eastern manner, is robbery in the gross."
2. *Scientific.* – "Elements of all sciences upon playing cards. The contents to be made the subject of conversation."
3. *Moral.* – "Inspire a general habit of applauding or condemning actions according to their *general* utility. Professional affections to be exploded. National affections to be encouraged, keeping clear of inhospitality. Family affections to be stationed in their proper place, viz., subordinate to natural ones."
4. "Inspire a contempt for ancient philosophy, or philosophy of words."
"The question between Christians and those who are not so, is a question of evidence. It is as unreasonable to make a difference of opinion on this question, one way or another, a matter of reproach, as the question, whether such a will was or was not made."

The following letter from Bentham to his father, indicates the nature of his occupations, and of his literary projects, in 1776: –

Bentham to his Father.
"HONORED SIR: I am now at work upon my capital work, I mean 'The Critical Elements of Jurisprudence.' I am not now, as heretofore,

barely collecting materials, but putting it into the form in which I propose that it should stand. I am working upon a plan which will enable me to detach a part and publish it separate from the rest. The part that I am now upon is the law of Personal Injuries: from thence I shall proceed to the law relative to such acts as are Injuries to property and reputation. This will include the whole of the criminal law relative to such offences as have determinate Individuals for their object. This part may be characterized by the name of the Law relative to Private Wrongs; the remainder, in that case, will come under the law relative to Public Wrongs; but a much clearer and more natural line will be drawn between the offences that respectively come under those divisions, than the technical mode of considering the subject would admit of Blackstone's drawing. Previous to these details, will come that part of the work which contains the general principles by which the execution of those details is governed. Of this preliminary part the plan is pretty well settled, and the materials in good part collected.

"By what I have seen and learned concerning Sam's work, I doubt not his doing great things in geometry. The rogue is pressing me so, I must be done; I have sent him upon the mare, thinking this would be a good opportunity of his having a couple of rides.

"I am, Dear Sir, yours most dutifully and affectionately,
(Signed)   "JERRY BENTHAM.
"*Fetcham*, 1st Oct. 1776."

Labors of this sort, however, did not satisfy the ambition of his father, who saw him desert the avenues to opulence and distinction, for the barren field of philosophy, with keen disappointment. He had fondly predicted, from the early promise of his son, a career of progressive honor at the bar and on the bench; to be crowned, perhaps, with the possession of the great seal – what then were his feelings, when he found that son manifesting the paltry desire to attain no higher station than that of a benefactor of mankind? It was, indeed, grievous for the old gentleman; but we do not learn that the world has since much regretted the choice. As for ourselves, we are disposed to speak of the change as one of the happiest events in history. That a person of the peculiar structure of mind of Bentham, with his acuteness, his rigidity, his independence, and his creative power, should have resolved to make himself an exception to the general run of lawyers; that he should have determined to pursue his profession, not as a means of profit or honor, but in order to point out its defects and suggest their remedies; that he should have relinquished the labor of writing briefs or pleading causes, for the sake of creating a vast inductive system of moral and political philosophy; that he should have thought the improvement of society of more consequence than his own individual advancement, are reasons for the gratitude and thanks of mankind. The boldness no less than the originality of his designs – of which, at this late day, our familiarity with the subjects hinders us from forming an adequate idea – would place him in the first rank of brave and independent thinkers. What Bacon was to the physical sciences, Bentham was to the science of law.

Bentham's first printed compositions were two letters, written for a paper called the Gazetteer, when he was twenty-three years old, and a defence of Lord Mansfield – whose character, however, he did not admire. But the first publication that gave him a name was an admirable and caustic criticism of Blackstone's introduction to his Commentaries. It was named a "Fragment on Government," and was originally intended to make part of a larger work on the same general subject. He sent it forth without his name, but the extraordinary acuteness and force of its logic, and the beauty of its style, brought it speedily into notice. It was successively ascribed to several of the most eminent and accomplished lawyers and writers of the times. Lord Mansfield, Lord Camden, and Lord Ashburton, were each supposed, by different persons, to have been the author of it. But at last, through the anxious desire of his father to obtain some alleviation for the long-suffering inflicted by the perversely disinterested course of his son, the secret took air. He as soon forced to repent of his weakness; for, says Bentham, "No sooner had the images of its reported illustrious father vanished – no sooner was it known that the bantling was the offspring of somebody known to nobody, than the rate of the sale underwent a sensible diminution." It was attacked with no little ferocity; anathemas were thundered against the presuming head of its author, and his opinions, political and religious, were called in question, with all the freedom and insolence of ribaldry. Indeed, so great was the opposition to him, that another work which he had prepared on Blackstone, entitled "Castrations to the Commentaries, being the 3d Chapter to the II. Book of that work, published, as it might have been" was suppressed from a fear of prosecution.

One effect of the publication of the "Fragment on Government," was to secure him the acquaintance and friendship of Lord Shelburne, afterwards Marquis of Lansdowne. The pleasantest days of his life were, perhaps, those passed at the delightful country seat, Bowood, of this amiable and liberal nobleman. It was a magnificent domain, in the midst of a picturesque and beautiful country. The owner, shortly afterward the Prime Minister of England, was possessed of the finest graces of the intellect, and the rarest virtues of the heart; and his immense wealth and princely establishment were alike at the service of his friends of all ranks. Many of the most distinguished men of the age were his guests; and many poets and philosophers, yet unknown to fame, shared his hospitality. There might be met the sages of the law, with Camden, Jekyll, and Dunning at their head; there were Franklin, Dumont, Linguet, and other no less noted men of science; there was that noble and estimable man and lawyer, Romilly; and Bankers, Barré, and the younger William Pitt, were there; all mingling on terms of equality in pleasant social intercourse – now enjoying a rubber at whist, and then discussing the merits of statesmen and the movements of courts. Bentham, when introduced into this brilliant circle, had the manners and habits of a recluse. He was shy, modest, and reserved. But there was a shrewdness in his remark, a penetration and solidity of judgment, and withal a depth of humor, that soon drew around him the master spirits of the assemblage. His nature opened under the genial influences of kindness and praise, and, in a little time, he found himself among the favorites of the household; sought by the men for his wisdom, and courted by the ladies for his pleasantry. Nor was he backward in returning the flatteries of the latter. One of them, however, touched him with a deeper feeling than that to which we give the name of admiration and esteem. In short, he fell deeply in love, and the history of his passion is a curious episode in his quiet career. His suit was rejected, and the incident seems to have been indelibly fixed in his mind. In the eightieth year of his age, we find him writing in this manner to the object of his early attachment:

"I am alive, – more than two months advanced in my eightieth year, more lively than when you presented me in ceremony with the flowers in the green lane. Since that day, not a single one has passed (and to speak of nights) in which you have not engrossed more of my thoughts than I could have wished. Yet, take me for all in all, I am more lively now than then; walking, though only for a few minutes and for health's sake, more briskly than most young men whom you see not unfrequently running. I have still the pianoforte harpsichord on which you played at —— ; as an instrument, though no longer useful, it is still curious, – as an article of furniture, not unhandsome:

as a legacy, will you accept it? I have a ring with some of my snow-white hair in it, and my profile, which everybody says is like. At my death you will have such another; should you come to want, it will be worth a good sovereign to you. * * * * *
Every minute of my life has been long counted, and I am plagued with remorse at the minutes which I have suffered you to steal from me. In proportion as I am a friend of mankind (if such I am, as I endeavor to be), you, if within my reach, would be an enemy."

Who can fully appreciate the bearing of this incident on the subsequent life of the man, on his high and noble public career, and on the destinies of nations to which he has so powerfully contributed to give their direction? Who will not see in it a subject for profound reflection, of the most deeply interesting character? Disappointed in his love, he gave to his race, he gave to the cause of truth, he gave to a sublime philanthropy and an expansive political philosophy, those mental energies, and those deep and deathless affections of the heart, which were thus debarred from the natural vent their first young impulse had sought. Have we not here the key to Bentham's whole life and character? Alas for him, the good and great old octogenarian, thus writing to the unforgotten object of the love of such a mind and such a heart! It has been, perhaps, our gain – but at what a cost to him! What fiction has ever presented a passage more profoundly touching, to the reflecting mind, than these simple and quiet lines we are tempted again to repeat: "I am alive – more than two months advanced in my 80th year, more lively than when you presented me in ceremony with the flowers in the green lane. *Since that day not a single one has passed (not to speak of nights) in which you have not engrossed more of my thoughts than I could have wished.*"

On the part of the lady, the impressions were not so deep. "I was present," says his biographer, "a short time before his death, when the answer came to this letter – that answer was cold and distant – it contained no reference to the state of former affections; and he was indescribably hurt and disappointed by it. I talked to him, however, of 'auld-lang-syne,' and reminded him of Burns' song and his beautiful reference to the times gone by. When I repeated, "We twa hae pu'ed the gowans fine,' he was cheered a little; the past recollection was brighter than the present thought – but he was for a long time silent and greatly moved. At last he said, 'Take me forward to the future, I entreat you – do not let me go back to the past – talk of something – find out something to remove my thoughts from the time of my youth.'"

We are glad that the name of the lady who could have returned a "cold and distant" answer to such a letter has not been given. Be it forgotten, so long as that of her noble, though unhappy lover, shall be remembered in the applauses and blessings of his kind!

With one more extract we close our article for the present, promising, if we have an opportunity, to renew it after the appearance of the sequel of Mr. Bowring's delightful memoir. The extract, being a letter addressed to Lady E. G., is an example of his playfulness and humor: –

"*Hendon, Middlesex, 27th November,* 1791.

"HONORED MADAM! – May it please your ladyship! I am the young man who was taken from behind the screen by my good Lady Warwick, in the room where the pianoforte is in Warwick castle, to wait upon your sweet person, and had the honor and happiness of accompanying you with the violin in one of Signor Bach's sonatas. I hope your ladyship's condescending goodness will excuse my freedom in addressing you, as I hereby make bold to do, wishing for the felicity of serving your ladyship in the capacity of musical instructer, or anything else I should be found capable of, being turned adrift upon the wide world, and out of place at this time. I served the Hon. Miss F—, whom belike your ladyship knows, – she being, as I am informed, your ladyship's cousin-german, – for ten long years, and hoped to have served her till death, had I not been, with grief be it spoken, forced to quit her service by hard usage. She was a dear lady, and a kind compassionate good lady, – as I have heard everybody say, and to be sure so it must be, as everybody says so, – to everybody but poor me. To be sure it must have been my own unworthiness, therefore it would be very unreasonable for me to complain. I am sober and honest, willing to turn my hand to anything, and not at all given to company keeping, as I am sure my said late honored lady, notwithstanding what has happened, will be ready to say for me. Dr. Ingenhousz, who is my lady's head philosopher, being somewhat stricken in years, I was in hopes of being promoted to his place, when Providence should please to call him away, considering that we are all mortal; but my evil star has ordered it otherwise. The times being hard, I am willing to serve for small wages, having had nothing given me to subsist upon, in all the ten years, except the direction of a letter, and a message or two, and they were given me by other people. As to playing on the pianoforte myself, I though it better not to trouble myself with any such thing, for fear of spoiling my teaching; by reason I have known your fine, tasty, fashionable, flourishing masters, who, instead of attending to their pupils, chose rather to keep playing themselves, for the sake of showing a fine finger. I am used to traveling, and am willing to attend your ladyship all the world over, as likewise to any part of England or Scotland; particularly the latter, which is the most delightful country upon earth.

"I hope your ladyship will pardon my making so bold; but I have a brother, a colonel by trade, who has a good mistress, who has given him leave to go about for a while and see whether he can do anything to mend himself. As it has become the fashion for ladies to practise shooting, I think that he may find employment by teaching them that, or anything else in the art of war – think him qualified, as there would be no objection to his teaching, – although I can't say I ever knew him draw a long bow, – to turn philosopher, as he has made greater bounces in his time than Philosopher Ingenhousz. Having learned metaphysics of the celebrated Miss V——, would be qualified as usher to a metaphysical academy, but would prefer private service. These few lines conclude with humble duty from,
"Honored madam,
"Your ladyship's most obedient,
"Humble servant to command.
"P.S. – O dear! O dear! well, what a lucky thing it was I happened to mention Scotland; it has brought the charmingest thought into my head that ever was. Did your ladyship ever hear of a place called Gretna Green? They have a way of playing duets there, and such duets, it beats all the concerts in the world; Signor Bach's music is nothing to it. There is no such thing as learning them at home: one must absolutely go there first to see the manner of it. There is a gentleman always, and a lady; and then a blacksmith in a black gown plays with his hammer dub–a–dub–dub, and yet it is but a duet after all. Well, now, as your ladyship, I have heard, likes travelling, and Scotland is the delighfulest country in the world, how comical it would be if your ladyship were to take a trip next Saturday to Gretna Green, and I were to attend your ladyship, as, to be sure, you could never think of going such a journey alone, and I would come slyly, just as it was dusk, and meet you just behind the Green house, and nobody should know anything about the matter, and I would have a chaise-and-four ready, and off we would go with a smack, smack, smack! to Gretna Green! And then Lady W. would cry – Where is Lady E.? and Lord W. would cry – Where is Lady E.? and nobody would know. And then all the servants would be called up, and there would be such doings, and all the while we should be playing duets at Gretna Green! and then we should come home again; and then there would be such a laugh; and the Lady W. would cry – How comical Mr. Bentham is! – I do vow and

declare there is never a man shall play duets with my E. but Mr. B.

"P.S. – Pray dear, sweet, good my lady – there's a dear lady – don't say a word to any living creature about this, as it would quite spoil the joke."

"*Dover Street, 29th November, 1791.*

"HONORED MADAM: This makes bold to inform you that my lady and I have made it up, and she has given me what is my due, and more too, and a dear, sweet, good lady she is; wherefore I have altered my mind, hoping no offence, and as I stay in my place, have no call to go with anybody to Gretna Green, unless it be with my lady. As everybody is willing to do the best they can for themselves, hope your ladyship won't be angry, as a rolling stone gathers no moss, as the saying is; and it cannot be expected a person should leave a good place, unless it were to better himself. Should anything amiss happen another time, should be very proud to serve your ladyship, or anybody. My brother being still disengaged, if agreeable, could venture to recommend him – and am,
 "Honored madam,
  "Your ladyship's very humble
   "Servant to command."

NOTES

[1] The works of Jeremy Bentham, now first collected. Part XIX, containing Memoirs of Bentham, by John Bowring, including Autobiographical Conversations and Correspondence. Edinburgh, 1842.

[2] See Democratic Review for 1840.

12

[G.H. Smith]

Review

The Works of Jeremy Bentham.
Published under the superintendence of his Executor,
John Bowring, M.P. Edinburgh: W. Tait

in

National Quarterly Review
vol. III, no. V (June 1861), pp. 51–70

Art. III.—*The Works of Jeremy Bentham.* Published under the superintendence of his Executor, John Bowring. M. P. Edinburgh : W. Tait.

For the last ten years before Bentham's death, there existed between him and Bowring the most familiar friendship, and the philosopher died with his head resting on the bosom of his friend. During that time, says the latter, "I believe not a thought, not a feeling of his, was concealed from me." It is needless to say more to show what an abundance of materials must have been placed at Dr. Bowring's disposal. The simple-hearted, communicative old man, well satisfied with himself, and comfortably persuaded that all he had ever said or done would be matter of interest to many enthusiastic admirers, was easily induced to give a full and particular account of all the incidents of his life. Thus he performed the part of his own Boswell; and although the egotism, necessary to such a performance, is by no means so agreeable as poor Bozzy's humble admiration for his great master, yet the work has been, if possible, even more completely executed. The character of Johnson is, however, a more agreeable one to contemplate. Under a rough exterior, his was a peculiarly genial and social nature. In spite of his rudeness, he knew how to perceive and esteem the good qualities of all sorts of men. He was the appreciative friend of most of the distinguished men of the day; and even under the rough exterior of poor Goldsmith, could detect the qualities of greatness. But in these same men Bentham could see nothing to admire. He held them all in great contempt, as being utterly benighted; or, worse—dishonest. There was but one standard by which he judged them all, and that was, how near they approached to his views of morals and legislation. In short, he seemed to have no admiration, no sympathy, for the many unquestionable virtues and other agreeable qualities which can exist in the heart of man independently of the Utilitarian Philosophy. To do the right thing was by no means sufficient for him; but it was also necessary that it should be done upon the greatest happiness-producing principle; in fine, *geniality*—a word including both appreciation and charity—was an element altogether lacking in his character. With few exceptions, he had no associations, no sympathies, except with those who adopted his philosophy and joined with him in his own peculiar pursuits. To him, *legislation* was the most important of all earthly pursuits; and all not engaged in it—and that, too, according to his method—were outcasts and aliens from his sympathies. He looked upon all such as passing their lives in a trivial manner, unworthy of the sympathy of a philosopher. Johnson he held to be "a pompous vamper of common-place morality—of phrases often trite, without being true." "I was angry," he says, "with Goldsmith for writing the Deserted Village. I liked nothing gloomy; besides, it was not true, for there were no such villages." Again: "I met Burke at Phil Metcalfe's. *He gave me a great disgust*. It was just at the dawn of the French Revolution. I imagined every body would acknowledge it was necessary that a bridle should be put on despotic power. All that Burke retorted was in a word—'Faction.'" "I remember," he says, "going to Twickenham church with my father and Mr. Reynolds, afterwards Sir Joshua. His conversation left no impression upon me. His countenance was not pleasing. There was a great talk about painting, and about his painting. But I knew nothing about painting, and cared nothing about him." In short, Bentham was acquainted more or less with all the many illustrious men that were contemporary with Johnson, but had for them no manner of interest or admiration. In the latter part of his life especially, he grew more and more impatient of intercourse with the world, and finally secluded himself entirely from all, except his own followers and admirers. In his residence at Queen's Square Place, he lived after the model of an old Greek philosopher, surrounded by reverential and believing disciples. His mode of life here is thus graphically described by Dr. Bowring:

"He dined at seven o'clock, in a room he called his shop......One, sometimes two, secretaries dined with him, who were honored with the name of 'reprobates.' Himself he liked to call 'the Hermit,' and his house 'the Hermitage.'........At eleven o'clock water was introduced, his night-cap brought in, which he tied under his chin, his watch delivered to the 'reprobate' who held the office of 'putter to bed,' his eyes washed, his habiliments doffed, and during all these proceedings, which lasted exactly an hour, he kept up a perpetual and amusing chit-chat; at twelve o'clock his guests were visited with 'ignominious expulsion.' He then withdrew into his room, where he slept on a hard bed......The 'reprobate' usually read to him till he fell asleep; but sometimes access was denied, and the 'reprobate' waited in the shop till he called out, Watch!

"He (Bentham) sometimes feigned to be in a great rage, I once heard him shout out, 'I cannot find the letter—curses! fury! rage! despair! I am seriously apprehensive I have sent the villain away with the wrong letter.' In all this there was not the slightest real passion. It was intended to make cursing ridiculous."

"When Riva Javia, the Buenos Ayres minister dined at his table, he (a not uncommon trick of foreigners) spat on the carpet. Up rose Mr. Bentham, ran into his bed-room, brought out a certain utensil, and placed it at his visitor's feet."

The cause of Bentham's egotism and eccentricity can be discerned in the circumstances of his life. He was born in the year 1748, in the month of February. From his earliest youth he exhibited great precocity, and was consistently educated in the notion that he was a great genius, and other boys great dunces. The effect of this was strengthened by the secluded manner of his early life. Until the age of fourteen, he had no companions of his own age, and the unsocial habit thus engendered clung to him through life. To use the expressive words of Dr. Bowring, he always "avoided the rush and shock of men." A morbid impatience of the opinions, the sentiments, the character of others, grew upon him with his years, until he took pleasure in the society of none except his admiring disciples. His life is a melancholy illustration of the truth that contact with the rough, everyday life of man, is necessary to the formation of a complete character. Without it, the result must always be egotism—a disposition to dwell alone upon ourselves, and those things with which we are occupied.

Among the few associations that Bentham formed of an ordinary kind was his acquaintance with Lord Shelburne's family. And who can tell how far that may have influenced his after life? His first acquaintance with Lord Shelburne was in 1781. Bentham was at that time thirty-three years of age. "I was lying," he says, "in my dog-hole in the temple, in obscurity, perfect obscurity, when a person entered, and said he was Lord Shelburne. He began to laud the 'Fragment' most outrageously, and invited me to his house; but my bashfulness and my pride prevented my going there. At last, after many weeks, I went, and staid some time. I was a great favorite with the ladies, and Lord Shelburne wished me to marry one of his family." Although the one proposed did not suit him, there was another whom he met at Lord Shelburne's that did. A young lady, then very young, whose name Dr. Bowring does not give, engaged but did not return his affections. His passion for her seems to have been very enduring. Dr. Bowring tells us that he has often heard Mr. Bentham talk of her with tears in his eyes. How his suit was met at the time is not related; but many years afterwards, when in his fifty-eighth year, he wrote to her, renewing his proposals. In a long, kind letter, she declines his offer. "My conscience acquits me," she says, in the usual style adopted by womankind on such occasions, "of ever designing to give pain to any human being, much less one whom I did and ever shall respect and remember. It is in your power, however, to make me easy, if you instantly, without the waste of a single day, return to those occupations from which the world will hereafter derive benefit, and yourself renown. I have enough to answer for already in interrupting your tranquillity (God knows how unintentionally!) —let me not be guilty of depriving mankind of your useful labors, of deadening the energy of such a mind as yours." Many years afterwards, at the age of eighty, the old man, writing to her sister, says: "Embrace ———; though it is for me, as it is by you, she will not be severe, and refuse her lips, as to me she did her hand, at a time perhaps not yet forgotten by her, any more than by me." "After the date of this letter," says Dr. Bowring, "he often spoke to me upon the subject—spoke as if he liked to expatiate upon it, and added: 'I have grown very garrulous about this to you.'" We confess that the old man, cherishing thus a hopeless love for fifty years—his almost only association with the common world—presents to us a touching spectacle; and though we admit his want of sympathy with the men and times he lived among, his egotism and his eccentricities, yet perish the hand that would throw the stone at him for this. Let it rather be remembered that he was honest and incorruptible, and devoted a long life to the interests of humanity; that he was eminently tender-hearted and faithful in the associations that he did form; and finally, that his genius has conferred great benefits upon the world.

The works of Jeremy Bentham are very voluminous. His first publication, "A Fragment on Government, or a Comment upon the Commentaries," was "an examination of what is delivered on the subject of Government in general, in the introduction to Sir William Blackstone's Commentaries." This work, published in 1776, attracted great attention, and gained for the author considerable reputation. His next was far more ambitious, being a work on the "Principles of Morals and Legislation." The rest of his works are either treatises upon particular subjects in the law, or specimen parts of a universal code, or, as he calls it, Pannomium. The work on the "Principles of Morals and Legislation" has always been regarded by Bentham and his followers as his greatest achievement. As the author of that work, it is claimed that he has originated a new philosophy—a philosophy destined to effect a revolution in social science. The principle of utility, it was acknowledged, was known long before; but Bentham claimed to have made such improvements in the development of it, as to make it, in effect, a new principle. "The Utilitarian Philosophy," says Dr. Bowring, "like the Baconian, has not tended so much to point out any new direction to the human intellect (a remark, by the way, as applied to Bacon, altogether untrue), as to keep it steady in a course of which it had previously a vague and slight notion, and from which it was every now and then straying." Mr. Bentham, in adopting the principle, makes but one material modification. He makes utility, not only the test, but the very essence of virtue, and as furnishing the only motive thereto. The actual end of action on the part of every individual at the moment of action, he asserts always to be *his* greatest happiness, according to his view of it at that moment; his proper end of action, he says, should be *his* real greatest happiness from that time to the end of his life. He afterwards explains this principle in a manner that renders it entirely unobjectionable, but at the same time, in effect, renders it altogether meaningless. The principle, as originally stated, is manifestly untrue. We do thousands of acts without a thought of our own happiness occurring. We do them, prompted by genuine love for others—a principle as universal and as real in the human heart, though not so powerful, as the love of ourselves. To say that every action is necessarily prompted by a regard to our own happiness, is to leave out of sight a great many other motives that exist in the heart of man, along with self-love, though sometimes nearly, but never entirely, swallowed up by it. Mr. Bentham's reasoning in support of his proposition against these facts, strikes us as in the highest degree trifling. Instead of the word "happiness," he prefers "pleasure." "The pursuit of pleasure," then, he holds to be the constant and never-varying motive of man. He did not confine the word, however, to sensuality, and mere corporeal enjoyment, but extended it to those objects and pursuits which the better part of mankind hold in esteem. Dropping the ordinary signification of the word "pleasure," he takes it to mean nearly the same thing as "volition"—"will."

"What it *pleases* man to do," says Dr. Bowring, "is simply what a man *wills* to do. What a man *wills* to do, or what he *pleases* to do, may be far from giving him enjoyment; yet, shall we say that in doing it, he is not following his own *pleasure?* A man drinks himself into a state of intoxication; here, whatever may be the ultimate balance of happiness, people can at least imagine present enjoyment, and will admit that the individual is pursuing what he calls his *pleasure*. A native of Japan, when he is offended, stabs himself, to prove the intensity of his feelings. It is difficult to see enjoyment in this case, or what is popularly called *pleasure;* yet the man obeyed his impulses, he has followed the dictates of his *will*—he has done that which it *pleased* him to do, or that which, as the balance appeared to him at the moment, was, in the question between stabbing and not stabbing, the alternative which gave him the more pleasure."

To take this view of the case reduces Mr. Bentham's proposition to a meaningless absurdity. The actual end of action, he says, on the part of every individual at the moment of action, is always his greatest happiness, according to his view of it that moment. Substitute the above definitions for " happiness," and the proposition reads : " The actual end of action on the part of every individual at the moment of action, is always what it *pleases* him to do—what he WILLS. This is incorrect. The end of action is *that which causes* him to will, whatever that may be. We see a man drowning: without a single thought of ourselves, without a single thought of any thing but the drowning man, we rescue him. If a thought of ourselves occurs at all, it is to deter us. The end of action is to save him from drowning; the motive an involuntary, instinctive sentiment, sensation, or feeling of our nature, that makes us desirous to cause happiness to another man. Certainly Mr. Bentham's principle, thus explained, is entirely unobjectionable. But the misfortune is, that while the Utilitarians defend it on these grounds, they use it always in the plain, selfish, false sense, which its words apparently express. In such a sense it is psychologically false. It is moreover to be noticed, that as Bentham was an atheist, he confines the principle altogether to the happiness to be enjoyed in this world, and, in striking the balance, makes no account of what may occur hereafter. Supposing that the proper end of action, on the part of every individual, is his own greatest happiness in this world alone, we do not see how we can adopt the "happiness of the whole," as the test of right.

Upon such an hypothesis, "our own happiness" would furnish not only the end of action, but the rule.

The principle must, however, be admitted to apply, as a test, to law. "The greatest happiness of the whole community ought to be the end or object of pursuit in every branch of the law." Mr. Bentham did not, however, claim originality in the mere announcement of this principle, but based his claims rather upon the manner in which he developed it, and brought it out in detail. The improvements thus supposed to be made, consist in an investigation and enumeration of all the different pleasures and pains, and a method of measuring the value of "a lot of pleasure or pain." This he treats with scholastic subtlety. His method in forming a judgment of whether a particular act is right or wrong—whether it conduces or not to the greatest happiness of the greatest number—is to enumerate on the one side all the pleasures that it would tend to produce, with the value of each indicated (probably by numbers); and on the other side, all the pains that it would tend to produce, with their value likewise indicated. Then, by an arithmetical calculation, the balance can be struck with infallible certainty. The error of this is, that it is impossible to determine the *value* of a *pleasure* or *pain*. It is different to different people. It cannot be determined by an enumeration of its different qualities, such as its intensity, its duration, &c. Besides, it is impossible to compare one pleasure with another, or with a pain, in this exact way. The things are what the mathematicians call incommensurable. Practically, the theory has never proved of any value. We doubt very much whether Mr. Bentham himself used it. But the great defect of Mr. Bentham's philosophy is rather omission than commission. It consists in entirely leaving out of view certain principles that lie at the very bottom of legal science, of which he appears to have been entirely ignorant. Further on we hope to make this apparent. At present we may remark, that succeeding philosophers seem generally to have concurred in the opinion that the "Principles of Morals and Legislation" contain very little that is original, and still less that is useful. The credit is, however, certainly due to him, that he roused the attention of the world to the abuses of the law. The parallel between Bentham and Bacon—made above by Dr. Bowring—is a very favorite one with the Utilitarians. We are told by Mr. R. Hildreth, the historian, another follower of Bentham (but, like Peter, afar off), that "in the judgment of an impartial posterity, Bentham will be placed with Bacon, as a genius of the first order," and still another enthusiastic disciple calls him "the great high priest of legislation, and the Lord Bacon of his age." Some points of resemblance must be admitted. The pride of intellect that inspired the " Franciscus de Verulamio sic cogitavit" of Bacon; the conviction that all received systems were worthless and vicious; that his own method was to regenerate science—all find their counterpart in Bentham, with the trifling exception that in him they were somewhat delusive.¹ In other respects we can hardly imagine a more perfect antithesis.

The Baconian philosophy holds induction to be the foundation of true science, and that all not with it in this respect, are against it. The Utilitarian, on the contrary, makes but little account of induction, but directs its labors rather to the ideas which the mind happens already to have received, than to the acquisition of new ideas by observation. And as the two systems differ in character, so also in fortune. Bacon's logic has been universally received; Bentham's as universally rejected. It would, however, be unjust to Mr. Bentham not to mention another point of contrast. The acquisitions of Bacon in the particular sciences, viewed by the present standard, are justly regarded as contemptible. But Bentham's practical observations on different subjects in the law with which he made himself acquainted, are generally sagacious and valuable, and entitle him to the gratitude of the world. There is no man who has effected so much towards the improvement of the law. The beneficial influence of his genius is perceptible every where in our statute-books. There are, besides, no other works so well calculated to remove the false notions still held in regard to this science—the professional prejudices engendered by practice in lawyers' minds—and to substitute an enlarged and liberal way of thinking. So that, as it may be said of Bentham, that a lawyer's knowledge of the law would have made him in this science the foremost man in the world, so we may say of the lawyers, that nothing would more tend to improve the law than some little knowledge on their part of the works of Jeremy Bentham.

We are told in Mr. Bowring's interesting memoirs of Jeremy Bentham, that when the latter was about seven years of age, his mind was much excited by the question, put to him one day at dinner by one of his father's guests—" What is genius ?"

"This question," says Mr. Bowring, "haunted young Bentham's mind for many years; until at the age of twenty, Helvetius' book, *De l'Esprit*, having fallen into his hands, it occurred to him that 'Genius was a word conjugate, derived from the word *gigno*, and consequently that it meant *invention* or *production*.' The effect of this discovery upon Mr. Bentham's mind is thus described by himself: 'Have *I* a genius for any thing? What can *I* produce?' was the first inquiry he made of himself. Then came another: 'What of all earthly pursuits is the most important?' 'Legislation,' was the answer Helvetius gave. 'Have *I* a genius for legislation?' Again and again he asked himself the question. He turned it over in his thoughts; he sought every symptom he could discover in his natural disposition or acquired habits; and finally gave himself the answer, fearfully and tremblingly —'Yes!'"

How far this notion of *genius* may have influenced the mind of Mr. Bentham, we cannot, of course, say; but certainly nothing could furnish a happier illustration of the character of his philosophy. Genius as applied to art—that is, to the use and application of knowledge—may mean *invention* or *production*. But thus defined, it can play no part in science, except that of corrupting it. In such a connection it leads us away from the very aim of science, which is *discovery*. This the whole history of philosophy shows. As applied to science, it can only mean capacity of perceiving the relations of things. In which respect, as is well remarked by Bacon, lies the greatest, and perhaps the radical difference between different men's minds in regard to philosophy. Consequently the materials upon which alone genius can usefully employ itself, are observed facts; and just in proportion as it rejects the use of observation, it wanders into error. "Man, the servant and interpreter of nature," says Bacon, "does, and understands as much, as he has actually or mentally observed of the order of nature: he neither knows nor is capable of more." To the observation of facts, then, philosophy looks as the source of all sound knowledge. To give to *genius* the meaning of *invention* or *production*, turns us away from this fundamental truth, and causes us to busy ourselves with recombining the notions which our minds have already happened to receive. The difference is, that in the one case we recognize the truth that our knowledge is absolutely bounded by our knowledge of the particular facts from which it is derived; and accordingly we base all our hopes upon observation and induction. In the other—to use the words of Bacon—we consider "those voluntary collections which the mind maketh of knowledge," as furnishing a sufficient collection of facts; and direct all our labor to *producing* new combinations of ideas thus already acquired. It is precisely this difference that exists between the new and the old philosophy. It is also precisely in this respect that Mr. Bentham's philosophy errs. It cannot, indeed, be asserted that he has not in some sort based his philosophy on facts. For this would be true of no system, worthy of the name, that has ever existed. But his error was, that he altogether mistook the class of facts, from which, in legal science, induction should be made. Facts are of two kinds, which may be described with sufficient accuracy for our purposes; the one, as *existing things* and their *qualities;* the other, as *events.* It is from the former class, and from a very small portion of it, that Mr. Bentham takes *his* facts. The nature of man, the motives which govern him, the nature of different kinds of pleasures and pains, in short, psychological facts arrived at by reflection—these furnish him with all the particulars upon which his philosophy is based. In his work upon the Principles of Morals and Legislation, he expressly assumes these as a sufficient basis for his philosophy. That this is fundamentally erroneous, will appear from a moment's consideration of the nature of law. A principle or rule of justice is but a generalization of what is just in particular cases. Hence, to lay down a principle, it is absolutely necessary to have a precedent knowledge of the cases upon which it is to operate.

Men are too apt to regard *justice* in the abstract—as something having an independent existence—as an existing thing. But the truth is, that there is a strict analogy between *justice* and the qualities of physical substances. As color, of which an abstract notion is formed by every one, can have no actual existence except in some particular subject of which it is a quality—as white, for instance, in marble or chalk: so justice can have an actual existence, only as connected with some particular case. We repeat, therefore, that our knowledge of *justice*—which we use as synonymous with the science of law, or the law as it should be—is derived altogether, either immediately or by tradition, from observations of what is just in particular cases; that is, from observations of the second class of facts above described. In determining whether the particular case is just or unjust, right or wrong, the principle of utility—a consideration of what will most conduce to human happiness—has its use. But it can operate no further than upon cases actually conceived of and presented to the mind. And in order to derive principles even from such cases, induction is necessary. Hence we perceive that Mr. Bentham's philosophy is based upon the absurd hypothesis, that from a psychological knowledge of the nature of man, and from "those voluntary collections of knowledge which the mind maketh, which is every man's reason," it is possible to arrive at a complete knowledge of the infinitely numerous and diversified events which compose the subject of the law. As to the knowledge which each man's mind happens to collect, it is indeed obtained from observation, but is defective and incomplete, and can by no means enable us to form an adequate conception of the infinite variety of events which have actually happened. To recognize this truth, it is only necessary to compare the conceptions of poets and novelists with actual events. How poorly do the incidents depicted by the most brilliant imagination compare with the inexhaustible variety of the events of real life! In all the various works of the greatest genius, we recognize in the main the same ideas differently combined. It is this which makes the peculiarity of each—this "which is every man's reason."

As for psychology, it can help us still less. To revert to our description of the two classes of facts, it is true that the former are causes of the latter. But even supposing that a knowledge of thousands of independent causes will enable us to conceive of all the effects which those causes will produce; yet it by no means follows that a knowledge of the nature of man will be sufficient to make us acquainted with all the events which compose the subject of law. To conceive of such a case as a trespass on land by a cow, it would be necessary to understand the nature of that animal also. Or to conceive of such an accident as a house falling down, it would be necessary to understand the principle of gravity, and various other qualities of brick and morter. In short, there are thousands of events which give rise to litigation, that happen independently of the agency of men; and consequently it would be necessary to add a complete knowledge of natural philosophy to that of psychology. And even then, when we consider that every particular combination of the innumerable causes with which we have become acquainted, will produce an event, it will need but a slight knowledge of the theory of permutations and combinations, to demonstrate, that our knowledge of events will just extend so far as our observation extends, and no further.

Hence, while Mr. Bentham assumed that a knowledge of the principle of utility, and of the pleasures and pains to which man is subject, furnished a sufficient basis for legal science, the fact was, that all he knew of that science was derived from a despised and unrecognized source—from a partial and accidental knowledge of that very class of facts, of which he made so little account; and, instead of being complete, as he imagined, was absolutely limited by his knowledge of that class of facts.

This remark is fully illustrated in the character of Mr. Bentham's work upon the "Principles of Morals and Legislation." The cases upon which the criminal law animadverts are comparatively few and simple, and are familiar to all. Every body is acquainted with such classes of events as murder, larceny, &c. Accordingly, Mr. Bentham, being well acquainted with these, and being, in the main, ignorant of the infinitely more numerous and diversified cases which compose the subjects of the civil laws, derives almost all his notions of the law exclusively from the former. And the whole treatise, though ambitiously intended to cover the whole field of the law, is, in effect, only a treatise upon the criminal branch of it.

We have dwelt at length upon this point, because this error seems to lie at the bottom of an opinion of Mr. Dugald Stewart, in which he was followed by Mr. Legaré.

"In those branches of study," says Mr. Stewart, "which are conversant about moral and political propositions, the nearest approach that I can imagine to a hypothetical science analogous to mathematics, is to be found in a code of municipal jurisprudence, or rather might be conceived to exist in such a code, if systematically carried into execution, agreeably to certain general or fundamental principles. Whether these principles should or should not be founded in justice or expediency, it is evidently possible, by reasoning from them consequentially, to create an artificial or conventional body of knowledge more systematic, and at the same time more complete in all its parts, than in the present state of knowledge any science can be rendered, which ultimately appeals to the eternal and immutable standards of truth and falsehood—of right and wrong."

This opinion, also, is evidently based upon the hypothesis hat it is possible, by mere *a priori* reasoning, to arrive at a knowledge of the events, from which arise the cases upon which the law is to operate. Evidently, by working upon the ideas which the mind happens to have acquired, "it is possible to create an artificial or conventional body of knowledge," but such a body of knowledge would necessarily be confined to a very limited proportion of the innumerable cases which occur in the course of human affairs. Such a body of knowledge, by different combinations of our ideas, might be made of infinite magnitude; but the great majority of cases which actually happen, would be left entirely unprovided for. We can only reason from our principles, by conceiving of particular cases, and it is impossible to foresee the cases which actually happen; and this seems to have been perceived by Bacon. "The laws," he says, "cannot provide against all cases, but are suited only to such as frequently happen; time, the wisest of all things, daily introducing new cases." And again: "The narrowness of human prudence cannot foresee all the cases that time may produce."

Mr. Bentham has altogether mistaken the diagnosis of the case. The only possible use of the principle of utility is to determine what is just in particular cases. Its use, even here, is limited. For where any case can be determined by received notions of justice, it is better to go no further back. Its only practical value, then, is to determine new cases—that is, cases to which no received principle of justice can be found to apply. It is, indeed, a common opinion that there are no such cases; that the known principles of justice are coextensive with human affairs; and that for every case that arises, there needs but the application of some one of those principles.

But the error of this opinion would immediately appear, were a collection made of all the known principles of justice, whether found in common use, or in the books of the philosophers. A lawyer's practice every day presents cases that could be determined by no one of those principles, or any deductions from them. The cause of error is, that men mistake capacity to perceive what is just in a particular case, for a precedent knowledge of some principle applicable to it; whereas it is a discovery of a new truth.

But in admitting the value of the utilitarian philosophy so far, it appears to us to resemble the adversaries of the giant and the dwarf—all of whom seem to have struck at the dwarf, and left the giant untouched. For with a particular case presented, it is comparatively easy to determine what justice demands, and consequently the errors in the law which have sprung from a wrong judgment of particular cases, are few in number and dwarfish in magnitude, compared with those which have arisen from incorrect abstraction and too hasty generalization. Indeed, as we shall hereafter show, the former generally have their origin in the latter.

With the foregoing principles clearly understood, it will be easy to form a judgment of the nature and value of Mr. Bentham's proposed innovations in the law. These innovations go to the very root of the matter. Every where in Mr. Bentham's works we see exhibited a most thorough contempt and hatred of the lawyers. To borrow an idea from Mr. Legaré, he proposed to begin, as Dick, the butcher, said to Jack Cade, by killing all the lawyers. He speaks of them as occupying to legal science a relation analogous to that of the schoolmen to science generally. Accordingly, he looked to his system to effect a revolution in legal science as radical and complete as that effected in other sciences, by the Baconian logic. The existing system of law he looked upon as fundamentally wrong—as rotten in the roots, and past all remedy but grubbing out. Accordingly he proposed to do away with it altogether, and to substitute a code of laws of his own making. The poor old man, as honest and as visionary as Don Quixote, imagined himself constituted, as it were by nature, a legislator for all nations. Possessed with this idea, he addressed himself to the authorities of France—to the Emperor of Russia—to the President of the United States—to the Governors of the United States separately, and the Governor of Pennsylvania in particular, and finally to "all civilized nations professing liberal opinions;" proposing to make out of hand for any of them desiring it, a complete and all-comprehensive code of law—or, in the Utilitarian jargon, Pannomium—which, if not perfect, should at least be a nearer approximation to perfection than had ever before been, or could hereafter be, effected by any or by all other men.

It is with the American letters that we are more particularly concerned. In these he urges, not only what he conceived to be the peculiar claims of his proposed Pannomium, but also his objections to the existing law. The proposition is at first sight one of stupendous, but, we believe, entirely unconscious, conceit. To understand the full extent of its boldness, it is necessary to consider (to make use of the just remark of Sir Matthew Hale) that our law "is not the product of the wisdom of some one man, or society of men, in any one age, but of the wisdom, counsel, experience, and observation of many ages of wise and observing men." For this Mr. Bentham proposed to substitute the lucubrations of his single brain. Like Don Quixote, in his plan for the rescue of the Algerine captive, he undertook to do singly what had before been effected only by the accumulated power of thousands.

In support of his proposition, he argues in effect as follows: "The law," he says, "instead of being the production of an intelligent legislator, acting with consistency and method, has been blundered out by a set of men, who, their course of action not being at their own command, but at the command of the plaintiffs in the several causes, were all along as completely destitute of power as under the influence of sinister interest; they could not but be of inclination to operate upon any clear and enlarged views of utility, or upon *any* comprehensive and consistent plan, good or bad." Consequently it must be radically vicious and defective. Especially it is deficient in the most essential quality of a good law—to use a word of his own—cognoscibility. That is, it is so scattered about in a thousand different volumes, that it is impossible for any one—even a lawyer—to know the law. Besides, there are many cases for which there is no law, until the case actually comes up for judgment. Then the judge makes a special law for the particular case, and says it has been law all the time. Thus, the law partakes of the odious nature of an *ex post facto* law. To remedy these defects, he proposed to make a code of laws, so complete as to provide beforehand for every possible case, and reduced to such a form, that every one would find it easy to understand and know the law.

All these objections of Mr. Bentham arise from an utter ignorance of the fundamental principles of legal science. Had he read the works of the lawyers, instead of despising them, it is probable, considering the unquestionable acuteness of his mind, that he would have perceived that they *have*, in the main, necessarily proceeded upon a comprehensive and consistent plan; and that plan the only right one—the plan of nature—the method by induction. The fundamental principle of the English law—Stare decisis—is but a mere practical statement of the principle of induction as applied to legal science. And in strict accordance with this principle the mass of the existing law has been produced. All who are acquainted with it know that the legislator has had very little to do with making it. Statutes form but a very small portion of the law. The rest is what Mr. Bentham, as a name implying all iniquities, calls *judge-made law*.

When a case was decided, it was held to be law for all similar cases. Law thus made is indeed liable to the objection that it partakes of the nature of an *ex post facto* law. But Mr. Bentham's objection to it on this ground, is but an illustration of our remark, that all his notions of the law are taken from the criminal law. The principle that an *ex post facto law* is odious, like the term itself, is confined to the criminal law. For while, for many obvious reasons, it would be iniquitous to punish a man for an act, lawful at the time of its commission; yet, from the nature of things, the principle cannot be applied, in its full extent, to the civil law. In regard to the latter, the most that justice requires, and the most that is possible, is, that the law existing when the case arose, shall not be changed. From what we have before remarked, it is obvious, that the extent of the law, at any given time, is absolutely limited to the cases that have previously happened, and cases similar to them. If any case comes under this description, it can be decided by the existing law. But if one arises which is not similar to precedent cases, there is necessarily no law for it; in such a case, if it is a question of criminal law, the accused must be acquitted; but if it is a question of civil law—that is, if it is a controversy between parties—it is still necessary that a decision should be made. The only rule, then, by which the court can decide, is natural justice. The judge decides the case as that requires, and a new principle is introduced into the law. The point that we are aiming to demonstrate is, not only that the law has been made in this way, but that from the nature of things it could not possibly have been otherwise; that it is, in the main, an absolute impossibility to make a law for a case, until that or some similar case has happened. The history, not only of our own, but of all law, proves this. The law has always been developed in exact proportion to the occurrence of new cases. There can no where be pointed out a single instance in which a law has been made until after the happening of some one of the class of cases upon which it is intended to operate. In early times, when business was simple and undiversified, and the cases of controversy between man and man limited in number and variety, the law also was limited in extent. But as civilization increased, and the business of mankind became more extensive and diversified, new cases occurred, and new principles were added to the law. Thus the ten tables of the Romans grew into the immense body of the civil law. They have been called the matrix—the source of the civil law; but it is impossible in any way to trace back the great mass of the civil law to such an origin. The true matrix—the true source—was natural justice, and the method of its production, as we have stated it.

Our own law is another illustration. In old times it was all contained in one or two small books; now, it can hardly be contained in a thousand. The great mass of its principles cannot be traced back to the law as it originally stood. On the contrary, the very occasions and manner of their successive introduction are related in the books of Reports.

As for Mr. Bentham's assertion, that the law has been perverted by the sinister interest of the lawyers, there can be no better proof of prejudice than such an assertion. Such an interest could only have operated in two ways—either by inducing lawyers to write books with the express purpose of rendering the law uncertain, which is a supposition too absurd to be seriously mentioned; or, by influencing the judges to give unjust decisions. Whatever might have been the interest of the lawyers to corrupt the law, certainly they could have had no opportunity of doing so, except by becoming judges; and by becoming judges their interest must have immediately ceased. Mr. Bentham, however, urges that the judges, being the creatures of the king, have always had his interest at heart, and not the interest of the people. Admitting this for the sake of the argument, the answer is obvious. Where the appointing power is in the hands of one man, his interest will be concerned in not one case out of thousands. Hence, it is absurd to suppose that such an influence could have had any very material effect upon the law. We have the high authority of Mr. Gibbon for saying, that this was true of the Roman law, even under the absolute despotism of the Cæsars. "The senate," he says, "under the reign of the Cæsars, was composed of magistrates and lawyers, and in questions of private jurisprudence the integrity of their judgment was seldom perverted by fear or interest."

Indeed—completely to answer Mr. Bentham's objection—it is a fact known to all acquainted with the decisions of the English judges, that, in deciding each case as it arose, they were in the main governed by the principle of utility. The books all show that, in most cases where this principle required a departure from received notions of justice, they pursued the former to the exclusion of the latter. Nay, they have sometimes erred by a too anxious observance of this principle—improperly laying down rules opposed to common notions, where the common notions were right. They indeed sometimes departed from the principle; but, as we have before remarked, the defects in the law springing from this source, bear no comparison with those produced by improper induction. Nine out of ten of the errors in the law result from extending precedents to cases not analogous.

It is easy, then, to dispose of Mr. Bentham's proposal to make a complete code of law, that should provide for every possible case. It would, doubtless, have been a very good thing, but it was simply impossible. It was equivalent to saying, that in all future developments of human affairs, no possible case could arise, which he was unable to foresee. It was the same thing as if one had proposed to make a treatise containing all the principles of chemistry—not only all that had been, but all that could ever after be discovered. For, in the one case and the other, the subject is infinite. This truth is well expressed by one of the despised race of lawyers: "It is impossible to make a finite rule of an infinite matter perfect."

It is impossible even to suppose that Mr. Bentham could have approximated to completeness, to any thing like the same extent as the existing law. For the law, as it now stands, extends to all cases such as have arisen in the courts of justice, which is the same thing as to say, that it is almost as extensive and complete as it is possible for it to be. But Mr. Bentham's Pannomium would have been limited by the knowledge—and very slight it was—which he himself happened to have of the cases which had previously occurred.

Thus far we have spoken in defence of the lawyers. We have given them the credit to which they are entitled; and have attempted to show the gross ignorance of fundamental principles that actuated Mr. Bentham's attacks upon them. We admit, however, that many prejudices and false notions have always existed in the profession, to the infinite detriment of the law. Especially we are compelled to acknowledge the force of Mr. Bentham's objection, that the law, in regard to form, is in a most deplorable condition. "Scattered" through thousands of volumes, it is impossible, even for a lawyer, to obtain any competent knowledge of it." Nay, in many cases, it is impossible for him, after the most diligent investigation, to tell with certainty what the law of a particular case may be. Mr. Bentham's proposition, however, to reduce it all to statute law, would only aggravate the evil. There is this essential difference between a written law and a precedent: the former is absolutely limited by the words used; the latter extends to every case presenting a similar reason, whether agreeing in name or not. As the law now stands, it extends to all cases, however differing in name and other circumstances, which present the same reason for decision as cases decided. Were it reduced to statute law—supposing it even to be perfectly well done—it would be confined to cases similar to those already decided, not only in principle but in name. Though the execution should be perfect, still it would be no improvement, but the contrary. But when we consider how such a work would probably be executed, to what hands intrusted, it seems to us that no greater misfortune could happen to the law. If there is one thing that a true friend of humanity should pray for, it is that legislatures may keep their rash hands from the civil law. With this branch of law, the legislature has never had—it should never have—any thing to do, except in the way of correction. The legislators of it have been the judges; and still to their hands alone can it safely be intrusted. Paradoxical as this may seem—opposed as it is to the common notion that the function of a judge is "jus dicere, non jus dare," it follows necessarily from the very nature of the civil law, and needs but to be stated in order to be perceived.

Upon some future occasion, we may attempt to show the true remedy for this and some other great evils in the law, and more especially to point out the false notions and prejudices of the profession—the idols or false images of the understanding, as Bacon calls them—to which they owe their origin. The latter we regard as by far the most important, according to the opinion of Lord Coke, that to trace an error to its fountain-head is to refute it. Being of the fraternity ourselves, and having for many years—at first with humble veneration—sat at the feet of the Gamaliels of the law, we have had at least a fair opportunity of understanding the character of their writings. We undertake the task, not from any feeling of peculiar fitness, but because no one, acquainted at the same time in some degree with the modern philosophy and with law, has to our knowledge, ever attempted it. For our law—less fortunate than its sister, the Roman law—has always fallen either into the hands of practising lawyers, unacquainted with philosophy, or, worse still, into the hands of philosophers unacquainted with law.